Glencoe Spanish 1

¡Buen viaje!

Conrad J. Schmitt
Protase E. Woodford

Glencoe

New York, New York   Columbus, Ohio   Chicago, Illinois   Peoria, Illinois   Woodland Hills, California

The McGraw·Hill Companies

Send all inquiries to:
Glencoe/McGraw-Hill
8787 Orion Place
Columbus, OH 43240-4027

ISBN: 0-07-846570-2 *(Student Edition)*
ISBN: 0-07-861951-3 *(Teacher Wraparound Edition)*

Printed in the United States of America.

8 9 10 071/055 10 09 08 07

About the Authors

Conrad J. Schmitt

Conrad J. Schmitt received his B.A. degree magna cum laude from Montclair State College, Upper Montclair, NJ. He received his M.A. from Middlebury College, Middlebury, VT. He did additional graduate work at Seton Hall University and New York University. Mr. Schmitt has taught Spanish and French at the elementary, junior, and senior high school levels, as well as at the undergraduate and graduate levels. In addition, he has traveled extensively throughout Spain, Central and South America, and the Caribbean.

Protase E. Woodford

Protase "Woody" Woodford has taught Spanish at all levels from elementary through graduate school. At Educational Testing Service in Princeton, NJ, he was Director of Test Development, Director of Language Programs, Director of International Testing Programs and Director of the Puerto Rico Office. He has served as a consultant to the United Nations Secretariat, UNESCO, the Organization of American States, the U.S. Office of Education, and many ministries of education in Asia, Latin America, and the Middle East.

For the Parent or Guardian

We are excited that your child has decided to study Spanish. Foreign language study provides many benefits for students in addition to the ability to communicate in another language. Students who study another language improve their first language skills. They become more aware of the world around them and they learn to appreciate diversity.

You can help your child be successful in his or her study of Spanish even if you are not familiar with that language. Encourage your child to talk to you about the places where Spanish is spoken. Engage in conversations about current events in those places. The section of their Glencoe Spanish book called **El mundo hispanohablante** on pages xxi–xxxiii may serve as a reference for you and your child. In addition, you will find information about the geography of the Spanish-speaking world and links to foreign newspapers at **spanish.glencoe.com**.

The methodology employed in the Glencoe Spanish books is logical and leads students step by step through their study of the language. Consistent instruction and practice are essential for learning a foreign language. You can help by encouraging your child to review vocabulary each day. As he or she progresses through the text, you will want to use the Study Tips on pages H16–H29 to help your child learn Spanish. If you have Internet access, encourage your child to practice using the activities, games, and practice quizzes at **spanish.glencoe.com**.

¡Buen viaje!

Lecciones preliminares

Objetivos

In these preliminary lessons you will learn to:

- ❖ greet people
- ❖ say good-bye to people
- ❖ express simple courtesies
- ❖ find out and tell the days of the week
- ❖ find out and tell the months of the year
- ❖ count from 1 to 30
- ❖ find out and tell the seasons

Capítulo 1

Objetivos

Un amigo o una amiga

Contenido

Capítulo 2

Objetivos

In this chapter you will learn to:

❖ **describe people and things**

❖ **talk about more than one person or thing**

❖ **tell what subjects you take in school and express some opinions about them**

❖ **tell time**

❖ **tell at what time an event takes place**

❖ **talk about Spanish speakers in the United States**

Alumnos y cursos

Capítulo 3 Las compras para la escuela

Objetivos

In this chapter you will learn to:

- ❖ identify and describe school supplies
- ❖ identify and describe articles of clothing
- ❖ shop for school supplies and clothing
- ❖ state color and size preferences
- ❖ speak to people formally and informally
- ❖ discuss differences between schools in the United States and in Spanish-speaking countries

Capítulo 4

Objetivos

In this chapter you will learn to:

❖ talk about going to school

❖ talk about some school activities

❖ greet people and ask how they feel

❖ tell how you feel

❖ describe where you and others go

❖ describe where you and others are

❖ discuss some differences between schools in the United States and schools in Spanish-speaking countries

En la escuela

Capítulo 5

Objetivos

In this chapter you will learn to:

✤ order food or a beverage at a café

✤ identify some food

✤ shop for food

✤ talk about activities

✤ talk about differences between eating habits in the United States and in the Spanish-speaking world

En el café

Capítulo 6

Objetivos

In this chapter you will learn to:

- ❖ **talk about your family**
- ❖ **describe your home**
- ❖ **tell your age and find out someone else's age**
- ❖ **tell what you have to do**
- ❖ **tell what you are going to do**
- ❖ **tell what belongs to you and to others**
- ❖ **talk about families in Spanish-speaking countries**

La familia y su casa

Capítulo 7   Deportes de equipo

Objetivos

In this chapter you will learn to:

❖ talk about team sports and other physical activities

❖ tell what you want to, begin to, and prefer to do

❖ talk about people's activities

❖ express what interests, bores, or pleases you

❖ discuss the role of sports in the Hispanic world

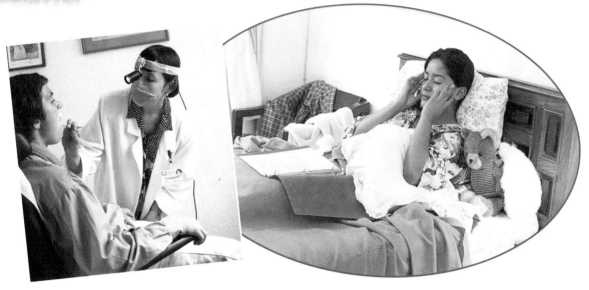

Capítulo 8

La salud y el médico

Objetivos

In this chapter you will learn to:

- ❖ explain a minor illness to a doctor
- ❖ describe some feelings
- ❖ have a prescription filled at a pharmacy
- ❖ describe characteristics and conditions
- ❖ tell where things are and where they're from
- ❖ tell where someone or something is now
- ❖ tell what happens to you or someone else

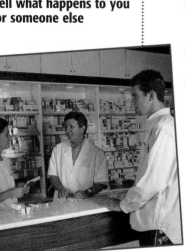

Capítulo 9

El verano y el invierno

Objetivos

In this chapter you will learn to:

* ❖ describe summer and winter weather
* ❖ talk about summer activities and sports
* ❖ talk about winter sports
* ❖ discuss past actions and events
* ❖ refer to people and things already mentioned
* ❖ talk about resorts in the Hispanic world

Capítulo 10 Diversiones culturales

Objetivos

In this chapter you will learn to:

❖ **discuss movies, museums, and theater**

❖ **discuss cultural events**

❖ **relate more past actions or events**

❖ **tell for whom something is done**

❖ **discuss some dating customs in the United States and compare them with those in Spanish-speaking countries**

❖ **talk about cultural activities that are popular in the Spanish-speaking world**

Capítulo 11 Un viaje en avión

Objetivos

In this chapter you will learn to:

❖ check in for a flight

❖ talk about some services on board the plane

❖ get through the airport after deplaning

❖ tell what you or others are currently doing

❖ tell what you know and whom you know

❖ discuss the importance of air travel in South America

Capítulo 12 Una gira

Objetivos

In this chapter you will learn to:

❖ **describe your personal grooming habits**

❖ **talk about your daily routine**

❖ **tell some things you do for yourself**

❖ **talk about a backpacking trip**

Capítulo 13 Un viaje en tren

Objetivos

In this chapter you will learn to:

❖ use expressions related to train travel

❖ purchase a train ticket and request information about arrival, departure, etc.

❖ talk about more past events or activities

❖ tell what people say

❖ discuss an interesting train trip in Spain and Peru

Capítulo 14 En el restaurante

Objetivos

In this chapter you will learn to:

❖ **order food or a beverage at a restaurant**

❖ **identify eating utensils and dishes**

❖ **identify more foods**

❖ **make a reservation at a restaurant**

❖ **talk about present and past events**

❖ **describe some cuisines of the Hispanic world**

Literary Companion

Video Companion

Contenido

Handbook

Guide to Symbols

Throughout **¡Buen viaje!** you will see these symbols, or icons. They will tell you how to best use the particular part of the chapter or activity they accompany. Following is a key to help you understand these symbols.

 Audio link This icon indicates material in the chapter that is recorded on compact disk.

 Recycling This icon indicates sections that review previously introduced material.

 Paired Activity This icon indicates sections that you can practice orally with a partner.

 Group Activity This icon indicates sections that you can practice together in groups.

 Un poco más This icon indicates additional practice activities that review knowledge from each chapter.

 ¡Adelante! This icon indicates the end of new material in each chapter. All remaining material is recombination and review.

 Literary Companion This icon appears in the review lessons to let you know that you are prepared to read the literature selection indicated if you wish.

 Interactive CD-ROM This icon indicates that the material is also on the Interactive CD-ROM.

El mundo hispanohablante

Spanish is the language of more than 350 million people around the world. Spanish had its origin in Spain. It is sometimes fondly called the "language of Cervantes," the author of the world's most famous novel and character, *Don Quijote.* The Spanish **conquistadores** and **exploradores** brought their language to the Americas in the fifteenth and sixteenth centuries. Spanish is the official language of almost all the countries of Central and South America. It is the official language of Mexico and several of the larger islands in the Caribbean. Spanish is also the heritage language of forty million people in the United States.

▼ España

▲ México

◀ Perú

▲ Chile

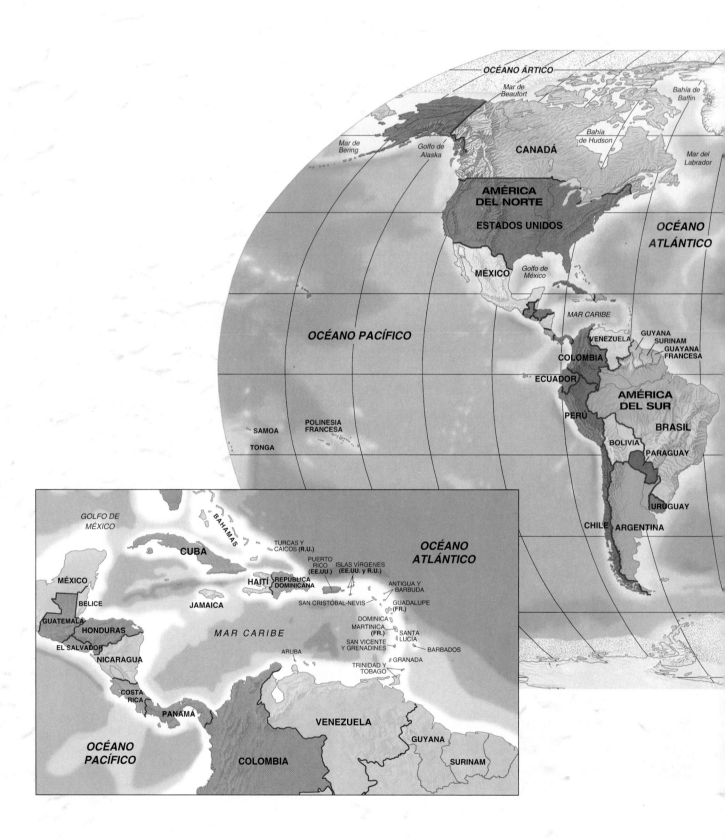

OCÉANO ÁRTICO

Mar de Beaufort

Bahía de Baffin

Mar de Bering

Golfo de Alaska

CANADÁ

Bahía de Hudson

Mar del Labrador

AMÉRICA DEL NORTE

ESTADOS UNIDOS

OCÉANO ATLÁNTICO

MÉXICO

Golfo de México

MAR CARIBE

VENEZUELA

GUYANA
SURINAM
GUAYANA FRANCESA

COLOMBIA

OCÉANO PACÍFICO

ECUADOR

PERÚ

AMÉRICA DEL SUR

BRASIL

SAMOA

POLINESIA FRANCESA

BOLIVIA

PARAGUAY

TONGA

URUGUAY

CHILE ARGENTINA

GOLFO DE MÉXICO

BAHAMAS

TURCAS Y CAICOS (R.U.)

OCÉANO ATLÁNTICO

CUBA

PUERTO RICO (EE.UU.)

ISLAS VÍRGENES (EE.UU. y R.U.)

MÉXICO

HAITÍ

REPÚBLICA DOMINICANA

ANTIGUA Y BARBUDA

BELICE

JAMAICA

SAN CRISTÓBAL-NEVIS

GUADALUPE (FR.)

GUATEMALA

DOMINICA

HONDURAS

MAR CARIBE

MARTINICA (FR.)

SANTA LUCÍA

EL SALVADOR

SAN VICENTE Y GRENADINES

BARBADOS

NICARAGUA

ARUBA

GRANADA

TRINIDAD Y TOBAGO

COSTA RICA

PANAMÁ

OCÉANO PACÍFICO

VENEZUELA

GUYANA

COLOMBIA

SURINAM

OCÉANO ÁRTICO

ENLANDIA
Mar de
Groenlandia
ISLANDIA
Mar de
Noruega
Mar de
Barents
Mar de Kara
Mar de Láptiev

Mar
del Norte

RUSIA
ASIA
Mar de
Ojotsk

EUROPA
KAZAJSTÁN
MONGOLIA

Mar Negro
GEORGIA
ARMENIA
UZBEKISTÁN
KIRGUIZITÁN
MELILLA
TURQUÍA
LÍBANO
SIRIA
TURKMENISTÁN
TAYIKISTÁN
CHINA
COREA
DEL NORTE
Mar
del
Japón
JAPÓN
CEUTA
AZERBAIJÁN
COREA
DEL SUR
MARRUÉCOS
TÚNEZ
ISRAEL
IRAK
IRÁN
AFGANISTÁN
MAR MEDITERRÁNEO
JORDANIA
NEPAL
BHUTÁN
OCÉANO
SAHARA
OCCIDENTAL
ARGELIA
LIBIA
EGIPTO
KUWAIT
PAKISTÁN
Mar de la
China
oriental
PACÍFICO
BAHREIN
TAIWÁN
QATAR
BO
RDE
MAURITANIA
MALÍ
NÍGER
CHAD
SUDÁN
ARABIA
SAUDITA
EMIRATOS
ÁRABES
UNIDOS
INDIA
BANGLADESH
MYANMAR
SENEGAL
OMÁN
LAOS
MARSHALL
MBIA
ÁFRICA
ERITREA
YEMEN
Golfo
de Bengala
Mar
de la China
meridional
GUINEA-
BISSAU
BURKINA
FASO
NIGERIA
DJIBOUTI
TAILANDIA
FILIPINAS
GUINEA
VIETNAM
MICRONESIA
RA LEONA
GHANA
BENIN
ETIOPÍA
SRI
LANKA
CAMBOYA
PALAU
TA DE MARFIL
LIBERIA
TOGO
REPÚBLICA
CENTROAFRICANA
CAMERÚN
BRUNEI
KIRIBATI
SAN TOMÉ E PRÍNCIPE
UGANDA
SOMALIA
MALDIVAS
MALAYSIA
GUINEA ECUATORIAL
GABÓN
KENYA
SINGAPUR
NAURÚ
RUANDA
REP. DEL
CONGO
REP. DEM.
DEL CONGO
BURUNDI
SEYCHELLES
OCÉANO
PAPÚA-
NUEVA
GUINEA
SALOMÓN
TUVALU
TANZANIA
ÍNDICO
INDONESIA
WALLIS Y
FUTUNA
ANGOLA
MALAWI
ZAMBIA
MOZAMBIQUE
ISLAS COMORES
Mar del
Coral
VANUATU
ISLAS
FIJI
NAMIBIA
ZIMBABWE
MADAGASCAR
MAURICIO
AUSTRALIA
NUEVA
CALEDONIA
BOTSWANA
REUNIÓN
OCÉANO
ATLÁNTICO
SUDÁFRICA
SWAZILANDIA
LESOTHO
Mar de
Tasmania
NUEVA
ZELANDIA

ANTÁRTIDA

NORUEGA
FINLANDIA
SUECIA
IRLANDA
REINO
UNIDO
DINAMARCA
ESTONIA
LETONIA
LITUANIA
RUSIA
RUSIA
PAÍSES
BAJOS
BELARÚS
BÉLGICA
ALEMANIA
POLONIA
LUXEMBURGO
OCÉANO
ATLÁNTICO
REPÚBLICA
CHECA
UCRANIA
FRANCIA
SUIZA
ESLOVAQUIA
MOLDOVA
AUSTRIA
HUNGRÍA
ANDORRA
ESLOVENIA
RUMANIA
PORTUGAL
CROACIA
ESPAÑA
MÓNACO
BOSNIA
HERZOGOVINA
YUGOSLAVIA
(Fed. Rep.)
GEORGIA
ITALIA
BULGARIA
Mar Negro
CEUTA
MELILLA
ALBANIA
MACEDONIA
Mar Mediterráneo
GRECIA
TURQUÍA
ÁFRICA
MALTA
SIRIA
CHIPRE
LÍBANO

España

Madrid

CAPITAL
Madrid

POPULATION
39,800,000

FUN FACT
The verdant hills of Galicia, the golden fields of Castilla, and the white villages of Andalucía as well as the industrial areas of Cataluña and the Basque Country are all a part of beautiful Spain. Once home to Iberians, Carthaginians, Romans, Celts, and Moors, Spain is the birthplace of Spanish—the language of many nations scattered on five continents of the globe. Madrid, in the exact center of the country, is considered a major cultural center of Europe.

México

Ciudad de México

CAPITAL
Ciudad de México

POPULATION
99,600,000

FUN FACT
Beautiful Mexico shares a border with the United States. This magnificent nation of Aztec, Mayan, and Spanish heritage is a country of contrasts: cosmopolitan cities such as Mexico City; industrial centers such as Monterrey; quaint towns such as Taxco and San Miguel de Allende; world-famous beaches like Acapulco and Cancún; as well as magnificent vestiges of pre-Columbian civilization in Chichén Itzá and Tulum.

Estados Unidos

Washington, D.C.

CAPITAL
Washington, D.C.

POPULATION
284,500,000

FUN FACT
The influence of Spanish and Mexican heritage has been evident in Texas and in the Southwest of the United States for generations. More recent is the proliferation of Hispanic or Latin cultures in all areas of the United States. New arrivals from the Caribbean, Central America, and South America bring their language, customs, music, and foods, adding to the rich cultural diversity of this "melting pot" country. Today Spanish is heard in New York, Chicago, Minneapolis, Denver, and Miami as well as El Paso, Phoenix, and Los Angeles.

Guatemala

CAPITAL
Guatemala

POPULATION
13,000,000

FUN FACT
Guatemala is a verdant country with a large indigenous population—descendants of the Mayans. Incredible ruined cities overgrown by jungle tell of a civilization that lasted for two thousand years and whose decline has never been definitively explained. Guatemala is considered by many to be one of the most beautiful countries in the world, with its volcanoes, mountains, jungles, and scenic cities and villages, such as Antigua, Panajachel, and Chichicastenango.

El Salvador

CAPITAL
San Salvador

POPULATION
6,400,000

FUN FACT
El Salvador is the smallest and most densely populated of the Central American republics. It is also the only one that has no Atlantic seaboard. The country is traversed by two mountain ranges with many impressive volcanic peaks.

Honduras

CAPITAL
Tegucigalpa

POPULATION
6,700,000

FUN FACT
Traditionally Honduras has been an agricultural country. One-third of the country is made up of rich farmlands. Its people are friendly and tranquil, with a pleasant smile for foreigners. The major cities are Teguciyulpa and San Pedro Sula. Like its neighbor Guatemala, Honduras has incredible ruins of the pre-Columbian civilizations such as those in Copán.

Nicaragua

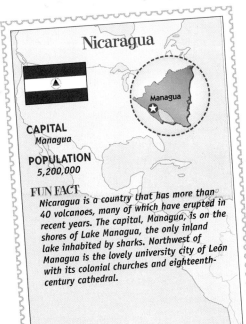

CAPITAL
Managua

POPULATION
5,200,000

FUN FACT
Nicaragua is a country that has more than 40 volcanoes, many of which have erupted in recent years. The capital, Managua, is on the shores of Lake Managua, the only inland lake inhabited by sharks. Northwest of Managua is the lovely university city of León with its colonial churches and eighteenth-century cathedral.

Costa Rica

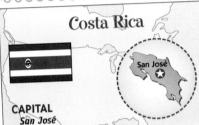

CAPITAL
San José

POPULATION
3,700,000

FUN FACT
Many consider Costa Rica a very special place. Its residents, Ticos, are polite, peaceful, and extremely friendly. Costa Rica has no army and prides itself on having more teachers than police officers. Costa Rica is a country of sun-drenched beaches on the Pacific, tropical jungles along the Caribbean coast, cosmopolitan cities such as San José, and high mountains in the central valley. Costa Rica is a tourist's paradise as well as home to many expatriates.

Panamá

CAPITAL
Panamá

POPULATION
2,900,000

FUN FACT
Panama is a country of variety—a variety of races, customs, natural wonders, and attractions. It is a country of tropical forests, mountains, beautiful beaches, excellent fishing, picturesque lakes, rivers, two oceans, and—the most incredible engineering feat—the Panama Canal. Panama is also the largest financial center of Latin America. All this in a mere 77,432 square kilometers!

Cuba

CAPITAL
La Habana

POPULATION
11,300,000

FUN FACT
Havana, the capital of Cuba, is known for its gorgeous colonial architecture. This lush island, not far from Florida, is one of the world's greatest producers of sugar cane. Cuba has been ruled by Fidel Castro since 1959 when he overthrew the dictator Fulgencio Batista.

La República Dominicana

CAPITAL
Santo Domingo

POPULATION
8,600,000

FUN FACT
The Dominican Republic shares with Haiti the island of Hispaniola in the greater Antilles. The oldest university in our hemisphere, la Universidad de Santo Domingo, was founded in Santo Domingo. The Dominicans are ardent fans or aficionados of baseball, and this rather small island nation has produced some of the finest major league players.

Puerto Rico

CAPITAL
San Juan

POPULATION
3,900,000

FUN FACT
Puerto Ricans have an endearing term for their beloved island—la isla del encanto—island of enchantment. A commonwealth of the United States, Puerto Rico is a lush, tropical island with beaches along its Atlantic and Caribbean shores and gorgeous mountains with Alpine-like views in its interior. Puerto Rico is the home of the beloved coquí—a little frog that lives only in Puerto Rico and who lets no one see him.

Venezuela

CAPITAL
Caracas

POPULATION
24,600,000

FUN FACT
Venezuela was the name given to this country by Spanish explorers in 1499, when they came across indigenous villages where people lived on the water and where all commerce was conducted by dugout canoes. The waterways reminded them of Venice, Italy. Caracas is a teeming cosmopolitan city of high-rises surrounded by mountains and tucked in a narrow nine-mile valley. Angel Falls in southern Venezuela is the highest waterfall in the world, reaching a height of 3,212 feet with an unbroken fall of 2,648 feet.

Colombia

CAPITAL
Bogotá

POPULATION
43,100,000

FUN FACT
Colombia covers over 440,000 square miles of tropical and mountainous terrain. Bogotá is situated in the center of the country in an Andean valley 8,640 feet above sea level. The Caribbean coast in the North boasts many beautiful beaches; the South is covered by jungle, and the southern port of Leticia is on the Amazon River.

Ecuador

CAPITAL
Quito

POPULATION
12,900,000

FUN FACT
Ecuador takes its name from the equator, which cuts right across the country. Ecuador is the meeting place of the high Andean sierra in the center, the tropical coastal plain to the west, and the Amazon Basin jungle to the east. Snowcapped volcanoes stretch some 400 miles from north to south. The beautiful colonial section of the capital, Quito, is sometimes called "the Florence of the Americas."

Perú

CAPITAL
Lima

POPULATION
26,100,000

FUN FACT
Peru, like Ecuador, is divided into three geographical areas—a narrow coastal strip of desert along the Pacific, the Andean highlands where nearly half the population lives, and the Amazon jungle to the east. Lima is on the coast, and for almost nine months out of the year it is enshrouded in a fog called la garúa. Peru is famous for its Incan heritage. Nothing can prepare visitors for the awe-inspiring view of the Incan city of Machu Picchu, an imposing architectural complex high in the Andes.

Bolivia

CAPITAL
La Paz

POPULATION
8,500,000

FUN FACT
Bolivia is one of two landlocked countries in South America. Mountains dominate the Bolivian landscape. La Paz is the highest city in the world at an altitude of 12,500 feet. Bolivia also has the world's highest navigable lake, Lake Titicaca, which is surrounded by the picturesque villages of the Aymara Indians.

Chile

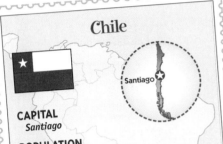

CAPITAL
Santiago

POPULATION
15,400,000

FUN FACT
Chile, a "string bean" country never more than 111 miles wide, stretches 2,666 miles from north to south along the Pacific Coast. The imposing Andes isolate it from Bolivia and Argentina. The northern part of the country is characterized by the super-arid Atacama desert, the South by the spectacular wind-swept glaciers and fjords of Patagonia. Over one-third of the country's population lives in the Santiago area.

Argentina

CAPITAL
Buenos Aires

POPULATION
37,500,000

FUN FACT
Argentina is often considered the most European country of South America. Buenos Aires is a beautiful city of parks, boutiques, restaurants, and wide boulevards. Argentina is famous for its beef from the cattle that graze on the huge estancias of the grassy Pampas. Farther south on the Chilean border is the gorgeous lake area with Swiss-like villages around Bariloche. To the south is Patagonia with its rocky countryside where the Welsh still graze sheep.

Paraguay

CAPITAL
Asunción

POPULATION
5,700,000

FUN FACT
Paraguay, like Bolivia, is landlocked. Asunción, situated on seven small hills on the east bank of the río Paraguay, is home to one-fifth of the country's total population. Located in the center of South America, this somewhat quaint city is nearly equidistant from the Atlantic and the Andes. The area to the west of the río Paraguay is called the Chaco—a very dry, hot, windy area of grasslands and scrubby forests.

Uruguay

CAPITAL
Montevideo

POPULATION
3,400,000

FUN FACT
Uruguay is the smallest country in South America. Most of the country's terrain is grazing land for sheep and cattle. Montevideo, situated where the río de la Plata empties into the Atlantic, is a rather peaceful city whose suburbs look more like beautiful resorts. The beaches of Uruguay's Atlantic coastline, particularly Punta del Este, attract many people from Brazil and Argentina.

Ceuta and Melilla

POPULATION
72,200

FUN FACT
Ceuta and Melilla, located on the north coast of Africa, comprise an autonomous community of Spain. Both of these modern cities are free ports and offer a beautiful blend of many cultures: Christian, Moslem, Hebrew, and Hindu.

Guinea Ecuatorial

CAPITAL
Malabo

POPULATION
500,000

FUN FACT
The Republic of Equatorial Guinea, on the West Coast of Africa between Gabon and Cameroon, was formerly called Spanish Guinea. The country is made up of some 10,000 square miles on the mainland and several small islands. Its capital, Malabo, is on the island of Bioko. Today two languages are spoken in Equatorial Guinea—Spanish and French.

Las Islas Filipinas

CAPITAL
Manila

POPULATION
77,200,000

FUN FACT
The Republic of the Philippines is an island nation in the South Pacific. The official language of the Philippines is Tagalog. Many people also speak Filipino—a language that has borrowed many words from Spanish. Spanish influence was extremely strong during the eighteenth and nineteenth centuries. Many Filipinos have Spanish names, and many can still speak Spanish.

La América del Sur

MAR CARIBE

OCÉANO ATLÁNTICO

Barranquilla
Cartagena
Maracaibo
Caracas
Lago de Maracaibo
Río Orinoco
Medellín
VENEZUELA
GUYANA
SURINAM
Santafé de Bogotá
GUAYANA FRANCESA
COLOMBIA
Cali
Río Magdalena
Ecuador
Otavalo
Quito
ECUADOR
Guayaquil
Cuenca
Islas Galápagos (Ecuador)
Río Amazonas
PERÚ
BRASIL
El Callao
Lima
Cuzco
CORDILLERA DE LOS ANDES
Lago Titicaca
BOLIVIA
La Paz
Cochabamba
Santa Cruz
Brasília
Sucre
Trópico de Capricornio
PARAGUAY
Asunción
CHILE
Río Paraná
Vicuña
Córdoba
OCÉANO PACÍFICO
Valparaíso
Santiago
Rosario
Buenos Aires
URUGUAY
Montevideo
La Plata
Río de la Plata
ARGENTINA
Mar del Plata
OCÉANO ATLÁNTICO
Puerto Montt
PATAGONIA
Estrecho de Magallanes
Islas Malvinas (R.U.)
Tierra del Fuego
Punta Arenas
Cabo de Hornos

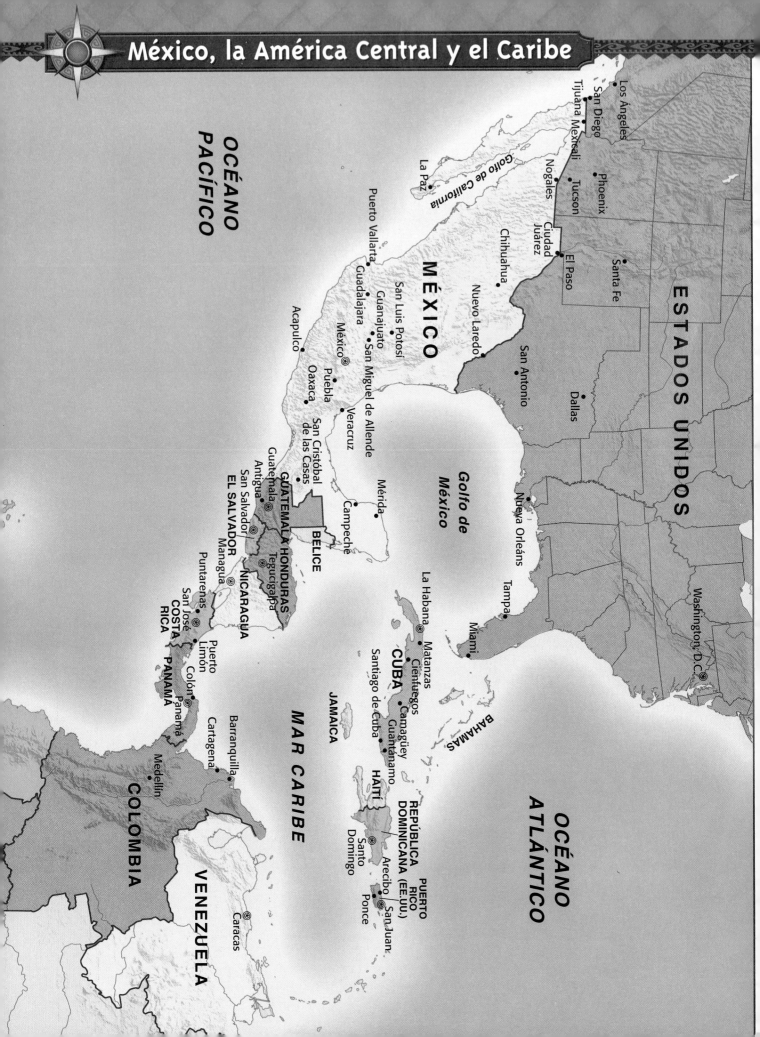

OCÉANO
PACÍFICO

OCÉANO
ATLÁNTICO

Golfo de California

Golfo de
México

MAR CARIBE

ESTADOS UNIDOS

M É X I C O

GUATEMALA

BELICE

HONDURAS

EL SALVADOR

NICARAGUA

COSTA
RICA

PANAMÁ

COLOMBIA

VENEZUELA

CUBA

JAMAICA

BAHAMAS

HAITÍ

REPÚBLICA
DOMINICANA

PUERTO
RICO (EE.UU.)

Los Ángeles
San Diego
Tijuana
Mexicali
Nogales
Tucson
Phoenix
Santa Fe
Ciudad
Juárez
El Paso
Chihuahua
Nuevo Laredo
San Antonio
Dallas
La Paz
Puerto Vallarta
Guadalajara
Guanajuato
San Luis Potosí
San Miguel de Allende
México
Puebla
Oaxaca
Acapulco
San Cristóbal
de las Casas
Veracruz
Mérida
Campeche
Nueva Orleáns
Tampa
Miami
La Habana
Matanzas
Cienfuegos
Camagüey
Santiago de Cuba
Guantánamo
Washington, D.C.
Guatemala
Antigua
San Salvador
Managua
Puntarenas
San José
Puerto
Limón
Colón
Panamá
Cartagena
Barranquilla
Medellín
Caracas
Tegucigalpa
Santo
Domingo
Arecibo
Ponce
San Juan

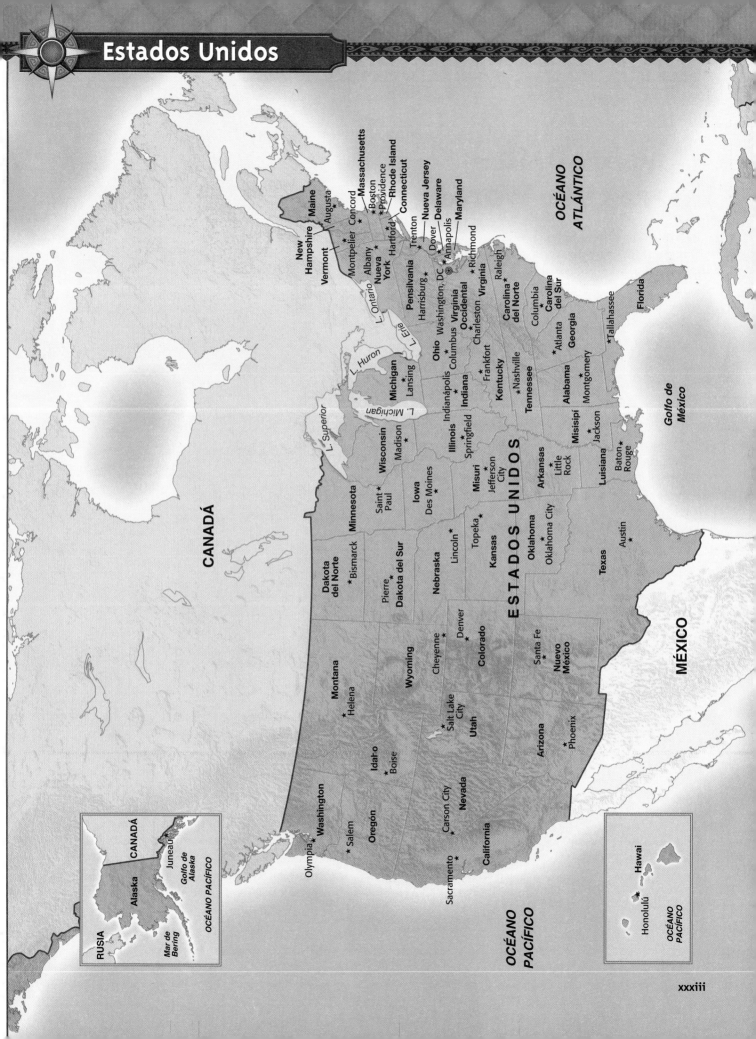

OCÉANO ATLÁNTICO

OCÉANO PACÍFICO

Golfo de México

CANADÁ

MÉXICO

ESTADOS UNIDOS

Maine
Augusta ★
New Hampshire
Vermont
Montpelier ★
Concord ★
Massachusetts
Boston ★
Providence ★
Rhode Island
Connecticut
Hartford ★
Albany ★
Nueva York
Trenton ★
Nueva Jersey
Dover ★
Delaware
Annapolis ★
Maryland
Washington, DC ®
Richmond ★
Virginia
Pensilvania
Harrisburg ★
Ohio
Columbus ★
Virginia Occidental
Charleston ★
Frankfort ★
Kentucky
Raleigh ★
Carolina del Norte
Columbia ★
Carolina del Sur
Atlanta ★
Georgia
Tallahassee ★
Florida
Indianápolis ★
Indiana
Springfield ★
Illinois
Nashville ★
Tennessee
Montgomery ★
Alabama
Jackson ★
Misisipi
Baton Rouge ★
Luisiana
Little Rock ★
Arkansas
Jefferson City ★
Misuri
Topeka ★
Kansas
Oklahoma City ★
Oklahoma
Austin ★
Texas
Santa Fe ★
Nuevo México
Phoenix ★
Arizona
Lincoln ★
Nebraska
Des Moines ★
Iowa
Madison ★
Wisconsin
Lansing ★
Michigan
Saint Paul ★
Minnesota
Bismarck ★
Dakota del Norte
Pierre ★
Dakota del Sur
Cheyenne ★
Wyoming
Denver ★
Colorado
Helena ★
Montana
Boise ★
Idaho
Salt Lake City ★
Utah
Carson City ★
Nevada
Salem ★
Oregón
Olympia ★
Washington
Sacramento ★
California
Honolulú ★

L. Ontario
L. Erie
L. Huron
L. Michigan
L. Superior

Why Learn Spanish?

The Spanish – Speaking World

Culture Knowing Spanish will open doors to you around the world. As you study the language, you will come to understand and appreciate the way of life, customs, values, and cultures of people from many different areas of the world. Look at the map on pages xxii–xxiii to see where Spanish is spoken, either as a first or second language.

Learning Spanish can be fun and will bring you a sense of accomplishment. You'll be really pleased when you are able to carry on a conversation in Spanish. You will be able to read the literature of Spain and Latin America, keep up with current events in magazines and newspapers from Spain and Latin America, and understand Spanish language films without relying on subtitles.

The Spanish language will be a source of enrichment for the rest of your life—and you don't have to leave home to enjoy it. In all areas of the United States there are Hispanic radio and television stations, Latin musicians, Spanish-language magazines and newspapers, and a great diversity of restaurants serving foods from all areas of the Spanish-speaking world. The Latin or Hispanic population of the United States today totals forty million people and is the fastest growing segment of the population.

Career Opportunities

Business Your knowledge of Spanish will also be an asset to you in a wide variety of careers. Many companies from Spain and Latin America are multinational and have branches around the world, including the United States. Many U.S. corporations have great exposure in the Spanish-speaking countries. With the growth of the Hispanic population in the U.S., bilingualism is becoming an important asset in many fields including retail, fashion, cosmetics, pharmaceutical, agriculture, automotive, tourism, airlines, technology, finance, and accounting.

You can use your Spanish in all these fields, not only abroad but also in the United States. On the national scene there are innumerable possibilities in medical and hospital services, banking and finance, law, social work, and law enforcement. The opportunities are limitless.

Language Link

Another benefit to learning Spanish is that it will improve your English. Once you know another language, you can make comparisons between the two and gain a greater understanding of how languages function. You'll also come across a number of Spanish words that are used in English. Just a few examples are: **adobe, corral, meseta, rodeo, poncho, canyon, llama, alpaca.** Spanish will also be helpful if you decide to learn yet another language. Once you learn a second language, the learning process for acquiring other languages becomes much easier.

Spanish is a beautiful, rich language spoken on many continents. Whatever your motivation is for choosing to study it, Spanish will expand your horizons and increase your job opportunities. **¡Viva el español! Y ¡buen viaje!**

El alfabeto español

a avión

b bebé

c cesta

d dedo

e elefante

f foto

g gemelos

h hamaca

i iglesia

j jabón

k kilo

l lago

m mono

n nariz

ñ ñame

o oso

p pelo

q queso

r rana

s sala

t té

u uva

uvas -grapes
plural

v vaca

w Washington, D.C.

x examen

y yeso

cast

z zapato

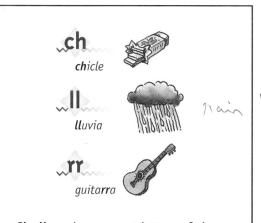

ch chicle

ll lluvia

rain Nubes clouds

rr guitarra

Ch, ll, and **rr** are not letters of the Spanish alphabet. However, it is important for you to learn the sounds they represent.

Lecciones preliminares

Bienvenidos

Objetivos

In these preliminary lessons you will learn to:

* ❖ greet people
* ❖ say good-bye to people
* ❖ express simple courtesies
* ❖ find out and tell the days of the week
* ❖ find out and tell the months of the year
* ❖ count from 1 to 30
* ❖ find out and tell the seasons

Calendario maya

Saludos

Greeting people

¡Hola!

Bien, gracias, ¿y tú?

¡Hola! ¿Qué tal?

Muy bien.

1 **¡Hola!** Get up from your desk. Walk around the classroom. Say hello to each classmate you meet.

2 **¿Qué tal?** Work with a classmate. Greet one another and find out how things are going.

Puerto Vallarta, México

BIENVENIDOS

Greeting people throughout the day

1. Some greetings are more formal than **¡Hola!** When you greet an older person, you may use one of the following expressions.

Buenos días, señora. **Buenas tardes, señorita.** **Buenas noches, señor.**

2. The titles **señor, señora,** and **señorita** are often used without the last name of the person.

> **Buenos días, señor.**
> **Buenas tardes, señora.**
> **Buenas noches, señorita.**

3 **Buenos días** Draw some figures on the board. Some will represent friends your own age and others will represent older people. Greet each of the figures on the board with the proper expression.

4 **Saludos** Look at these photographs of young people in Spain and Mexico. As they greet one another, they do some things that are different from what we do when we greet each other. What do you notice in the photographs?

Saying good-bye

Adiós, José.

Adiós, Gloria.

Chao, Patricia.

Chao, Roberto.
¡Hasta luego!

1. The common expression to use when saying good-bye to someone is
¡Adiós!

2. If you plan to see the person again soon, you can say **¡Hasta pronto!** or
¡Hasta luego! If you plan to see the person the next day, you can say
¡Hasta mañana!

3. An informal expression you often hear, particularly in Spain and in
Argentina, is **¡Chao!**

1 **¡Chao!** Go over to a classmate and say good-bye to him or her.

2 **¡Hasta luego!** Work with a classmate. Say **¡Chao!** to one another
and let each other know that you will be getting together again soon.

3 **¡Adiós!** Say good-bye to your Spanish teacher. Then say good-bye
to a friend. Use a different expression with each person.

Conversando más

—¡Hola, Julio!
—¡Hola, Verónica! ¿Qué tal?
—Bien, ¿y tú?
—Muy bien, gracias.

—Chao, Julio
—Chao, Verónica. ¡Hasta luego!

  ¡Hola, amigo(a)! Work with a classmate. Have a conversation in Spanish. Say as much as you can to one another.

Salamanca, España

Ordering food politely

There are several ways to express *you're welcome*.

> **No hay de qué.**
> **De nada.**
> **Por nada.**

CAFÉ HAITI GALERIAS NACIONALES LTDA.
CAFETERIA, TE, HELADERIA Y SIMILARES
San Antonio 53- Fono: 633 15 36
SANTIAGO CENTRO- R.U.T.89.560.800-9

CAFÉ *Haití*

1 CORTADO GRANDE
$ 360 (IVA Incluido)

Fecha:

496969

BOLETA VENTA Cliente
Impresos T.G Fono 6396150

1 **La cortesía** With a classmate, practice reading the conversation above. Be as animated and polite as you can.

2 Una cola, por favor. You are at a café in Manzanillo, Mexico.
Order the following things from the waiter or waitress (your partner).
Be polite when you order.

1. un sándwich

2. una gaseosa

3. una limonada

4. un café

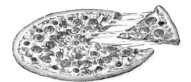

5. una pizza

3 Tacos, enchiladas, tamales You are in a Mexican restaurant.
Order the following foods from the waiter or waitress (your partner).
Be polite to each other.

1. un taco

2. una enchilada

3. un tamal

Guanajuato,
México

Preliminar D

La fecha

Telling the days of the week

lunes	martes	miércoles	jueves	viernes	sábado	domingo
1	2	3	4	5	6	7
8	9	10	11	12	13	14

To find out and give the day of the week, you say:

—¿Qué día es hoy?

—Hoy es lunes.

1 ⚙ **¿Qué día es?** Answer in Spanish.

1. ¿Qué día es hoy?

2. ¿Qué día es mañana?

3. ¿Cuáles son los días del fin de semana o del *weekend*?

Telling the months

Finding out and giving the date

¿Cuál es la fecha de hoy?

Hoy es el doce de septiembre.

SEPTIEMBRE
12

When giving the date, you use **primero** for the first day of the month. For other days you use **dos, tres, cuatro,** etc.

Avenida 9 de Julio,
Buenos Aires, Argentina

Celebración del
Cinco de Mayo

...ing the seasons

la primavera

el verano

el invierno

el otoño

2 **¿Cuántos?** Answer in Spanish.

1. ¿Cuántos días hay en una semana, siete o cuatro?
2. ¿Cuántos meses hay en un año, siete o doce?
3. ¿Cuántas estaciones hay en un año, cuatro o doce?

3 **¿En qué mes?** Each of you will stand up in class and give your birthday **(cumpleaños)** in Spanish. Listen carefully and keep a record of how many classmates were born in the same month. Then tell, in Spanish, in which month the greatest number of students were born. In which month were the fewest born?

4 **La estación, por favor.** Tell in which season the following months are. Answer in Spanish.

1. ¿En qué estación es mayo?
2. ¿En qué estación es enero?
3. ¿En qué estación es julio?
4. ¿En qué estación es octubre?

Vocabulario

Greeting people

¡Hola!	Buenas noches.
Buenos días.	¿Qué tal?
Buenas tardes.	Muy bien.

Identifying titles

señor
señora
señorita

Saying good-bye

¡Adiós!	¡Hasta pronto!
¡Chao!	¡Hasta mañana!
¡Hasta luego!	

Being courteous

Por favor.	De (Por) nada.
Gracias.	No hay de qué.

How well do you know your vocabulary?

- Choose an expression from the list to begin a conversation.
- Have a classmate respond.
- Take turns.

Identifying the days of the week

lunes	sábado
martes	domingo
miércoles	hoy
jueves	mañana
viernes	el fin de semana

Identifying the months of the year

enero	julio
febrero	agosto
marzo	septiembre
abril	octubre
mayo	noviembre
junio	diciembre

Identifying the seasons

la primavera	el otoño
el verano	el invierno

Other useful expressions

¿Qué día es hoy?	¿Cuál es la fecha?

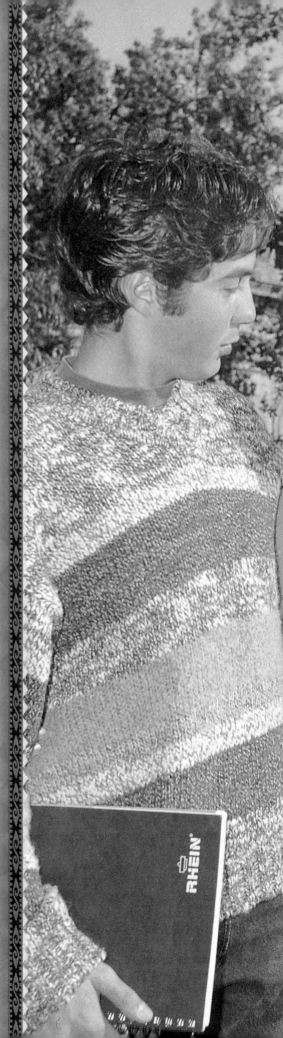

Capítulo 1

Un amigo o una amiga

Objetivos

In this chapter you will learn to:

❖ ask or tell who someone is

❖ ask or tell what something is

❖ ask or tell where someone is from

❖ ask or tell what someone is like

❖ describe yourself or someone else

❖ talk about a famous Spanish novel and some Latin American heroes

Francisco de Goya *Muchachos trepando a un árbol*

¿Quién es?

el muchacho   Nando

la muchacha   Pepita

el amigo   la amiga

el alumno   la alumna

¿Qué es?

una escuela
un colegio

¿Qué es un colegio?
Un colegio es una escuela secundaria.
Es una escuela secundaria en Latinoamérica.

Guadalupe es mexicana.
Guadalupe es de San Miguel de Allende.
Ella es alumna en un colegio.
Es alumna en el Colegio Juárez.
Guadalupe es una amiga de José Antonio.

¿Cómo es el muchacho?

alto   bajo

 guapo

 feo

 rubio

 moreno

 pelirrojo

 gracioso, cómico

 serio

 ambicioso

 perezoso

¿Cómo es la muchacha?

alta   baja

 bonita, linda

 fea

 rubia

 morena

 pelirroja

 graciosa, cómica

 seria

 ambiciosa

 perezosa

Anita es alta. No es baja.
Ella es muy bonita, muy linda.

José es rubio.
Él es guapo. No es feo.

Nota There are many ways to express *good-looking, handsome,* or *pretty* in Spanish. The word **guapo(a)** can be used to describe a boy or a girl. The words **bonito, lindo, hermoso,** and **bello** all mean *pretty.* They can describe a pretty girl or a pretty item. The word **feo** in Spanish is not as strong as the word *ugly* in English. To get a friend's attention, you could even say jokingly, **¡Oye, feo!**

The following words are used to express degrees.

Él es guapo.
Es bastante guapo.
Es muy guapo.

Ella es bonita.
Es bastante bonita.
Es muy bonita.

lario

...alabra necesito?

Historieta Un muchacho mexicano
Contesten. (*Answer.*)

1. ¿Es Manolo mexicano o colombiano?
2. ¿Es de San Miguel de Allende o de Bogotá?
3. ¿Es alumno en el Colegio Juárez?
4. ¿Es el Colegio Juárez un colegio mexicano?
5. ¿Es Manolo un amigo de Alicia Gómez?

2 Historieta Una muchacha americana
Contesten. (*Answer.*)

1. ¿Es Debbi una muchacha americana?
2. ¿Es ella de Miami?
3. ¿Es ella alumna en una escuela secundaria de Miami?
4. ¿Es ella una alumna seria?
5. ¿Es Debbi una amiga de Bárbara Jones?

3 ¿Quién? ¿Manolo o Debbi?
Contesten. (*Answer.*)

1. ¿Quién es de San Miguel de Allende?
2. ¿Quién es de Miami?
3. ¿Quién es alumno en el Colegio Juárez?
4. ¿Quién es alumna en una escuela secundaria de Miami?

Miami, la Florida

Barcelona, España

4 Historieta ¿Cómo es Fernando?
Contesten según la foto. (*Answer according to the photo.*)

1. ¿Cómo es Fernando? ¿Es alto o bajo?
2. ¿Cómo es Fernando? ¿Es gracioso o serio?
3. ¿Cómo es Fernando? ¿Es guapo o feo?
4. ¿Cómo es Fernando? ¿Es rubio o moreno?

5 Todo lo contrario Contesten según el modelo.
(Answer according to the model.)

¿Es alta Teresa?

No, de ninguna manera. Es bastante baja.

1. ¿Es muy seria Teresa?
2. ¿Es pelirroja Teresa?
3. ¿Es baja Teresa?
4. ¿Es muy ambiciosa Teresa?

Málaga, España

6 ¿Quién es? Work with a classmate. Choose one of the photographs below, but don't tell which one. Describe the student in the photo. Your partner has to guess which person you are describing. Take turns.

1.

2.

3.

4.

7 Juego ¿Es un muchacho o una muchacha?

Work with a classmate. Describe someone in the class. First your partner will tell whether you're describing a boy or a girl and will then guess who it is. Take turns.

UN POCO MÁS

*For more practice using words from **Palabras 1**, do Activity 1 on page H2 at the end of this book.*

¡Hola!
Yo soy Roberto. Roberto Davidson.
Soy de California.
Soy un alumno serio.
Soy un amigo de Carmen.

Carmen es una amiga
muy buena.
Ella es una persona
muy simpática.

¿Quién es y cómo es?

Oye, Roberto. ¿Quién es?

Es muy flaco, ¿no?
¿Y él? ¿Quién es?

Ay, Jaime. Es el famoso don Quijote.
Don Quijote es de la Mancha,
en España.

Es el compañero de d
Es Sancho Panza. Sanc
flaco como don Quijote

flaco

gordo

Los números

0	cero	11	once	21	veintiuno
1	uno	12	doce	22	veintidós
2	dos	13	trece	23	veintitrés
3	tres	14	catorce	24	veinticuatro
4	cuatro	15	quince	25	veinticinco
5	cinco	16	dieciséis	26	veintiséis
6	seis	17	diecisiete	27	veintisiete
7	siete	18	dieciocho	28	veintiocho
8	ocho	19	diecinueve	29	veintinueve
9	nueve	20	veinte	30	treinta
10	diez				

Nota Words that look alike and have similar meanings in Spanish and English are called "cognates." It is very easy to guess the meaning of cognates. But, **¡Cuidado!** *(Watch out!)* because even though they look alike and mean the same thing, they are pronounced differently. Here are some cognates. Take care to pronounce them correctly.

fantástico
tímido
sincero

honesto
generoso

San Francisco, California

...sito?

...chacho

...Collins o

...s de San Francisco,
...uadalajara, México?
...dad es Jim? ¿Es americano

...umno Jim? ¿En un colegio
...o en una escuela secundaria
...ornia?
...o es Jim? ¿ Es serio o gracioso?

...on Quijote.
...ho no es
... Es gordo.

9 **¿Cómo es la muchacha?**
Describan a cada muchacha. *(Describe each girl.)*

1. Ana

2. Alicia

3. Isabel

4. Victoria

5. Beatriz

6. Juanita

Una alumna mexicana

10 Historieta Gabriela Torre[s]
Completen. *(Complete.)*

Gabriela Torres es de México. [...]
No es americana. Gabriela es alum[na] [...]
__2__ mexicano. No es alumna en un[a] [...]
secundaria americana. Gabriela no es [...]
Ella es bastante __4__. ¿Es ella muy ser[ia] [...]
de ninguna manera. Gabriela es muy __[5]__
Ella es una amiga __6__.

11 ¿Quién es? Think of a student in the class.
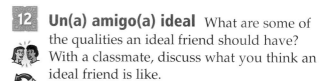
A classmate will ask you questions about the
person and try to guess who it is. Take turns.

12 Un(a) amigo(a) ideal What are some of
the qualities an ideal friend should have?
With a classmate, discuss what you think an
ideal friend is like.

El Zócalo, Ciudad de México

cabulario

s, la graciosa

una

r thing

...ella es ___1___.

...na en un

...a ___3___

...baja.

...a? No,

una

...ing is a noun. In Spanish, every noun ...or feminine. Many Spanish nouns end in ...s that end in **o** are masculine, and almost all ...ninine.

...articles. The English word *the* is called a definite ...used to refer to a definite or specific person or ...e school. The word *a (an)* is called an indefinite article ...s to any person or thing, not a specific one—a girl, a school.

...te articles in Spanish are **el** and **la. El** is used with a masculine ...d **la** is used with a feminine noun. The indefinite articles are ...d **una. Un** is used with a masculine noun and **una** is used with a ...ninine noun.

el muchacho	**la muchacha**	**un muchacho**	**una muchacha**
el colegio	**la escuela**	**un colegio**	**una escuela**

¿Cómo lo digo?

13 **Historieta** **El muchacho y la muchacha**

Contesten con **sí.** (*Answer with* sí.)

1. ¿Es americano el muchacho?
2. ¿Y la muchacha? ¿Es ella americana?
3. ¿Es bastante guapo el muchacho?
4. ¿Es muy bonita la muchacha?

Una amiga y un amigo,
California

14 Historieta El muchacho mexicano y la muchacha americana Completen con **el** o **la.** (*Complete with* el *or* la.)

__1__ muchacho es mexicano. __2__ muchacha es americana. __3__ muchacho mexicano es Paco y __4__ muchacha americana es Linda. __5__ muchacha es morena y __6__ muchacho es moreno. __7__ muchacha es alumna en __8__ Escuela Belair en Houston. __9__ muchacho es alumno en __10__ Colegio Hidalgo en Guanajuato.

Guanajuato, México

15 Historieta Un muchacho y una muchacha
Completen con **un** o **una.** (*Complete with* un *or* una.)

Roberto es __1__ muchacho americano y Maricarmen es __2__ muchacha chilena. Roberto es __3__ alumno muy serio. Pero es __4__ muchacho muy gracioso. Él es alumno en __5__ escuela secundaria en Nueva York. Maricarmen es __6__ alumna muy seria también. Ella es alumna en __7__ colegio chileno en Santiago.

Santiago, Chile

Adjetivos en el singular
Describing a person or thing

1. A word that describes a noun is an adjective. The highlighted words in the following sentences are adjectives.

> **El muchacho pelirrojo es muy guapo.**
> **La muchacha morena es una alumna muy buena.**

2. In Spanish, an adjective must agree with the noun it describes or modifies. If the noun is masculine, then the adjective must be in the masculine form. If the noun is feminine, the adjective must be in the feminine form. Many singular masculine adjectives end in **o,** and many singular feminine adjectives end in **a.**

un muchacho gracioso	**una muchacha graciosa**
un alumno serio	**una alumna seria**

SPANISH *Online*

For more information about Santiago and other cities in the Spanish-speaking world, go to the Glencoe Spanish Web site: spanish.glencoe.com

¿Cómo lo digo?

16 **Historieta** **Elena y Eduardo**
Contesten. *(Answer.)*

1. ¿Es Elena americana o venezolana?
2. Y Eduardo, ¿es él americano o venezolano?
3. ¿Es moreno o rubio el muchacho?
4. Y la muchacha, ¿es ella rubia o morena?
5. ¿Es Elena una alumna seria?
6. ¿Es ella alumna en una escuela americana?
7. Y Eduardo, ¿es él un alumno serio también?
8. ¿Es él alumno en un colegio venezolano?

Nueva York

17 **¿Quién es gracioso?** Describan. *(Here are some adjectives that describe people. Choose a classmate and an adjective that describes that person. Then make up a sentence about him or her.)*

moreno   alto   rubio

serio   americano   gracioso

bajo   cómico   fantástico   tímido

Caracas, Venezuela

San Miguel de Allende, México

18 **¿Quién es y cómo es?** Show a classmate this photo of Isabel García, a new friend you made in San Miguel de Allende, Mexico. One of your classmates wants to know all about Isabel. Answer his or her questions.

19 **¿Quién es y cómo es?** Here's a photo of Pablo Gómez, another friend you met on your trip. He's from Guanajuato. Answer your classmate's questions about him.

Guanajuato, México

Presente del verbo **ser** en el singular
Identifying a person or thing

1. The verb *to be* in Spanish is **ser**. Study the following forms of this verb.

SER	
yo	soy
tú	eres
él	es
ella	es

(not ser)
Estar – are doing
continous present tense

2.

Yo soy Eugenio.

Tú eres Juan.

Él es Alejandro.

Ella es una alumna seria.

| You use **yo** to talk about yourself. | You use **tú** to address a friend. | You use **él** or the person's name to talk about a boy or a man. | You use **ella** or the person's name to talk about a girl or a woman. |

Note that the form of the verb changes with each person.

3. Since the form of the verb changes with each person, the subjects **yo, tú, él,** and **ella** can be omitted.

> **Soy Paco.**
> **Eres mexicano, ¿no?**
> **Es alumna.**

4. To make a sentence negative, you simply put **no** in front of the verb.

> **Antonio es mexicano. Él no es colombiano.**
> **Yo soy de Bogotá. No soy de Cali.**

Bogotá, Colombia

Estructura

¿Cómo lo digo?

20 **¡Qué coincidencia!** Practiquen la conversación. *(Practice the conversation.)*

—¡Hola!
—¡Hola! ¿Quién eres?
—¿Quién? ¿Yo?
—Sí, tú.
—Pues, soy Julia. Julia Rivera. Y tú, ¿quién eres?
—Yo soy Emilio. Emilio Ortega.
—¿Eres americano, Emilio?
—No, no soy americano.
—¿No? ¿De dónde eres?
—Soy de México.
—¡Yo soy de México también!
—¡Increíble!

21 **Julia Rivera y Emilio Ortega** Hablen de Julia y Emilio.
(Based on the conversation, tell what you know about Julia and Emilio.)

22 **Yo soy...** Contesten personalmente.
(Answer about yourself.)

1. ¿Eres americano(a) o cubano(a)?
2. ¿Eres alumno(a)?
3. ¿Eres alumno(a) en una escuela secundaria?
4. ¿De dónde eres?
5. ¿Cómo eres? ¿Eres alto(a) o bajo(a)?
6. ¿Eres muy serio(a) o bastante gracioso(a)?

Ponce, Puerto Rico

23 **Historieta** José, ¿eres... ?
Pregúntenle a José Fuentes si es...
(Ask José Fuentes if he is . . .)

1. puertorriqueño
2. de Ponce
3. alumno en un colegio de Ponce
4. un amigo de Inés García

24 **Historieta** Inés, ¿eres...?

Pregúntenle a Inés García si es...

(*Ask Inés García if she is . . .*)

1. de Chile
2. de Santiago
3. alumna en un colegio
4. una amiga de José Fuentes

Santiago, Chile

San Miguel de Allende, México

25 **En un café** You've just met a student your own age at a café in San Miguel de Allende, Mexico. Have a conversation to get to know one another better.

26 **Un(a) amigo(a) nuevo(a)**

A classmate will think of someone in class you both know and pretend that that person is his or her new boyfriend or girlfriend. Ask as many questions as you can to try to find out who the new boyfriend or girlfriend is.

27 **Juego** **¡Soy una persona fantástica!** Have a contest with a classmate to see which one of you can boast the most. Say something good about yourself and then your partner will "one-up" you.

ALUMNA 1: **Yo soy simpática.**

ALUMNA 2: **Yo soy simpática. Y soy generosa también.**

Andas bien. ¡Adelante!

Conversación

¿De dónde eres?

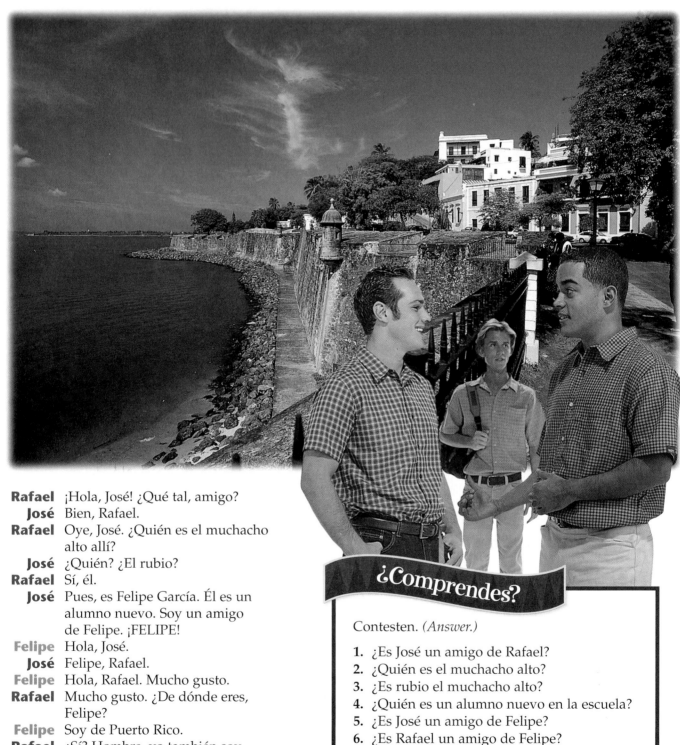

Rafael	¡Hola, José! ¿Qué tal, amigo?
José	Bien, Rafael.
Rafael	Oye, José. ¿Quién es el muchacho alto allí?
José	¿Quién? ¿El rubio?
Rafael	Sí, él.
José	Pues, es Felipe García. Él es un alumno nuevo. Soy un amigo de Felipe. ¡FELIPE!
Felipe	Hola, José.
José	Felipe, Rafael.
Felipe	Hola, Rafael. Mucho gusto.
Rafael	Mucho gusto. ¿De dónde eres, Felipe?
Felipe	Soy de Puerto Rico.
Rafael	¿Sí? Hombre, yo también soy puertorriqueño.

¿Comprendes?

Contesten. (*Answer.*)

1. ¿Es José un amigo de Rafael?
2. ¿Quién es el muchacho alto?
3. ¿Es rubio el muchacho alto?
4. ¿Quién es un alumno nuevo en la escuela?
5. ¿Es José un amigo de Felipe?
6. ¿Es Rafael un amigo de Felipe?
7. ¿De dónde es Felipe?
8. Y Rafael, ¿de qué nacionalidad es?

Vamos a hablar más

A **¿Quién es?** Think of someone in the class, but don't tell who it is. Say just one thing about the person and let your partner take a guess. If he or she guesses incorrectly, give another hint. Continue until your partner guesses correctly. Take turns.

B  **¿Quién soy yo?** Play a guessing game. Think of someone in the class. Pretend you're that person and describe yourself. A classmate has to guess who you are.

Pronunciación

Las vocales a, o, u

When you speak Spanish, it is important to pronounce the vowels carefully. The vowel sounds in Spanish are very short, clear, and concise. The vowels in English have several different pronunciations, but in Spanish they have only one sound. Imitate carefully the pronunciation of the vowels **a, o,** and **u.** Note that the pronunciation of **a** is similar to the *a* in *father,* **o** is similar to the *o* in *most,* and **u** is similar to the *u* in *flu.*

a	o	u
Ana	o	uno
baja	no	mucha
amiga	Paco	mucho
alumna	amigo	muchacho

Repeat the following sentences.

> **Ana es alumna.**
> **Adán es alumno.**
> **Ana es amiga de Adán.**

Lecturas culturales

El Quijote

El Quijote es una novela famosa de la literatura española. El autor de *El Quijote* es Miguel de Cervantes Saavedra.

El Quijote es la historia del famoso caballero andante[1], don Quijote de la Mancha. La Mancha es una región de España.

Don Quijote es alto y flaco. Sancho Panza es el compañero o escudero[2] de don Quijote. ¿Es alto y flaco como don Quijote? No, de ninguna manera. Sancho es bajo y gordo. Sancho Panza es una persona muy graciosa. Es muy cómico. ¿Y don Quijote? De ninguna manera. No es cómico. Él es muy serio y es muy honesto y generoso. Pero según[3] Sancho Panza, don Quijote es muy tonto[4]. Y según don Quijote, Sancho es perezoso.

[1]caballero andante *knight errant*
[2]escudero *knight's attendant*
[3]según *according to*
[4]tonto *foolish*

Sancho Panza y
don Quijote

La Mancha, España

¿Comprendes?

A ¿Es don Quijote o Sancho Panza?
Decidan. (*Decide whether each sentence describes Don Quijote or Sancho Panza.*)

1. Es bajo.
2. Es alto.
3. Es muy gracioso.
4. Es gordo.
5. Es flaco.
6. Es muy serio.
7. Es un caballero andante.
8. Es honesto y generoso.
9. Es un escudero.

B Palabras afines Busquen cinco palabras afines en la lectura. (*Find five cognates in the reading.*)

Don Quijote de Pablo Picasso

Lectura opcional 1

Una alumna venezolana

Alicia Bustelo es una muchacha venezolana. Ella es de Caracas, la capital de Venezuela. Alicia es alta y es una muchacha bastante bonita. Es muy graciosa. Pero es también una alumna muy seria. Es alumna en el Colegio Simón Bolívar. En Latinoamérica un colegio es una escuela secundaria. El Colegio Simón Bolívar es una escuela muy buena.

VENEZUELA
Caracas

AMÉRICA DEL SUR

Plaza Simón Bolívar, Caracas

¿Comprendes?

Latinoamérica Busquen la información en la lectura. *(Find the information in the reading.)*
1. the name of a Latin American country
2. the name of a Latin American capital
3. the name of a Latin American hero
4. the term for the Spanish-speaking countries of the Americas

Lectura opcional ②

Simón Bolívar

Simón Bolívar y José de San Martín

María Iglesias es una muchacha venezolana. Ella es de Caracas, la capital. Es alumna en el Colegio Simón Bolívar. Y la plaza principal de Caracas es la Plaza Simón Bolívar. Simón Bolívar es un héroe famoso de la América del Sur.

José Ayerbe no es venezolano. Él es peruano. Es de Lima, la capital de Perú. Es alumno en el Colegio San Martín. Y la plaza principal de Lima es la Plaza San Martín. San Martín es otro héroe famoso de la América del Sur.

Simón Bolívar y José de San Martín luchan contra[1] España por la independencia de los países[2] de la América del Sur. Simón Bolívar es el gran[3] «libertador» de los países del norte del continente sudamericano y San Martín es el libertador de los países del sur.

[1]luchan contra *fight against*   [2]países *countries*   [3]gran *great*

José de San Martín

¿Comprendes?

A Héroes   Den ejemplos. (*Give examples.*)
Many schools in Spain and in Latin America are named after heroes. Is the same true in the United States? Give some examples.

B El libertador   Expliquen. (*Explain.*)
What is the meaning of the word **libertador** or *liberator* in English? What does a liberator do?

C Historia de Estados Unidos
Contesten. (*Answer.*)
Who is considered the liberator of the United States? What did he fight for?

Conexiones
Las ciencias sociales

La geografía

Geography is the scientific study of the Earth's surface. It deals with all of Earth's features, particularly the natural forces that create these features and cause them to change. It is also the study of where people, animals, and plants live and how rivers, deserts, and other of Earth's features affect their lives. It is a subject that has interested human beings since earliest times.

Look at the map of South America. Notice how many geographical terms you will be able to recognize in Spanish. Now find out how easy it is to read about geography in Spanish.

El río Tajo, España

El desierto Atacama, Chile

La geografía

Hay cuatro puntos cardinales: el norte, el sur, el este y el oeste.

Hay siete continentes: la América del Norte, la América del Sur, Europa, África, Asia, Australia y la Antártida.

El océano Atlántico es muy grande. Es inmenso. El océano Pacífico es muy grande también.

España es parte de una península. Puerto Rico es una isla. El español es la lengua[1] de España. Es la lengua de Puerto Rico también. El español es una lengua muy importante. Es la lengua de países[2] en la América del Sur, en la América Central, en el Caribe, en la América del Norte y en Europa.

[1]lengua *language*   [2]países *countries*

Montevideo, Uruguay

Los Andes, Argentina

¿Comprendes?

A **Un poco de geografía** Escojan la palabra. *(Choose the correct word to complete each sentence. You may use a word more than once.)*
1. Europa es un ____.
2. España no es una isla. España es parte de una ____.
3. Puerto Rico es una ____.
4. Cuba es otra ____.
5. El Sahara es un ____ de África y el Atacama es un ____ de la América del Sur.

isla

continente

desierto

océano

península

B **Estrategias** Adivinen. *(Guess the meaning of the following words.)* Often you can guess the meaning of words because of other knowledge you have. You may not know the meaning of **el río** but when you see **el río Misisipí** or **el río Hudson,** you can probably figure out what **río** means.
1. el **río** Hudson
2. la **bahía** Chesapeake
3. el **lago** Superior, el **lago** Erie
4. el **golfo** de México
5. el **mar** Mediterráneo

¡Te toca a ti!

Use what you have learned

1 Un amigo nuevo

✔ *Describe a male friend and answer questions about him*

Work with a classmate. Here's a picture of your new friend, Carlos Álvarez. He's from Barcelona, Spain. Say as much as you can about him and answer any questions your partner may have about Carlos.

2 Una alumna nueva

✔ *Ask a female friend questions and tell her about yourself*

Inés Figueroa (a classmate) is a new girl in your school. You want to get to know her better and help her feel at home. Find out as much as you can about her. Tell Inés about yourself, too.

Barcelona, España

3 Oye, ¿quién es?

✔ *Ask someone questions about another person*

You and a friend (a classmate) are in a café in San Juan, Puerto Rico. You see an attractive girl or boy across the room. It just so happens your friend knows the person. Ask your friend as many questions as you can to find out more about the boy or girl you're interested in.

San Juan,
Puerto Rico

ESCRIBIR

4 Un amigo español
✔ *Write a postcard telling about yourself*

The following is a postcard you just received from a new pen pal.
First read the postcard. Then answer it. Give Jorge similar information
about yourself.

¡Hola!
Soy Jorge Pérez Navarro. Soy de Madrid, la
capital de España. Soy español. Soy alumno
en el Colegio Sorolla. Soy rubio y bastante
alto. Soy bastante gracioso. No soy muy
serio. Y no soy tímido. De ninguna manera.
Hasta pronto,
Jorge

Plaza de Cibeles, Madrid, España

Writing Strategy

Freewriting One of the easiest ways to begin any kind of
personal writing is simply to begin—to let your thoughts flow and
write the first thing that comes to mind. Sometimes as you think
of one word, another word will come to mind. If you get stuck,
take several minutes to think of another word or phrase. Such
brainstorming and freewriting are sometimes the best sources
when doing any type of writing about yourself.

HABLAR

5 ¿Quién soy yo?

ESCRIBIR

On a piece of paper, write down as
much as you can about yourself in
Spanish. Your teacher will collect the
descriptions and choose students to
read them to the class. You will all try
to guess who's being described.

Assessment

Vocabulario

1 **Escojan.** *(Choose.)*

1.
   a. serio
   b. gracioso

2.
   a. guapo
   b. feo

3.
   a. morena
   b. rubia

4.
   a. ambiciosa
   b. perezosa

5.
   a. alto
   b. bajo

To review **Palabras 1**, turn to pages 14-15.

To review **Palabras 2**, turn to pages 18-19.

2 **Completen.** *(Complete.)*

6. Roberto es ____ en una escuela secundaria.
7. Roberto no es ____. Él es bastante serio.
8. Carmen es una ____ de Roberto. Ella es una ____ muy simpática.
9. Sancho Panza es ____. No es flaco.

Estructura

3 **Completen con el o la.** *(Complete with* el *or* la.*)*

10–11. ____ muchacho es americano y ____ muchacha es mexicana.
12. Ella es alumna en ____ Colegio de Santa Teresa.

4 **Completen con un o una.** *(Complete with* un *or* una.*)*

13–14. ____ colegio es ____ escuela secundaria.

To review definite and indefinite articles, turn to page 22.

5 Completen. *(Complete.)*

15. El muchacho es ____. (pelirrojo)
16. La muchacha es ____ también. (pelirrojo)
17. Ella es muy ____. (gracioso)
18. Pero él es bastante ____. (serio)

To review adjectives, turn to page 23.

6 Completen con **ser.** *(Complete with* ser.*)*

19. El muchacho ____ cubano.
20. Yo ____ americano(a).
21. Y tú, ¿de dónde ____?

To review ser in the singular, turn to page 25.

7 Contesten con **no.** *(Answer with* no.*)*

22. ¿Es muy tímida la muchacha?
23. ¿Eres argentino(a)?

To review negative sentences, turn to page 25.

Cultura

8 Escojan. *(Choose the correct completion.)*

24. Don Quijote es ____.
    a. escudero   **b.** alto y flaco   **c.** bajo y gordo
25. El autor de *El Quijote* es ____.
    a. Shakespeare   **b.** Sancho Panza   **c.** Cervantes

To review this cultural information, turn to pages 30-31.

Tell all you can about this illustration.

Identifying a person or thing

el muchacho   la alumna
la muchacha   la persona
el amigo   el colegio
la amiga   la escuela
el alumno

Describing a person

alto(a)	moreno(a)	cómico(a)	tímido(a)
bajo(a)	rubio(a)	serio(a)	sincero(a)
guapo(a)	pelirrojo(a)	ambicioso(a)	honesto(a)
bonito(a)	flaco(a)	perezoso(a)	generoso(a)
lindo(a)	gordo(a)	bueno(a)	simpático(a)
feo(a)	gracioso(a)	fantástico(a)	ser

Stating nationality

americano(a)   mexicano(a)
chileno(a)   puertorriqueño(a)
colombiano(a)   venezolano(a)
cubano(a)

How well do you know your vocabulary?

- Choose five words that describe a good friend.
- Use these words to write several sentences about him or her.

Finding out information

¿quién?   ¿de qué nacionalidad?
¿qué?   ¿no?
¿cómo?
¿de dónde?

Expressing degrees

bastante
muy
no, de ninguna manera

Other useful expressions

secundario(a)

VIDEOTUR

Episodio 1

In this video episode, you will meet six friends from different Spanish-speaking countries. Get to know Alejandra, Julián, Claudia, Alberto, Vicky, and Fernando as they themselves become acquainted. See page 492 for more about the adventures of our new friends.

Capítulo 2

Alumnos y cursos

Objetivos

In this chapter you will learn to:

- describe people and things
- talk about more than one person or thing
- tell what subjects you take in school and express some opinions about them
- tell time
- tell at what time an event takes place
- talk about Spanish speakers in the United States

Juan Carlos Liberti *Concierto barroco*

¿Quiénes son?

PUERTO RICO
• Ponce

las alumnas

las amigas

los alumnos

los amigos

¿Qué son?

Marta y Adela son puertorriqueñas.
Juan y Ricardo son puertorriqueños también.
Los cuatro amigos son de Ponce.
Ellos son alumnos en la misma escuela.
Son muy inteligentes.

¿Cómo son las clases?

la clase

el profesor

los alumnos

la profesora

Es una clase pequeña.
¿Cuántos alumnos hay en la clase?
Hay pocos alumnos en la clase.
Es una clase aburrida.

Es una clase grande.
Hay muchos alumnos en la clase.
Es una clase interesante.

El curso de español no es difícil. Es fácil.

El curso de matemáticas es bastante difícil (duro).

Nota Once again you will see how many Spanish words you already know because they are cognates. You should have no trouble guessing the meaning of these words.

el curso	inteligente	dominicano
la clase	interesante	ecuatoriano
el profesor, la profesora	popular	panameño

¿Qué palabra necesito?

1 **Historieta** **Los cuatro amigos argentinos**

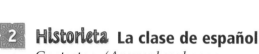

Contesten. (*Answer.*)

1. ¿Son amigas Sara y Julia?
2. ¿Son amigos David y Alejandro?
3. ¿Son argentinos o mexicanos los cuatro amigos?
4. ¿Son de Buenos Aires o de Puebla?
5. ¿Son ellos alumnos muy buenos?

2 **Historieta** **La clase de español**

Contesten. (*Answer based on your own experience.*)

1. ¿Es grande o pequeña la clase de español?
2. ¿Hay muchos o pocos alumnos en la clase de español?
3. ¿Quién es el profesor o la profesora de español?
4. ¿De qué nacionalidad es él o ella?
5. ¿Cómo es el curso de español? ¿Es un curso interesante o aburrido?
6. ¿Es fácil o difícil el curso de español?
7. ¿Son muy inteligentes los alumnos en la clase de español?
8. ¿Son ellos alumnos serios?
9. ¿Cuántos alumnos hay en la clase de español?

Plaza San Martín, Buenos Aires, Argentina

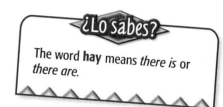

¿Lo sabes?

The word **hay** means *there is* or *there are.*

Una clase de español

3 De ninguna manera

Sigan el modelo. *(Follow the model.)*

Son interesantes, ¿no?

No, de ninguna manera.

Entonces, ¿cómo son?

Son aburridos.

1. Son pequeños, ¿no?
2. Son aburridos, ¿no?
3. Son fáciles, ¿no?
4. Son altos, ¿no?
5. Son bonitos, ¿no?

4 ¿Cómo es la clase?
With a classmate, look at the photograph. Take turns asking each other questions about it. Use the following question words: **¿qué? ¿quién? ¿cómo? ¿de dónde? ¿cuántos?**

5 La escuela ideal
Get together with a classmate. Describe what for each of you is an ideal school. Say as much as you can about the teachers, classes, and students. Determine whether you agree.

Los cursos escolares

Las ciencias
la biología
la química
la física

Las matemáticas
la aritmética
el álgebra
la geometría
el cálculo

Las lenguas
el español
el inglés
el francés
el alemán
el latín

Las ciencias sociales
la historia
la geografía

**Otras asignaturas
o disciplinas**
la educación física
la música
el arte
la economía doméstica
la informática

¿Qué son?

¡Hola, todos!
Nosotros somos americanos.
Uds. son americanos también, ¿no?
¿Son Uds. alumnos de español?
Nosotros, sí. Y somos alumnos muy buenos.

Más números

31	treinta y uno	**36**	treinta y seis	**50**	cincuenta
32	treinta y dos	**37**	treinta y siete	**60**	sesenta
33	treinta y tres	**38**	treinta y ocho	**70**	setenta
34	treinta y cuatro	**39**	treinta y nueve	**80**	ochenta
35	treinta y cinco	**40**	cuarenta	**90**	noventa

Vocabulario

¿Qué palabra necesito?

6 Ciencias, lenguas o matemáticas
Contesten con **sí** o **no**. (*Answer with sí or no.*)

1. La biología es una ciencia.
2. La historia y la geografía son matemáticas.
3. El cálculo es una lengua.
4. El latín y el francés son lenguas.
5. El arte y la música son cursos obligatorios.

7 Cursos fáciles y difíciles Contesten.
(*Answer based on your own experience.*)

1. ¿Es el español un curso difícil o fácil?
2. ¿Es grande o pequeña la clase de español?
3. ¿Qué cursos son fáciles?
4. ¿Cuántos cursos son fáciles?
5. ¿Qué cursos son difíciles?
6. ¿Cuántos cursos son difíciles?
7. ¿Qué cursos son interesantes?
8. ¿Qué cursos son aburridos?

8 Historieta Alumnos americanos
Contesten. (*Answer.*)

1. ¿De qué nacionalidad son los alumnos?
2. ¿Son alumnos en una escuela secundaria?
3. ¿Son alumnos de química?
4. ¿Son alumnos buenos o malos en la química?

9 ¿Qué curso o asignatura es?
Identifiquen el curso. (*Identify the course.*)

1. el problema, la ecuación, la solución, la multiplicación, la división
2. la literatura, la composición, la gramática
3. un microbio, un animal, una planta, el microscopio, el laboratorio
4. el círculo, el arco, el rectángulo, el triángulo
5. el piano, el violín, la guitarra, el concierto, la ópera, el coro
6. las montañas, los océanos, las capitales, los recursos naturales
7. la pintura, la estatua, la escultura
8. el fútbol, el básquetbol, el béisbol, el voleibol, el tenis

Una clase de ciencias

10 **¡Qué clase tan difícil!** Divide into groups of three or four. In each group rate your courses as **fácil, difícil, regular, interesante, aburrido, fantástico.** Tally the results and report the information to the class.

SPANISH *Online*

For more information about Córdoba and other cities in the Spanish-speaking world, go to the Glencoe Spanish Web site: spanish.glencoe.com

11 **En España** You are spending the summer with a family in Córdoba in southern Spain. Tell your Spanish "brother" or "sister" (your partner) all you can about your Spanish class and your Spanish teacher. Answer any questions he or she may have.

Córdoba, España

12 *Juego* **Un número secreto** Think of a number between 1 and 99. Your partner will try to guess the number you have in mind. Use a hand gesture to indicate whether the number you are thinking of is higher or lower. Continue until your partner guesses the correct number. Take turns.

Estructura

Sustantivos, artículos y adjetivos en el plural
Describing more than one

1. Plural means *more than one.* In Spanish, the plural of most nouns is formed by adding an **s**.

SINGULAR	PLURAL
el muchacho	**los muchachos**
el colegio	**los colegios**
la amiga	**las amigas**
la escuela	**las escuelas**

2. The plural forms of the definite articles **el** and **la** are **los** and **las.** The plural forms of the indefinite articles **un** and **una** are **unos** and **unas.**

SINGULAR	PLURAL
el curso	**los cursos**
la alumna	**las alumnas**
un amigo	**unos amigos**
una amiga	**unas amigas**

3. To form the plural of adjectives that end in **o, a,** or **e,** you add **s** to the singular form.

El alumno es serio.	**Los alumnos son serios.**
La alumna es seria.	**Las alumnas son serias.**
La lengua es interesante.	**Las lenguas son interesantes.**

4. To form the plural of adjectives that end in a consonant, you add **es.**

El curso es fácil.	**Los cursos son fáciles.**
La lengua es fácil.	**Las lenguas son fáciles.**

COLEGIO EXTERNADO DE SAN JOSE
SAN SALVADOR.

EXAMEN DE 2a. QUINCENA III TRIMESTRE
I N G L E S.
TURNO VESPERTINO.

NOMBRE: Diana Aída Martínez Cortez   # 22 SECC: B 10/.

I PARTE: Tranlate into English.

- La casa esta limpia.   The house is clean
- El policia es fuerte.   The policeman is strong,
- El doctor es guapo.   The doctor is handsome
- Rose es gorda.   Rose is fat
- El carro es caro.   The car is expensive.   3√

¿Cómo lo digo?

 13 Historieta Amigos nuevos

Contesten con **sí.** (*Answer with* sí.)

1. ¿Son amigos nuevos los dos muchachos?
2. ¿Son chilenos los dos muchachos?
3. ¿Son ellos alumnos en un colegio en Santiago, Chile?
4. ¿Son alumnos serios?
5. ¿Son ellos muchachos populares?

Santiago, Chile

 14 ¿Cómo son?

Describan a las personas. (*Describe the people.*)

1. David, Domingo

2. Inés, Susana

3. Paco, Eduardo

4. Isabel, Carmen

 15 Historieta La señora Ortiz Completen.
(*Complete with an appropriate word.*)

La señora Ortiz es una profesora muy __1__. Las clases de
la señora Ortiz son __2__. Las clases de la señora Ortiz no son __3__.
Los alumnos de la señora Ortiz son __4__. No son __5__.

Estructura

 ## Presente de **ser** en el plural
Talking about more than one

1. You have already learned the singular forms of the verb **ser.** Review the following.

SER	
yo	soy
tú	eres
él	es
ella	es

2. Now study the plural forms of the verb **ser.**

SER	
nosotros(as)	somos
ellos	son
ellas	son
Uds.	son

3.

Nosotros somos amigos.

Ellos son americanos.

When you talk about yourself and another person or other people, you use the **nosotros(as)** form.

You use **ellos** when talking about two or more males or a mixed group of males and females.

Ellas son simpáticas.

¿Uds. son amigos?

Sí, somos amigos.

You use **ellas** when talking about two or more females.

When talking to more than one person, you use **ustedes,** the plural form for **tú. Ustedes** is commonly abbreviated as **Uds.**

¿Cómo lo digo?

16 **Somos alumnos americanos.**

Practiquen la conversación. *(Practice the conversation.)*

—¿Son ustedes americanos?

—Sí, somos americanos.

—¿Son ustedes alumnos?

—Sí, somos alumnos. Y somos alumnos serios.

—¿En qué escuela son ustedes alumnos?

—Somos alumnos en la Escuela Jorge Wáshington. Y ustedes, ¿son alumnas?

—Sí, somos alumnas en la Escuela Martin Luther King.

Completen según la conversación. *(Complete based on the conversation.)*

Los muchachos __1__ americanos. Ellos __2__ alumnos. __3__ alumnos muy serios. __4__ alumnos buenos. __5__ alumnos en la Escuela Jorge Wáshington. Las muchachas __6__ americanas también. __7__ alumnas en la Escuela Martin Luther King.

17 **Él, ella y yo** Contesten. *(Answer.)*

1. ¿Son ustedes amigos?
2. ¿Son ustedes alumnos serios?
3. ¿Son ustedes graciosos?
4. ¿En qué escuela son ustedes alumnos?

5. ¿Son ustedes alumnos en la misma clase de español o en clases diferentes?
6. ¿Son ustedes alumnos buenos en español?

18 **¿Qué son ustedes?** Formen preguntas según el modelo.
(Form questions based on the model.)

americanos   cubanos

—María y José, ¿son ustedes americanos o cubanos?
—Somos cubanos.

1. chilenos   mexicanos

2. bajos   altos

3. morenos   rubios

La República Dominicana

19 **Historieta** **El amigo de Carlos**

Completen con **ser.** *(Complete with ser.)*

Yo __1__ un amigo de Carlos. Carlos __2__ muy simpático. Y él __3__ gracioso. Carlos y yo __4__ dominicanos. __5__ de la República Dominicana.

La República Dominicana __6__ parte de una isla en el mar Caribe. Nosotros __7__ alumnos en un colegio en Santo Domingo. Santo Domingo __8__ la capital de la República Dominicana. Nosotros __9__ alumnos de inglés. La profesora de inglés __10__ la señora Drake. Ella __11__ americana.

La clase de inglés __12__ bastante interesante. Nosotros __13__ muy buenos en inglés. Nosotros __14__ muy inteligentes.

¿Y ustedes? Ustedes __15__ americanos, ¿no? ¿De dónde __16__ ustedes? ¿__17__ ustedes alumnos en una escuela secundaria? ¿__18__ ustedes alumnos de español?

20 **¿De qué nacionalidad son?** Work in groups of four. Two of ... together and choose a city from the map below. The other two ... ... Take turns. Follow the model.

Sí, somos de Santo Domingo.

La hora
Telling time

1. To find out the time, you ask:

   ¿Qué hora es?

2. To tell time, you say:

Es la una.

Son las dos.

Son las diez.

Son las doce.

Es el mediodía.

Es la medianoche.

Es la una y diez.

Son las tres y cinco.

Son las cuatro
y veinticinco.

Son las cinco
menos veinte.

Son las seis
menos diez.

Son las diez
menos cinco.

Son las dos
y cuarto.

Son las siete
menos cuarto.

Son las seis y media.

3. To indicate A.M. and P.M. in Spanish, you use the following expressions.

Son las ocho de la mañana.   **Son las tres de la tarde.**   **Son las once de la noche.**

4. To ask and tell at what time something (such as a party) takes place you say:

—¿A qué hora es la fiesta?
—La fiesta es a las nueve.

¿Cómo lo digo?

21 **¿Qué hora es?** Digan la hora. *(Tell the time on each clock.)*

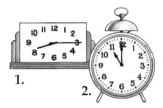

1.   2.   3.   4.   5.   6.

22 **El horario escolar** Digan la hora de la clase. *(Tell the time of each class.)*

23 **¿A qué hora** Find out from a partner what time he or she has a particular class. He or she will respond with the time. Take turns.

For more practice telling time, do Activity 2 on page H3 at the end of this book.

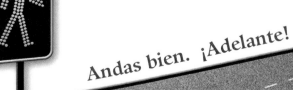
Andas bien. ¡Adelante!

Conversación

¿De qué nacionalidad son ustedes?

Patricio ¿De dónde son ustedes?
Manuel ¿Nosotros? Somos americanos.
Patricio ¿Ah, sí? ¿De dónde?
Manuel Somos de Tejas, de San Antonio.
¿De qué nacionalidad son ustedes?
Patricio Somos mexicanos. Somos de Coyoacán.
Manuel ¿Coyoacán?
Patricio Sí, es una colonia de la Ciudad
de México, la capital.

¿Comprendes?

Contesten. (*Answer.*)

1. ¿De dónde son los muchachos americanos?
2. ¿De dónde son los muchachos mexicanos?
3. ¿Cuál es la capital de México?
4. ¿Cuál es una ciudad en el estado de Tejas?
5. ¿Cuál es una parte de la Ciudad de México?

Vamos a hablar más

A **En México** Work in groups of four. Two of you are visiting Mexico and you meet two Mexican students in a café. Find out as much about each other and your schools as you can.

Guanajuato, México

B **Juego** **¿Qué clase es?** Work with a classmate. He or she gives you a one-sentence description of a class. Guess what class it is. If you're wrong, your partner will give you another hint. Continue until you guess the class being described. Take turns.

Pronunciación

Las vocales e, i

The sounds of the Spanish vowels **e** and **i** are short, clear, and concise. The pronunciation of **e** is similar to *a* in *mate*. The pronunciation of **i** is similar to the *ee* in *bee* or *see*. Imitate the pronunciation carefully.

e	i
Elena	Isabel
peso	Inés

Repeat the following sentences.

Elena es una amiga de Felipe.
Inés es tímida.
Sí, Isabel es italiana.

Lecturas culturales

El español en Estados Unidos 🔄 🎧

Reading Strategy

Using titles and subtitles Look at titles and subtitles before you begin to read. They will usually help you know what a reading selection will be about. Having an idea of what a reading will be about will help you understand better as you read.

Mexicanoamericanos

¡Hola! Somos Alejandro Chávez y Guadalupe Garza. Somos alumnos en una escuela secundaria de Pueblo, Colorado. Somos alumnos en una escuela secundaria americana. Pero para nosotros el español no es una lengua extranjera[1]. ¿Por qué[2]? Porque nosotros somos de ascendencia[3] mexicana. Somos mexicanoamericanos.

[1]extranjera   *foreign*
[2]¿Por qué?   *Why?*
[3]ascendencia   *background, descent*

Jóvenes de ascendencia mexicana

Miami, la Florida

Jóvenes de ascendencia cubana

Cubanoamericanos

Nosotros somos Raúl Ugarte y Marta Dávila. Somos de Miami, en la Florida. Como muchas personas en Miami, somos de ascendencia cubana. Somos cubanoamericanos.

En Estados Unidos hay unos cuarenta millones de hispanohablantes[4]. El español es una lengua muy importante en Estados Unidos.

[4]hispanohablantes *Spanish speakers*

¿Comprendes?

A Alejandro Chávez y Guadalupe Garza
Contesten. (*Answer.*)
1. ¿Quiénes son Alejandro Chávez y Guadalupe Garza?
2. ¿Dónde son alumnos?
3. ¿De dónde son ellos?
4. Para Alejandro y Guadalupe, ¿es el español una lengua extranjera?
5. ¿Por qué no? ¿Qué son ellos?

B Raúl Ugarte y Marta Dávila
Corrijan. (*Correct the false statements.*)
1. Raúl Ugarte y Marta Dávila son de ascendencia mexicana.
2. Ellos son mexicanoamericanos.
3. Ellos son de San Antonio, Tejas.
4. Hay unos cuarenta millones de hispanohablantes en Cuba.

Lectura opcional ❶

San Antonio

San Antonio es una ciudad[1] muy bonita de Tejas. Es una ciudad muy histórica. Es la ciudad favorita de muchos turistas. San Antonio es una ciudad bilingüe. Hay mucha gente[2] de ascendencia mexicana en San Antonio. Hay muchos mexicanoamericanos.

[1]ciudad *city*
[2]gente *people*

El Álamo, San Antonio

El río, San Antonio

¿Comprendes?

A **¿Cómo es San Antonio?**
Contesten con **sí** o **no**.
(Answer with sí or no.)
1. San Antonio es una ciudad bastante fea.
2. Hay monumentos históricos en San Antonio.
3. San Antonio es una ciudad de México.
4. Hay muchos hispanohablantes en San Antonio.
5. Hay muchos mexicanoamericanos en San Antonio.

B **En español, por favor.**
Busquen las palabras afines en la lectura.
(Find the following cognates in the reading.)
1. favorite   3. bilingual
2. historic   4. tourists

Lectura opcional ②

Coyoacán

La Ciudad de México es hoy día[1] la ciudad más grande del mundo[2]. Coyoacán es una colonia en la zona sur de la ciudad. Es una colonia bonita y tranquila. Es elegante también. Muchos residentes o habitantes de Coyoacán son personas famosas.

[1]hoy día *these days*
[2]mundo *world*

Coyoacán, México

¿Comprendes?

A La Ciudad de México
Completen. (*Complete.*)
1. _____ es la ciudad más grande del mundo.
2. _____ es una colonia de la Ciudad de México.
3. Coyoacán es una colonia en la zona _____ de la ciudad.
4. Hay muchas personas _____ en Coyoacán.

B En español, por favor. Busquen las palabras afines en la lectura. (*Find the following cognates in the reading.*)
1. zone
2. tranquil, calm
3. elegant
4. residents
5. inhabitants

MUSEO   Nº 13376
Frida Kahlo
LONDRES Nº 247
COL. DEL CARMEN
COYOACAN
ADMISION: N$ 5.00

El Museo de Frida Kahlo, Coyoacán

Conexiones

Las ciencias sociales

La sociología

Sociology is the study of society in all its aspects. A society is composed of many groups. All of us belong to a number of groups. We belong to a family group, a language group, and an ethnic or racial group.

The large Spanish-speaking world is one of great diversity. There are many ethnic groups living in Spain and in Latin America. Let's take a look at some of these groups.

Grupos étnicos de Latinoamérica

En Latinoamérica hay muchos grupos étnicos. ¿Cuáles son los grupos étnicos de Latinoamérica?

Influencia africana

En la región del Caribe hay mucha influencia africana. En Puerto Rico, Cuba, la República Dominicana, Panamá y en la costa norte de la América del Sur, la influencia negra es notable. Hay mucha gente[1] de ascendencia africana. Hay también mucha gente de raza mixta—de sangre[2] blanca y negra.

Influencia india o indígena

En México, Guatemala y la región andina—de los Andes—hay muchos indios. En Ecuador, Perú y Bolivia, hay muchos descendientes de los incas. En México y Guatemala hay muchos descendientes de los mayas. Hay también muchos mestizos, personas con una mezcla[3] de sangre india y blanca.

Criollos

¿Y quiénes son los criollos? Los criollos son los blancos nacidos[4] en las colonias—los españoles nacidos en América.

[1]gente *people*   [2]sangre *blood*   [3]mezcla *mixture*   [4]nacidos *born*

La almendra del cacao
de Diego Rivera

¿Comprendes?

A En español Busquen las palabras afines en la lectura.
(Find the cognates in the reading.)

B La palabra, por favor. Pareen. *(Match.)*

1. área de las Américas donde el español es la lengua oficial
2. una persona de África
3. la región de los Andes
4. los indios del Perú, Ecuador y Bolivia
5. los indios de México y Guatemala
6. una persona con una mezcla de sangre india y blanca

   a. mestizo
   b. Latinoamérica
   c. africano
   d. andina
   e. descendientes de los incas
   f. descendientes de los mayas

¡Te toca a ti!

Use what you have learned

HABLAR

1 Nosotros(as)

✔ *Describe yourself and someone else*

Work with a classmate. Together prepare a speech that you are going to present to the class. To help you organize your presentation, use the following as a guide.

- tell who you are
- tell where you're from
- give the name of your school
- describe one of your classes

HABLAR

2 La escuela ideal

✔ *Talk about school*

Work with a classmate. Describe what for each of you is an ideal school. Say as much as you can about the teachers, classes, and students.

Salón de clase, San Miguel de Allende, México

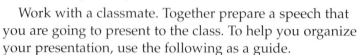

```
                    *** LICEO SALVADOREÑO ***

                       INFORME   DE   NOTAS

    22 - MANUEL ERNESTO MARTINEZ CORTEZ
                                          PROF. RODRIGO RAMIREZ SANTOS

    TERCERA AREA                                     Nota   30%   3ra.   Nota Obs.
                           1ra.  2da.  Act  Activ.  P.O.               Area   ACUM.
    Nombre materia         Area  Area  10%   40%    50%

                                                     88    26.4   2.6    4.8
                           0.9   1.3   10    34      44    86    25.8   2.6    5.1
    EDUCACION EN LA FE      1.2   1.3   31    46      87    26.1   2.6    4.8
    LENGUAJE               1.0   1.2   8     33      46    97    29.1   2.9    5.5
    ESTUDIOS SOCIALES      1.4   1.2   10    38      49    87    26.1   2.6    5.2
    INGLES                 1.2   1.4   10    37      40    83    24.9   2.5    5.2
    MATEMATICAS            1.3   1.4   9     38      36    95    28.5   2.9    5.3
    CIENCIA,SALUD Y MEDIO A 1.2   1.2   9     36      50   100    30.0   3.0    5.8
    EDUCACION ESTETICA     1.4   1.4   10    40      50    86    25.8   2.6    5.1
    EDUCACION FISICA       1.2   1.3   10    31      45    95    28.5   2.9    5.5
    MECANOGRAFIA           1.3   1.3   9     36      50
    COMPUTACION


                                                  FIRMA ENCARGADO
```

ESCRIBIR
3 Un correo electrónico
✔ *Write about your classes and friends*

Answer an e-mail message from a student in Colombia who wants to know about your life in the United States. Give him or her as many details as possible about school, classes, and friends.

San Andrés, Colombia

ESCRIBIR
4 Clases y profesores

You've been in school for about a month. You've had a chance to get to know what your courses are like and to become familiar with your teachers. Create a journal entry in which you write about your classes and your teachers. Try to write about your classes— the days and times of each, whether there are many or few students, whether the class is big or small, what the class is like, who the teacher is, and what he or she is like. When you have finished, reread your journal entry. Did you discover anything about your courses or your teachers that you hadn't thought of before?

Writing Strategy

Keeping a journal There are many kinds of journals you can keep, each having a different purpose. One type of journal is the kind in which you write about daily events and record your thoughts and impressions about these events. It's almost like "thinking out loud." By keeping such a journal, you may find that you discover something new that you were not aware of.

Assessment

Vocabulario

1 ¿Sí o no? *(True or false?)*

1. Hay muchos alumnos en una clase pequeña.
2. Una clase aburrida es muy interesante.
3. Marta y Tomás son alumnos en el Colegio Rubén Torres. Son alumnos en la misma escuela.

To review **Palabras 1**, turn to pages 44–45.

2 Den lo contrario. *(Give the opposite.)*

4. difícil
5. interesante
6. pequeño

3 Identifiquen. *(Identify.)*

¿Qué curso es?

To review **Palabras 2**, turn to pages 48–49.

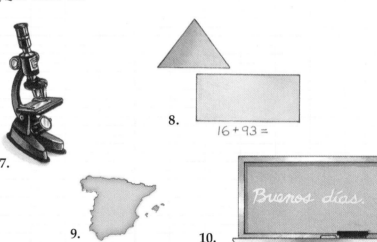

8. $16 + 93 =$

7.

9.

10. *Buenos días.*

Estructura

4 Completen con el plural. *(Complete with the plural.)*

To review plurals, turn to page 52.

11. El alumno es muy inteligente.
    ____ alumno__ ____ muy inteligente__.
12. La amiga de Carlos es puertorriqueña.
    ____ amiga__ de Carlos ____ puertorriqueña__.
13. El curso de matemáticas es fácil.
    ____ curso__ de matemáticas ____ fácil__.
14. La muchacha rubia es chilena.
    ____ muchacha__ rubia__ ____ chilena__.

5 **Completen con ser.** *(Complete with* ser.*)*

15. ¿De qué nacionalidad ____ ustedes?
16. Ustedes ____ alumnos en la misma escuela, ¿no?
17. Sí, (nosotros) ____ alumnos en el Colegio Hidalgo.
18. Nosotros ____ mexicanos.

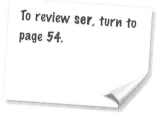
To review **ser**, turn to page 54.

Cultura

6 **Completen.** *(Complete.)*

19–20. Hay muchos mexicanoamericanos y cubanoamericanos en Estados Unidos. Los mexicanoamericanos son de ascendencia ____ y los cubanoamericanos son de ascendencia ____.

To review this cultural information, turn to pages 62-63.

Tell all you can about this illustration.

Vocabulario

Identifying a person or thing

el profesor
la profesora

la clase
el curso

Identifying school subjects

las ciencias
  la biología
  la química
  la física
las matemáticas
  la aritmética
  el álgebra
  la geometría
  el cálculo
las ciencias sociales
  la historia
  la geografía

las lenguas
  el inglés
  el español
  el francés
  el alemán
  el latín
otras asignaturas o disciplinas
  la educación física
  la música
  el arte
  la economía doméstica
  la informática

VIDEOTUR

Episodio 2

In this video episode, you will join
Alberto and Claudia in time for class. See
page 493 for more information.

Describing teachers and courses

inteligente
interesante
aburrido(a)
pequeño(a)
grande

fácil
difícil, duro(a)
popular
obligatorio(a)

How well do you know your vocabulary?

- Choose your favorite school subject. Choose words to describe this subject.
- Use these words to describe the subject and your teacher.

Identifying other nationalities

argentino(a)
dominicano(a)

ecuatoriano(a)
panameño(a)

Finding out information

¿quiénes?

¿cuántos(as)?

Agreeing and disagreeing

sí, también
no, de ninguna manera

Other useful expressions

hay
mucho
poco

mismo(a)
todos(as)

Capítulo 3

Las compras para la escuela

Objetivos

In this chapter you will learn to:

- ❖ identify and describe school supplies
- ❖ identify and describe articles of clothing
- ❖ shop for school supplies and clothing
- ❖ state color and size preferences
- ❖ speak to people formally and informally
- ❖ discuss differences between schools in the United States and in Spanish-speaking countries

Joaquín Torres-García *Abstract Art in Five Tones and Complementaries*

Los materiales escolares

la mochila

un cuaderno, un bloc

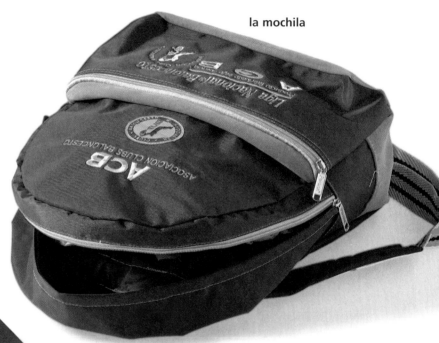

una carpeta

un libro

una calculadora

un marcador

un bolígrafo, una pluma

un disquete

una hoja de papel

una goma de borrar

un lápiz,
dos lápices

En la papelería

Alejandro necesita materiales escolares.
Busca un cuaderno en la papelería.

Alejandro mira un cuaderno.
Mira un bolígrafo también.

¿El cuaderno?
¿Cuánto es, por favor?

Noventa pesos.

la dependienta,
la empleada

Alejandro habla con la dependienta.

la caja

Alejandro compra el cuaderno.
El cuaderno cuesta noventa pesos.
Alejandro paga noventa pesos.
Paga en la caja.

Alejandro lleva los materiales escolares
en una mochila.

Vocabulario

¿Qué palabra necesito?

1 Los materiales escolares
Preparen una lista de materiales escolares importantes. *(Make a list of important school supplies.)*

2 Historieta En la papelería
Contesten. *(Answer.)*

1. ¿Necesita la muchacha materiales escolares?
2. ¿Busca los materiales escolares en la papelería?
3. ¿Mira ella un bolígrafo?
4. ¿Habla con el dependiente?
5. ¿Compra el bolígrafo?
6. ¿Paga en la caja?

Una papelería, Santiago, Chile

grafoplas

3 CARPETAS

Blíster de 3 carpetas con gomas y solapa TECNIGRAF,

€2,85

3 Historieta De compras
Escojan. *(Choose.)*

1. Diego ____ materiales escolares.
   a. paga   **b.** habla   **c.** necesita
2. Él ____ un bolígrafo y un cuaderno.
   a. mira   **b.** cuesta   **c.** habla
3. Diego ____ con el empleado.
   a. paga   **b.** habla   **c.** mira
4. Él necesita ____ para la computadora.
   a. un disquete   **b.** un bloc   **c.** un lápiz
5. Diego ____ en la caja.
   a. paga   **b.** compra   **c.** lleva
6. Él ____ los materiales escolares en una mochila.
   a. compra   **b.** mira   **c.** lleva

4 Historieta Una calculadora, por favor.

Contesten. *(Answer.)*

Una papelería, Málaga, España

1. ¿Con quién habla Casandra en la papelería?
2. ¿Qué necesita ella?
3. ¿Qué busca?
4. ¿Compra la calculadora?
5. ¿Cuánto cuesta la calculadora?
6. ¿Dónde paga Casandra?

5 En la papelería
Work with a classmate. You're buying the school supplies below. Take turns being the customer and the salesperson.

18 pesos
45 pesos
10 pesos
99 pesos
4 pesos

6 Juego ¿Qué es?
Play a guessing game. Your partner will hide a school supply behind his or her back. Guess what he or she is hiding. Take turns.

La ropa

una blusa

una gorra

un traje

un pantalón corto

una chaqueta

un pantalón
largo

un T-shirt,
una camiseta

una camisa

una falda

36

la talla,
el tamaño

los zapatos

38 M 6750032

el número

una corbata

un blue jean

los calcetines

un par de tenis

La muchacha lleva un
     T-shirt y un blue jean.
Lleva un par de tenis.
Lleva una chaqueta.
No lleva una falda.

¿Qué desea Ud.?

Una blusa, por favor.

Sí, señorita. ¿Qué talla usa Ud.?

Treinta y cuatro.

¿Qué número usa (calza) Ud.?

Treinta y ocho.

Gloria habla con la dependienta.
La dependienta trabaja en la tienda de ropa.

Rubén compra un par de zapatos.
Él habla con el dependiente.

La camisa cuesta mucho.
Es muy cara.

1.200 pesos

35 pesos

La gorra no cuesta mucho.
Cuesta poco.
Es bastante barata.

Los colores

¿De qué color es?

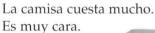

anaranjado(a) verde de color marrón

blanco(a)

gris

rosado(a)

rojo(a)

amarillo(a)

negro(a) azul

Más números

100	ciento, cien	600	seiscientos
200	doscientos	700	setecientos
300	trescientos	800	ochocientos
400	cuatrocientos	900	novecientos
500	quinientos	1000	mil

150	ciento cincuenta
790	setecientos noventa
1800	mil ochocientos

Vocabulario

¿Qué palabra necesito?

7 ¿Qué es? Identifiquen. (Identify.)

1.

2.

3.

4.

5.

6.

Madrid, España

8 Historieta En la tienda de ropa

Contesten según se indica.
(Answer according to the cues.)

1. ¿Con quién habla Eugenio?
   (con la dependiente)
2. ¿Dónde trabaja la dependiente?
   (en la tienda de ropa)
3. ¿Qué necesita Eugenio? (un T-shirt)
4. ¿Qué talla usa? (treinta y ocho)
5. ¿De qué color es el T-shirt? (blanco)
6. ¿Cuánto es? (cinco pesos)
7. ¿Cuesta mucho? (no, poco)
8. ¿Es caro? (no, barato)
9. ¿Compra Eugenio el T-shirt? (sí)
10. ¿Dónde paga? (en la caja)

9 ¿De qué color es? Completen con el color. (Complete with the color.)

1. Tomás compra
   un pantalón ____.
2. Ana compra una
   blusa ____.
3. Emilio compra
   una camisa ____.

4. Paco compra una
   gorra ____.
5. Adriana compra una
   falda ____.
6. César compra zapatos
   de color ____.

10 **¿Qué es?** With a classmate, take turns asking each other what each of the following items is. Then ask questions about each one. Find out how much it costs and tell what you think about the price. Is it a real bargain—**¿una ganga?**

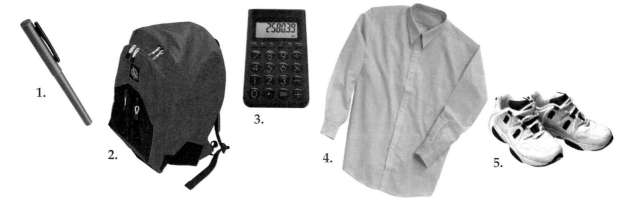

1.
2.
3.
4.
5.

11 **¿Quién es?** Work in small groups. One person tells what someone in the class is wearing. The others have to guess who it is. If several people are wearing the same thing, you will have to give more details.

12 **En la tienda de ropa** With a classmate, look at the photograph. Ask one another questions about it. Answer each other's questions. Then work together to make up sentences about the photograph. Put the sentences in logical order to form a paragraph.

13 **Juego** **¿Cuál es el número?** Give some numbers in a mathematical pattern but leave one out. Your partner will try to figure out what the missing number is. Take turns. You can use the model as a guide.

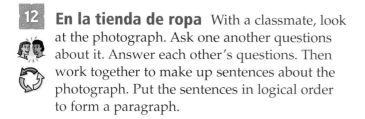

doscientos, cuatrocientos, _____, ochocientos

seiscientos

Estructura

Presente de los verbos en -ar en el singular
Telling what people do

1. All verbs, or action words, in Spanish belong to a family, or conjugation. Verbs whose infinitive ends in **-ar** (**hablar:** *to speak,* **comprar:** *to buy*) are called first conjugation verbs.

necesitar	comprar
buscar	hablar
mirar	pagar

2. Spanish verbs change their endings according to the subject. Study the following forms.

INFINITIVE	hablar	comprar	mirar	ENDINGS
STEM	habl-	compr-	mir-	
yo	hablo	compro	miro	-o
tú	hablas	compras	miras	-as
él	habla	compra	mira	-a
ella	habla	compra	mira	-a

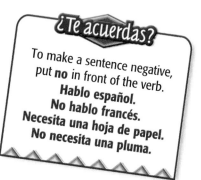
3. Since the ending of the verb in Spanish indicates who performs the action, the subjects (**yo, tú, él, ella**) are often omitted.

Hablo español.

Hablas español.

Habla español.

Use **-o** when you talk about yourself.

Use **-as** when you talk to a friend.

Use **-a** when you talk about someone.

¿Qué palabra necesito?

14 **Historieta** **En la papelería**
Contesten. *(Answer.)*

1. ¿Necesita Andrea materiales escolares?
2. ¿Busca ella un bolígrafo?
3. ¿Compra un bolígrafo en la papelería?
4. ¿Habla ella con la empleada?
5. ¿Paga ella en la caja?
6. ¿Lleva los materiales escolares en una mochila?

Una papelería, Caracas, Venezuela

15 **Historieta** **Llevo un blue jean.**
Contesten personalmente. *(Answer about yourself.)*

1. ¿Llevas un blue jean?
2. ¿Necesitas un nuevo blue jean?
3. ¿Compras el blue jean en una tienda de ropa?
4. ¿Con quién hablas en la tienda?
5. ¿Qué talla usas?
6. ¿Dónde pagas?
7. ¿Pagas mucho?
8. ¿Cuánto pagas?

16 **Historieta** **Necesito un par de tenis, por favor.**
Contesten según se indica. *(Answer according to the cues.)*

1. ¿Qué necesitas? (un par de tenis)
2. ¿Dónde buscas los tenis? (en la zapatería)
3. ¿Qué número usas? (treinta y seis)
4. ¿Miras un par de tenis? (sí)
5. ¿Compras los tenis? (sí)
6. ¿Cuánto pagas? (quinientos pesos)
7. ¿Dónde pagas? (en la caja)

CONVERSION DE TALLAS

Ropa de señora — Vestidos y abrigos						
Estados Unidos	6	8	10	12	14	16
España	36	38	40	42	44	46
Sudamérica	34	36	38	40	42	44
Ropa de señora — Blusas y jersey						
Estados Unidos	30	32	34	36	38	40
España	38	40	42	44	46	48
Sudamérica	38	40	42	44	46	48
Ropa de caballeros — Trajes						
Estados Unidos	34	36	38	40	42	44
España	44	46	48	50	52	54
Sudamérica	44	46	48	50	52	54
Calzado — señoras						
Estados Unidos	4	5	6	7	8	9
España	34/35	35/36	36/37	38/39	39/40	41/42
Sudamérica	2	3	4	5	6	7
Calzado — caballeros						
Estados Unidos	8	8½	9	9½	10	10½
España	41	42	43	43	44	45
Sudamérica	6	6½	7	7½	8	8½

17 **Perdón, ¿qué necesitas?** Sigan el modelo. *(Follow the model.)*

Necesito un bolígrafo.

Perdón, ¿qué necesitas?

1. Necesito una hoja de papel.
2. Busco una goma de borrar.
3. Compro un disquete.
4. Llevo una mochila.

Estructura

18 Historieta **En la tienda de ropa** Completen. *(Complete.)*

Casandra __1__ (necesitar) una blusa. Ella __2__ (buscar) una blusa
verde. En la tienda de ropa Casandra __3__ (hablar) con una amiga.

—Casandra, ¿qué __4__ (buscar)?

—Yo __5__ (buscar) una blusa.

—¿__6__ (Necesitar) un color especial?

—Sí, verde.

—¿Qué talla __7__ (usar)?

—Treinta y seis.

—¿Por qué no __8__ (hablar) con la dependienta?

—¡Buena idea!

Casandra __9__ (hablar) con la dependienta.
Ella __10__ (mirar) varias blusas verdes. Casandra
__11__ (comprar) una blusa que es muy bonita.
Ella __12__ (pagar) en la caja.

Marbella, España

19 **¿Trabajas o no?** Find out from a classmate whether he or she works. Try to find out where and when. Tell the class about your friend's work.

20 **¿Qué necesitas?** You're talking on the phone with a good friend. The new school year **(la apertura de clases)** is about to begin. You need lots of things. Have a conversation with your friend. You may want to use some of the following words and expressions.

¿qué talla?

la papelería

ropa

necesitar

¿de qué color?

la tienda de ropa

materiales escolares

comprar

¿cuánto cuesta?

*For more practice using words from **Palabras 1** and **2** and **-ar** verbs, do Activity 3 on page H4 at the end of this book.*

 Tú o **usted**

Talking formally and informally

1. In Spanish, there are two ways to say *you*. You can use **tú** when talking to a friend, to a person your own age, or to a family member. **Tú** is called the informal or familiar form of address.

> **José, ¿hablas español?** **Carolina, ¿qué necesitas?**

2. You use **usted** when talking to an older person, a person you do not know very well, or anyone to whom you wish to show respect. The **usted** form of address is polite, or formal. **Usted** is usually abbreviated **Ud.** **Usted** takes the same verb ending as **él** or **ella**.

> **Señor, ¿habla usted inglés?**
> **Señora, usted trabaja en la papelería, ¿no?**

¿Qué palabra necesito?

 21 **¿Tú o usted?** Pregunten. (*Ask the following people what they need and what they are looking for. Use* **tú** *or* **usted** *as appropriate.*)

1.   2.   3.   4.   5.

 22 **Claudia y el señor** Sigan el modelo. (*Follow the model.*)

> Necesito una hoja de papel. →
> —Y tú, Claudia, ¿qué necesitas?
> —¿Y qué necesita usted, señor?

1. Necesito un cuaderno.   3. Compro una camisa.
2. Busco una goma de borrar. 4. Hablo español.

Andas bien. ¡Adelante!

Conversación

En la tienda de ropa

OFERTA $150

Empleada	Sí, señor. ¿Qué desea usted?
Cliente	Necesito una camisa.
Empleada	Una camisa. ¿De qué color, señor?
Cliente	Una camisa blanca.
Empleada	De acuerdo. ¿Qué talla usa usted?
Cliente	Treinta y seis.
	(After looking at some shirts)
Cliente	¿Cuánto es, por favor?
Empleada	Ciento cincuenta pesos.
Cliente	Bien. ¿Pago aquí o en la caja?
Empleada	En la caja, por favor.

¿Comprendes?

Contesten. *(Answer.)*

1. ¿Con quién habla el cliente?
2. ¿Qué necesita?
3. ¿Qué talla usa?
4. ¿Mira el señor una camisa?
5. ¿Cuánto es la camisa?
6. ¿Compra el señor la camisa?
7. ¿Dónde paga?

Vamos a hablar más

For more information about schools in the Spanish-speaking world, go to the Glencoe Spanish Web site:
spanish.glencoe.com

A **Para la apertura de clases** Ask a classmate what school supplies he or she needs at the beginning of the new school year and where he or she usually **(generalmente)** buys them. Then tell the class what you find out.

B **En las tiendas** Work with a classmate. Take turns playing the roles of the salesperson and the customer in the following situations.

- **En la papelería** You want to buy two pens—preferably red ones—, a notebook, and a calculator.

- **En la tienda de ropa** You want to buy a blue shirt for your friend. They have his size, but only in white.

- **En la zapatería** You need a pair of brown shoes. The ones the salesperson shows you are expensive.

C **¿Qué lleva?**

Have one student leave the room. The others will choose a classmate to describe. The student who left comes back in and has to guess which classmate the others have chosen by asking questions about his or her clothes. Use the model as a guide.

¿Lleva un blue jean azul y una camiseta roja?

¿Lleva un par de tenis negros?

¡Es Tomás!

No.

Sí.

Pronunciación

Las consonantes l, f, p, m, n

The pronunciation of the consonants **l, f, p, m,** and **n** is very similar in both Spanish and English. However, the **p** is not followed by a puff of breath as it often is in English. Repeat the following sentences.

> **Lolita es linda y elegante.**
> **La falda de Felisa no es fea.**
> **Paco es una persona popular.**
> **La muchacha mexicana mira una goma.**
> **Nando necesita un cuaderno nuevo.**

Lecturas culturales

Reading Strategy

Using pictures and photographs Before you begin to read, look at pictures, photographs, or any other visuals that accompany a reading. By doing this, you can often tell what the reading selection is about before you actually read it.

Un alumno madrileño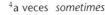

   Julio Torres es de Madrid. Él es alumno en el Liceo Joaquín Turina en Madrid. Un liceo o colegio es una escuela secundaria en España. En Madrid, la apertura de clases[1] es a fines de[2] septiembre. Julio necesita muchas cosas para la apertura de clases. Necesita materiales escolares. En una papelería compra un libro, un bolígrafo, tres lápices y varios cuadernos. Compra también un disquete para la computadora.

   Pero Julio no necesita ropa nueva para la escuela. ¿Por qué? Porque Julio no lleva un blue jean o una camiseta a la escuela. Él lleva un uniforme. Es obligatorio llevar uniforme a la escuela. Un muchacho lleva un pantalón negro y una camisa blanca. En algunas[3] escuelas es necesario llevar chaqueta y corbata también. Una muchacha lleva una falda y una blusa. Y a veces[4] es necesario llevar una chaqueta. ¿Qué opinas? ¿Es una buena idea llevar uniforme a la escuela?

[1]apertura de clases *opening of school*
[2]a fines de *at the end of*
[3]algunas *some*
[4]a veces *sometimes*

A Un alumno madrileño

Contesten. *(Answer.)*

1. ¿De dónde es Julio Torres?
2. ¿En qué escuela es alumno?
3. ¿Cuándo es la apertura de clases en Madrid?
4. ¿Qué necesita Julio para la apertura de clases?
5. ¿Dónde compra las cosas que necesita?
6. ¿Necesita Julio ropa nueva para la escuela?
7. ¿Qué lleva él a la escuela?
8. ¿Qué lleva una muchacha a la escuela?

Colegio de Nuestra Señora de la Consolación, Madrid

B Julio Torres   Busquen la información en la lectura. *(Find the information in the reading.)*

1. de dónde es Julio Torres
2. la escuela de Julio
3. cuándo es la apertura de clases en Madrid
4. las cosas que compra Julio
5. lo que es obligatorio llevar a la escuela
6. lo que Julio no lleva a la escuela
7. el uniforme típico de un muchacho
8. el uniforme típico de una muchacha

C Discusión   ¿Qué opinas? *(What is your opinion?)*
¿Es una buena idea llevar uniforme a la escuela?

El Retiro, Madrid

Lectura opcional ①

La ropa indígena

La ropa que lleva la población india o indígena de Latinoamérica es muy interesante y muy bonita.

En Guatemala, por ejemplo, la ropa cambia o varía de un pueblo[1] a otro. El traje que lleva una señora de Santiago de Atitlán no es el mismo traje que lleva una señora de Chichicastenango.

La india de Guatemala no lleva sombrero. Pero la india del Perú, sí. Ella lleva sombrero.

La india del famoso pueblo de Otavalo en el Ecuador lleva dos faldas de lana[2] oscura con una blusa muy brillante. El señor otavaleño lleva un pantalón blanco, una camisa blanca y un poncho azul.

[1]pueblo *town*   [2]lana *wool*

¿Comprendes?

La ropa indígena
Identifiquen. *(Identify.)*
Some articles of clothing retain their Spanish names in English. Look at the photographs to find out what they are.

huaraches

sarape

poncho

Lectura opcional 2

Un diseñador famoso

El famoso diseñador de ropa Oscar de la Renta es de Santo Domingo, la capital de la República Dominicana. Los estilos de de la Renta son muy elegantes y lujosos. Los trajes de gala de de la Renta son muy caros. La fama de Oscar de la Renta es mundial[1].

Oscar de la Renta es también una persona muy buena y muy humana. En la República Dominicana, de la Renta funda un orfanato[2] y un tipo de «Boys' Town». El «Boys' Town» es para niños desamparados[3]. Funda también una escuela especial para sordos[4].

[1]mundial *worldwide*
[2]orfanato *orphanage*
[3]niños desamparados *homeless children*
[4]sordos *deaf people*

¿Comprendes?

A En español, por favor. Busquen las palabras afines en la lectura. *(Find the cognates in the reading.)*

B Oscar de la Renta Contesten. *(Answer.)*
1. ¿De dónde es Oscar de la Renta?
2. ¿Por qué es él un hombre (señor) muy famoso?

Conexiones
La tecnología

La computadora

Some years ago computers began to revolutionize the way people conduct their lives. They have changed the way we view the world and, in reality, they've changed the world. Computers have a place in our homes, in our schools, and in our world of business. If you are interested in computers, you may want to familiarize yourself with some basic computer vocabulary in Spanish. Then read the information about computers on the next page.

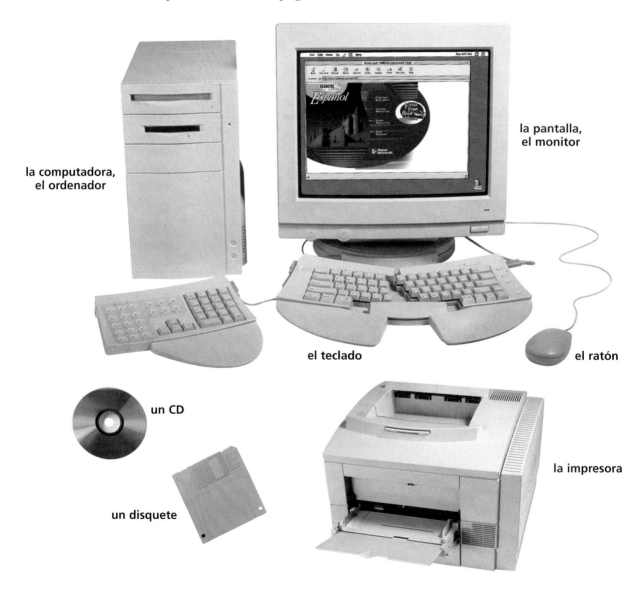

la pantalla, el monitor

la computadora, el ordenador

el teclado

el ratón

un CD

un disquete

la impresora

Conecta la computadora y ¡a trabajar!

Una computadora procesa datos. El hardware es la computadora y todo el equipo[1] conectado con la computadora. El software son los programas de la computadora. Un programa es un grupo o conjunto de instrucciones.

La computadora almacena[2] datos. Envía o transmite los datos a un disco. La computadora calcula, compara y copia datos. Pero la computadora no piensa[3]. El operador o la operadora de la computadora entra las instrucciones y la computadora procesa la información.

[1]equipo *equipment*   [2]almacena *stores*   [3]piensa *think*

El Internet—¡Conecta al mundo!

Con el Internet hay acceso al mundo[4] entero. Hay información sobre la historia, la economía, el arte, la música y muchas otras áreas de interés. Cuando navegas por la red[5], es posible conectar con los centros de noticias. Es posible enviar correo[6] electrónico y conversar con amigos en otras partes del mundo. Cuando estamos conectados a la red por cable o por satélite nuestras comunicaciones son casi instantáneas. Los satélites llevan los mensajes hasta 20 veces más rápido que el modem. Y las conexiones DSL llevan los mensajes de 50 a 150 veces más rápido que el modem. Cada día los avances tecnológicos resultan en comunicaciones más fáciles y más rápidas. Y hay la posibilidad de crear una página Web. Sí, ¡el mundo entero en una pantalla!

[4]mundo *world*   [5]red *Net*   [6]correo *mail*

¿Comprendes?

A En español, por favor.
Busquen las palabras en la lectura.
(Find the following words in the reading.)

1. hardware
2. software
3. program
4. data
5. satelite
6. surf the Net
7. Web page
8. e-mail (electronic mail)
9. to process information
10. access
11. computer operator

B Una página Web Look at the monitor on page 94. If you have access to the Internet either at home or at school, go to **spanish.glencoe.com ¡a practicar el español!**

Los alumnos navegan por la red.

¡Te toca a ti!

Use what you have learned

HABLAR

1 En la papelería

✔ *Identify and shop for school supplies*

With a classmate, take turns playing the parts of a student shopping and a salesperson in a stationery store. Tell some supplies you need and find out how much each item costs. The salesperson will give you the information.

150 pesos

95 pesos

30 pesos

87 pesos

5 pesos

120 pesos

HABLAR

2 Lo que llevo yo

✔ *Identify and describe articles of clothing*

Work with a classmate. Each of you will describe what you typically wear to school.

HABLAR

3 Regalos

✔ *Shop for clothing*

You have just spent a few weeks in Spain and want to buy some articles of clothing as gifts for several friends. Make a list of what you want to buy. Go to the different stores to buy the items you want. With a classmate, take turns being the customer and salesperson at the stores where you are purchasing the items on your list.

Madrid, España

ESCRIBIR
4 Necesito ropa
✔ *Order clothing from a catalogue and give the size and color you need*

You want to order from the catalogue. Write a letter stating which items, what color, and what size.

Pantalón corto de vestir, en varios colores.

€11,99

B - MOCASINES planos con forma de zuecos y pequeño talón de 1.5 cm. Empeine pespunteado de color crudo por el exterior. Exterior y plantilla en piel de serraje acabado ante.

| malva | 580.1030 | negro | 580.3374 |
| beige | 580.3036 | | |

35, 36, 37   **3.795 pesos**
38, 39, 40, 41   **4.195 pesos**

B - desde **3.795** Mocasines **35 41**

PIEL DE SERRAJE

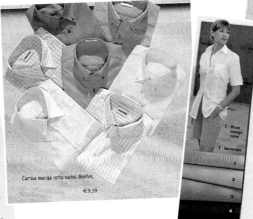

Camisa manga corta varios diseños.
€9,59

C - BLUSA. 100% algodón. **MANGA CORTA CON VUELTA.**
blanco   810.0638
38, 40   **1.995 pesos**
42, 44, 46   **2.195 pesos**
48, 50, 52   **2.395 pesos**
54   **2.595 pesos**

E - BERMUDAS. largo desde el tiro 20 cm, boquilla 30 cm aprox.
1. malva 280.1116   4. marino 280.4409
2. beige 280.0118   5. negro 280.3468
3. caqui 280.2528
36, 38, 40   **2.495 pesos**
42, 44, 46   **2.695 pesos**

Writing Strategy

Preparing for an interview
An interview is one way to gather information for a story or a report. A good interviewer should prepare questions ahead of time. In preparing the questions, think about what you hope to learn from the interview. The best interview questions are open-ended. Open-ended questions cannot be answered with *yes* or *no*. They give the person being interviewed more opportunity to "open up" and speak freely.

HABLAR
ESCRIBIR
5 Guadalupe Álvaro

It is the beginning of a new school year. Your first assignment for the school newspaper is to write an article about a new exchange student, Guadalupe Álvaro. Guadalupe is from Salamanca, Spain.

You decide to interview Guadalupe before writing your article. To prepare for the interview, write down as many questions as you can. Ask her about her personal life, school life in her country, her friends, etc. After you have prepared your questions, conduct the interview with a partner who plays the role of Guadalupe. Write down your partner's answers to your questions. Then organize your notes and write your article.

¿De dónde?
¿Cuánto? ¿Cómo?
¿Quién? ¿Dónde?
¿Qué?

Vocabulario

1 **Identifiquen.** *(Identify.)*

¿Qué es?

1.

2.

3.

To review **Palabras 1,** turn to pages 76–77.

2 **Completen.** *(Complete.)*

4. Alejandro _____ con la dependienta en la papelería.
5. El cuaderno _____ noventa pesos.
6. Alejandro paga en la _____.

3 **Identifiquen.** *(Identify.)*

To review **Palabras 2,** turn to pages 80–81.

7.

8.

9.

4 Completen. *(Complete.)*

10. La muchacha _____ un blue jean y un T-shirt.

11. La camisa no cuesta mucho. Es bastante _____.

12. Rubén compra un par de _____, número 38.

Estructura

5 Completen. *(Complete.)*

13. ¿Cuánto _____ (tú)? (pagar)

14. Yo _____ un nuevo blue jean. (necesitar)

15. ¿Dónde _____ tú el blue jean? (comprar)

16. La dependienta _____ en la tienda de ropa. (trabajar)

6 Escojan. *(Choose.)*

17. ¿Dónde _____, señor?
    a. trabajas   b. trabaja usted

18. Amigo, ¿qué _____?
    a. buscas   b. busca usted

Cultura

7 Contesten. *(Answer)*

19. ¿Qué es un colegio o un liceo en España?

20. En España, ¿qué lleva un alumno o una alumna a la escuela?

To review -ar verbs in the singular, turn to page 84.

To review tú and usted, turn to page 87.

To review this cultural information, turn to page 90.

La Ciudad de México

Tell all you can about this illustration.

Vocabulario

Identifying school supplies

los materiales escolares	el marcador	el libro
la mochila	la goma de borrar	la hoja de papel
el lápiz, los lápices	el cuaderno, el bloc	la calculadora
el bolígrafo, la pluma	la carpeta	el disquete

Identifying articles of clothing

la ropa	el blue jean, los blue jeans	la gorra
el pantalón	la falda	los calcetines
la camisa	la blusa	los zapatos
la corbata	la chaqueta	los tenis, un par de tenis
el T-shirt, la camiseta	el traje	

Describing clothes

largo(a)	corto(a)

Identifying colors

¿De qué color es?	anaranjado(a)
blanco(a)	rojo(a)
negro(a)	rosado(a)
gris	verde
azul	de color marrón
amarillo(a)	

> ### How well do you know your vocabulary?
> - Identify the words and expressions that describe what you do to get ready for a new school year.
> - Use as many words as you can from your list to write a story to tell about your preparation for going back to school.

Identifying some types of stores

la papelería	la tienda de ropa

Shopping

el/la dependiente(a)	necesitar
el/la empleado(a)	buscar
la caja	mirar
la talla, el tamaño	comprar
el número	pagar
barato(a)	usar, calzar
caro(a)	llevar
mucho	hablar
poco	trabajar

VIDEOTUR

Episodio 3

In this video episode, you will accompany Vicky and Julián on a shopping expedition. See page 494 for more information.

Other useful expressions

¿Qué desea usted?	¿Cuánto es?, ¿Cuánto cuesta?

4

En la escuela

Objetivos

In this chapter you will learn to:
- ❖ talk about going to school
- ❖ talk about some school activities
- ❖ greet people and ask how they feel
- ❖ tell how you feel
- ❖ describe where you and others go
- ❖ describe where you and others are
- ❖ discuss some differences between schools in the United States and schools in Spanish-speaking countries

Diego Rivera *Alfabetización*

Llegar a la escuela

a pie

en carro, en coche

en el bus escolar

Los alumnos llegan a la escuela.
¿Cuándo llegan a la escuela?
¿A qué hora llegan?
Llegan a eso de las ocho menos cuarto.
No llegan a las ocho menos cuarto en punto.

Algunos van a la escuela a pie.
Algunos van en carro.
Otros toman el bus escolar.

En la escuela

entrar en la escuela

Los alumnos entran en la escuela.

la sala de clase,
el salón de clase

Los alumnos están en la sala de clase.
Los alumnos estudian.
La profesora enseña.

Vocabulario

¿Qué palabra necesito?

1 Historieta ¡A la escuela!

Contesten. *(Answer.)*

1. ¿Llegan los alumnos a la escuela?
   ¿Adónde llegan los alumnos?
   ¿Quiénes llegan a la escuela?
2. ¿Llegan a la escuela a eso de las ocho menos cuarto?
   ¿Cuándo llegan a la escuela?
   ¿A qué hora llegan a la escuela?
3. ¿Van algunos alumnos a la escuela a pie?
   ¿Cómo van a la escuela?
   ¿Adónde van a pie?
4. ¿Toman otros alumnos el bus escolar?
   ¿Qué toman?
   ¿Adónde toman el bus escolar?
   ¿Cómo llegan ellos a la escuela?

Colegio San José, Estepona, España

Autobuses escolares, Málaga, España

2 Historieta En la escuela

Contesten según se indica.
(Answer according to the cues.)

1. ¿Dónde están los alumnos? (en clase)
2. ¿Quiénes estudian? (los alumnos)
3. ¿Estudian mucho? (sí)
4. ¿Quién no estudia? (la profesora)
5. ¿Quién enseña? (la profesora)

UN POCO MÁS ➤ *For more practice using words from **Palabras 1**, do Activity 4 on page H5.*

3 Historieta ¡A la escuela, todos!

Completen. (*Complete.*)

Los alumnos __1__ a la escuela. Llegan a eso de las __2__ menos cuarto—a las ocho menos veinte o a las ocho menos trece. No __3__ a las ocho menos cuarto en punto. Algunos van a la escuela a __4__. Algunos __5__ en carro. Y otros __6__ el bus escolar.

Los alumnos entran en la __7__ de clase a eso de las ocho. Cuando entran en la clase, hablan con el __8__. Los alumnos __9__ mucho en la escuela. Pero el profesor no __10__; él __11__.

Toman el bus escolar, Quito, Ecuador

4 Entrevista

Work with a classmate. Pretend you are on the staff of your school newspaper and have been assigned to interview a Mexican exchange student about a school day in his or her hometown. Interview him or her.

Tec de Monterrey, Ciudad de México

En la clase

un examen

una nota buena,
una nota alta

una nota mala,
una nota baja

escuchar

hablar

la pizarra, el pizarrón

Los alumnos miran la pizarra.
Miran al profesor también.

El profesor habla.
El profesor explica la lección.
Los alumnos escuchan al profesor.
Prestan atención.
Cuando el profesor habla, los alumnos escuchan.

Los alumnos toman apuntes.

el lunes—examen

Ahora la profesora da un examen.
Los alumnos toman el examen.

Elena saca una nota buena.

La fiesta del Club de español

cantar

una merienda

bailar

El Club de español da una fiesta.
Muchos alumnos van a la fiesta.
Escuchan discos compactos y casetes.
Los miembros del club bailan y cantan.
Toman una merienda también.

un video

un DVD

un CD

Más números

1000	mil	1200	mil doscientos
2000	dos mil	1492	mil cuatrocientos noventa y dos
2002	dos mil dos	1814	mil ochocientos catorce
2500	dos mil quinientos	1898	mil ochocientos noventa y ocho
3000	tres mil	1,000,000	un millón
3015	tres mil quince	2,000,000	dos millones
3650	tres mil seiscientos cincuenta		

Vocabulario

¿Qué palabra necesito?

 5 Historieta En clase Contesten. (*Answer.*)

1. ¿Miran los alumnos la pizarra?
2. ¿Habla la profesora?
3. ¿Escuchan los alumnos?
4. ¿Prestan atención cuando la profesora habla?
5. ¿Toman los alumnos apuntes en un cuaderno?
6. ¿Estudian mucho los alumnos?
7. ¿Trabajan ellos mucho?
8. ¿Da la profesora un examen?
9. ¿Toman los alumnos el examen?
10. ¿Sacan notas buenas o malas en el examen?

Colegio San José, Estepona, España

6 Historieta La escuela Completen. (*Complete.*)

Los alumnos llegan a la escuela y luego van a ___1___. Los alumnos ___2___ mucho en la escuela y los profesores ___3___. Los alumnos toman ___4___ en un cuaderno. Cuando el profesor habla, los alumnos ___5___ atención. El profesor da un ___6___ y los alumnos toman el ___7___. Algunos alumnos sacan notas ___8___ y otros sacan notas ___9___. Una nota buena es una nota ___10___ y una nota mala es una nota ___11___.

7 Historieta El Club de español Contesten con **sí** o **no**. (*Answer with* sí *or* no.)

1. ¿Da una fiesta el Club de español?
2. ¿Van muchos alumnos a la fiesta?
3. ¿Bailan en la fiesta?
4. ¿Cantan también?
5. ¿Preparan los miembros del club una merienda?
6. ¿Toman una merienda?

 8 En clase
With a classmate, look at the photograph. Take turns saying as much as you can about it.

 9 ¿Es importante el año? Think of a year that has some significance. Say the year in Spanish for your partner, who will write it down. Tell him or her whether the number is correct. Have your partner tell you (in English, if necessary) why that year is important. Take turns.

Tres músicos de Pablo Picasso

Ministerio de Cultura
Museo Nacional del Prado

Serie P № 808805

SPANISH Online

For more information about Pablo Picasso and other Hispanic artists, go to the Glencoe Spanish Web site:
spanish.glencoe.com

Estructura

Presente de los verbos en -ar en el plural
Talking about things people do

1. You have already learned the singular forms of regular **-ar** verbs. Now study the plural forms.

INFINITIVE	hablar	estudiar	tomar	ENDINGS
STEM	habl-	estudi-	tom-	
nosotros(as)	hablamos	estudiamos	tomamos	-amos
ellos, ellas, Uds.	hablan	estudian	toman	-an

2.

Hablamos español.

When you talk about yourself and someone else, you use **-amos.**

José y Casandra estudian mucho.

When you talk about two or more people, you use **-an.**

3. In most parts of the Spanish-speaking world, except for some regions of Spain, there is no difference between formal and informal address in the plural.

Uds. toman muchos apuntes.

When speaking to more than one person, you use the **ustedes** form of the verb. Note that **Uds.** is an abbreviation of **ustedes.**

4. Now review all the forms of the present tense of the regular **-ar** verbs.

INFINITIVE	hablar	estudiar	tomar	ENDINGS
STEM	habl-	estudi-	tom-	
yo	hablo	estudio	tomo	-o
tú	hablas	estudias	tomas	-as
él, ella, Ud.	habla	estudia	toma	-a
nosotros(as)	hablamos	estudiamos	tomamos	-amos
vosotros(as)	*habláis*	*estudiáis*	*tomáis*	*-áis*
ellos, ellas, Uds.	hablan	estudian	toman	-an

¿Cómo lo digo?

 10 **Historieta** **En la escuela**

Sigan el modelo.
(Follow the model.)

> llegar ⟶
> **Los alumnos llegan.**

1. llegar a la escuela a las ocho
2. llevar los materiales escolares en una mochila
3. entrar en la sala de clase
4. hablar con el profesor
5. prestar atención
6. tomar apuntes
7. estudiar mucho
8. sacar notas buenas

Colegio San José, Estepona, España

 11 **Historieta** **¿Y ustedes?** Contesten personalmente.
(Answer about yourself and a friend.)

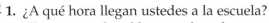
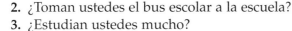

1. ¿A qué hora llegan ustedes a la escuela?
2. ¿Toman ustedes el bus escolar a la escuela?
3. ¿Estudian ustedes mucho?
4. ¿Toman ustedes un curso de español?
5. ¿Hablan ustedes mucho en la clase de español?
6. ¿Escuchan ustedes al profesor cuando habla?
7. ¿Miran ustedes un video?
8. ¿Escuchan ustedes CDs?

12 Historieta Sí, estudiamos. Sigan el modelo. *(Follow the model.)*

Uds. necesitan estudiar.

Pero, estudiamos.

1. Ustedes necesitan estudiar mucho.
2. Ustedes necesitan mirar el video.
3. Ustedes necesitan escuchar los casetes.
4. Ustedes necesitan trabajar.
5. Ustedes necesitan prestar atención.
6. Ustedes necesitan escuchar al profesor cuando habla.

13 Historieta En un colegio de Perú Completen. *(Complete.)*

Emilio __1__ (ser) un muchacho peruano. Él __2__ (estudiar) en un colegio en Trujillo. Los amigos de Emilio __3__ (llevar) uniforme a la escuela. Uno de los amigos de Emilio __4__ (hablar):

—Sí, todos nosotros __5__ (llevar) uniforme a la escuela.

__6__ (Llevar) un pantalón negro, una camisa blanca yuna corbata negra. ¿__7__ (Llevar) ustedes uniforme a la escuela en Estados Unidos?

Los amigos de Emilio __8__ (tomar) muchos cursos. Y Emilio también __9__ (tomar) muchos cursos. Algunos cursos __10__ (ser) fáciles y otros __11__ (ser) difíciles. Los amigos de Emilio __12__ (hablar):

—Nosotros __13__ (tomar) nueve cursos. En algunos cursos nosotros __14__ (sacar) notas muy buenas y en otros __15__ (sacar) notas bajas.

Un amigo __16__ (preguntar):

—¡Oye, Emilio! ¿En qué cursos __17__ (sacar) tú notas buenas y en qué cursos __18__ (sacar) tú notas malas?

Emilio __19__ (contestar):

—Cuando yo __20__ (trabajar) y __21__ (estudiar) yo __22__ (sacar) notas buenas en todos los cursos.

Plaza de Armas, Trujillo, Perú

14 Una clase Ask a classmate about one of his or her classes. Then he or she will ask you about one of your classes. The following are some words or expressions you may want to use.

enseñar

aburrido · profesor · ¿quién? · hablar

grande · escuchar · mirar

pequeño · ¿cómo?

interesante · tomar

apuntes · ¿a qué hora?

exámenes · prestar

15 Un día típico With a classmate look at the illustrations. Take turns talking about them.

1.

2.

3.

4.

16 ¿Cuándo? ¿En clase, después de las clases o en una fiesta?
Work with a classmate. He or she will suggest an activity. You will tell where or when you and your friends typically take part in the activity. Take turns.

Estructura

Presente de los verbos ir, dar, estar
Describing people's activities

1. The verbs **ir** *(to go)*, **dar** *(to give)*, and **estar** *(to be)* are irregular. An irregular verb does not conform to the regular pattern. Note the similarity in the irregular **yo** form of these verbs.

   yo   voy   doy   estoy

2. The other forms of these verbs are the same as those you have learned for regular **-ar** verbs.

INFINITIVE	ir	dar	estar
yo	voy	doy	estoy
tú	vas	das	estás
él, ella, Ud.	va	da	está
nosotros(as)	vamos	damos	estamos
vosotros(as)	*vais*	*dais*	*estáis*
ellos, ellas, Uds.	van	dan	están

¿Cómo lo digo?

17 Historieta Voy a la escuela.
Contesten. *(Answer.)*

1. ¿Vas a la escuela?
2. ¿A qué hora vas a la escuela?
3. ¿Vas a la escuela a pie?
4. ¿Vas en el bus escolar?
5. ¿Vas en carro?
6. ¿Cómo vas?
7. ¿Estás en la escuela ahora?
8. ¿En qué clase estás ahora?

San Juan, Puerto Rico

18 **Perdón, ¿adónde vas?** Sigan el modelo. *(Follow the model.)*

> Voy a la escuela.   Perdón, ¿adónde vas?

1. Voy a la clase de español.
2. Voy a la clase de biología.
3. Voy a la cafetería.
4. Voy al laboratorio.
5. Voy al gimnasio.
6. Voy a la papelería.

19 **¿Dónde están ustedes?** Preparen una conversación. *(Prepare a conversation.)*

> Tomamos una merienda. (en la cafetería)
> —¿Dónde están ustedes? ¿En la cafetería?
> —Sí, estamos en la cafetería.

1. Tomamos un sándwich. (en la cafetería)
2. Miramos un DVD. (en la clase de español)
3. Compramos un cuaderno. (en la papelería)
4. Estudiamos biología. (en el laboratorio)
5. Damos una fiesta. (en el Club de español)

Santurce, Puerto Rico

20 **Historieta La escuela**
Contesten. *(Answer.)*

1. ¿A qué hora van ustedes a la escuela?
2. ¿Cómo van?
3. ¿Están ustedes en la escuela ahora?
4. ¿En qué clase están?
5. ¿Está el/la profesor(a)?
6. ¿Da él/ella muchos exámenes?
7. ¿Da él/ella exámenes difíciles?
8. ¿Qué profesores dan muchos exámenes?

La Torre del Oro,
Sevilla, España

Estructura

Las contracciones al y del
Expressing direction and possession

1. The preposition **a** means *to* or *toward*. **A** contracts with the article **el** to form one word: **al**. The preposition **a** does not change when used with the other articles **la, las,** and **los**.

> **a + el = al**
>
> **En la escuela voy al laboratorio.**
> **Después voy a la cafetería.**
> **Y después voy a las tiendas.**

2. The preposition **a** is also used before a direct object that refers to a specific person or persons. It is called the "personal **a**" and has no equivalent in English.

> **Miro la televisión.**   **Miro al profesor.**
> **Escucho el CD.**   **Escucho a los amigos.**

3. The preposition **de** can mean *of, from,* or *about.* Like **a,** the preposition **de** contracts with the article **el** to form one word: **del**. The preposition **de** does not change when used with the other articles **la, las,** and **los**.

> **de + el = del**
>
> **Él habla del profesor de español.**
> **Es de la ciudad de Nueva York.**
> **Él es de Estados Unidos.**

4. You also use the preposition **de** to indicate possession.

> **Es la calculadora del profesor.**
> **Son los bolígrafos de Teresa y Sofía.**
> **Son los cuadernos de Juan y Fernando.**
> **Son los exámenes de los alumnos de la clase de español.**

La alumna usa una máquina de braille.

¿Cómo lo digo?

21 **Historieta** **¿Qué o a quién?** Contesten con **sí.** (*Answer with* sí.)

1. ¿Miras el video?
2. ¿Miras la pizarra?
3. ¿Miras al muchacho?
4. ¿Miras a la muchacha?

5. ¿Escuchas el CD?
6. ¿Escuchas la música?
7. ¿Escuchas al profesor?
8. ¿Escuchas a las profesoras?

22 Historieta ¿Adónde vas? Preparen una conversación.
(Prepare a conversation based on each illustration.)

—¿Adónde vas?
—¿Quién? ¿Yo?
—Sí, tú.
—Pues, voy a la escuela.

1.

2.

3.

4.

5.

23 Historieta Roberta Smith
Contesten. *(Answer.)*

1. ¿Es Roberta de la ciudad de Nueva York?
2. ¿Es Roberta de Estados Unidos?
3. ¿Habla Roberta del curso de biología?
4. ¿Habla del profesor de biología?
5. Y después de las clases, ¿habla Roberta con los amigos?
6. ¿Hablan de la escuela?
7. ¿Hablan de los cursos que toman?
8. ¿Hablan de la fiesta del Club de español?

Andas bien. ¡Adelante!

Conversación

La fiesta del Club de español

Rubén   Hola, amigo. ¿Qué tal? ¿Cómo estás?
Héctor   Bien. ¿Y tú?
Rubén   Muy bien. Oye, ¿adónde vas el viernes?
Héctor   ¿El viernes? Pues, voy a la fiesta del
          Club de español. ¿Tú no vas, hombre?
Rubén   Sí, voy. ¿Por qué no vamos juntos?
Héctor   ¿Por qué no? ¡Buena idea!
Rubén   En la fiesta bailamos, cantamos.
Héctor   Sí, y tomamos una merienda—
          ¡tacos y enchiladas!

¿Comprendes?

Contesten. *(Answer.)*

1. ¿Con quién habla Rubén?
2. ¿Cómo están los dos muchachos?
3. ¿Adónde va Héctor el viernes?
4. ¿Va Rubén también?
5. ¿Quién da la fiesta?
6. ¿Van juntos los dos muchachos?
7. ¿Bailan en la fiesta?
8. ¿Cantan?
9. ¿Toman una merienda?
10. ¿Qué toman?

Vamos a hablar más

A **Para ser un(a) alumno(a) bueno(a)** Work with a classmate. Prepare a list of things one has to do to be a good student. Take turns telling each other what you have to do. Each will respond to the other's advice. Use the models as a guide.

ALUMNO 1: **Necesitas estudiar.**
ALUMNO 2: **Pues, estudio.**

ALUMNO 1: **Es necesario estudiar.**
ALUMNO 2: **Sí, y yo no estudio.**

B **¿Bailan o qué?** With a classmate, look at the places below. Choose one and tell several things students usually do in that place. Take turns.

 1.

 2.

3.

 4.

C **Un día típico** Work with a classmate. Each of you will tell about your typical school-day activities. When you finish, identify those things that both of you do.

Pronunciación

La consonante t

The **t** in Spanish is pronounced with the tip of the tongue pressed against the upper teeth. It is not followed by a puff of air.

ta	**te**	**ti**	**to**	**tu**
taco	Teresa	tienda	toma	tú
canta	interesante	tiempo	tomate	estudia
está	casete	latín	Juanito	estupendo

Repeat the following sentences.

Tito necesita siete disquetes de la tienda.
Tú tomas apuntes en latín.
Teresa invita a Tito a la fiesta.

Lecturas culturales

Escuelas del ♻ 🎧 mundo hispano

Paula y Armando son dos amigos peruanos. Son de Miraflores. Miraflores es un suburbio bonito de Lima.

Paula y Armando no van a la misma escuela. Paula va a una academia privada y Armando va a un colegio privado. Muchas escuelas privadas en España y Latinoamérica no son para muchachos y muchachas. No son mixtas. Pero la mayoría[1] de las escuelas públicas son mixtas.

Hay otra diferencia interesante entre una escuela norteamericana y una escuela hispana. Aquí los alumnos van de un salón a otro. El profesor o la profesora de álgebra enseña en un salón y el profesor o la profesora de español enseña en otro. En España y Latinoamérica, no. Los alumnos no van de un salón a otro. Pasan la mayor parte[2] del día en el mismo salón. Son los profesores que «viajan[3]» o van de una clase a otra.

[1]mayoría *majority*
[2]mayor parte *greater part*
[3]viajan *travel*

Colegio de Nuestra Señora del Carmen, Miraflores, Perú

Miraflores, Perú

Una vista de Miraflores

¿Comprendes?

A ¿En Latinoamérica o en Estados Unidos?

Decidan. *(Decide whether each statement describes more accurately a school in Latin America or one in the United States.)*

1. Los muchachos y las muchachas van a la misma escuela.
2. Los alumnos van de un salón a otro.
3. Los profesores van de un salón a otro.

B Las escuelas de Paula y Armando

Contesten. *(Answer.)*

1. ¿De dónde son Paula y Armando?
2. ¿Van a la misma escuela?
3. ¿Va Paula a una escuela pública o privada?
4. ¿Y Armando? ¿Va él a una escuela pública o privada?
5. ¿Son mixtas la mayoría de las escuelas privadas en Latinoamérica?
6. ¿Dónde pasan la mayor parte del día los alumnos hispanos?
7. ¿Quiénes «viajan» de una clase a otra?

C En español, por favor.

Busquen las palabras afines. *(Find the cognates in the reading.)*

Lectura opcional ①

Harvard University, Massachusetts

Una conferencia universitaria

En la universidad los profesores dan conferencias a los estudiantes. Hay una conferencia universitaria muy histórica y famosa. Es famosa porque es la primera[1] conferencia universitaria de las Américas. Y la primera conferencia que da un profesor en una universidad de América es una conferencia en español.

¿Por qué en español? Es en español porque el profesor da la conferencia en la Universidad de Santo Domingo. La universidad más antigua[2] de las Américas es la Universidad de Santo Domingo (1538). La universidad más antigua de Estados Unidos es Harvard (1636).

[1]primera *first* [2]más antigua *oldest*

Antigua Universidad de Santo Domingo

¿Comprendes?

En inglés, por favor. Expliquen. (*Explain the significance of the information presented in the reading.*)

¿Lo sabes?

The Spanish word **conferencia** is a false cognate. It looks like the English word *conference*, but it actually means *lecture*.

Lectura opcional ②

Gabriela Mistral (1889–1957)

    Gabriela Mistral es una poeta famosa. Es de Vicuña. Vicuña es un pequeño pueblo rural de Chile. De joven[1], Gabriela Mistral enseña en varias escuelas primarias en áreas rurales de Chile. Ella pasa unos años[2] como directora de una escuela en Punta Arenas, en el extremo sur de la Patagonia chilena. Hoy la escuela lleva el nombre[3] de la maestra y poeta—el Liceo Gabriela Mistral. Es una maestra excelente y es también una poeta excelente. Como poeta, Gabriela Mistral recibe un gran honor. Gana[4] el Premio Nóbel de Literatura.

[1]De joven *As a young woman*
[2]años *years*
[3]nombre *name*
[4]Gana *She wins*

Liceo Gabriela Mistral, Punta Arenas

¿Comprendes?

A Gabriela Mistral ¿Sí o no? *(True or false?)*
1. Gabriela Mistral es novelista.
2. Gabriela Mistral es venezolana.
3. Ella es de Santiago, Chile.
4. Ella enseña en muchas áreas urbanas de Chile.
5. Ella enseña en varias escuelas secundarias.

B No es así. Corrijan. *(Correct the statements in Activity A that are not correct.)*

C Un poco de geografía Busquen en el mapa. *(On the map of South America on page xxxi, locate* Punta Arenas *and* la Patagonia. *Patagonia is in two countries. What countries are they?)*

Conexiones
Las ciencias naturales

La biología

Sciences are an important part of the school curriculum. If you like science, it would be fun to be able to read some scientific material in Spanish. You will see how easy it is. It's easy because you already have some scientific background and knowledge. The knowledge you already have helps you understand what you are reading. In addition, many scientific terms are cognates. The following is a short selection in Spanish about biology.

Plantas, Puerto Montt, Chile

La biología

La biología es la ciencia que estudia los animales y las plantas. Es el estudio de la estructura de los organismos vivos. El/La biólogo(a) es el/la científico(a) que estudia la biología.

El microscopio

Los biólogos trabajan en un laboratorio. Un instrumento importante para los biólogos es el microscopio. El microscopio permite a los biólogos observar objetos muy pequeños, muy diminutos. Con el microscopio los biólogos observan y analizan células, microbios y bacterias.

Una clase de biología, Buenos Aires

Llamas, Puerto Montt, Chile

La célula

¿Qué es una célula? La célula es el elemento básico y más importante de los seres vivientes[1]. Generalmente una célula es microscópica. Consiste en una masa llamada[2] «protoplasma» envuelta[3] en una membrana. Un microbio es un ser monocelular vegetal o animal. El microbio es solamente visible con el microscopio.

[1]seres vivientes *living creatures*
[2]llamada *called*
[3]envuelta *wrapped, encased*

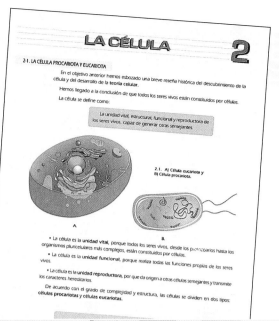

¿Comprendes?

A Palabras científicas

Hagan una lista. *(Make a list of science terms you recognize.)*

B La biología ¿Sí o no? *(True or false?)*

1. La biología es la ciencia que estudia los elementos químicos.
2. Los biólogos estudian los animales y las plantas.
3. Un vegetal es un animal.
4. Los biólogos trabajan en un laboratorio.
5. Los biólogos usan un telescopio.
6. Hay muchas cosas que son visibles solamente con el microscopio.
7. Una célula es bastante grande.
8. Un microbio es un ser de una sola célula—es monocelular.

C Estudio de palabras Adivinen. *(Note that the following words are all related to one another. If you know the meaning of one of them, you can guess the meaning of the others.)*

1. la biología, el biólogo, biológico
2. observar, la observación, el observador
3. analizar, el análisis, analítico
4. la célula, celular
5. el microscopio, microscópico

Una clase de biología, Buenos Aires

¡Te toca a ti!

Use what you have learned

Barcelona, España

HABLAR

1 En el café
✔ *Talk about school life in the United States*

You're seated at a café in Barcelona. You're chatting with a friend (your partner). He or she has some questions about school life in the United States. Have a conversation. Be sure to answer his or her questions.

HABLAR

2 Diferencias
✔ *Talk about differences between schools in the United States and the Spanish-speaking world*

Your school is going to have an exchange student from Spain. Based on what you have learned about schools in the Spanish-speaking world, tell some things the exchange student will find that are different. Tell also what he or she will find that is similar.

Tec de Monterrey,
Ciudad de México

ESCRIBIR

3 La rutina típica
✔ *Write about a typical school day*

You can now go back to the e-mail you sent your new friend on page 69 and add more details about what a typical school day is like in the United States.

ESCRIBIR

4 Una fiesta del Club de español

✔ *Write about some typical party activities*

Write a brief letter to a friend of yours who is also studying Spanish. Tell him or her that you're a member of your school's Spanish Club. Describe to your friend a typical Spanish Club party.

Writing Strategy

Ordering ideas You can order ideas in a variety of ways when writing. Therefore, you must be aware of the purpose of your writing in order to choose the best way to organize your material. When describing an event, it is logical to put the events in the order in which they happen. Using a sensible and logical approach helps readers develop a picture in their minds.

ESCRIBIR

5 Una fiesta

In the most recent letter from your Spanish pen pal, Gloria Velázquez, she described a party she had for her best friend. She told you what she had to do to prepare for the party and what her friends did at the party. She wants to know whether the types of parties she has are similar to the ones teenagers give here in the United States. Write her a letter explaining what you do to prepare for a party and what the parties are like. Include as many details as you can. These words may be helpful to you: **dar, invitar, necesitar, preparar, llegar, estar, hablar, tomar, escuchar, bailar, cantar.**

Madrid, España

EN LA ESCUELA

ciento ventinueve **129**

Assessment

Vocabulario

1 **Completen.** *(Complete.)*

1. Los alumnos no van a la escuela a pie. Toman el ____.
2. ¿____ llegan los alumnos a la escuela? Llegan a las ocho en punto.
3–4. En la escuela los alumnos ____ y la profesora ____.

2 **Contesten.** *(Answer.)*

5. ¿Quién habla en la sala de clase?
6. ¿Quiénes escuchan y prestan atención?
7. ¿Qué miran los alumnos?

3 **Completen.** *(Complete.)*

8–9. La profesora ____ un examen y los alumnos ____ el examen.
10. El Club de español da una ____.
11. Los miembros del club bailan y ____ durante la fiesta.

Estructura

4 **Completen.** *(Complete.)*

12–13. Los alumnos ____ atención cuando el profesor ____. (prestar, hablar)
14–15. Nosotros ____ mucho y ____ notas buenas. (estudiar, sacar)
16. ¿En qué ____ ustedes los materiales escolares? (llevar)

5 **Contesten.** *(Answer.)*

17. ¿Vas a la escuela a pie o en carro?
18. ¿Estás en la escuela ahora?

To review **Palabras 1**, turn to pages 104–105.

To review **Palabras 2**, turn to pages 108–109.

To review the plural of **-ar** verbs, turn to pages 112–113.

To review **ir** and **estar**, turn to page 116.

6 Escojan. *(Choose.)*

19. Ahora nosotros ____ en la cafetería.

    a. estás   **b.** están   **c.** estamos

20. Pero en cinco minutos (nosotros) ____ a la clase de biología.

    a. va   **b.** vamos   **c.** van

21. Los miembros del Club de español ____ una fiesta el viernes.

    a. da   **b.** dan   **c.** damos

To review **ir, dar,** and **estar,** turn to page 116.

7 Completen. *(Complete.)*

22. No es la calculadora ____ profesor. Es la calculadora de los alumnos.

23. Ellos van ____ colegio en el bus escolar.

To review the contractions with **a** and **de,** turn to page 118.

Cultura

8 ¿Sí o no? *(True or false?)*

24. En una escuela mixta hay muchachos y muchachas. Muchas escuelas públicas en España y Latinoamérica son mixtas.

25. En las escuelas de España y Latinoamérica los alumnos van de un salón de clase a otro como aquí en Estados Unidos.

To review this cultural information, turn to page 122.

Alumnos en San Juan, Puerto Rico

Tell all you can about this illustration.

Getting to school

llegar
ir a pie
en el bus escolar
en carro, en coche
entrar en la escuela

Identifying classroom objects

la sala (el salón) de clase
la pizarra, el pizarrón

Discussing classroom activities

estar en clase	prestar atención
estudiar	tomar apuntes
enseñar	dar un examen
mirar	sacar notas buenas (altas)
escuchar	sacar notas malas (bajas)

Discussing the Spanish Club

el Club de español	un DVD
el miembro	la merienda
la fiesta	bailar
la música	cantar
un CD	preparar
un video	dar una fiesta

Finding out information

¿a qué hora?
¿cuándo?
¿adónde?

How well do you know your vocabulary?

- Choose words from the list that describe a typical school day.
- Use these words to write about or tell what you do at school.

Other useful expressions

a eso de	algunos(as)
en punto	ahora
otros(as)	también

VIDEOTUR

Episodio 4

In this video episode, you will spend an interesting math class with Vicky and Fernando. See page 495 for more information.

Conversación

La apertura de clases

Julio   Anamari, ¿cómo estás?

Anamari   Muy bien, Julio. ¿Y tú?

Julio   Bien. ¿Adónde vas?

Anamari   Voy a la papelería. Necesito comprar algunas cosas para la apertura de clases.

Julio   ¡Ay, septiembre, una vez más y la apertura de clases! ¡Es increíble!

Estepona, España

¿Comprendes?

A **Anamari y Julio** Contesten. (*Answer.*)
1. ¿Con quién habla Anamari?
2. ¿Cómo está Julio?
3. ¿Son amigos Julio y Anamari?
4. ¿Son alumnos?
5. ¿Adónde va Anamari? ¿Qué necesita?
6. ¿De qué hablan los dos amigos?

B **¿Qué compra Anamari?** Preparen una lista de los materiales escolares que Anamari compra para la apertura de clases. (*Prepare a list of school supplies that Anamari buys for the beginning of school.*)

Estructura

Verbos, sustantivos, artículos y adjetivos

1. Review the forms of regular **-ar** verbs.

HABLAR	hablo	hablas	habla	hablamos	*habláis*	hablan
LLEVAR	llevo	llevas	lleva	llevamos	*lleváis*	llevan

2. Review the irregular verbs you have learned so far.

SER	soy	eres	es	somos	*sois*	son
IR	voy	vas	va	vamos	*vais*	van
ESTAR	estoy	estás	está	estamos	*estáis*	están
DAR	doy	das	da	damos	*dais*	dan

3. An adjective must agree with the noun it describes. Remember that adjectives that end in **o** have four forms. Adjectives that end in a consonant have two forms.

el amigo sincero	los amigos sinceros	la amiga sincera	las amigas sinceras
el curso difícil	los cursos difíciles	la clase difícil	las clases difíciles

1 **Entrevista** Contesten personalmente.
(Answer about yourself.)

1. ¿Vas a una escuela secundaria?
2. ¿Estás en la escuela ahora?
3. ¿Cuántos cursos tomas?
4. ¿Habla mucho la profesora?
5. ¿Son buenos los alumnos de español?
6. ¿Escuchan ustedes cuando la profesora habla?
7. ¿Sacan ustedes notas buenas?
8. ¿Dan los profesores muchos exámenes?

2 **Julio y Anamari** Work with a classmate. Look at the photo of Julio and Anamari. They are from Málaga, Spain. Say as much as you can about Julio. Then say as much as you can about Anamari. Take turns.

3 **Los amigos** Look at the photo of a group of friends from Estepona, Spain, on page 134. With a classmate, talk about the group. Ask one another questions about some of the people in the photo.

Literary Companion

You may wish to read the poem from *Versos sencillos* by José Martí. This literary selection is found on pages 470–471.

Entérate México

Los secretos precolombinos

Hay misterios sobre dos ciudades en ruinas, declaradas Patrimonio Mundial de la Humanidad[1] por la UNESCO.

La Pirámide del Sol

Teotihuacán

■ El nombre original de la ciudad es un misterio. Es un misterio también la lengua de los habitantes de la ciudad—igual que la escritura[2].

■ Sus monumentos principales datan de 200 después de Cristo.

■ Los aztecas dan el nombre de Teotihuacán a la ciudad. Teotihuacán significa "Ciudad de los Dioses". Antes de la llegada de los aztecas la ciudad está abandonada por unos 700 años.

■ En la ciudad hay dos pirámides famosas—la Pirámide del Sol[3] y la Pirámide de la Luna[4]. La Pirámide del Sol es muy grande. Es de una altura de 66 metros y una base de 225 metros. La pirámide tiene[5] dos millones de ladrillos[6].

■ En la ciudad hay estatuas de cabezas[7] grandes. Una es del dios Quetzalcóatl.

Chichén Itzá

Chichén Itzá

La pirámide maya Castillo

■ La antigua ciudad de Chichén Itzá es una ciudad importante entre 300 y 900 antes de Cristo. Los habitantes de Chichén Itzá son los mayas. Ellos levantan las grandes construcciones de la ciudad sin usar bestias de carga (animales) ni rueda[8].

■ ¡Una cosa muy interesante! La pirámide Castillo de Kukulcán tiene una escalinata[9] de 365 peldaños[10]—un peldaño para cada día del año. La antigua civilización maya domina las matemáticas y ellos inventan un calendario muy exacto, muy preciso.

■ En los equinoccios[11] una sombra[12] forma una serpiente en la escalinata. Según[13] una leyenda la serpiente es el dios maya Kukulcán. El nombre que los aztecas dan a Kukulcán es Quetzalcóatl.

[1]Patrimonio Mundial de la Humanidad: *World Heritage Sites*
[2]escritura: *writing*
[3]sol: *sun*
[4]luna: *moon*
[5]tiene: *has*
[6]ladrillos: *bricks*
[7]cabezas: *heads*
[8]rueda: *wheel*
[9]escalinata: *staircase*
[10]peldaños: *stairs*
[11]equinoccios: *the Equinoxes*
[12]sombra: *shadow*
[13]según: *according to*

Un vistazo a Diego Rivera

Los últimos detalles sobre la vida del pintor y muralista que a los tres años sabe dibujar[1].

Autorretrato

Una obra del pintor

El estudio de Rivera   Rivera y Kahlo

■ Diego Rivera nace en 1892. Su nombre completo es Diego María Concepción Juan Nepomuceno Estanislao de la Rivera y Barrientos Acosta y Rodríguez.

■ Arriba he su autorretrato[2].

■ En las pinturas o murales de Rivera, él pinta escenas del pasado precolombino, la historia mexicana y la vida del campesino[3].

■ Se casa con[4] Frida Kahlo. Se divorcian y pronto se casan de nuevo. Frida Kahlo es una artista famosa también. Durante un tiempo ellos tienen un estudio uno al lado del otro. Diego Rivera muere[5] en 1957.

[1]dibujar: *sketch*
[2]autorretrato: *self-portrait*
[3]vida del campesino: *life of a peasant*
[4]se casa con: *he marries*
[5]muere: *dies*

Calendario de fiestas

Muchas fiestas tradicionales varían según[1] el lugar donde se celebran.

Las Posadas—del 16 al 24 de diciembre

Durante las Posadas hay desfiles[2]. La gente va de una casa a otra como María y José cuando buscan alojamiento[3] en Belén. Los participantes en los desfiles llevan el mismo tipo de ropa que María, José y los pastores. El desfile termina en una casa donde todos celebran una fiesta con una piñata.

Las Posadas

El Día de la Independencia— el 16 de septiembre

Los mexicanos celebran el Día de la Independencia para conmemorar el día que comienza la lucha por la independencia de México, el 16 de septiembre de 1810. Hay desfiles, fuegos artificiales[4], fiestas con comida típica, bailes folklóricos y música de mariachi.

El Día de la Independencia

El Día de los Muertos[5]—el 2 de noviembre

Las familias mexicanas van a las tumbas en el cementerio para honrar a sus parientes muertos. Tocan música y llevan flores[6] y comida tradicional. Llevan esqueletos de azúcar[7] y pan[8] de muertos. Pero no es un tiempo de luto[9]. Es un tiempo de alegría[10].

El Día de los Muertos

[1]según: *according to*
[2]desfiles: *parades*
[3]alojamiento: *lodging*
[4]fuegos artificiales: *fireworks*
[5]muertos: *dead*
[6]flores: *flowers*
[7]azúcar: *sugar*
[8]pan: *bread*
[9]luto: *mourning*
[10]alegría: *joy*

SUCESOS

■ **Maná,** la banda de rock, tiene[1] mucho interés en la ecología. El grupo trabaja para proteger millas y millas de la costa del Pacífico de México. Trabajan para proteger la población de tortugas[2] amenazadas[3] por cazadores[4] de huevos[5].

Maná

■ El legendario actor **Anthony Quinn** interpreta muchos roles étnicos como Zorba el griego[6]. Es de Chihuahua, México. Su madre mexicana es de ascendencia indígena y su padre es mexicanoirlandés.

Anthony Quinn

[1]tiene: *has*
[2]tortugas: *turtles*
[3]amenazadas: *threatened*
[4]cazadores: *hunters*
[5]huevos: *eggs*
[6]griego: *Greek*

Una receta sana

mi cocina

Croquetas de avena[1]

Ingredientes

4 huevos
2 tazas[2] de avena
1 cebolla
2 ramitos de perejil[3]
3–4 chiles, sin semillas[4] (opcional)
sal y pimienta al gusto[5]
aceite de oliva para freír

Preparación

Batir[6] los huevos, añadir[7] la avena y mezclar[8]. Picar[9] la cebolla y el perejil finamente. Incorporarlos a la mezcla de avena y huevo. Añadir sal, pimienta y los chiles. En una sartén[10], calentar el aceite de oliva. Formar pequeñas tortas[11] y aplastarlas[12] hasta lograr un disco de $1\frac{1}{2}$ o 2 pulgadas de diámetro. Freírlas, secarlas[13] en un papel de cocina[14] y luego servirlas.

[1]avena: *oat*
[2]tazas: *cups*
[3]ramitos de perejil: *sprigs of parsley*
[4]sin semillas: *without seeds*
[5]al gusto: *to taste*
[6]batir: *beat*
[7]añadir: *add*
[8]mezclar: *mix*
[9]picar: *chop up*
[10]sartén: *frying pan*
[11]tortas: *cakes*
[12]aplastarlas: *squash them*
[13]secarlas: *dry them*
[14]papel de cocina: *paper towel*

Salma Hayek

Salma Hayek nace con estrella[1]

De pequeña, el sueño[2] de Salma Hayek es de ser actriz. Nace en Coatzacoalcos de madre mexicana y padre libanés. Durante su adolescencia pasa unos años en Houston, Texas con su tía pero regresa a México para ir a la universidad. En contra de la voluntad y los deseos de su familia deja[3] sus estudios para ser actriz. En muy poco tiempo es una actriz famosa con un papel (o rol) importante en una telenovela[4] mexicana. Pero Salma deja todo para ir a Hollywood.

Ella estudia inglés, toma clases de interpretación[5], va a audiciones y por fin tiene un papel secundario en un filme. Pero no es muy famosa en EE.UU. hasta tener un papel importante en el filme *Desesperado* con Antonio Banderas. Luego Hayek aparece en numerosos filmes incluyendo *El coronel no tiene quien le escriba* basado en la novela del famoso autor colombiano Gabriel García Márquez.

Desde 1999 Hayek produce varios filmes con su propia compañía. Uno es *Frida*. Ella misma juega un papel[6] importante en el filme que trata de[7] la vida de la pintora mexicana Frida Kahlo. Por su interpretación en el filme Hayek fue[8] nominada al Óscar. Y, es ella la primera latina inmortalizada con una estatua de cera[9] en el Museo de Cera de Madame Tussaud en Nueva York.

---

[1]nace con estrella: *was born with luck*

[2]sueño: *dream*

[3]deja: *she gives up*

[4]telenovela: *soap opera*

[5]interpretación: *acting*

[6]juega un papel: *plays a part*

[7]trata de: *deals with*

[8]fue: *was*

[9]cera: *wax*

Cuarón

Alfonso Cuarón, director
Alfonso Cuarón es director de películas hollywoodenses (filmes) como *A Little Princess* y *Great Expectations*. Además rodea[1] películas en México. Pero Cuarón hace[2] historia cuando es seleccionado para ser director de *Harry Potter and the Prisoner of Azkaban.* Es la tercera parte de la famosa serie de películas basadas en las aventuras de Harry Potter. Es quizás la primera (1ª) vez en la historia del cine que un latino tenga[3] la oportunidad y responsabilidad de ser director de un filme tan espectacular—un filme cuyo éxito de taquilla[4] fue[5] garantizado antes de comenzar la producción.

García Bernal

Gael García Bernal, actor
Es nativo de Guadalajara. Varias veces trabaja en películas que tienen el honor de ser candidatas al Óscar.

Luna

Diego Luna, actor
Desde la infancia él es amigo de Gael García Bernal. En la película *Frida*, con Salma Hayek, él interpreta el papel del primer novio[6] de Frida Kahlo.

---

[1]rodea: *he films*

[2]hace: *makes*

[3]tenga: *has*

[4]filme cuyo éxito de taquilla: *film whose box office success*

[5]fue: *was*

[6]novio: *boyfriend*

En la tele y la radio

Ana María Canseco

Ana María Canseco da su mejor sonrisa[1] como copresentadora del show *Despierta América* (Univisión). Si da una interviú a un cantante, prueba algún plato[2] o habla de la moda o algo política, siempre es encantadora, muy simpática.

María Hinojosa es autora, corresponsal de CNN, y presentadora de programas de National Public Radio. De su nuevo libro *Raising Raúl* dice[3] "Habla de encontrar nuestras voces[4] como mujeres[5] y encontrar cosas en común que van más lejos de[6] la raza y la cultura."

María Hinojosa

[1]su mejor sonrisa: *her best smile*

[2]prueba algún plato: *trying a dish*

[3]dice: *she says*

[4]encontrar nuestras voces: *finding our voices*

[5]mujeres: *women*

[6]van más lejos de: *go further than*

música

Café Tacuba

Lo mejor del año

La firma[1] de autógrafos de **Café Tacuba**, siempre es "un desmadre," lo que en el argot[2] es un "caos[3]." Nada extraño[4] para el grupo que cruza fronteras con un sonido original, producto de la fusión de ritmos mexicanos con rock, punk, ska, reggae y balada.

Los Tucanes de Tijuana

Los Tucanes[5] de Tijuana no son tucanes y no son de Tijuana. Pero su nombre refleja el carácter imaginativo de este grupo importante de la música regional mexicana. Tienen muchos aficionados y seguidores[6] que compran millones de sus discos.

En el CD *Shaman* del famoso músico **Carlos Santana**, figura la valiosa colaboración de **Michelle Branch** con la canción "The Game of Love." Además de Branch, Plácido Domingo, entre varios otros, colabora en este CD del guitarrista y cantante mexicano.

Santana y Branch

[1]firma: *signing*

[2]argot: *slang*

[3]caos: *chaos*

[4]nada extraño: *nothing unusual*

[5]tucanes: *a type of bird*

[6]aficionados y seguidores: *fans and followers*

Nuestros Hits

Bajo el azul de tu misterio / Jaguares.
Este super álbum doble de rock contiene 10 temas grabados[1] y 11 en concierto. Con un trabajo de guitarras excelente y el timbre agridulce[2] de las interpretaciones es el grupo uno de los más universales y mexicanos de todos los tiempos.

El más grande homenaje a los Tigres del Norte / varios.
Si en el pasado medio mundo[3] respeta y escucha a los Tigres del Norte, después de este homenaje[4] el otro medio mundo va a adorar a los Tigres del Norte. Los Lobos y Café Tacuba, entre otros grupos, presentan la música y las letras[5] de los Tigres del Norte—y la realidad del México de la frontera[6].

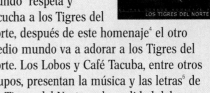

[1]grabados: *recorded*

[2]timbre agridulce: *bittersweet ring*

[3]mundo: *world*

[4]homenaje: *tribute*

[5]letras: *lyrics*

[6]frontera: *border*

Capítulo 5

En el café

Objetivos

In this chapter you will learn to:

❖ order food or a beverage at a café

❖ identify some food

❖ shop for food

❖ talk about activities

❖ talk about differences between eating habits in the United States and in the Spanish-speaking world

Bernardita Zegers *Don Diego y doña Patricia*

En el café

el mesero,
el camarero

una mesa libre

el menú

una mesa
ocupada

la mesa

Rafael va al café.
Él va al café con Catalina.
Ellos van juntos.
Buscan una mesa.
Ven una mesa libre.

Catalina lee el menú.

Para beber

los refrescos

un café solo

un café con leche

una gaseosa,
una soda

un té helado

una limonada

Para comer

una sopa

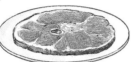
el jamón

el queso

una ensalada

una tortilla

el postre

un bocadillo,
un sándwich

papas fritas

una hamburguesa

un pan dulce

un helado
de vainilla

un helado
de chocolate

Antes de comer

Sí, señores, ¿qué desean Uds.?

Para mí, un café
con leche, por favor.

Y para mí,
una cola.

Los clientes hablan con el mesero.
El mesero escribe la orden.

Después de comer

La cuenta, por favor.

Sí, señor. Enseguida.

¿Está incluido el servicio?

Sí, señor.

la
cuenta

Nota When learning a language, try to guess the meaning of unfamiliar words. The other words in the sentence provide the context and will help you understand words you do not know.

Elena estudia español en la escuela. *Aprende* el español en la escuela. Elena lee un menú en español. Ella *comprende* el menú. *Comprende* porque *aprende* el español en la escuela. Elena comprende, habla, lee y escribe el español. Es una alumna buena. *Recibe* notas muy buenas.

Vocabulario

¿Qué palabra necesito?

1 Historieta Al café Contesten. *(Answer.)*

1. ¿Adónde van los amigos?
2. ¿Qué buscan?
3. ¿Están ocupadas todas las mesas?
4. ¿Ven una mesa libre?
5. ¿Toman la mesa?
6. ¿Lee Gabriela el menú?
7. ¿Con quién hablan los amigos?
8. ¿Quién escribe la orden?
9. ¿Qué bebe Gabriela?
10. ¿Qué bebe Tomás?
11. ¿Toman un refresco los amigos?

Caracas, Venezuela

2 Historieta En el café Contesten. *(Answer.)*

1. Los amigos van ____.
   a. al café   b. a la cafetería de la escuela
2. Buscan ____.
   a. una mesa ocupada   b. una mesa libre
3. Los amigos leen ____.
   a. el menú   b. la orden

4. El mesero ____ la orden.
   a. lee   b. escribe
5. Para ____ hay café, té y cola.
   a. comer   b. beber
6. El cliente paga ____.
   a. el menú   b. la cuenta

3 ¿Qué toma José? Sigan el modelo. *(Follow the model.)*

José bebe una gaseosa.

José come un bocadillo de jamón y queso.

1.

2.

3.

4.

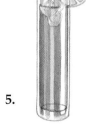

5.

4 **Historieta** **Una experiencia buena**
Contesten. *(Answer.)*

1. ¿Va Linda a un café?
2. ¿Va a un café en Jerez?
3. ¿Va con un grupo de alumnos americanos?
4. ¿Habla Linda con el camarero?
5. ¿Lee Linda el menú?
6. ¿Es en español el menú?
7. ¿Comprende Linda el menú?
8. ¿Y comprende Linda al camarero cuando él habla?
9. ¿Por qué comprende Linda? ¿Aprende ella el español en la escuela?
10. ¿Habla, lee y comprende Linda el español?

Jerez, España

5 **Al café** Work in small groups. You're in a café in Mexico City. One of you will be the server. Have a conversation from the time you enter the café until you leave. You will get a table, order, get the check, and pay.

6 **¿Qué toman los amigos?** Look at the photographs below. With a classmate, take turns telling one another what's happening in each one.

Madrid, España

En el mercado

las manzanas

las naranjas

la lechuga

los plátanos

los tomates

las papas

las judías verdes

las frutas

las zanahorias

los guisantes

las habichuelas, los frijoles

los vegetales

los mariscos

la carne

los huevos

el pollo

el pescado

¿A cuánto están los guisantes hoy?

A cincuenta el kilo.

Medio kilo, por favor.

¿Algo más, señora?

No, nada más, gracias.

La señora va de compras.
Va de compras en México.
La señora vive en México.

En el supermercado

Venden:

un bote (una lata) de atún

productos congelados

una bolsa de papas fritas

un paquete de arroz

Las comidas

el desayuno

el almuerzo

la cena

Vocabulario

¿Qué palabra necesito?

Málaga, España

7 Historieta Al mercado

Contesten. (*Answer.*)

1. ¿Van ustedes al mercado?
2. ¿Compran ustedes comida en el mercado?
3. En el mercado, ¿venden vegetales y frutas?
4. ¿Venden carne y pescado también?
5. ¿Quiénes venden, los clientes o los empleados?
6. ¿Van ustedes al supermercado también?
7. En el supermercado, ¿venden productos en botes, paquetes y bolsas?
8. ¿Venden también muchos productos congelados?

San Miguel de Allende, México

8 Historieta De compras Completen según la foto. (*Complete according to the photo.*)

La señora está en el mercado. La señora va a un mercado en México porque ella __1__ en México. Habla con la empleada. Compra una docena de __2__. Hoy los huevos están a __3__ pesos la docena. La señora compra los huevos pero no necesita __4__ más.

9 ¿El desayuno, el almuerzo o la cena? Contesten con **sí** o **no**. (*Answer with* sí *or* no.)

1. En el desayuno comemos cereales, huevos, pan dulce, yogur y pan tostado con mermelada.
2. En la cena comemos un biftec.
3. En el desayuno comemos un bocadillo de pollo con papas fritas y una ensalada de lechuga y tomate.
4. En la cena comemos carne o pescado, papas o arroz, un vegetal y un postre.

10 Lo contrario

Escojan lo contrario. *(Choose the opposite.)*

1. algo
2. ocupado
3. para beber
4. leer
5. comprar
6. enseñar

a. escribir
b. aprender
c. nada
d. libre
e. vender
f. para comer

Málaga, España

11 Al mercado

Visit a Hispanic market in your community with your classmates. If you don't know the names of some foods that appeal to you, ask the vendor. Choose a few items and find out how much you owe. Be sure to speak Spanish. If there isn't a Latin American market in your community, set one up in your classroom. Bring in photos of food items. Take turns pretending to be the vendor and the customers.

12 Las comidas para mañana

Work with a classmate. Prepare a menu for tomorrow's meals—**el desayuno, el almuerzo y la cena.** Based on your menus, prepare a shopping list.

13 ¿Qué compras en el mercado?

You're at an open-air food market in Ecuador. Make a list of the items you want to buy. With a classmate, take turns being the vendor and the customer as you shop for the items on your lists.

Un mercado del altiplano, Ecuador

Estructura

Presente de los verbos en -er e -ir
Describing people's activities

You have already learned that many Spanish verbs end in **-ar.** These verbs are referred to as first conjugation verbs. Most regular Spanish verbs belong to the **-ar** group. The other two groups of regular verbs in Spanish end in **-er** and **-ir.** Verbs whose infinitive ends in **-er (comer, beber, leer, vender, aprender, comprender)** are second conjugation verbs. Verbs whose infinitive ends in **-ir (vivir, escribir, recibir)** are third conjugation verbs. Study the following forms. Note that the endings of **-er** and **-ir** verbs are the same except for the **nosotros** and **vosotros** forms.

-ER VERBS			ENDINGS
INFINITIVE	comer	leer	
STEM	com-	le-	
yo	como	leo	-o
tú	comes	lees	-es
él, ella, Ud.	come	lee	-e
nosotros(as)	comemos	leemos	-emos
vosotros(as)	*coméis*	*leéis*	*-éis*
ellos, ellas, Uds.	comen	leen	-en

-IR VERBS			ENDINGS
INFINITIVE	vivir	escribir	
STEM	viv-	escrib-	
yo	vivo	escribo	-o
tú	vives	escribes	-es
él, ella, Ud.	vive	escribe	-e
nosotros(as)	vivimos	escribimos	-imos
vosotros(as)	*vivís*	*escribís*	*-ís*
ellos, ellas, Uds.	viven	escriben	-en

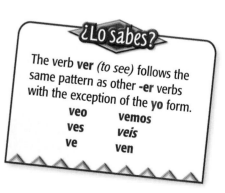

¿Lo sabes?

The verb **ver** *(to see)* follows the same pattern as other **-er** verbs with the exception of the **yo** form.

veo	vemos
ves	*veís*
ve	ven

¿Cómo lo digo?

14 Historieta Un menú español

Lean y contesten. *(Read and answer.)*

PABLO	Linda, ¿lees el menú en español?
LINDA	¡Sí, claro!
PABLO	Pero, ¿comprendes un menú en español?
LINDA	Sí, comprendo. ¿Por qué preguntas?
PABLO	Pero no eres española. Y no vives aquí en Madrid. ¿Lees el español? ¿Cómo es posible?
LINDA	Pues, aprendo el español en la escuela en Nueva York. En clase hablamos mucho. Leemos y escribimos también.
PABLO	Pues, yo aprendo el inglés aquí en Madrid. Hablo un poco, pero cuando leo no comprendo casi nada. Comprendo muy poco.

Madrid, España

1. ¿Qué lee Linda?
2. ¿En qué lengua lee el menú?
3. ¿Comprende el menú?
4. ¿Es de España Linda?
5. ¿Vive ella en Madrid?
6. ¿Por qué comprende? ¿Dónde aprende ella el español?
7. En la clase de español, ¿hablan mucho los alumnos?
8. ¿Leen y escriben también?
9. ¿Qué lengua aprende Pablo en Madrid?
10. ¿Comprende él cuando lee algo en inglés?

15 **Historieta** **En un café** Completen. *(Complete.)*

En el café los clientes __1__ (ver) al mesero. Ellos __2__ (hablar) con el mesero. Los clientes __3__ (leer) el menú y __4__ (decidir) lo que van a comer o beber. Los meseros __5__ (tomar) la orden y __6__ (escribir) la orden en una hoja de papel o en un bloc pequeño. Los meseros no __7__ (leer) el menú. Los clientes __8__ (leer) el menú. Y los clientes no __9__ (escribir) la orden. Los meseros __10__ (escribir) la orden.

16 **Yo** Contesten personalmente. *(Answer about yourself.)*

1. ¿Dónde vives?
2. En casa, ¿hablas inglés o español?
3. ¿Aprendes el español en la escuela?
4. En la clase de español, ¿hablas mucho?
5. ¿Lees mucho?
6. ¿Escribes mucho?
7. ¿Comprendes al profesor o a la profesora cuando él o ella habla?
8. ¿Comprendes cuando lees?

17 **¿Qué comen todos?** Sigan el modelo. *(Follow the model.)*

carne ⟶
—Teresa come carne.
—Yo como carne también. / Yo no como carne.
   Y tú, ¿comes carne o no?

1. vegetales
2. pescado
3. mariscos
4. ensalada
5. postre
6. pollo
7. huevos

Cádiz, España

For more practice using words from *Palabras 1* and *2* and *-er* verbs, do Activity 5 on page H6 at the end of this book.

18 Nosotros Contesten personalmente.
(Answer about yourself and a friend.)

1. ¿Dónde viven ustedes?
2. ¿A qué escuela asisten ustedes. (van ustedes)?
3. ¿Escriben ustedes mucho en la clase de español?
4. ¿Escriben ustedes mucho en la clase de inglés?
5. ¿Leen ustedes mucho en la clase de español?
6. ¿En qué clase leen ustedes novelas y poemas?
7. ¿Aprenden ustedes mucho en la clase de español?
8. ¿Comprenden ustedes cuando el profesor o la profesora habla?
9. ¿Ven ustedes un video en la clase de español?
10. Recibimos notas buenas en español. ¿Reciben ustedes notas buenas también?

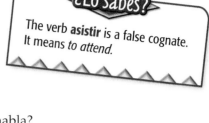

¿Lo sabes?

The verb **asistir** is a false cognate. It means *to attend*.

19 ¿Toman ustedes un refresco? Sigan el modelo. *(Follow the model.)*

una cola ⟶

—Nosotros bebemos una cola. / No bebemos una cola.
¿Y ustedes? ¿Beben una cola o no?

1. café solo   4. limonada
2. café con leche   5. té
3. leche

20 ¿Qué comes? With a classmate, take turns finding out what each of you eats for breakfast, lunch, and dinner.

Café Luna

sándwich	14 pesos
tamal	10 pesos
enchilada	11 pesos
café	2 pesos
limonada	3 pesos

21 ¿Cuánto es, por favor? You are at a little café in South America. Your classmate is the waiter or waitress. Order something you want to eat and drink. Then find out how much it is. The waiter or waitress can refer to the menu to tell you how much you owe.

22 El curso de inglés Have a discussion with a classmate about your English class. Tell as much as you can about what you do and learn in class. You may want to use some of the following words: **aprender, leer, recibir, escribir, comprender.**

Andas bien. ¡Adelante!

En la terraza de un café

Julia Carlos, hay mucha gente en el café.

Carlos Sí, veo que no hay muchas mesas libres.

Julia Verdad, pero allí hay una. ¿Ves? ¡Vamos!

Carlos ¡Vale!

(Llegan a la mesa y Julia lee el menú.)

Mesero Señores, ¿desean ustedes tomar algo?

Julia Sí, para mí una limonada, por favor.

Carlos Y para mí un café con leche.

Mesero Sí, señores. Enseguida.

(Julia y Carlos hablan mientras toman el refresco.)

Carlos ¿Qué lees, Julia?

Julia Leo una novela de Isabel Allende. Es excelente.

(Unos momentos después)

Carlos Mesero, la cuenta, por favor.

Mesero Sí, señor.

¿Comprendes?

Contesten. *(Answer.)*

1. ¿Dónde están Julia y Carlos?
2. ¿Hay mucha gente en el café?
3. ¿Qué ve Julia?
4. ¿Qué lee Julia?
5. ¿Con quién hablan Carlos y Julia?
6. ¿Qué desea Julia?
7. ¿Y Carlos?
8. ¿Qué novela lee Julia?
9. ¿Cómo es la novela?

Vamos a hablar más

A **En el café** Work in groups of three or four. You're all friends from Madrid. After school you go to a café where you talk about lots of things—school, teachers, friends, etc. One of you will play the role of the waiter or waitress at the café. You have to interrupt the conversation once in a while to take the orders and serve.

B **¿Qué preparamos?** Work in groups of three or four. The Spanish Club is having a party and you're planning the menu. You want to have one dish with meat and one without meat, since there are quite a few students who are vegetarians **(vegetarianos)**. Look at the menu the club members have prepared and decide what you have to buy at the supermarket.

para comer:
sándwiches
hamburguesas
ensaladas
fruta
para beber:
- refrescos
café

Pronunciación

La consonante d

The pronunciation of **d** in Spanish varies according to its position in the word. When a word begins with **d** (initial position) or follows the consonants **l** or **n,** the tongue gently strikes the back of the upper front teeth.

da	de	di	do	du
da	dependiente	difícil	domingo	dulce
merienda	vende	andino	condominio	

When **d** appears within the word between vowels (medial position), **d** is extremely soft. Your tongue should strike the lower part of your upper teeth, almost between the upper and lower teeth.

da	de	di	do	du
privada	modelo	estudio	helado	educación
ensalada	cuaderno	medio	congelado	

When a word ends in **d** (final position), **d** is either extremely soft or omitted completely—not pronounced.

nacionalidad   ciudad

Repeat the following sentences.

Diego da el disco compacto a Donato en la ciudad.
El dependiente vende helado y limonada.
Adela compra la merienda en la tienda.

Lecturas culturales

En un café en Madrid

Reading Strategy

Guessing meaning from context It's easy to understand words you have already studied. There are also ways to understand words you are not familiar with. One way is to use the context—the way these words are used in the sentence or reading—to help you guess the meaning of those words you do not know.

José Luis vive en Madrid. Después de las clases, los amigos de José Luis van juntos, en grupo, a un café. En el otoño y en la primavera, ellos van a un café al aire libre[1]. Pasan una hora o más en el café. Toman un refresco y a veces comen un bocadillo o un pan dulce. En el café, hablan y hablan. Hablan de la escuela, de los amigos, de la familia. Y a veces miran a la gente que pasa.

Paseo de la Castellana, Madrid

[1] al aire libre *outdoor*

Madrid, España

Después de una hora o más, van a casa. Cuando llegan a casa, ¿comen o cenan enseguida, inmediatamente? No, no comen inmediatamente. En España, no cenan hasta las diez o las diez y media de la noche. Pero en España y en algunos países latinoamericanos la comida principal es la comida del mediodía.

Estepona, España

¿Comprendes?

A José Luis Contesten con **sí** o **no.** *(Answer with* sí *or* no.*)*
1. José Luis es un muchacho de la Ciudad de México.
2. José Luis va solo al café.
3. En el invierno, José Luis y un grupo de amigos van a un café al aire libre.
4. En el café, toman un refresco.
5. Hablan de muchas cosas diferentes.
6. Pasan solamente unos minutos en el café.
7. Cuando llegan a casa, los muchachos comen enseguida con la familia.
8. La comida principal es la cena.

B La verdad, por favor. Corrijan las oraciones falsas de la Actividad A. *(Correct the false statements from Activity A.)*

Lectura opcional 1

Las horas para comer

El desayuno

En España y en los países de Latinoamérica, la gente suele[1] comer más tarde que aquí en Estados Unidos. Como nosotros, toman el desayuno a eso de las siete o las ocho de la mañana. A eso de las diez van a un café o a una cafetería donde toman otro café con leche y un churro o pan dulce.

El almuerzo

El almuerzo es a la una o, en el caso de España, a eso de las dos de la tarde. Hoy día la mayoría[2] de la gente no va a casa a tomar el almuerzo. Toman el almuerzo en la cafetería de la escuela o en la cafetería donde trabajan. Si no, comen en un café o en un restaurante. Muchos no van a casa a tomar el almuerzo porque hay mucho tráfico. Tarda (toma) demasiado tiempo[3].

La cena

En la mayoría de los países latinoamericanos la gente suele cenar a las ocho y media o a las nueve de la noche. Pero, en España, no. En España la cena es a las diez o a las diez y media.

[1]suele *tend to* [3]demasiado tiempo *too much time*
[2]mayoría *majority*

Buenos Aires, Argentina

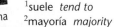

¡A comer en el mundo hispano! Contesten. *(Answer.)*

1. ¿Dónde suele comer la gente más tarde, en Estados Unidos o en los países hispanos?
2. ¿A qué hora toman el desayuno en los países hispanos?
3. ¿A qué hora toman ustedes el desayuno?
4. ¿A qué hora es el almuerzo?
5. ¿Dónde toma la gente el almuerzo?
6. ¿Van muchos a casa?
7. ¿Por qué no van a casa?
8. ¿A qué hora cenan en Latinoamérica?
9. Y en España, ¿a qué hora cenan?
10. ¿A qué hora cenan ustedes?

Lectura opcional 2

Málaga, España

¿Mercado o supermercado?

En los países hispanos hay muchos mercados. Algunos son mercados al aire libre. En el mercado la gente compra los alimentos o comestibles[1] que necesitan para las tres comidas. Los productos que venden en los mercados están muy frescos[2]. ¡Qué deliciosos!

Hay también supermercados—sobre todo (particularmente) en las grandes ciudades y en los alrededores[3] de las grandes ciudades. En los supermercados venden muchos productos en lata, en paquete o en bolsa. En los supermercados hay un gran surtido[4] de productos congelados.

[1]comestibles *foods*
[2]frescos *fresh*
[3]alrededores *outskirts*
[4]surtido *assortment*

Estepona, España

¿Comprendes?

A De compras para la comida Completen. *(Complete.)*
1. En los países hispanos hay ____.
2. En los mercados la gente compra ____.
3. Los productos del mercado están ____.
4. Hay supermercados en ____.
5. En los supermercados venden ____.

B Otra expresión Busquen una expresión equivalente en la lectura.
(Find an equivalent expression in the reading for the italicized words.)
1. En *las naciones* hispanas hay muchos mercados al aire libre.
2. La gente compra *los alimentos* que necesitan.
3. Están muy frescos. ¡Y qué ricos y *sabrosos*!
4. Venden productos *enlatados*.
5. Hay *una gran selección*.

Conexiones

Las matemáticas

La aritmética

When we go shopping or out to eat, it is often necessary to do some arithmetic. We either have to add up the bill ourselves or check the figures someone else has done for us. In a café or restaurant we want to figure out how much tip we should leave. In order to do this we have to do some arithmetic.

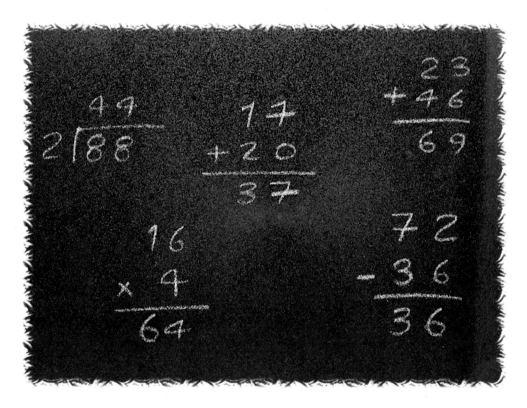

We seldom do a great deal of arithmetic in a foreign language. We normally do arithmetic in the language in which we learned it. It is fun, however, to know some basic arithmetical terms in case we have to discuss a bill or a problem with a Spanish-speaking person.

Before we learn some of these terms in Spanish, let's look at some differences in numbers. Note how the numbers 1 and 7 are written in some areas of the Spanish-speaking world.

Also note the difference in the use of the decimal point in some countries.

La aritmética

sumar   +
restar   −
multiplicar   x
dividir   ÷

Para resolver un problema oralmente

Suma dos y dos.
> Dos y dos son cuatro. $2 + 2 = 4$

Resta dos de cinco.
> Cinco menos dos son tres. $5 - 2 = 3$

Multiplica dos por cinco.
> Dos por cinco son diez. $2 \times 5 = 10$

Divide quince entre tres.
> Quince entre tres son cinco. $15 \div 3 = 5$

El diez por ciento de ciento cincuenta pesos son quince pesos.

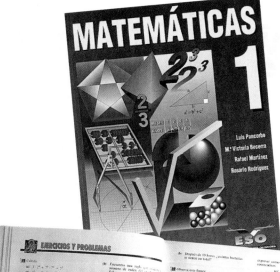

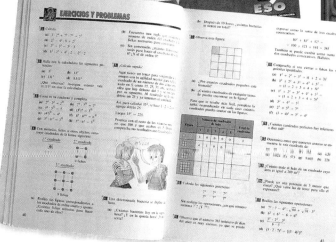

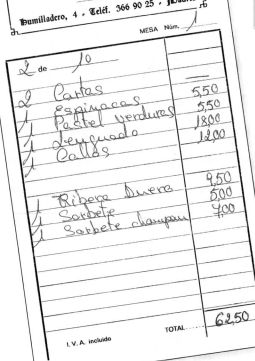

¿Comprendes?

A ¿Cuánto es? Resuelvan los problemas aritméticos en voz alta. (*Solve the following problems aloud.*)

1. $2 + 2 = 4$
2. $14 + 6 = 20$
3. $30 - 8 = 22$
4. $20 - 4 = 16$
5. $4 \times 4 = 16$
6. $8 \times 3 = 24$
7. $27 \div 9 = 3$
8. $80 \div 4 = 20$

B La respuesta, por favor. Contesten en español. (*Do the following problems in Spanish.*)

1. Suma 5 y 2.
2. Suma 20 y 3.
3. Resta 3 de 10.
4. Resta 8 de 25.
5. Multiplica 5 por 3.
6. Multiplica 9 por 4.
7. Divide 9 entre 3.
8. Divide 16 entre 2.

C La cuenta, por favor. Sumen.
(*Add the bill in Spanish.*)

¡Te toca a ti!

Use what you have learned

1 En el café
✔ *Order something to eat and drink at a café*

Work with a classmate. You're in a café on the Gran Vía in Madrid. One of you is the customer. The other is the waiter or waitress. Have a conversation. Say as much as you can to each other.

2 En el mercado
✔ *Buy food from a vendor at a market*

You are spending a semester studying in Spain. You are going to prepare a dinner for your "Spanish family." Decide what you need to buy at the market. Then have a conversation with a classmate who will be the clerk at the food store.

SPANISH Online

For more information about the Gran Vía and other interesting parts of Madrid, go to the Glencoe Spanish Web site: spanish.glencoe.com

3 Juego Una competición
✔ *Use quantities correctly with food*

See which one of you can make up the most expressions using the following words.

un kilo   un paquete   una botella   una bolsa

una lata   una docena

4 El menú

✔ *Plan a meal*

Write a menu in Spanish for your school cafeteria.

Estepona, España

5 Un anuncio

✔ *Write an advertisement for a supermarket*

Using these supermarket ads as a guide, write similar food advertisements in Spanish for your local supermarket. Choose any three foods you would like to feature.

Writing Strategy

Visualizing Many writers have a mental picture of what they want to write before they actually begin to write. The mental picture helps organize what they want to say. It also helps them visualize what they want to describe in their writing. Closing your eyes and visualizing what you want to write can make the writing experience more pleasant. When writing in a foreign language, you must limit your mental picture to what you know how to say.

6 Un café

You have been asked to write a short article about a visit to a café. Look at this photo. Pretend this is the mental picture you have of the restaurant you are going to write about. Look at it for several minutes and then write a paragraph about it.

Vocabulario

1 **Identifiquen.** *(Identify.)*

1.
2.
3.

4.
5.

To review **Palabras 1**, turn to pages 142–143.

2 **Completen la conversación.** *(Complete the conversation.)*

En el café

6. **Mesero** Sí, señores. ¿Qué _____ ustedes?

   Cliente Un café con leche y una limonada, por favor.

   (Después)

7. **Cliente** Mesero, la _____, por favor.

   Mesero Sí, señor. Enseguida.

8. **Cliente** ¿Está incluido el _____?

   Mesero Sí, señor.

3 **Identifiquen.** *(Identify.)*

9.
10.

11.
12.

To review **Palabras 2**, turn to pages 146–147.

4 **Completen.** *(Complete.)*

13–14. Las tres comidas del día son el _____, el almuerzo y la _____.

Estructura

5 **Completen.** *(Complete.)*

15–16. Nosotros _____ soda y ustedes _____ limonada. (beber)

17–18. Yo _____ muchos vegetales y mi amigo _____ muchas frutas. (comer)

19. Nosotros _____ en Estepona pero el profesor _____ en Málaga. (vivir)

To review -er and -ir verbs, turn to page 150.

6 **Completen.** *(Complete.)*

20–21. Nosotros aprend_____ mucho en la escuela y recib_____ notas muy buenas.

22–23. Nosotros le_____ novelas pero no escrib_____ novelas.

Cultura

7 **¿Sí o no?** *(True or false?)*

24. Los cafés son muy populares en España.

25. En España la gente cena a las seis. Cuando llegan a casa comen enseguida.

To review this cultural information, turn to pages 156–157.

Valldemossa, España

Tell all you can about this illustration.

Getting along in a cafe

el café	la orden	leer
la mesa	la cuenta	comer
el/la mesero(a),	libre	beber
el/la camarero(a)	ocupado(a)	¿Qué desean ustedes?
el menú	ver	¿Está incluido el servicio?

Identifying snacks and beverages

los refrescos	un yogur	una tortilla
una gaseosa, una soda	una sopa	una ensalada
un café solo, con leche	un bocadillo, un sándwich	el postre
un té helado	el jamón	un helado de vainilla,
una limonada	el queso	de chocolate
el cereal	una hamburguesa	un pan dulce
el pan tostado	papas fritas	

Shopping for food

el mercado	una bolsa	¿A cuánto está(n)?
el supermercado	un kilo	algo más
un bote, una lata	congelado(a)	nada más
un paquete	vender	

Identifying foods and meals

los vegetales	la carne
los guisantes	el biftec
las habichuelas,	los mariscos
los frijoles	el pescado
las judías verdes	el pollo
las zanahorias	el huevo
las papas	el atún
la lechuga	el arroz
las frutas	las comidas
las naranjas	el desayuno
las manzanas	el almuerzo
los plátanos	la cena
los tomates	

> ### How well do you know your vocabulary?
> - Choose words for specific foods you enjoy.
> - Create a menu using these words.

Other useful expressions

juntos(as)	aprender
antes de	escribir
después de	recibir
enseguida	vivir
comprender	

VIDEOTUR

Episodio 5

In this video episode, you will join Alejandra and Julián at a café. See page 496 for more information.

Capítulo 6

La familia y su casa

Objetivos

In this chapter you will learn to:

- ❖ talk about your family
- ❖ describe your home
- ❖ tell your age and find out someone else's age
- ❖ tell what you have to do
- ❖ tell what you are going to do
- ❖ tell what belongs to you and to others
- ❖ talk about families in Spanish-speaking countries

María Izquierdo *Mis sobrinas*

Vocabulario

PALABRAS 1

La familia

los abuelos

Don Luis Guerrero — el abuelo

Doña Antonia Guerrero — la abuela

los padres — los tíos

Sr. Ramos — el esposo, el marido — el padre

Sra. Ramos — la esposa, la mujer — la madre

Sr. Guerrero — el tío

Sra. Guerrero — la tía

los hijos

Marcos — el hijo — el hermano — el nieto

Lourdes — la hija — la hermana — la nieta

Tomás — el sobrino — el primo

Isabel — la sobrina — la prima

Tico — el gato

Merlín — el perro

Es la familia Moliner. Son de Quito.
El señor y la señora Moliner tienen dos hijos.
Tienen un hijo, Felipe, y una hija, Verónica.
Los Moliner tienen un gato, Tico.
La familia no tiene un perro.

¿Cuántos años tienen los hijos?
Felipe, el hijo, tiene dieciséis años.
Verónica, la hija, tiene catorce años.
Son jóvenes. No son viejos (ancianos).

el regalo

Hoy es el 28 de noviembre.
Es el cumpleaños de Verónica.
Los Moliner van a dar una fiesta
    para Verónica.
Van a invitar a todos sus parientes
    (los tíos, los abuelos) a la fiesta.
Los amigos van a llevar regalos
    para Verónica.

Vocabulario

¿Qué palabra necesito?

1 Historieta La familia Rodríguez de España

Contesten. *(Answer.)*

1. ¿Vive la familia Rodríguez en España?
2. ¿Tienen dos hijos los señores Rodríguez?
3. ¿Es grande o pequeña la familia Rodríguez?
4. ¿Cuántos años tiene Antonio?
5. ¿Cuántos años tiene Maricarmen?
6. ¿Tienen los Rodríguez un gato o un perro?

Madrid, España

2 Los parientes Completen. *(Complete.)*

1. El hermano de mi padre es mi ____.
2. La hermana de mi padre es mi ____.
3. El hermano de mi madre es mi ____.
4. La hermana de mi madre es mi ____.
5. El hijo de mi tío o de mi tía es mi ____.
6. La hija de mis tíos es mi ____.
7. Los hijos de mis tíos son mis ____.
8. Los padres de mis padres son mis ____.

3 Y yo Escojan. *(Choose.)*

1. Yo soy ____ de mis abuelos.
   a. el nieto   b. la nieta
2. Yo soy ____ de mis padres.
   a. el hijo   b. la hija
3. Yo soy ____ de mis tíos.
   a. el sobrino   b. la sobrina
4. Yo soy ____ de mis primos.
   a. el primo   b. la prima

Lima, Perú

4 **Historieta** **El cumpleaños de Luisa**
Contesten según se indica. *(Answer according to the cues.)*

1. ¿Qué es hoy? (el cumpleaños de Luisa)
2. ¿Cuántos años tiene hoy? ¿Cuántos años cumple? (quince)
3. ¿Qué dan sus padres en su honor? (una fiesta)
4. ¿A quiénes invitan a la fiesta? (a sus amigos y a sus parientes)
5. ¿Qué va a recibir Luisa? (muchos regalos)

5 **La familia Guzmán** With a classmate, look at the picture of the Guzmán family. Take turns saying as much as you can about each person in the photo.

6 **Juego** **¿Cúal de los parientes es?** Give a definition in Spanish of a relative. Your partner will then tell which relative you're referring to. Take turns.

la madre de mi madre

Es la abuela.

La casa

la casa

el jardín

el garaje

alrededor de

JUAN ELCANO

la calle

la recámara

el cuarto de baño

el cuarto

el dormitorio

la sala

la cocina

el comedor

Es la casa de la familia Moliner.
Alrededor de la casa hay un jardín.
El garaje está cerca de la casa.
Los Moliner viven en una casa
   privada (particular).
Tienen un carro.
El carro está en el garaje.
La casa está en la calle Juan Elcano.

La casa de los Moliner tiene siete cuartos.

las noticias

el periódico

el libro

la revista

una emisión deportiva

una película

Después de la cena, la familia va a la sala.
En la sala ellos leen.
Y ven la televisión.

Una casa de apartamentos (departamentos)

el décimo piso
el noveno piso
el octavo piso
el séptimo piso
el sexto piso
el quinto piso
el cuarto piso
el tercer piso
el segundo piso
el primer piso
la planta baja

Los García tienen un apartamento en
el quinto piso.
Suben al apartamento en el ascensor.
No toman la escalera.
Toman el ascensor.

Vocabulario

¿Qué palabra necesito?

7 Historieta La casa de los Baeza
Contesten. (*Answer. Make up a story.*)

1. ¿Tienen los Baeza una casa bonita?
2. ¿Está en la calle Silva la casa?
3. ¿Cuántos cuartos tiene la casa?
4. ¿Tiene dos pisos la casa?
5. ¿Qué cuartos están en la planta baja?
6. ¿Qué cuartos están en el primer piso?
7. ¿Tienen los Baeza un carro?
8. ¿Está en el garaje el carro?
9. ¿Está el garaje cerca de la casa?
10. ¿Hay un jardín alrededor de la casa?

Málaga, España

8 Historieta Actividades en casa
Completen. (*Complete.*)

1. La familia prepara la comida en la ____.
2. La familia come en ____ o ____. A veces comen en ____ y a veces comen en ____.
3. Después de la cena, la familia va o pasa a ____.
4. En la sala leen ____, ____ o ____. No escriben cartas.
5. En la sala ven ____.
6. Ven ____, ____ o ____ en la televisión.

Madrid, España

9 Historieta ¿Es verdad o no? Contesten con **sí** o **no**.
(Answer with sí or no.)

1. Una casa pequeña tiene sólo dos cuartos.
2. Un apartamento grande tiene dos cuartos.
3. La casa de apartamentos es alta.
4. Una casa privada o particular tiene sólo uno o dos pisos y una casa de apartamentos tiene muchos pisos.
5. En una casa privada la familia sube de un piso a otro en el ascensor.
6. La familia toma la escalera para subir de un piso a otro en una casa particular.

Santiago, Chile

Málaga, España

El Viejo San Juan, Puerto Rico

10 Mi casa Work with a classmate. One of you lives in a private house and the other lives in an apartment building. Ask each other as many questions as you can about your homes. Answer each other's questions, too.

11 La rutina de mi familia Get together with a classmate and discuss the routine your family follows after school or after work. You may want to use some of the following words.

comer mirar preparar escribir

tomar leer ver

Estructura

Presente de **tener**
Telling what you and others have

1. The verb **tener** (*to have*) is irregular. Study the following forms.

INFINITIVE	tener
yo	tengo
tú	tienes
él, ella, Ud.	tiene
nosotros(as)	tenemos
vosotros(as)	*tenéis*
ellos, ellas, Uds.	tienen

2. You also use the verb **tener** to express age in Spanish.

¿Cuántos años tienes?
Tengo dieciséis años.
¿Cuántos años tiene usted?

¿Cómo lo digo?

12 **¿Cómo es tu familia?** Contesten personalmente.
(*Answer about yourself.*)

1. ¿Tienes un hermano?
2. ¿Cuántos hermanos tienes?
3. ¿Tienes una hermana?
4. ¿Cuántas hermanas tienes?
5. ¿Tienes un perro?
6. ¿Tienes un gato?
7. ¿Tienes muchos amigos?
8. ¿Tienes una familia grande o pequeña?

Los Ángeles, California

13 **¿Tienes un hermano?** Practiquen la conversación.
(Practice the conversation.)

¿Cuántos años tiene ella?

Ernesto, ¿tienes un hermano?

Tiene catorce años.

¿Uds. tienen un perro?

No, no tengo un hermano. Tengo una hermana.

Y tú, ¿cuántos años tienes?

No, perrito no tenemos. Pero tenemos una gata adorable.

Yo tengo dieciséis.

14 **Ernesto y Teresa** Hablen de Ernesto y Teresa.
(In your own words, tell all about Ernesto and Teresa.)

15 **¿Qué tienes?** Formen preguntas con **tienes**.
(Form questions with tienes.*)*

1. un hermano
2. una hermana
3. primos
4. un perro
5. un gato
6. muchos amigos

Santiago, Chile

16 **¿Qué tienen ustedes?** Sigan el modelo.
(Follow the model.)

una casa o un apartamento ⟶
—Marcos y Adela, ¿ustedes tienen una casa o un apartamento?
—Tenemos una casa. / Tenemos un apartamento.

1. un perro o un gato
2. un hermano o una hermana
3. un sobrino o una sobrina
4. una familia grande o pequeña
5. una bicicleta o un carro
6. CDs o videos

UN POCO MÁS

*For more practice using **tener**, do Activity 6 on page H7 at the end of this book.*

17 Historieta La familia Sánchez

Completen con **tener.** (*Complete with* tener.)

Aquí __1__ (nosotros) una foto de la familia Sánchez. La familia Sánchez __2__ un piso (apartamento) muy bonito en Madrid. El piso __3__ seis cuartos y está en Salamanca, una zona bastante elegante de Madrid. Los Sánchez __4__ una casa de campo en Chinchón también. La casa de campo en Chinchón es un pequeño chalé donde los Sánchez pasan los fines de semana o los *weekend* y sus vacaciones. La casa de campo __5__ cinco cuartos.

Hay cuatro personas en la familia Sánchez. Carolina __6__ nueve años y su hermano Gerardo __7__ once años. Gerardo y Carolina __8__ un perrito encantador, Chispa. Adoran a su Chispa.

¿Tú __9__ un perro? ¿Tú __10__ un gato? ¿Tu familia __11__ un apartamento o una casa? ¿Ustedes también __12__ una casa de campo donde pasan los fines de semana como los Sánchez?

La Plaza, Chinchón, España

For more information about the Salamanca quarter of Madrid and Chinchón, go to the Glencoe Spanish Web site: spanish.glencoe.com

18   **Tengo tres hermanos.** With a classmate, take turns telling one another some things about your family. Tell whether you have a large or small family; tell the numbers of brothers and sisters you have and their ages, etc.

Tener que; Ir a
Telling what you have to and are going to do

1. **Tener que** + *infinitive* (**-ar, -er,** or **-ir** form of the verb) means *to have to.*

   Tengo que comprar un regalo.

2. **Ir a** + *infinitive* means *to be going to.* It is used to express what is going to happen in the near future.

   Vamos a llegar mañana.
   Ella va a cumplir quince años.

¿Cómo lo digo?

19 Historieta ¡Cuánto tengo que trabajar!

Contesten personalmente. *(Answer about yourself.)*

1. ¿Tienes que trabajar mucho en la escuela?
2. Antes de la apertura de clases, ¿tienes que comprar materiales escolares?
3. ¿Tienes que comprar ropa también?
4. ¿Tienes que estudiar mucho?
5. ¿Tienes que leer muchos libros?
6. ¿Tienes que tomar apuntes?
7. ¿Tienes que escribir mucho?

20 Historieta Voy a dar una fiesta.

Contesten con **sí.** (*Answer with* sí.)

1. ¿Vas a dar una fiesta?
2. ¿Vas a dar la fiesta para Ángel?
3. ¿Ángel va a cumplir diecisiete años?

4. ¿Vas a invitar a sus amigos?
5. ¿Van ustedes a bailar durante la fiesta?
6. ¿Van a comer?

Estepona, España

21 Historieta ¡Tenemos tanto que hacer!

Sigan el modelo. (*Follow the model.*)

> **ver la televisión / preparar la comida** ⟶
> **No vamos a ver la televisión porque
> tenemos que preparar la comida.**

1. escuchar discos compactos / estudiar
2. hablar por teléfono / escribir una composición
3. tomar seis cursos / sacar notas buenas
4. tomar apuntes / escuchar al profesor
5. ir a la fiesta / trabajar

22 Tengo que...

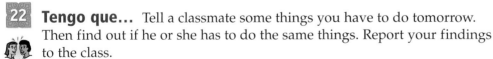

Tell a classmate some things you have to do tomorrow.
Then find out if he or she has to do the same things. Report your findings
to the class.

23 No voy a...

Tell a classmate some things you're not going to do
tomorrow because you have to do something else. Tell what you have to
do. Your classmate will let you know if he or she is in the same situation.

Adjetivos posesivos
Telling what belongs to whom

1. You use possessive adjectives to show possession or ownership. Like other adjectives, the possessive adjective must agree with the noun it modifies. The possessive adjectives **mi, tu,** and **su** have only two forms: singular and plural.

mi libro y **mi** revista	**mis** libros y **mis** revistas
tu libro y **tu** revista	**tus** libros y **tus** revistas
su libro y **su** revista	**sus** libros y **sus** revistas

2. The possessive adjective **su** can mean *his, her, their,* or *your.* Its meaning is usually obvious from the way it is used in the sentence. However, if it is not clear, **su** can be replaced by a prepositional phrase.

el libro ⎰ **de él** / **de ella** / **de Ud.** **el libro** ⎰ **de ellos** / **de ellas** / **de Uds.**

3. The possessive adjective **nuestro** (*our*) has four forms.

nuestro apartamento	**nuestros** libros
nuestra casa	**nuestras** revistas

> **¿Lo sabes?**
>
> **Vuestro** is the possessive adjective used with **vosotros** in parts of Spain. **Vuestro,** like **nuestro,** has four forms.

Marbella, España

Estructura

¿Cómo lo digo?

24 Historieta Mi familia y mi casa

Contesten personalmente. *(Answer about yourself.)*

1. ¿Dónde está tu casa o tu apartamento?
2. ¿Cuántos cuartos tiene tu casa o tu apartamento?
3. Tu apartamento o tu casa, ¿es grande o pequeño(a)?
4. ¿Cuántas personas hay en tu familia?
5. ¿Dónde viven tus abuelos?
6. Y tus primos, ¿dónde viven?

25 Tengo una pregunta para ti. Sigan el modelo. *(Follow the model.)*

la casa ⟶
Lupita, ¿dónde está tu casa?

1. el hermano
2. la hermana
3. los primos
4. los libros
5. la escuela
6. el/la profesor(a) de español

26 La verdad es que... Preparen una conversación.
(Make up a conversation.)

—**¿Tienes tú mi libro?** ⟶
—**No. De ninguna manera. No tengo tu libro.
La verdad es que tú tienes tu libro.**

1.

2.

3.

4.

27 ¿Cómo son sus parientes? Sigan el modelo. *(Follow the model.)*

el hermano de Susana ⟶
Su hermano es muy simpático.

1. el hermano de Pablo
2. la amiga de Pablo
3. el primo de Carlos y José
4. la tía de Teresa y José
5. los tíos de Teresa y José
6. los padres de usted

28 Historieta **Nuestra casa y nuestra escuela**
Contesten personalmente. *(Answer about yourself.)*

1. Su casa (la casa de ustedes), ¿es grande o pequeña?
2. ¿Cuántos cuartos tiene su casa?
3. ¿Su casa está en la ciudad o en el campo?
4. ¿En qué calle está su escuela?
5. Su escuela, ¿es una escuela intermedia o una escuela superior?
6. En general, ¿sus profesores son simpáticos?
7. ¿Son interesantes sus cursos?
8. ¿Son grandes o pequeñas sus clases?

Lima, Perú

29 Mi hermano y yo... Work with a classmate. Tell him or her about yourself and a sibling, or your friend if you don't have a sibling. Then ask your classmate questions about his or her family. Here are some words you may want to use.

casa
perro
escuela
amigo
gato
jardín
carro
amiga
clase

Andas bien. ¡Adelante!

¿Vas a la fiesta?

Tadeo ¿Vas a la fiesta de José Luis el viernes?

Jaime ¡Ah! ¡Es verdad! José Luis va a dar una fiesta.

Tadeo ¡Hombre! ¿No vas?

Jaime Pues, tengo que ir de compras. Tengo que comprar un regalo para mi hermana.

Tadeo ¿Tienes una hermana?

Jaime Sí, y va a cumplir quince años.

Tadeo ¿Ustedes van a dar una fiesta?

Jaime ¡Claro! Vamos a tener una celebración.

Tadeo Pero, no es mañana, ¿verdad?

Jaime No. Su fiesta es el sábado.

Tadeo Pues, tienes que ir a la fiesta de José Luis.

¿Comprendes?

Contesten. (*Answer.*)

1. ¿Con quién habla Tadeo?
2. ¿Adónde tiene que ir Jaime?
3. ¿Qué tiene que comprar?
4. ¿Por qué tiene que comprar un regalo para su hermana?
5. ¿Cuántos años tiene su hermana?
6. ¿Cuántos años va a cumplir el sábado?
7. ¿Van a dar una fiesta?
8. ¿Cuándo es la fiesta de su hermana?
9. ¿Cuándo es la fiesta de José Luis?

Vamos a hablar más

A **¿Qué casa?** You and your family are planning to spend a month in Peru. Which of the houses or apartments, as described in the newspaper ads, would suit your family best? Explain why.

B **¡Qué familia!** Work with a classmate. Make up an imaginary family. Describe each family member and tell what he or she has to do. Be as creative as possible.

ALQUILER DE CASAS DEPARTAMENTOS Y RESIDENCIAS
En Lima, Callao y balnearios

1A.- CASAS

01 $ 1,500 2 chalets 21 Benavides colegio Humboldt Juana Larco Dammert 4 dorm. escritorio 9780150 o 9435188

01 CHACARILLA Maravillosa residencia 1 planta piscina 4 dormitorios 4 baños ideal diplomaticos funcionarios $ 2200 telefono 4613661.

ALQUILO casa 5 baños 3 salas comedor cocina 3 cocheras piscina 2 bares amoblada area de servicio lavanderia preferencia extranjeros Tf. 4469062 - 9940537

CHALET 2 plantas $ 300 Pueblo Libre 3 dormitorios sala comedor 2 baños lavanderia Telef. 4443394.

1B.- DEPARTAMENTOS

07 ALOJAMIENTO Temporal suite Los Pinos Pardo Miraflores departamentos full equipo 1 2 dormitorios cochera directo con departamentos cable VHS limpieza seguridad privacidad excelente ubicacion desde $ 45 diarios reservas 2421354 - 2421503 - 4477745

04 ALOJAMIENTO temporal San Isidro departamento independiente completamente equipado Tv cable limpieza diaria minimo 1 semana T. 421-8092

02 VISTA AL MAR departamento nuevo 3 dormitorios 2 cocheras piscina jacuzzi c/s muebles $ 2,000 T. 445-8748

Pronunciación

Las consonantes b, v

There is no difference in pronunciation between a **b** and a **v** in Spanish. The **b** or **v** sound is somewhat softer than the sound of an English *b*. When making this sound, the lips barely touch. Imitate the following carefully.

ba	**be**	**bi**	**bo**	**bu**
bajo	bebé	bicicleta	bonito	bueno
bastante	escribe	bien	recibo	bus
trabaja	recibe	biología	árbol	aburrido

va	**ve**	**vi**	**vo**	**vu**
vamos	verano	vive	vosotros	vuelo
nueva	venezolano	violín	voleibol	

Repeat the following sentences.

> El joven vive en la avenida Bolívar en Bogotá.
> Bárbara trabaja los sábados en el laboratorio de biología.
> La joven ve la bicicleta nueva en la televisión.

AVENIDA BOLÍVAR

Lecturas culturales

La familia hispana 🔄 🎧

Reading Strategy

Using background knowledge When you are first assigned a reading, quickly look at the accompanying visuals to determine what the reading is about. Once you know what the topic is, spend a short time thinking about what you already know about it. If you do this, the reading will be easier to understand.

Estepona, España

Cuando un joven hispano habla de su familia, no habla solamente de sus padres y de sus hermanos. Habla de toda su familia—sus abuelos, tíos, primos, etc. Incluye también a sus padrinos—a su padrino y a su madrina.

¿Quiénes son los padrinos? Los padrinos son los que asisten al bebé durante el bautizo[1]. En la sociedad hispana, los padrinos forman una parte íntegra de la familia. Y la familia es una unidad muy importante en la sociedad hispana. Cuando hay una celebración familiar como un bautizo, una boda[2] o un cumpleaños, todos los parientes van a la fiesta. Y los padrinos también van a la fiesta.

[1]bautizo *baptism*   [2]boda *wedding*

San Juan, Puerto Rico

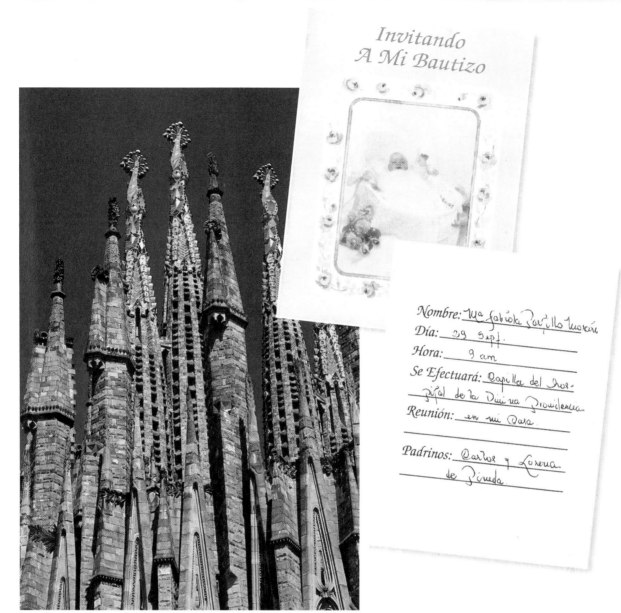

La Sagrada Familia, Barcelona, España

Invitando A Mi Bautizo

Nombre: Ma. Fabiola Parrillo Morán
Día: 29 Sept.
Hora: 9 am
Se Efectuará: Capilla del Hospital de la Divina Providencia
Reunión: en mi Casa

Padrinos: Carlos y Lorena de Pineda.

¿Comprendes?

La familia hispana Contesten. *(Answer.)*
1. Cuando una persona hispana habla de su familia, ¿de quiénes habla?
2. ¿Quiénes son los padrinos?
3. ¿Son una parte importante de la familia los padrinos?
4. ¿Cuáles son algunas celebraciones familiares?
5. ¿Quiénes asisten a una celebración familiar?

*En Tus
Quince Años*

La quinceañera

En Estados Unidos celebramos la *Sweet Sixteen*. La *Sweet Sixteen* es una fiesta en honor de la muchacha que cumple dieciséis años.

En una familia hispana hay una gran celebración en honor de la quinceañera. ¿Quién es la quinceañera? La quinceañera es la muchacha que cumple quince años. La familia siempre da una gran fiesta en su honor. Todos los parientes y amigos asisten a la fiesta.

La quinceañera recibe muchos regalos. A veces los regalos son extraordinarios—como un viaje[1] a Europa o a Estados Unidos, por ejemplo. Y si la quinceañera vive en Estados Unidos es a veces un viaje a Latinoamérica o a España.

[1]viaje *trip*

Una quinceañera, México

¿Comprendes?

¿Una costumbre hispana o estadounidense? Lean las frases. *(Read the statements and tell whether each more accurately describes a Hispanic or an American custom. In some cases, it may describe a custom of both cultures.)*

1. Dan una fiesta en honor de una muchacha que cumple quince años.
2. Dan una fiesta en honor de la muchacha que cumple dieciséis años.
3. La muchacha recibe regalos para su cumpleaños.
4. La fiesta es principalmente para los amigos jóvenes de la muchacha.
5. Toda la familia asiste a la fiesta—los abuelos, los tíos, los padrinos.

Lectura opcional ②

Las Meninas de
Diego Velázquez

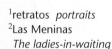

Las Meninas

Todos tenemos fotos de nuestra familia, ¿no? Muchos tenemos todo un álbum. No hay nada más adorable que la foto de un bebé—sobre todo (especialmente) si el bebé es un hijo, sobrino o nieto, ¿verdad?

Muchas familias tienen retratos[1] de su familia—sobre todo, las familias nobles. Aquí tenemos el famoso cuadro *Las Meninas*[2]. El cuadro *Las Meninas* es del famoso artista español del siglo XVII, el pintor Diego Velázquez.

En su cuadro, *Las Meninas,* vemos a la hija del Rey[3] con sus damas y su perro. Vemos al pintor mismo de pie delante de su caballete[4]. Y en el cuadro hay algo maravilloso. Más atrás en el espejo[5] vemos el reflejo del Rey y la Reina. En el cuadro vemos a toda la familia real[6]: al padre, el Rey; a la madre, la Reina; a la hija, la princesa.

[1]retratos *portraits*
[2]Las Meninas
   The ladies-in-waiting
[3]Rey *King*
[4]caballete *easel*
[5]espejo *mirror*
[6]real *royal*

¿Comprendes?

A **Una familia real** Contesten. (*Answer.*)
1. ¿Qué tienen muchas familias?
2. ¿Qué es una colección de fotos?
3. ¿Son adorables las fotos de un bebé?
4. ¿Tienen muchas familias retratos familiares también?
5. ¿Quién es el pintor de *Las Meninas?*
6. ¿Es español o latinoamericano Velázquez?
7. La muchacha en el cuadro, ¿es hija de quién?
8. ¿Dónde está el pintor en el cuadro?
9. ¿De quiénes hay un reflejo en el espejo?
10. ¿A quiénes vemos en el cuadro?

B **Las Meninas** Busquen a las personas en el cuadro.
(*Find the following people in the painting.*)
1. el artista
2. la hija del Rey
3. las meninas o damas de la princesa
4. el Rey
5. el perro de la princesa
6. la madre de la princesa, la Reina

Conexiones

Las bellas artes

El arte

One may know a great deal or just a little about art. But almost everyone has at least some interest in art. How often have we heard, "I may not know anything about art, but I certainly know what I like"?

There is no doubt that many of the world's great artists have come from Spain and Latin America. Do you recognize any of the following names?

El Greco, Velázquez, Murillo, Goya, Zurbarán, Sorolla, Picasso, Dalí, Miró, Rivera, Orozco, Siqueiros, Kahlo, Tamayo, Botero.

Let's first read some information about art and then enjoy some famous works of Spanish and Latin American artists.

Autorretrato de Frida Kahlo

La pintura

El pintor

Antes de pintar, el pintor o artista tiene que preparar su lienzo. Tiene que colocar el lienzo en el caballete. El pintor escoge o selecciona el medio en que va a pintar. Los medios más populares son la acuarela[1], el óleo y el acrílico. El artista aplica los colores al lienzo con un pincel o una espátula.

El motivo o tema

Para el observador, el individuo que mira el cuadro, el motivo o tema de una obra de arte es el principal elemento de interés. Es la materia que pinta el artista—una persona, un santo, una escena, una batalla, un paisaje[2].

El estilo

El estilo es el modo de expresión del artista. En términos generales, clasificamos el estilo en figurativo o abstracto. Una obra figurativa presenta una interpretación literal o realista de la materia. El observador sabe[3] enseguida lo que ve en el cuadro.

Una obra de arte abstracto enfatiza o da énfasis al diseño más que a la materia. El artista no pinta la escena misma. Pinta algo que representa la escena o materia.

Aquí vemos unas obras famosas de algunos maestros de España y Latinoamérica.

[1]acuarela *watercolor*   [2]paisaje *landscape*   [3]sabe *knows*

El tres de mayo de Francisco de Goya

Zapatistas de José Clemente Orozco

El entierro del Conde de Orgaz
de El Greco

¿Comprendes?

El cuadro favorito Identifiquen su favorito. *(Identify your favorite.)*

Look at the paintings and tell which one is your favorite. Explain why it's your favorite.

¡Te toca a ti!

Use what you have learned

Una residencia bonita

✔ *Describe a home or an apartment*

You are trying to sell one of the apartments or houses listed in the ads. Say as much as you can to convince your client (your classmate) to buy one.

BOSQUES DE LAS LOMAS. En venta, moderno, impecable, 377 m2, finos acabados. Areas recreativas, alberca, salón de fiestas, cancha de tenis, jardines, vigilancia las 24 horas.

TETELA DEL MONTE. Excelente, colonial mexicano. Arq. Sánchez. 1,500 m2 terreno, 500 m2 construcción, 4 rec., 3.5 baños, alberca, palapa

Una casa de apartamentos

✔ *Talk about families and where they live*

With a classmate, look at this plan of the fourth floor of an apartment building. A different family lives in each apartment. Give each family a name. Then say as much as you can about the families and their activities. Don't forget to describe their apartment. Give as many details as possible.

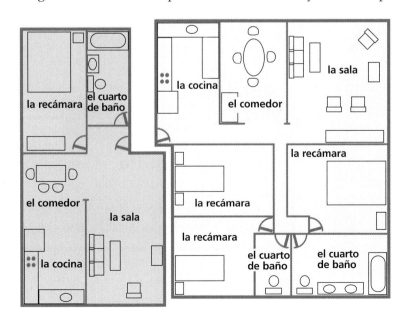

3 La quinceañera

ESCRIBIR

✔ *Invite a friend to a birthday party*

Your best friend Anita will soon be fifteen years old. Write out an invitation to her birthday party.

4 Mi familia y yo

ESCRIBIR

✔ *Describe yourself and your family*

You plan to spend next year as an exchange student in Argentina. You have to write a letter about yourself and your family to the agency in your community that selects the exchange students. Make your description as complete as possible.

Writing Strategy

Ordering details There are several ways to order details when writing. The one you choose depends on your purpose for writing. When describing a physical place, sometimes it is best to use spatial ordering. This means describing things as they actually appear—from left to right, from back to front, from top to bottom, or any other combination of logical order that works.

5 La casa de mis sueños

ESCRIBIR

Write a description of your dream house. Be as complete as you can.

Fuengirola, España

Assessment

Vocabulario

1 **Identifiquen.** *(Identify.)*

1. la madre de mi madre
2. el hermano de mi madre
3. el hijo de mi tío
4. la hija de mis padres
5. la esposa de mi padre

To review **Palabras 1,** turn to pages 170–171.

2 **Completen.** *(Complete.)*

6. Hoy es el ____ de Verónica. Hoy tiene quince años.
7. Los amigos tienen ____ para Verónica.

3 **Identifiquen.** *(Identify.)*

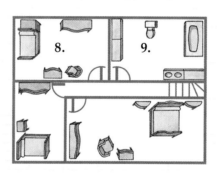
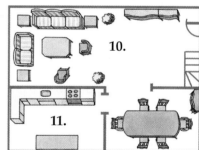

4 **Escojan.** *(Choose.)*

12. Después de la cena, papá lee ____.
    a. la televisión   **b.** el periódico   **c.** una emisión
13. Ellos ____ al quinto piso en el ascensor.
    a. toman   **b.** ven   **c.** suben

To review **Palabras 2,** turn to pages 174–175.

Estructura

5 **Contesten.** *(Answer.)*

14. ¿Cuántos años tienes?
15. ¿Tiene tu familia una casa o un apartamento?
16. ¿Tienen ustedes un perro?

To review **tener**, turn to page 178.

6 **Completen con tener.** *(Complete with* tener.*)*

17–18. —Yo ____ tres hermanos.
    —Perdón, Enrique. ¿Cuántos hermanos ____?

7 **Completen.** *(Complete.)*

19. Yo ____ compr__ un regalo para Sarita porque mañana es su cumpleaños.
20. Yo no ____ com__ mucho durante la fiesta.

To review **tener que** and **ir a**, turn to page 181.

8 **Escojan.** *(Choose.)*

21. ¿Dónde está el carro de Jorge? ____ carro está en el garaje.
    a. Mi   **b.** Su   **c.** Nuestro
22. ¿Cuántos años tiene tu hermana? ____ hermana tiene trece años.
    a. Mi   **b.** Nuestra   **c.** Tu
23. —¿Ustedes tienen un perro?
    —Sí, y ____ perro es adorable.
    a. su   **b.** nuestro   **c.** nuestros

To review possessive adjectives, turn to page 183.

Cultura

9 **Contesten.** *(Answer.)*

24. Cuando una persona hispana habla de su familia, ¿de quiénes habla?
25. ¿Quiénes asisten al bebé durante el bautizo y luego forman parte de la familia?

To review this cultural information, turn to page 188.

Tell all you can about this illustration.

Vocabulario

Identifying family members

la familia
los parientes
el padre
la madre
el esposo, el marido
la esposa, la mujer
el/la hijo(a)
el/la hermano(a)
el/la abuelo(a)

el/la nieto(a)
el/la tío(a)
el/la sobrino(a)
el/la primo(a)
el gato
el perro
joven
viejo(a), anciano(a)

Talking about family affairs or events

el cumpleaños
el regalo
la celebración

tener
cumplir… años
invitar

Identifying rooms of the house

la sala
el comedor
la cocina
el cuarto, el dormitorio, la recámara
el cuarto de baño

How well do you know your vocabulary?
- Identify the cognates.
- Use as many of them as you can to write a story.

Talking about a home

la casa
el apartamento,
   el departamento
la calle
el jardín
el garaje
el carro
la planta baja

el piso
el ascensor
la escalera
privado(a), particular
alrededor de
cerca de
subir

Discussing some home activities

el periódico
la revista
el libro
la película

la emisión deportiva
las noticias
ver la televisión
escribir una carta

VIDEOTUR

Episodio 6

In this video episode, you will join Claudia and Francisco as they celebrate Claudia's cousin's birthday. See page 497 for more information.

Capítulo 7

Deportes de equipo

Objetivos

In this chapter you will learn to:

* talk about team sports and other physical activities
* tell what you want to, begin to, and prefer to do
* talk about people's activities
* express what interests, bores, or pleases you
* discuss the role of sports in the Hispanic world

Ángel Zarraga *Futbolistas en el llano*

El fútbol

la cabeza

el estadio

la jugadora

el espectador, la espectadora

el balón

el campo de fútbol

el brazo

la mano derecha

la mano izquierda

el portero, la portera

la portería

la pierna

la rodilla

el pie

el equipo

Hay un partido hoy.
Hay un partido entre el Real Madrid y
    el Barcelona.
El Real Madrid juega contra el Barcelona.

el tablero indicador   el tanto

Los jugadores juegan (al) fútbol.
Un jugador lanza el balón.
Tira el balón con el pie.
El portero guarda la portería.

El segundo tiempo empieza.
Los dos equipos vuelven al campo.
El tanto queda empatado en cero.

El portero no puede bloquear (parar)
    el balón.
El balón entra en la portería.
González mete un gol.
Él marca un tanto.

El Real Madrid gana el partido.
El Barcelona pierde.
Pero el Barcelona no pierde siempre.
A veces gana.

Vocabulario

¿Qué palabra necesito?

1 **Historieta** **Un partido de fútbol** Contesten. (*Answer.*)

1. ¿Cuántos equipos de fútbol hay en el campo de fútbol?
2. ¿Cuántos jugadores hay en cada equipo?
3. ¿Qué tiempo empieza, el primero o el segundo?
4. ¿Vuelven los jugadores al campo cuando empieza el segundo tiempo?
5. ¿Tiene un jugador el balón?
6. ¿Lanza el balón con el pie o con la mano?
7. ¿Para el balón el portero o entra el balón en la portería?
8. ¿Mete el jugador un gol?
9. ¿Marca un tanto?
10. ¿Queda empatado el tanto?
11. ¿Quién gana, el Real Madrid o el Barcelona?
12. ¿Qué equipo pierde?
13. ¿Siempre pierde?

El estadio Atahualpa, Quito, Ecuador

2 Historieta El fútbol

Contesten según se indica. *(Answer according to the cues.)*

1. ¿Cuántos jugadores hay en el equipo de fútbol? (once)
2. ¿Cuántos tiempos hay en un partido de fútbol? (dos)
3. ¿Quién guarda la portería? (el portero)
4. ¿Cuándo mete un gol el jugador? (cuando el balón entra en la portería)
5. ¿Qué marca un jugador cuando el balón entra en la portería? (un tanto)
6. En el estadio, ¿qué indica el tablero? (el tanto)
7. ¿Cuándo queda empatado el tanto? (cuando los dos equipos tienen el mismo tanto)

El equipo de Chile,
La Copa mundial

3 Un partido de fútbol
Work with a classmate. Take turns asking and answering each other's questions about the photograph below.

El béisbol

el campo de béisbol

el jardinero

el pícher, el lanzador

el bateador

el bate

la base

el platillo

el cátcher, el receptor

El pícher lanza la pelota.

la pelota

el guante

el jugador de béisbol

El cátcher devuelve la pelota.

El bateador batea.
Batea un jonrón.
El jugador corre de una base a otra.

En un juego de béisbol hay nueve entradas. Si después de la novena entrada el tanto queda empatado, el partido continúa.

La jugadora atrapa la pelota. Atrapa la pelota con el guante.

El básquetbol, El baloncesto

driblar con el balón

la cancha de básquetbol

el cesto, la canasta ········

encestar

el balón

meter el balón en el cesto

tirar el balón

pasar el balón

¿Qué palabra necesito?

Monterrey, México

4 **Historieta** **El béisbol**
Escojan. *(Choose.)*

1. Juegan al béisbol en ____ de béisbol.
   a. un campo   **b.** una pelota
   c. una base
2. El pícher ____ la pelota.
   a. lanza   **b.** encesta   **c.** batea
3. El receptor atrapa la pelota en ____.
   a. una portería   **b.** un cesto
   c. un guante
4. El jugador ____ de una base a otra.
   a. tira   **b.** devuelve   **c.** corre
5. En un partido de béisbol hay ____ entradas.
   a. dos   **b.** nueve   **c.** once

San Juan, Puerto Rico

5 **Historieta** **El baloncesto**
Contesten. *(Answer.)*

1. ¿Es el baloncesto un deporte de equipo o un deporte individual?
2. ¿Hay cinco o nueve jugadores en un equipo de baloncesto?
3. Durante un partido de baloncesto, ¿los jugadores driblan con el balón o lanzan el balón con el pie?
4. ¿El jugador tira el balón en el cesto o en la portería?
5. ¿El encestado (canasto) vale dos puntos o seis puntos?

6 ¿Qué deporte es? Escojan. *(Choose.)*

el béisbol

el baloncesto

el fútbol

1. El jugador lanza el balón con el pie.
2. Hay cinco jugadores en el equipo.
3. Hay nueve entradas en el partido.
4. El jugador corre de una base a otra.
5. El portero para o bloquea el balón.
6. El jugador tira el balón y encesta.

7 *Juego* ¿Qué deporte es? Work with a classmate. Give him or her some information about a sport. He or she has to guess what sport you're talking about. Take turns.

FÁBRICA DE UNIFORMES DEPORTIVOS

La casa de las urgencias
27 años de experiencia nos respaldan

Pedidos al interior de la República
y en los Estados Unidos

Fabricante de balones de Futbol, Voli,
Basket, Pelotas de Beisball, Gorras,
Playeras y todo para el deporte.

UNIFORMES SUBLIMADOS DE EQUIPOS NACIONALES
Y EXTRANJEROS A PRECIOS MUY BAJOS. CONSÚLTANOS

SCHUMANN No. 165-2o PISO, COL, VALLEJO MÉXICO D.F. 07870

55-17-24-25 /57-59-21-71 / 55-17-53-29

Estructura

Verbos de cambio radical **e → ie** en el presente
Telling what you want or prefer

1. There are certain groups of verbs in Spanish that have a stem change in the present tense. The verbs **empezar** *(to begin)*, **comenzar** *(to begin)*, **querer** *(to want)*, **perder** *(to lose)*, and **preferir** *(to prefer)* are stem-changing verbs. The **e** of the stem changes to **ie** in all forms except **nosotros** and **vosotros.** The endings are the same as those of regular verbs. Study the following forms.

INFINITIVE	empezar	querer	preferir
yo	empiezo	quiero	prefiero
tú	empiezas	quieres	prefieres
él, ella, Ud.	empieza	quiere	prefiere
nosotros(as)	empezamos	queremos	preferimos
vosotros(as)	*empezáis*	*queréis*	*preferís*
ellos, ellas, Uds.	empiezan	quieren	prefieren

2. The verbs **empezar, comenzar, querer,** and **preferir** are often followed by an infinitive.

> **Ellos quieren ir al gimnasio.**
> **¿Por qué prefieres jugar al fútbol?**

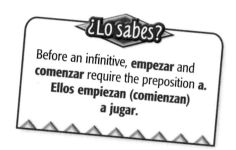

¿Lo sabes?

Before an infinitive, **empezar** and **comenzar** require the preposition **a.**
Ellos empiezan (comienzan) a jugar.

Lima, Perú

¿Cómo lo digo?

8 **Historieta** **Queremos ganar.** Contesten. *(Answer.)*

1. ¿Empiezan ustedes a jugar?
2. ¿Empiezan ustedes a jugar a las tres?
3. ¿Quieren ustedes ganar el partido?
4. ¿Quieren ustedes marcar un tanto?
5. ¿Pierden ustedes a veces o ganan siempre?
6. ¿Prefieren ustedes jugar en el parque o en la calle?

Buenos Aires, Argentina

9 **Historieta** **El partido continúa.**
Sigan el modelo. *(Follow the model.)*

> **el segundo tiempo / empezar** →
> **El segundo tiempo empieza.**

1. los jugadores / empezar a jugar
2. los dos equipos / querer ganar
3. ellos / preferir marcar muchos tantos
4. Sánchez / querer meter un gol
5. el portero / querer parar el balón
6. el equipo de Sánchez / no perder

10 **Historieta** **¿Un(a) aficionado(a) a los deportes?**
Contesten personalmente. *(Answer about yourself.)*

1. ¿Prefieres jugar al béisbol o al fútbol?
2. ¿Prefieres jugar con un grupo de amigos o con un equipo formal?
3. ¿Prefieres jugar en el partido o prefieres mirar el partido?
4. ¿Prefieres ser jugador(a) o espectador(a)?
5. ¿Siempre quieres ganar?
6. ¿Pierdes a veces?

11 **Historieta ¿Baloncesto o béisbol?** Completen. *(Complete.)*

Rosita ___1___ (querer) jugar al baloncesto. Yo ___2___ (querer) jugar al béisbol. Y tú, ¿___3___ (preferir) jugar al baloncesto o ___4___ (preferir) jugar al béisbol? Si tú ___5___ (querer) jugar al béisbol, tú y yo ___6___ (ganar) y Rosita ___7___ (perder). Pero si tú ___8___ (querer) jugar al baloncesto, entonces tú y Rosita ___9___ (ganar) y yo ___10___ (perder).

12 **¿Qué prefieres?** With a partner, look at the illustrations below. They each depict two activities. Find out from your partner which activity he or she prefers to do and which one he or she doesn't want to do. Take turns.

1.

2.

3.

4.

5.

Verbos de cambio radical o → ue en el presente

Describing more activities

1. The verbs **volver** *(to return to a place)*, **devolver** *(to return a thing)*, **poder** *(to be able)*, and **dormir** *(to sleep)* are also stem-changing verbs. The **o** of the stem changes to **ue** in all forms except **nosotros** and **vosotros**. The endings are the same as those of regular verbs. Study the following forms.

INFINITIVE	volver	poder	dormir
yo	vuelvo	puedo	duermo
tú	vuelves	puedes	duermes
él, ella, Ud.	vuelve	puede	duerme
nosotros(as)	volvemos	podemos	dormimos
vosotros(as)	volvéis	podéis	dormís
ellos, ellas, Uds.	vuelven	pueden	duermen

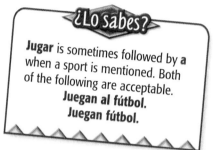

¿Lo sabes?

Jugar is sometimes followed by **a** when a sport is mentioned. Both of the following are acceptable.
Juegan al fútbol.
Juegan fútbol.

2. The **u** in the verb **jugar** changes to **ue** in all forms except **nosotros** and **vosotros**.

    jugar   **juego, juegas, juega, jugamos,** *jugáis,* **juegan**

¿Cómo lo digo?

13 **Historieta** **Un partido de béisbol**
Contesten. *(Answer.)*

1. ¿Juegan ustedes al béisbol?
2. ¿Juegan ustedes con unos amigos o con el equipo de la escuela?
3. ¿Vuelven ustedes al campo después de cada entrada?
4. ¿Pueden ustedes continuar el partido si el tanto queda empatado después de la novena entrada?
5. ¿Duermen ustedes bien después de un buen partido de béisbol?

La Liga mexicana

Estructura

14 Historieta En la clase de español

Contesten. (*Answer.*)

1. ¿Juegas al Bingo en la clase de español?
2. ¿Juegas al Loto en la clase de español?
3. ¿Puedes hablar inglés en la clase de español?
4. ¿Qué lengua puedes o tienes que hablar en la clase de español?
5. ¿Duermes en la clase de español?
6. ¿Devuelve el/la profesor(a) los exámenes pronto?

Una clase de español en Estados Unidos

San Juan, Puerto Rico

15 Historieta Sí, pero ahora no puede. Completen. (*Complete.*)

Yo __1__ (jugar) mucho al fútbol y Diana __2__ (jugar) mucho también, pero ahora ella no __3__ (poder).

—Diana, ¿por qué no __4__ (poder) jugar ahora?

—No __5__ (poder) porque __6__ (querer) ir a casa.

Sí, Diana __7__ (querer) ir a casa porque ella __8__ (tener) un amigo que __9__ (volver) hoy de Puerto Rico y ella __10__ (querer) estar en casa. Pero mañana todos nosotros __11__ (ir) a jugar. Y el amigo puertorriqueño de Diana __12__ (poder) jugar también. Su amigo __13__ (jugar) muy bien.

16 Quiero pero no puedo.

A classmate will ask you if you want to do something or go somewhere. Tell him or her that you want to but you can't because you have to do something else. Tell what it is you have to do. Take turns asking and answering the questions.

For more practice using stem-changing verbs, do Activity 7 on page H8 at the end of this book.

Interesar, aburrir y gustar
Expressing what interests, bores, or pleases you

1. The verbs **interesar** and **aburrir** function the same in Spanish and in English. Study the following examples.

¿Te aburre el arte?	*Does art bore you?*
No, el arte me interesa.	*No, art interests me.*
¿Te aburren los deportes?	*Do sports bore you?*
No, los deportes me interesan.	*No, sports interest me.*

¿Lo sabes?

Mí and **ti** are used after a preposition: **para mí y para ti**
A mí me gustan.
¿A ti también?

2. The verb **gustar** in Spanish functions the same as **interesar** and **aburrir**. **Gustar** conveys the meaning *to like*, but its true meaning is *to please*. The Spanish equivalent of *I like baseball* is *Baseball pleases me*. Study the following examples.

¿Te gusta el béisbol? Ah, sí, me gusta mucho.
¿Te gustan los deportes? Sí, me gustan mucho.

3. The verb **gustar** is often used with an infinitive to tell what you like to do.

¿Te gusta jugar al fútbol? Sí, me gusta jugar.
¿Te gusta comer? Sí, me gusta comer.

¿Cómo lo digo?

17 **¿Qué cursos te interesan y qué cursos te aburren?**
 Contesten. *(Answer.)*

1. ¿Te interesa la historia?
2. ¿Te interesa la geografía?
3. ¿Te interesa la biología?
4. ¿Te interesa la educación física?
5. ¿Te interesan las matemáticas?
6. ¿Te interesan las ciencias?
7. ¿Te interesan las lenguas?

Colegio San José, Estepona, España

18 **¿Te interesa o te aburre?** Sigan el modelo. *(Follow the model.)*

> **la biología** →
> **La biología me interesa. No me aburre.**

1. el álgebra
2. la geometría
3. la historia
4. el español
5. la geografía

19 **¿Te interesan o te aburren?**
Sigan el modelo. *(Follow the model.)*

> **las películas** →
> —**¿Te interesan las películas o te aburren?**
> —**Las películas me interesan. No me aburren.**

1. los partidos de fútbol
2. las películas románticas
3. las emisiones deportivas
4. las noticias

20 **Los deportes** Contesten. *(Answer.)*

1. ¿Te gusta el fútbol?
2. ¿Te gusta el béisbol?
3. ¿Te gusta el voleibol?
4. ¿Te gusta más el béisbol o el fútbol?
5. ¿Te gusta más el voleibol o el básquetbol?

DEPORTES

FÚTBOL

Los siguientes partidos de FÚTBOL corresponden a la Liga Nacional de Primera División.
Se recomienda consulten fechas por posibles cambios de fechas. / Please check dates for any changes.

● **ESTADIO SANTIAGO BERNABÉU**
P.º DE LA CASTELLANA, 104.
TEL.: 91 344 00 52. (METRO: SANTIAGO BERNABÉU).

4 Oct.
Real Madrid - Tenerife.

25 Oct.
Real Madrid - Racing.

● **ESTADIO VICENTE CALDERÓN**
VIRGEN DEL PUERTO, 67.
TEL.: 91 366 47 07. (METRO: PIRÁMIDES Y MARQUÉS DE VADILLO).

18 Oct.
Atlético de Madrid - Tenerife.

21 **Los alimentos** Contesten. *(Answer.)*

1. ¿Te gusta la ensalada?
2. ¿Te gusta un sándwich de jamón y queso?
3. ¿Te gusta la sopa?
4. ¿Te gusta la carne?
5. ¿Te gustan las tortillas?
6. ¿Te gustan las enchiladas?
7. ¿Te gustan los frijoles?
8. ¿Te gustan los tomates?

22 **¿Te gusta la ropa?** Sigan el modelo. *(Follow the model.)*

—¿Te gusta la gorra?
—Sí, a mí me gusta.

1.

2.

3.

4.

5.

6.

23 **¿Qué te gusta hacer?** Contesten. *(Answer.)*

1. ¿Te gusta cantar?
2. ¿Te gusta bailar?
3. ¿Te gusta comer?
4. ¿Te gusta leer?
5. ¿Te gusta más hablar o escuchar?
6. ¿Te gusta más jugar o ser espectador(a)?

24 **¿Qué te interesa?** Work with a classmate. Take turns telling those things that interest you and those that bore you. Decide which interests you have in common.

25 **Gustos** Get together with a classmate. Tell one another some things you like and don't like. Some categories you may want to explore are: **comida, ropa, cursos, deportes, actividades.** Decide whether you and your classmates have any of the same likes and dislikes.

Andas bien. ¡Adelante!

Conversación

¿Quieres jugar?

Anita Tomás, ¿prefieres el béisbol o el fútbol?

Tomás ¿Yo? Yo prefiero el fútbol. Me gusta más que el béisbol.

Anita ¿Juegas al fútbol?

Tomás Sí, juego. Pero la verdad es que me gusta más ser espectador que jugador.

Anita ¿Es bueno el equipo de tu escuela?

Tomás Sí, tenemos un equipo estupendo.

Anita ¿Son campeones?

Tomás No, pero van a ganar el campeonato.

¿Comprendes?

Contesten. (*Answer.*)

1. ¿Prefiere Tomás el béisbol o el fútbol?
2. ¿Juega mucho al fútbol?
3. ¿Qué prefiere ser?
4. ¿Es bueno el equipo de su escuela?
5. ¿Qué va a ganar el equipo?

Vamos a hablar más

A **No soy muy aficionado(a) a...** Work with a classmate. Tell him or her what sport you don't want to play because you don't like it. Tell what you prefer to play. Then ask your classmate questions to find out what sports he or she likes.

B **Un partido de fútbol** You are at a soccer match with a friend (your classmate). He or she has never been to a soccer match before and doesn't understand the game. Your friend has a lot of questions. Answer the questions and explain the game. You may want to use some of the following words.

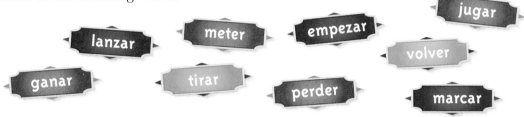

jugar

lanzar meter empezar

volver

ganar tirar perder marcar

Pronunciación

Las consonantes s, c, z

The consonant **s** is pronounced the same as the *s* in *sing*. Repeat the following.

sa	se	si	so	su
sala	base	sí	peso	su
pasa	serio	simpático	sopa	Susana
saca	seis	siete	sobrino	

The consonant **c** in combination with **e** or **i** (**ce, ci**) is pronounced the same as an **s** in all areas of Latin America. In many parts of Spain, **ce** and **ci** are pronounced like the *th* in English. Likewise, the pronunciation of **z** in combination with **a, o, u** (**za, zo, zu**) is the same as an **s** throughout Latin America and as a **th** in most areas of Spain. Repeat the following.

za	ce	ci	zo	zu
cabeza	cero	cinco	zona	zumo
empieza	encesta	ciudad	almuerzo	Zúñiga

Repeat the following sentences.

> González enseña en la sala de clase.
> El sobrino de Susana es serio y sincero.
> La ciudad tiene cinco zonas.
> Toma el almuerzo a las doce y diez en la cocina.

Lecturas culturales

El fútbol

La Liga española

Estamos en el estadio Santiago Bernabéu en Madrid. ¡Qué emoción! El Real Madrid juega contra el Atlético de Madrid. Quedan[1] dos minutos en el segundo tiempo. El partido está empatado en cero. ¿Qué va a pasar[2]? Da Silva pasa el balón a Casero. Casero lanza el balón con el pie izquierdo. El balón vuela[3]. El portero quiere parar el balón. ¿Puede o no? No, no puede. El balón entra en la portería. Casero mete un gol y marca un tanto. En los últimos dos minutos del partido, el equipo de Casero y da Silva gana. El Real Madrid derrota[4] al Atlético de Madrid uno a cero. El Real Madrid es triunfante, victorioso. Casero y da Silva son sus héroes.

La Copa mundial

Casero y da Silva son jugadores muy buenos y van a jugar en la Copa mundial. Pero da Silva no va a jugar con el mismo equipo que Casero. ¿Por qué? Porque da Silva no es español. Es de Brasil y en la Copa él va a jugar con el equipo de Brasil. Casero va a jugar con el equipo de España porque es español.

Cada cuatro años las estrellas[5] de cada país forman parte de un equipo nacional. Hay treinta y dos equipos nacionales que juegan en la Copa mundial. Los equipos de los treinta y dos países de todas partes del mundo compiten[6] para ganar la Copa y ser el campeón del mundo.

[1]Quedan *Remain* [3]vuela *flies* [5]estrellas *stars*
[2]pasar *happen* [4]derrota *defeats* [6]compiten *compete*

Reading Strategy

Scanning for specific information Scanning for specific information means reading to find out certain details without concerning yourself with the other information in the passage. Some examples of scanning are looking up words in a dictionary or searching a television listing to find out when certain programs are on. Another example of scanning is reading articles to find out something specific, such as sports results.

El estadio Santiago Bernabéu

A Lo mismo
Escojan la palabra equivalente.
(Choose the equivalent term.)

1. la mayoría
2. el vocabulario
3. lanzar
4. el campeón
5. triunfante
6. el jugador
7. parar

a. victorioso
b. tirar
c. el/la que gana
d. la mayor parte
e. no permitir pasar, bloquear
f. las palabras
g. el miembro del equipo

B Lo contrario
Escojan la palabra contraria. *(Choose the opposite term.)*

1. el/la jugador(a)
2. últimos
3. izquierdo
4. gana
5. entra

a. primeros
b. derecho
c. el/la espectador(a)
d. pierde
e. sale

C El partido de fútbol
Contesten. *(Answer.)*

1. ¿A qué juegan los dos equipos?
2. ¿Cuántos minutos quedan en el segundo tiempo?
3. ¿Quién pasa el balón?
4. ¿Quién lanza el balón?
5. ¿Cómo lanza el balón?
6. ¿Puede parar el balón el portero?
7. ¿Qué mete Casero?
8. ¿Qué marca?
9. ¿Qué equipo es victorioso?
10. ¿Quiénes son los héroes?

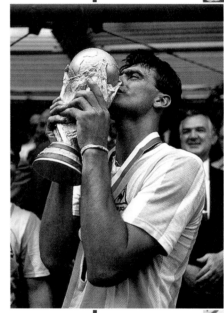

La Copa mundial

D La Copa mundial
Sí o no? *(True or false?)*

1. Los equipos juegan en la Copa mundial cada año.
2. Todos los jugadores de un equipo son de la misma nacionalidad.
3. Cada equipo que juega en la Copa representa un país.
4. Los equipos de veintidós naciones juegan en la Copa mundial.
5. Todos los equipos son de Europa.

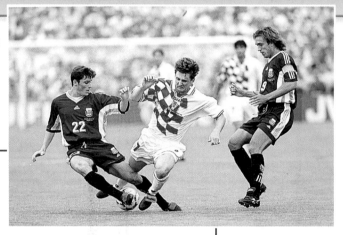

Argentina contra Croacia

Lectura opcional ①

Deportes populares

El fútbol

El fútbol es un deporte muy popular en todos los países hispanos. Los equipos nacionales tienen millones de aficionados. Cuando el equipo de un país juega contra el equipo de otro país, el estadio está lleno[1] de espectadores.

El béisbol

El béisbol no es un deporte popular en todos los países hispanos. Es popular en sólo algunos. El béisbol tiene o goza de popularidad en Cuba, Puerto Rico, la República Dominicana, Venezuela, Nicaragua, México y Panamá. Como el béisbol es esencialmente un deporte norteamericano, la mayoría del vocabulario del béisbol es inglés: las bases, el pícher, el out, el jonrón.

Muchos jugadores de béisbol de las Grandes Ligas son hispanos. Entre 1919 y hoy más de cien jugadores latinos juegan en la Serie Mundial.

[1]lleno *full*

La Liga mexicana

¿Comprendes?

A **¿Es la verdad o no?** Contesten con **sí** o **no.** (*Answer with* sí *or* no.)
1. El fútbol es un deporte popular en todas partes de Latinoamérica.
2. Casi todos los países tienen su equipo nacional de fútbol.
3. Cuando un equipo nacional juega contra otro equipo nacional—un equipo de otro país—hay muy poca gente en el estadio; hay muy pocos espectadores.
4. El béisbol es también un deporte popular en todos los países hispanos.
5. El béisbol es muy popular en los países del Caribe.
6. Muchos beisbolistas famosos de las Grandes Ligas de Estados Unidos son de origen hispano o latino.

B **Las nacionalidades** Completen. (*Complete.*)
1. Un puertorriqueño es de ____.
2. Un cubano es de ____.
3. Un panameño es de ____ y un nicaragüense es de ____.
4. Un mexicano es de ____ y un dominicano es de la ____.

El país vasco, España

Lectura opcional 2

Miami, la Florida

El «jai alai» o la pelota vasca

Jai alai es una palabra vasca. El país vasco es una región del norte de España y del sudoeste de Francia. El jai alai tiene otro nombre— la pelota vasca. El jai alai es un juego vasco popular.

Juegan al jai alai o a la pelota vasca en una cancha. Los jugadores son «pelotaris». Llevan un pantalón blanco, una camisa blanca, una faja roja y alpargatas. Tienen una cesta. Usan la cesta para lanzar y recibir la pelota.

En la cancha de jai alai hay tres paredes[1]. El frontón es la pared delantera[2]. «Frontón» es también el nombre de toda la cancha. El jugador lanza la pelota con la cesta contra la pared. Cuando la pelota pega[3] contra el frontón y rebota[4] hacia el jugador, el «pelotari» tiene que devolver la pelota. ¡Y la pelota viaja[5] a unas ciento cincuenta millas por hora!

[1]paredes *walls*   [4]rebota *rebounds*
[2]delantera *front*   [5]viaja *travels*
[3]pega *hits*

faja

cesta

alpargatas

¿Comprendes?

Jai alai Completen. (*Complete.*)
1. El jai alai o la ____ es un juego popular vasco.
2. Los pelotaris son ____ de jai alai.
3. Llevan un pantalón ____, una camisa ____ y una faja ____.
4. Los pelotaris no llevan zapatos cuando juegan. Llevan ____.
5. Los pelotaris usan una ____ para lanzar y recibir la pelota.
6. El ____ es la cancha de jai alai.
7. En una cancha de jai alai hay tres ____.
8. El jugador tiene que ____ la pelota cuando pega contra el frontón.
9. En un juego de jai alai la pelota viaja a unas ____ millas por hora.

Conexiones
Las ciencias sociales

La arqueología

Archeology is a fascinating field. Archeologists travel to every corner of the globe searching for places to excavate and study the ruins of ancient civilizations. There have been interesting archeological discoveries in Latin America where many pre-Columbian civilizations existed long before the arrival of the Spaniards. Let's read about some of these archeological sites. A few famous ones revealed some interesting information about sports and games in pre-Columbian cultures.

Copán, Honduras

Chichén Itzá, México

La arqueología

La arqueología es el estudio de los monumentos y artefactos de la antigüedad. Los arqueólogos excavan y estudian los objetos antiguos hechos o producidos por seres humanos. En Latinoamérica hay muchos sitios arqueológicos famosos. Algunos tienen canchas de pelota que datan del siglo ocho.

Honduras y México

En Copán en Honduras y en Chichén Itzá en México hay ruinas de varias canchas de pelota. La cancha en Copán data del año 775 después de Cristo. Es interesante notar que los juegos de los mayas de Copán y los juegos de los mayas de Chichén Itzá son bastante similares. Los indios usan una pelota grande de goma[1] y no pueden tocar[2] la pelota con las manos. El juego es una diversión[3] pero en Chichén Itzá tiene también sentido religioso. Después del juego sacrifican a los jugadores que ganan.

[1]goma *rubber*   [2]tocar *touch*   [3]diversión *amusement*

Puerto Rico

Recientemente hay una excavación arqueológica cerca de Ponce en Puerto Rico. ¿Y qué descubren? Descubren una cancha de pelota. Y el juego que juegan los indios taínos de Puerto Rico es parecido o similar al juego de los mayas de Centroamérica. El juego de los taínos es el batú. El batú es un juego de diversión pero tiene también sentido religioso. En el juego hay dos bandos o equipos. Juegan con una pelota de goma. Uno de los bandos lanza la pelota al otro bando. El otro bando tiene que devolver la pelota. Y no pueden usar las manos. Tienen que lanzar la pelota con la pierna, la rodilla o el brazo pero no pueden tocar la pelota con la mano. El equipo que deja rodar[4] la pelota por el suelo[5] el mayor número de veces[6] pierde el juego.

[4]deja rodar *lets roll*
[5]suelo *ground*
[6]mayor número de veces
greatest number of times

SPANISH Online

For more information about archeological sites in the Spanish-speaking world, go to the Glencoe Spanish Web site:
spanish.glencoe.com

Ponce, Puerto Rico

¿Comprendes?

¡A discutir! Discutan. *(Discuss with your classmates.)*
There are many interesting and unbelievable things in this reading selection. This is particularly true when one realizes that the games took place centuries ago and that there is quite a distance between these areas of Central America and Puerto Rico. Discuss some of these interesting facts. You may wish to have your discussion in English.

¡Te toca a ti!

Use what you have learned

1 **Soy muy aficionado(a) a...**

✔ *Describe your favorite sport*

Name a sport you really like. Then give a description of that sport.

2 **Una entrevista con el capitán**

✔ *Ask someone questions about a sports team*

You are to interview the captain (your classmate) of one of the school's sports teams for the local Spanish language television station. Try to find out as much information as possible. Then change roles.

3 **Los deportes**

✔ *Compare the sports you like and don't like*

Get together with a classmate. Take turns describing sports you like and don't like.

4 *Juego* **¡Adivina quién es!**

✔ *Talk about your favorite sports hero*

Think of your favorite sports hero. Tell a classmate something about him or her. Your classmate will ask you three questions about your hero before guessing who it is. Then reverse roles and you guess who your classmate's hero is.

DON BALON LA REVISTA NÚMERO 1 DEL FÚTBOL

Un reportaje

✔ *Write a description of a sporting event*

Work in groups of three. One of you is the captain of one of the school's teams. The other two are sports reporters for a Spanish newspaper. The two reporters will prepare an interview with the captain about the team's last game. The reporters will edit the information they get from the interview and write their report for tomorrow's paper. The report can be in the present tense.

Horario deportivo

✔ *Post a schedule of sporting events*

Your Spanish class has a Web site. Prepare your school's schedule of sporting events for the coming month in Spanish to post at your site.

Writing Strategy

Gathering information If your writing project deals with a topic you are not familiar with, you may need to gather information before you begin to write. Some of your best sources are the library, the Internet, and people who know something about the topic. Even if you plan to interview people about the topic, it may be necessary to do some research in the library or on the Internet to acquire enough knowledge to prepare good interview questions.

La Copa mundial

Many of you already know that the World Cup is a soccer championship. Try to give a description of the World Cup as best you can in Spanish. If you are not familiar with it, you will need to do some research. It might be interesting to take what you know or find out about the World Cup and compare it to the World Series in baseball. Gather information about both these championships and write a report.

Vocabulario

1 **Escojan.** *(Choose.)*

To review
Palabras 1, turn to
pages 202–203.

1. El campo de fútbol está en ____.
   a. la portería   **b.** el tablero   **c.** el estadio
2. Los ____ miran el partido.
   a. porteros   **b.** espectadores   **c.** jugadores
3. El portero ____ el balón.
   a. bloquea   **b.** marca   **c.** gana
4. En un partido de fútbol, el jugador tira o lanza el balón con ____.
   a. la mano   **b.** el tablero   **c.** el pie

2 **Completen.** *(Complete.)*

To review **Palabras 2**, turn to pages 206–207.

5. En un juego de béisbol, el pícher ____ la pelota.
6. Otro jugador batea y ____ de una base a otra.
7. La jugadora atrapa la pelota con el ____.
8. Hay nueve ____ en un juego de béisbol.
9. En un juego de básquetbol, el jugador ____ con el balón.
10. El jugador de básquetbol marca un tanto cuando ____.

Estructura

3 **Contesten.** *(Answer.)*

11. ¿Quieres jugar al fútbol?
12. ¿Quieren ustedes ganar?
13. ¿Prefieres el fútbol o el básquetbol?
14. ¿Qué deporte prefieren ustedes?
15. ¿Puedes ver el partido en la televisión?
16. ¿Pueden ustedes hablar con los jugadores?

To review stem-changing verbs, turn to pages 210 and 213.

4 **Completen.** *(Complete.)*

17–18. Ellos ____ al béisbol y nosotros ____ al fútbol. (jugar)
19. ¿Tú ____ a jugar a qué hora? (empezar)

5 **Completen.** *(Complete.)*

20–21. Me gust__ mucho los deportes. No me aburr__.
22. ¿Te interes__ más ver una película o una emisión deportiva?

To review **interesar**, **aburrir**, and **gustar**, turn to page 215.

Cultura

6 **¿Sí o no?** *(True or false?)*

23. El estadio Santiago Bernabéu es un equipo de fútbol español.
24. Todos los jugadores del Real Madrid, un equipo español, son españoles.
25. Todos los jugadores de un equipo que juega en la Copa mundial tienen que ser de la misma nacionalidad.

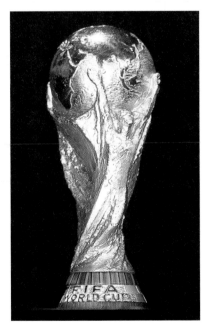

La Copa de la FIFA

To review this cultural information, turn to page 220.

DEPORTES DE EQUIPO

Tell all you can about this illustration.

Vocabulario

Identifying sports

el fútbol	el básquetbol,
el béisbol	el baloncesto

Describing a sports event in general

el estadio	el equipo	lanzar
el/la espectador(a)	el tablero indicador	perder
el campo	el tanto	ganar
la cancha	empatado(a)	entre
el partido	empezar, comenzar	contra
el/la jugador(a)	tirar	

Describing a football game

el fútbol	el/la portero(a)	bloquear	marcar un tanto
el balón	la portería	parar	meter un gol
el tiempo	jugar		

Describing a baseball game

el béisbol	el jardinero	la base	batear
el/la bateador(a)	el guante	la entrada	correr
el pícher, el lanzador	el platillo	la pelota	atrapar
el cátcher, el receptor	el jonrón	el bate	devolver

Describing a basketball game

el básquetbol,	driblar
el baloncesto	pasar
el cesto, la canasta	encestar
	meter

Expressing likes and interests

gustar	aburrir
interesar	

Identifying some parts of the body

el pie	la mano
la pierna	el brazo
la rodilla	la cabeza

Other useful expressions

poder	a veces
querer	siempre
volver	izquierdo(a)
preferir	derecho(a)

How well do you know your vocabulary?

- Choose a sport from the list.
- Ask classmates to give you as many words as they can associated with the sport you chose.

VIDEOTUR

Episodio 7

In this video episode, you will join Julián and Alberto as they sign up for a new extracurricular activity. See page 498 for more information.

Conversación

Un partido importante

Julio   Alberto, Carlos y yo vamos al Café Miramar. ¿Quieres ir con nosotros?

Alberto   No, Julio, no puedo porque quiero ver el partido.

Julio   ¿De qué partido hablas?

Alberto   Los Osos juegan contra los Tigres y mi equipo favorito son los Osos.

Julio   ¿Vas al estadio a ver el partido?

Alberto   No. Las entradas (los boletos) cuestan mucho. Voy a ver el partido en la televisión.

Julio   ¿A qué hora empieza?

Alberto   A las siete y media. ¿Quieres ver el partido también?

Julio   Sí. ¿Dónde vives?

Alberto   Vivo en la calle Central, número 32.

Julio   Bien. ¡Hasta pronto!

¿Comprendes?

Los tres amigos Contesten. *(Answer.)*

1. ¿Adónde quieren ir los dos muchachos?
2. ¿Invitan a Alberto?
3. ¿Puede ir Alberto?
4. ¿Por qué no?
5. ¿Por qué no va al estadio?
6. ¿Dónde va a ver el partido?
7. ¿A qué hora empieza?
8. ¿Van los muchachos a casa de Alberto?

Estructura

Verbos en -er, -ir

Review the forms of regular **-er** and **-ir** verbs.

COMER	como	comes	come	comemos	*coméis*	comen
VIVIR	vivo	vives	vive	vivimos	*vivís*	viven

Tú y tus amigos
Contesten. *(Answer.)*

1. ¿Qué comes cuando vas a un café?
2. ¿Qué bebes cuando estás en un café?
3. ¿Qué aprenden tú y tus amigos en la escuela?
4. ¿Qué leen ustedes en la clase de inglés?
5. ¿Qué escriben ustedes?
6. ¿Comprenden los alumnos cuando el profesor de español habla?
7. ¿Reciben ustedes notas buenas en todas las asignaturas?

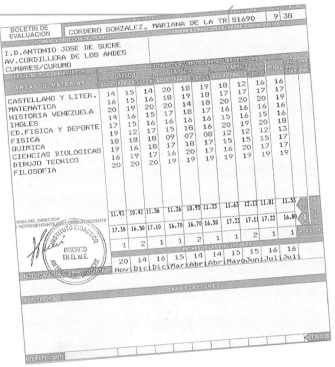

Verbos de cambio radical

1. Review the forms of stem-changing verbs.

e → ie

EMPEZAR	empiezo	empiezas	empieza	empezamos	*empezáis*	empiezan
PERDER	pierdo	pierdes	pierde	perdemos	*perdéis*	pierden

o → ue

VOLVER	vuelvo	vuelves	vuelve	volvemos	*volvéis*	vuelven
PODER	puedo	puedes	puede	podemos	*podéis*	pueden

2. Review the forms of the verb **tener.** Note that this verb also has a change in the stem.

TENER	tengo	tienes	tiene	tenemos	*tenéis*	tienen

Historieta **Un juego de béisbol**

Completen. *(Complete.)*

El juego de béisbol __1__ (empezar) a las tres y media. Habla Teresa:

—Hoy yo __2__ (querer) ser la pícher.

La verdad es que Teresa __3__ (ser) una pícher muy buena. Ella __4__ (jugar) muy bien. Nosotros __5__ (tener) un equipo bueno. Todos nosotros __6__ (jugar) bien. Nuestro equipo no __7__ (perder) mucho. Hoy yo __8__ (tener) que jugar muy bien porque nuestro equipo no __9__ (poder) perder. __10__ (Tener) que ganar.

3 **Entrevista** Contesten personalmente.
(Answer about yourself.)

1. ¿Cuántos años tienes?
2. ¿Cuántos hermanos tienes?
3. ¿Cuántos años tienen ellos?
4. ¿Tienen ustedes un perro o un gato?

Adjetivos posesivos

Review the forms of possessive adjectives.

mi, mis	**nuestro, nuestra, nuestros, nuestras**
tu, tus	
su, sus	**su, sus**

4 **Historieta** **Nuestra casa**

Completen. *(Complete.)*

Vivo en __1__. __2__ casa está en la calle __3__. __4__ padres tienen un carro. Y yo tengo una bicicleta. __5__ carro está en el garaje y __6__ bicicleta está en el garaje también. Nosotros tenemos un perro. __7__ perro está en el jardín. El jardín alrededor de __8__ casa es bonito. Mi hermano y __9__ amigos siempre juegan en el jardín.

Málaga, España

Verbos como **interesar, aburrir, gustar**

Review the construction for verbs such as **gustar**, **interesar**, and **aburrir**.

¿Te gusta el arte?
{
Sí, me gusta el arte.
El arte me interesa mucho.
No me aburre nada.
}

¿Te gustan los deportes?
{
Los deportes, sí, me gustan mucho.
Los deportes me interesan.
No me aburren nada.
}

5 **Información** Den cuantas respuestas posibles.
(*Give as many answers as possible.*)

1. ¿Qué te gusta?
2. ¿Qué te interesa?
3. ¿Qué te aburre?

6 **Una fiesta familiar** With a classmate, look at the illustration. Take turns describing the illustration, giving as much detail as you can.

Literary Companion

You may wish to read the adaptation of «**Una moneda de oro**» by Francisco Monterde. This literary selection is found on pages 472–477.

Monumentos naturales e históricos

Argentina tiene nueve lugares que la UNESCO considera Patrimonio de la Humanidad. Entre ellos se destacan:

Quebrada de Humahuaca

Quebrada de Humahuaca
Montañas de intensos colores que el ser humano habita[1] desde hace 10 mil años.

Parque Nacional de Ischigualasto Más conocido como el "Valle de la Luna", es un terreno de formas fantásticas y fósiles de vegetales, dinosaurios y otros animales de hace 180 millones de años.

Cueva[2] de las Manos Cueva de la provincia de Santa Cruz, con más de 800 impresiones de manos y otras pinturas rupestres[3], a la que los científicos calculan unos 9,300 a 13,000 años de antigüedad.

Parque Nacional Los Glaciares En la provincia de Santa Cruz hay 47 glaciares mayores. El más conocido e imponente[4] es el Perito Moreno.

Cataratas[5] del Iguazú Son las cataratas más anchas[6] del mundo, entre Argentina, Paraguay y Brasil.

Éstas son algunas de las maravillas de Chile:

Isla de Pascua[7] Isla del Pacífico; aún hoy la cultura de sus antiguos[8] habitantes se considera muy avanzada, especialmente por la arquitectura y los conocimientos[9] de astronomía.

Valparaíso Se la llama Perla del Pacífico. Los chilenos la consideran su capital cultural. Toda ella es un museo, con tranvías y ascensores[10] para ascender por los cerros[11].

Isla de Chiloé Tiene palafitos[12], que son construcciones de madera, y varias iglesias declaradas Patrimonio de la Humanidad.

Isla de Pascua

Colonia del Sacramento

En Uruguay tienes que visitar esta joya de ciudad:

Colonia del Sacramento Es la única ciudad fundada por los portugueses en las costas del Río de la Plata. Todas las tardes, los jóvenes de esta ciudad colonial se reúnen a charlar y a ver las maravillosas puestas de sol[13] sobre el río.

Y si vas por Paraguay, no olvides visitar estos bellos lugares:

Ciudad del Este Es parte del complejo de parques donde se hallan las Cataratas del Iguazú.

Misiones de Jesús de Tavarangue y Santísima Trinidad Estas construcciones se consideran Patrimonio de la Humanidad desde 1993.

---

[1] habita: *inhabits*
[2] cueva: *cave*
[3] pinturas rupestres: *cave paintings*
[4] imponente: *impressive*
[5] cataratas: *waterfalls*
[6] anchas: *wide*
[7] Isla de Pascua: *Easter Island*
[8] antiguos: *ancient*
[9] conocimientos: *knowledge*
[10] ascensores: *elevators*
[11] cerros: *hills*
[12] palafitos: *stilt houses*
[13] puestas de sol: *sunsets*

el mundo salvaje

Gigantes del reino vegetal en Chile

Los bosques de araucarias se consideran monumentos nacionales en Chile. Algunos de estos árboles tienen 600 a 1,200 años de edad.

La Patagonia argentina

■ ¿Te imaginas un bosque hecho piedra? El bosque petrificado de Jaramillo mide 10,000 hectáreas y en él se encuentran los árboles petrificados más grandes del mundo.

■ Si tienes que ir a Usuahia, la capital de Tierra del Fuego, vas a estar en la ciudad más austral[1] del planeta.

■ ¿Te interesan las ballenas? Ver jugar a estos gigantes horas y horas con sus crías[2] es un espectáculo[3] que se disfruta[4] desde las playas de Península de Valdés.

■ Al pingüino de magallanes no le preocupa el frío. No hay nadie como este animalito para soportar[5] las bajas temperaturas.

Piedras semipreciosas del Uruguay

Muchas ágatas y amatistas que adornan joyas[6] y decorados en todo el mundo son uruguayas.

Araucarias de Chile

La Patagonia

Amatista

[1] austral: *southernmost*	[4] se disfruta: *one enjoys*
[2] crías: *calves*	[5] soportar: *withstand*
[3] espectáculo: *show*	[6] joyas: *jewelry*

SUCESOS

Mariel Davesa vive contra viento y marea[1]. Es campeona nacional de *windsurf* en Estados Unidos.

Eva Perón es un personaje de la política argentina. Es tema de una ópera y Madonna la representa en la película *Evita*.

Un día, **Pablo Neruda** escribe a un amor: "Puedo escribir los versos más tristes esta noche". Hoy grupos de rock como **Maná** y **Los Fabulosos Cadillacs** y cantantes como **Alejandro Sanz** y **Beto Cuevas** rinden tributo[2] en un CD a este famoso poeta chileno.

[1] contra viento y marea: *against all odds*
[2] rinden tributo: *pay tribute*

Beto Cuevas

Empanadas a la Ferro

micocina

Candela comparte una sabrosa tradición

A la argentina Candela Ferro, presentadora de "Ocurrió así" (Telemundo), le gusta cocinar para sus amigos. ¿Su receta preferida? ¡Empanadas! Las empanadas son un plato típico del Cono sur. La preparación varía según la región. ¡Anímate a prepararlas!

Ingredientes
Discos
> 2 tazas de harina de trigo
> ½ taza de manteca[1]
> 1 huevo pequeño
> 1 cdta. de pimentón rojo dulce[2]
> ½ cdta. de sal
> agua tibia

Relleno
> ½ taza de aceitunas deshuesadas[3]
> 6 huevos duros en rodajas
> 1 lb. de carne de res molida
> 1 cebolla
> 1 pimiento morrón[4] cortado finito
> 2 dientes de ajo
> ½ taza de pasas o ciruelas[5]
> sal y pimienta al gusto
> 2 cucharadas de aceite de oliva

Preparación

Masa: Batir el huevo con el pimentón, sal y agua. Mezclar la harina con la manteca y la mezcla de huevo. Formar una bola con la masa y dejarla reposar. Dividir la masa, amasar[6] y hacer los discos.

Relleno: Calentar el aceite en una sartén. Sofreír[7] la cebolla, el ajo y el pimiento. Agregar la carne y sofreírla. Poner los huevos, las aceitunas y las pasas.

Armar las empanadas. Ponerlas al horno, precalentado a 200 grados, hasta que estén doradas, y ¡buen provecho!

[1] manteca: *Arg.: butter*
[2] pimentón rojo dulce: *sweet paprika*
[3] aceitunas deshuesadas: *pitted olives*
[4] pimiento morrón: *canned roasted peppers*
[5] pasas o ciruelas: *raisins or prunes*
[6] amasar: *knead*
[7] sofreír: *sautee*

Isabel Allende

Una vida de cuento

A Isabel Allende la llaman la Scherezada latinoamericana. Como el personaje de *Las mil y una noches*, esta escritora chilena sabe tejer[1] un cuento tras otro y encantar[2] a grandes y chicos. Dos de sus novelas son ya películas: *La casa de los espíritus* y *De amor y de sombra*. ¿Sabes que todos los 8 de enero empieza un nuevo libro? Hoy tiene un estudio muy bien montado[3] en Sausalito, California, pero en sus comienzos, ¡escribía[4] por las noches en la cocina de su casa!

Isabel Allende es una excelente escritora y una gran recicladora[5]. ¡Tiene el poder de convertir a sus familiares y amigos en personajes de novelas! Sus abuelos, por ejemplo, son dos de los personajes de *La casa de los espíritus*, su primera novela. En *Paula*, su hija del mismo nombre es personaje y motivo[6] del libro. ¡Incluso la novela *Afrodita* es el producto de un sueño en el que aparece su amigo Antonio Banderas!

Si todavía no conoces *El Reino del Dragón de Oro*, su libro más reciente, tienes que hacerlo pronto y dejarte encantar.

[1] tejer: *weave*
[2] encantar: *charm*
[3] montado: *equipped*
[4] escribía: *would write*
[5] recicladora: *recycler*
[6] motivo: *inspiration*

Primera novela de Allende, publicada ya en 27 idiomas

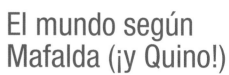

El mundo según Mafalda (¡y Quino!)

Joaquín Salvador Lavado, conocido como Quino, es el genial creador de Mafalda, personaje de una tira cómica[1], leída[2] y querida en todo el mundo. Los personajes principales de Mafalda son niños, pero Quino dice que siempre se dirige[3] a los adultos. Mafalda es sinónimo de imaginación y visión crítica y cuestionadora de la vida. Sus numerosos premios[4] lo confirman. En 1977, la UNICEF ilustra con Mafalda y sus amigos la Declaración de los Derechos del Niño. ¿Te interesa conocer a Mafalda? Arriba tienes una muestra[5].

[1] tira cómica: *comic strip*
[2] leída: *read*
[3] dirige: *addresses*
[4] premios: *awards*
[5] muestra: *example*

Quino

Justo para ti

Justo Lamas

Damas y caballeros… ¡aquí viene Justo! ¡Sí, **Justo Lamas,** el que canta "La bamba", "Magdalena" y "Cielito lindo"! Verlo actuar[1] es asistir[2] a algo más que un concierto. Sus actuaciones[3] derrochan[4] inspiración a la par[5] que permiten aprender español. Ha grabado tres discos compactos: "Justo para ti", "Un día especial" y "Vivir". El cantautor[6] siempre tiene algo importante que comunicar: "Si piensas que la vida a veces te lastima[7], despierta[8], tú puedes, confía[9]…" dice en "No hay camino sin salida".

[1] actuar: *perform*
[2] asistir: *attend*
[3] actuaciones: *performances*
[4] derrochan: *radiate*
[5] a la par: *at the same time*
[6] cantautor: *singer-songwriter*
[7] lastima: *hurts*
[8] despierta: *wake up*
[9] confía: *trust*

¿Argentina o mexicana?

Dorismar

Al decir música argentina, se piensa en tango, rock o folklore. **Dorismar** quiere algo diferente: Canta música grupera[1], ¡y lo hace muy bien! Cuando no está de gira[2] con Los Tucanes de Tijuana o actúa en telenovelas, esta joven argentina prefiere la tranquilidad de su apartamento en Miami.

[1] música grupera: *Mexican regional music*
[2] gira: *tour*

De sur a norte

Desde la década de los setenta, **Alejandro Lerner** canta y vive "todo a pulmón"[1], como se titula[2] una de sus canciones. El legendario Carlos Santana sabe cuánto vale este argentino, y por eso cantan juntos en la gira del famoso guitarrista por Estados Unidos.

Alejandro Lerner

[1] todo a pulmón: *with my best efforts*
[2] titula: *entitled*

Reto[1] de a dos

El tango, baile de argentinos y uruguayos, se impone[2] cada vez más en fiestas y salones de todo el mundo. No es sólo un baile. Es más que un ritmo, ¡es un rito![3] Su influencia llega hasta el lenguaje de todos los días.

Carlos Saura, el director de cine español, muestra en su película "Tango", pasos de bailes espectaculares. La música de la película es de Lalo Schifrin, compositor argentino muy reconocido por su tema de la serie de televisión "Misión imposible".

Escena de "Tango"

Un toque de lunfardo

El tango tiene su propio idioma[4]: el lunfardo. ¿Te interesa saber un poco de lunfardo? Estas son palabras que dicen los jóvenes argentinos y uruguayos.

al divino botón: *inútilmente*[5]
bronca: *enojo*[6]
guita: *dinero*
laburo: *trabajo*
macanudo: *excelente*
morfar: *comer*

El tango

[1] reto: *challenge*
[2] impone: *gains recognition*
[3] rito: *ritual*
[4] idioma: *language*
[5] inútilmente: *uselessly*
[6] enojo: *anger*

Capítulo 8

La salud y el médico

Objetivos

In this chapter you will learn to:

- ❖ explain a minor illness to a doctor
- ❖ describe some feelings
- ❖ have a prescription filled at a pharmacy
- ❖ describe characteristics and conditions
- ❖ tell where things are and where they're from
- ❖ tell where someone or something is now
- ❖ tell what happens to you or someone else

Pablo Picasso *Head of a Medical Student*

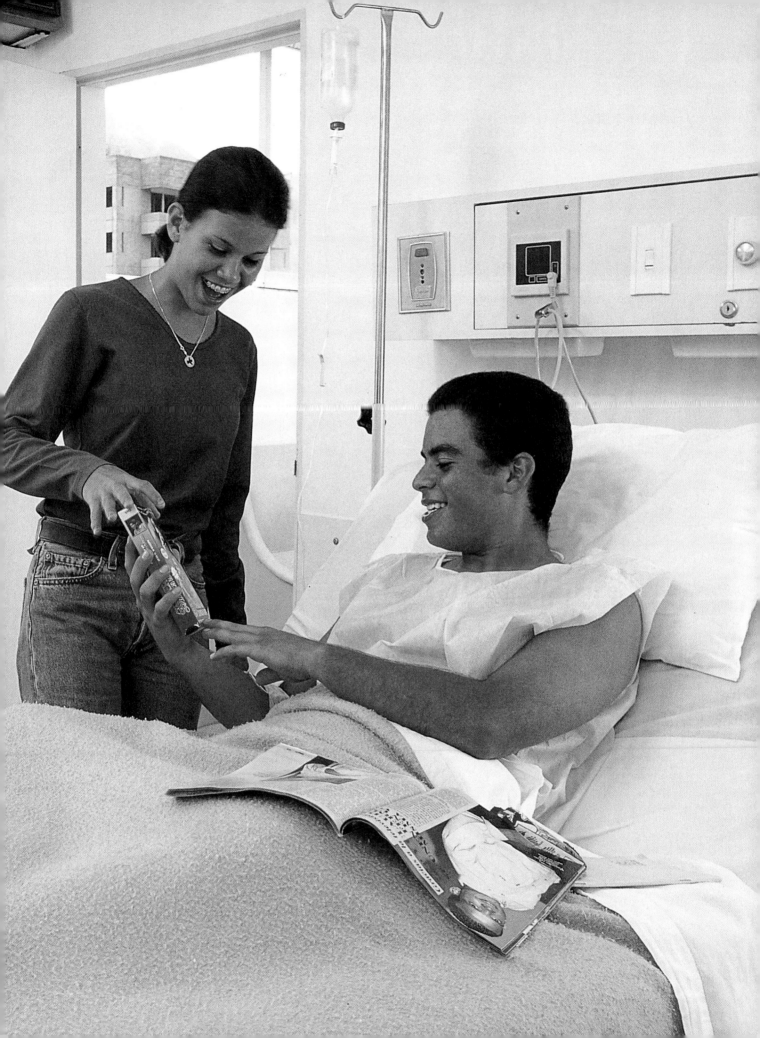

¿Cómo está?

enfermo

cansada

contento

triste

nervioso

El pobre muchacho está enfermo.
Tiene fiebre.
Tiene la gripe.

la cama

la fiebre

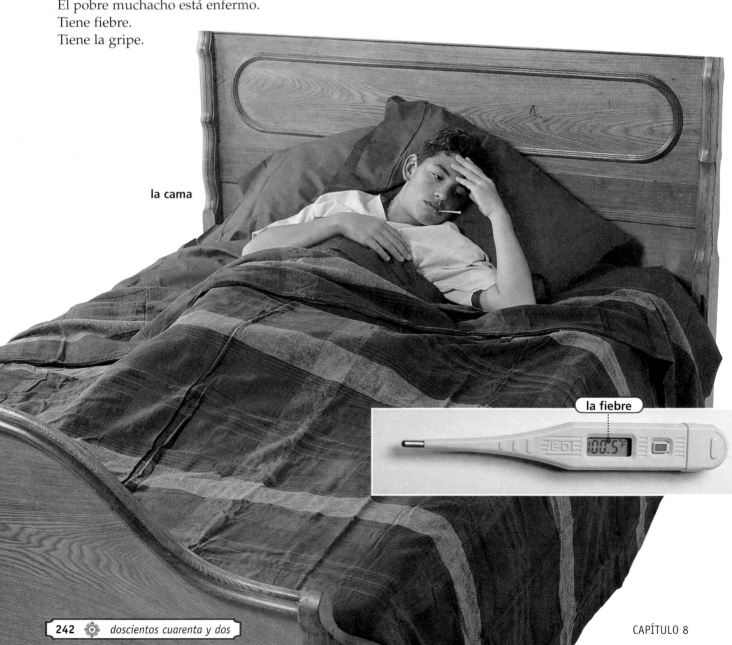

La muchacha tiene catarro.
Está resfriada.

El muchacho tiene tos.
Tiene dolor de garganta.

La muchacha tiene dolor de cabeza.

El muchacho tiene dolor de estómago.

El enfermo tiene que guardar cama.
Tiene escalofríos porque tiene fiebre.
Él está de mal humor.
No está de buen humor.

¿Qué palabra necesito?

1 **Historieta** **El pobre joven está enfermo.**
Contesten.

1. ¿Está enfermo el pobre muchacho?
2. ¿Tiene la gripe?
3. ¿Tiene tos?
4. ¿Tiene dolor de garganta?
5. ¿Tiene fiebre?
6. ¿Tiene escalofríos?
7. ¿Tiene dolor de cabeza?
8. ¿Está siempre cansado?

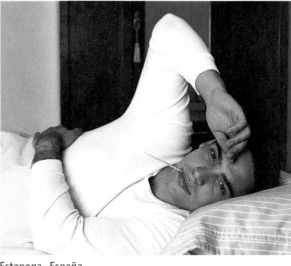

Estepona, España

2 **Historieta** **La pobre muchacha** Contesten.

San Miguel de Allende, México

1. ¿Está enferma la muchacha?
2. ¿Tiene tos?
3. ¿Estornuda mucho?
4. ¿Tiene dolor de cabeza?
5. ¿Está resfriada?
6. ¿Está en cama?
7. ¿Tiene que guardar cama?
8. ¿Qué opinión tienes? ¿Qué crees?
   ¿Está la muchacha de buen humor o
   de mal humor?

TOA...¡PARA TOA LA TOS!

Toa...
adulto e infantil

TOA tiene un agradable sabor y además te permite seguir activo.

Y para sus niños... ¡TOA INFANTIL!

3 **¿Cómo está?** Contesten según las fotos.

1. ¿Cómo está el joven?
   ¿Está triste o contento?

2. Y la joven, ¿cómo está?
   ¿Está triste o contenta?

3. El señor, ¿está bien o está enfermo?

4. Y la señora, ¿está nerviosa o está tranquila?

4 **¿Cómo estás tú?** Contesten personalmente.

1. ¿Cómo estás hoy?
2. Cuando estás enfermo(a), ¿estás de buen humor o estás de mal humor?
3. Cuando tienes dolor de cabeza, ¿estás contento(a) o triste?
4. Cuando tienes catarro, ¿siempre estás cansado(a) o no?
5. Cuando tienes catarro, ¿tienes fiebre y escalofríos?
6. Cuando tienes la gripe, ¿tienes fiebre y escalofríos?
7. ¿Tienes que guardar cama cuando tienes catarro?
8. ¿Tienes que guardar cama cuando tienes fiebre?

5 **¿Qué te pasa?** Work with a classmate. Ask your partner what's the matter—**¿Qué te pasa?** He or she will tell you. Then suggest something he or she can do to feel better. **¿Por qué no… ?** Take turns.

En la consulta del médico

la consulta del médico,
el consultorio

el médico

los ojos

la boca

la médica

Jaime está en el consultorio.
La médica examina a Jaime.
Examina sus ojos.
Después Jaime abre la boca.
La médica cree que Jaime
  tiene la gripe.

Me duele la cabeza.

Me duele la garganta.

Me duele el estómago.

En la farmacia

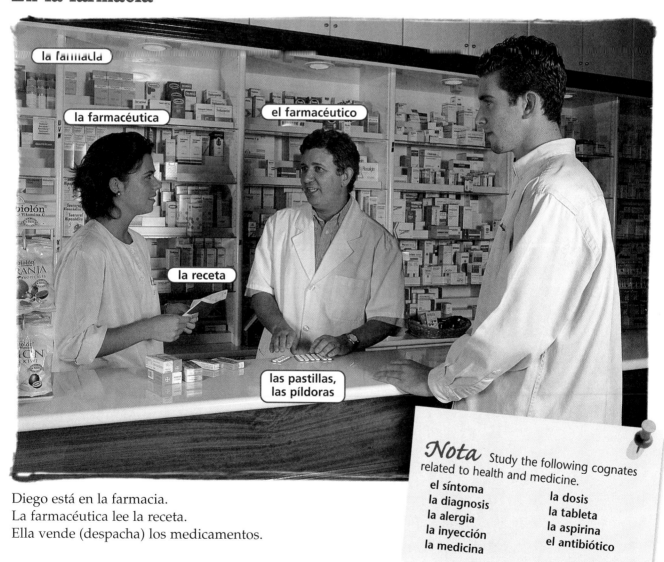

la farmacia

la farmacéutica

el farmacéutico

la receta

las pastillas, las píldoras

Diego está en la farmacia.
La farmacéutica lee la receta.
Ella vende (despacha) los medicamentos.

Nota Study the following cognates related to health and medicine.

el síntoma
la diagnosis
la alergia
la inyección
la medicina

la dosis
la tableta
la aspirina
el antibiótico

Vocabulario

¿Qué palabra necesito?

6 **¿Qué te pasa?** Preparen una conversación según el modelo.

—¿Qué te pasa? ¿Tienes dolor de garganta?
—Sí, me duele mucho. ¡Qué enfermo(a) estoy!

Me duele la garganta.

Me duele el estómago.

Me duele la cabeza.

1.

2.

San Miguel de Allende, México

7 **Historieta** En el consultorio
Contesten.

1. ¿Dónde está Alberto? ¿En la consulta de la médica o en el hospital?
2. ¿Quién está enfermo? ¿Alberto o la médica?
3. ¿Quién examina a Alberto? ¿La médica o la farmacéutica?
4. ¿Qué examina la médica? ¿La cabeza o la garganta?
5. ¿Qué tiene que tomar Alberto? ¿Una inyección o una pastilla?
6. ¿Quién receta los antibióticos? ¿La médica o la farmacéutica?
7. ¿Adónde va Alberto con la receta? ¿A la clínica o a la farmacia?
8. ¿Qué despacha la farmacéutica? ¿Los medicamentos o las recetas?

8 **Historieta** **Alberto está enfermo, el pobre.**
Corrijan las oraciones.

1. Alberto está muy bien.
2. Alberto está en el hospital.
3. Alberto examina a la médica.
4. Alberto abre la boca y la médica examina los ojos.
5. La médica habla con Alberto de sus síntomas.
6. La farmacéutica receta unos antibióticos.
7. Alberto va al consultorio con la receta.
8. La médica despacha los medicamentos.

9 **Buenos días, doctor.** Look at the illustration. Pretend you're the patient. Tell the doctor how you're feeling.

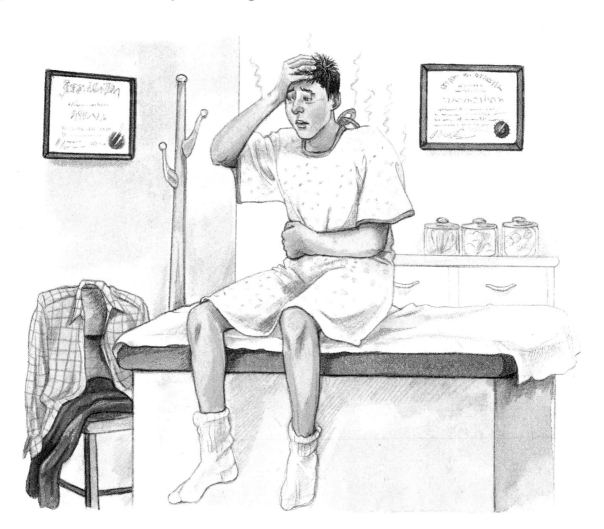

10 **En la consulta del médico** Work with a classmate. You're sick with a cold or the flu. The doctor (your partner) will ask you questions about your symptoms. Answer the doctor's questions as completely as you can. Then change roles.

Estructura

Ser y estar
Characteristics and conditions

1. In Spanish there are two verbs that mean *to be*. They are **ser** and **estar.** These verbs have very distinct uses. They are not interchangeable. **Ser** is used to express a trait or characteristic that does not change.

> **Ella es muy sincera.**
> **La casa de apartamentos es muy alta.**

2. **Estar** is used to express a temporary condition or state.

> **Eugenio está enfermo.**
> **Está cansado y nervioso.**

La familia está contenta,
San Miguel de Allende

¿Cómo lo digo?

11 **Al contrario** Sigan el modelo.

Roberto es rubio.

Al contrario. No es rubio.
Roberto es moreno.

1. Teresa es morena.
2. Justo es alto.
3. Héctor es feo.
4. Catalina es muy seria.
5. La clase de biología es aburrida.
6. Los cursos son fáciles.
7. Nuestro equipo de fútbol es malo.
8. Su familia es grande.

12 Tu escuela y tus clases Contesten.

1. ¿Cómo es tu escuela?
2. ¿Quién en la clase de español es rubio?
3. ¿Quién es moreno?
4. ¿Cuál es un curso interesante?
5. ¿Cuál es una clase aburrida?
6. ¿El equipo de qué deporte es muy bueno?

13 ¿Cómo está o cómo es? Describan a la persona en cada foto.

1. Antonia

2. Jorge

3. Beatriz

4. Teresa

5. Susana

14 ¿Cómo eres? Den una descripción personal.

INFOR-MED

La Medicina cada día avanza más en el desarrollo de nuevas formas de proteger la salud del ser humano. ¡Manténgase informado al respecto!

15 **Historieta Están enfermos.**

Completen con la forma correcta de **ser** o **estar**.

Rubén y Marisol __1__ enfermos. Rubén no tiene energía. __2__ muy cansado. __3__ triste. Y Marisol tiene tos. Su garganta __4__ muy roja. La mamá de Rubén y Marisol __5__ muy nerviosa. Su papá __6__ nervioso también porque sus dos hijos __7__ enfermos. Pero su médico __8__ muy bueno. El doctor Rodríguez __9__ muy inteligente. Su consultorio __10__ muy moderno. El doctor Rodríguez examina a Rubén y a Marisol. El médico habla:

—Ustedes no __11__ muy enfermos. Tienen la gripe. Aquí tienen unos antibióticos. Los antibióticos __12__ muy buenos.

Ahora todos __13__ muy contentos y los padres no __14__ nerviosos. No __15__ nerviosos porque Rubén no __16__ muy enfermo y Marisol no __17__ muy enferma. Dentro de poco, sus hijos van a __18__ muy bien.

16 **¿Por qué?** There is usually a reason for everything. Talk to a classmate. He or she will ask you how you're feeling. Answer and explain why you are feeling as you are. Some of the following words may be helpful to you.

nervioso   triste   cansado   de mal humor

de buen humor   contento   melancólico

*For more practice using words from **Palabras 1** and **ser** and **estar**, do Activity 8 on page H9 at the end of this book.*

 17 **Virtudes y defectos** Work in small groups. Make a list of characteristics and personality traits. Divide them into two groups— **características positivas (virtudes)** and **características negativas (defectos).** Then have some fun. Make up a description of a person with many virtues. Make up another description of a person with many defects or faults. Be as creative as possible.

Ser y estar
Origin and location

1. The verb **ser** is used to express where someone or something is from.

> **La muchacha es de Cuba.**
> **El café es de Colombia.**

2. **Estar** is used to express where someone or something is located.

> **Los alumnos están en la escuela.**
> **Los libros están en el salón de clase.**

San Andrés, Colombia

¿Cómo lo digo?

 18 **¿De dónde es?** Contesten según el modelo.

> ¿Es cubano el muchacho?
> Sí, creo que es de Cuba.

1. ¿Es colombiana la muchacha?
2. ¿Es guatemalteco el muchacho?
3. ¿Es puertorriqueña la joven?
4. ¿Es española la profesora?
5. ¿Es peruano el médico?
6. ¿Son venezolanos los amigos?
7. ¿Son chilenas las amigas?
8. ¿Son costarricenses los jugadores?

19 Historieta Una carta a un amigo

Completen la carta.

Caracas, Venezuela

Hola David,

¿Qué tal? ¿Cómo ___1___? Yo ___2___ muy bien. Yo ___3___ Alejandro Salas. ___4___ de Venezuela. Mi casa ___5___ en Caracas, la capital. ___6___ en la calle Rómulo Gallegos. Nuestro apartamento ___7___ moderno. Y ___8___ bastante grande. ___9___ en el quinto piso del edificio. El edificio ___10___ muy alto. Tiene muchos pisos. Me gusta nuestro apartamento.

David, ¿cómo ___11___ tu casa? ¿ ___12___ muy grande y moderna? Y tu familia, ¿ ___13___ grande o pequeña?

20 ¿De dónde es y dónde está ahora? Contesten.

1. Bernardo es de México pero ahora está en Venezuela.
   ¿De dónde es Bernardo?
   ¿Dónde está ahora?
   ¿De dónde es y dónde está?

2. Linda es de Estados Unidos pero ahora está en Colombia.
   ¿De dónde es Linda?
   ¿Dónde está ahora?
   ¿De dónde es y dónde está?

3. La señora Martín es de Cuba pero ahora está en Puerto Rico.
   ¿De dónde es la señora Martín?
   ¿Dónde está ella ahora?
   ¿De dónde es y dónde está?

21 **Entrevista** Contesten personalmente.

1. ¿Estás en la escuela ahora?
2. ¿Dónde está la escuela?
3. ¿En qué clase estás?
4. ¿En qué piso está la sala de clase?
5. ¿Está el/la profesor(a) en la clase también?
6. ¿De dónde es él/ella?
7. ¿Y de dónde eres tú?
8. ¿Cómo estás hoy?
9. Y el/la profesor(a), ¿cómo está?
10. ¿Y cómo es?

22 **Historieta** **Un amigo, Ángel**
Completen con **ser** o **estar**.

West New York, New Jersey

Ángel __1__ un amigo muy bueno. __2__ muy atlético y __3__ muy inteligente. Además __4__ sincero y simpático. Casi siempre __5__ de buen humor. Pero hoy no. Al contrario, __6__ de mal humor. __7__ muy cansado y tiene dolor de cabeza. __8__ enfermo. Tiene la gripe. __9__ en casa. __10__ en cama.

La casa de Ángel __11__ en la calle 60. La calle 60 __12__ en West New York. West New York no __13__ en Nueva York. __14__ en Nueva Jersey. Pero la familia de Ángel no __15__ de West New York. Sus padres __16__ de Cuba y sus abuelos __17__ de España. Ellos __18__ de Galicia, una región en el noroeste de España. Galicia __19__ en la costa del Atlántico y del mar Cantábrico. Ángel tiene una familia internacional.

Pero ahora todos __20__ en West New York y __21__ contentos. Muchas familias en West New York __22__ de ascendencia cubana. El apartamento de la familia de Ángel __23__ muy bonito. __24__ en el tercer piso y tiene una vista magnífica de la ciudad de Nueva York.

Estructura

Me, te, nos
Telling what happens to whom

Me, te, and **nos** are object pronouns. Note that the pronoun is placed right before the verb.

¿**Te** ve el médico?
Sí, el médico me **ve**. Me **examina**.
¿**Te** da una receta?
Sí, me **da** una receta.
Cuando tenemos la gripe, el médico nos **receta** antibióticos.

¿Cómo lo digo?

23 Historieta En el consultorio
Contesten.

1. ¿Estás enfermo(a)?
2. ¿Vas a la consulta del médico?
3. ¿Te ve el médico?
4. ¿Te examina?
5. ¿Te habla el médico?
6. ¿Te da una diagnosis?
7. ¿Te receta unas pastillas?
8. ¿Te despacha los medicamentos la farmacéutica?

Prevención y Tratamiento del Tabaquismo por el Farmacéutico

24 Una invitación Completen.

—Aquí tienes una carta.
  ¿Quién __1__ escribe?
—Carlos __2__ escribe.
—¿Ah, sí?
—Sí, __3__ invita a una fiesta.
—¿__4__ invita a una fiesta?
—Sí, Carlos siempre __5__
  invita cuando tiene una
  fiesta.

Los Integrantes de la Promoción XXVIII
de
Institutos Educacionales Asociados
Tienen el gusto de invitarle a la fiesta que ofrecen
con motivo de su Graduación,
el Miércoles 30 de Julio

Recepción:
Hotel Tamanaco
Salón "Naiguatá"

Hora: 8:30 p.m.
Traje formal.
1 Persona.

Indispensable la presentación de esta tarjeta.

25 **Preguntas y más preguntas** Work with a partner. Have some fun making up silly questions and giving answers. For example, **¿Te da una receta tu amigo cuando es tu cumpleaños?** Use as many of the following words as possible. Be original!

me | te | da | tu amigo(a) | invita

tu abuelo(a) | tu mamá | nos | habla | enseña

compra | comprende | el/la farmacéutico(a)

el/la médico(a) | tu papá | el/la mesero(a)

tu profesor(a)

Facultad de Farmacia, Universidad de Madrid

Andas bien. ¡Adelante!

Conversación

En la consulta del médico

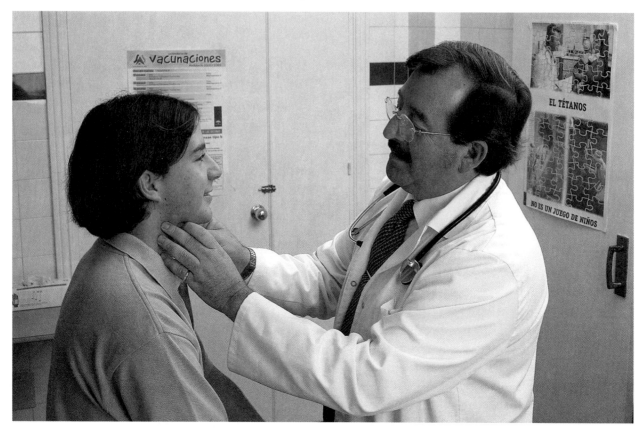

Alejandro Buenos días, doctor López.
Doctor Buenos días, Alejandro. ¿Qué te pasa? ¿Qué tienes?
Alejandro Doctor López, ¡qué enfermo estoy!
Doctor ¿Me puedes explicar tus síntomas?
Alejandro Pues, tengo fiebre. Y tengo escalofríos.
Doctor ¿Te duele la garganta?
Alejandro ¿La garganta? Me duele todo— la garganta, la cabeza.
Doctor Bien, Alejandro. ¿Puedes abrir la boca? *(Después de mirar)* Ya veo. Tienes la garganta muy roja.
Alejandro ¿Qué tengo, doctor?
Doctor No es nada serio. Tienes la gripe. Te voy a recetar unos antibióticos. Dentro de dos días vas a estar muy bien.

¿Comprendes?

Contesten.

1. ¿Dónde está Alejandro?
2. ¿Con quién habla?
3. ¿Cómo está Alejandro?
4. ¿Qué tiene?
5. ¿Tiene dolor de garganta?
6. ¿Tiene dolor de cabeza?
7. ¿Abre la boca Alejandro?
8. ¿Qué examina el médico?
9. ¿Cómo está la garganta?
10. ¿Qué cree el médico que Alejandro tiene?

Vamos a hablar más

A **¿Debes o no debes ser médico(a)?** Work with a classmate. Interview one another and decide who would be a good doctor. Make a list of questions for your interview. One question you may want to ask is: **¿Tienes mucha o poca paciencia?**

B **Juego** **¿Quién es?** Play a guessing game with a classmate. Give some features and characteristics of someone in the class. Then tell how the person appears to be today. Your partner will guess who it is you are talking about. Then your partner will describe someone and it will be your turn to guess.

ALUMNO 1: **Es morena y alta. Está contenta hoy.**

ALUMNO 2: **¡Es Alicia!**

ALUMNO 1: **Sí, es ella.**

Pronunciación

La consonante c

You have already learned that **c** in combination with **e** or **i (ce, ci)** is pronounced like an **s**. The consonant **c** in combination with **a, o, u (ca, co, cu)** has a hard **k** sound. Since **ce, ci** have the soft **s** sound, **c** changes to **qu** when it combines with **e** or **i (que, qui)** in order to maintain the hard **k** sound. Repeat the following.

ca	que	qui	co	cu
cama	que	equipo	como	cubano
casa	queso	aquí	médico	
catarro	parque	química	cocina	
cansado	pequeño	tranquilo		
cabeza				
boca				

Repeat the following sentences.

El médico cubano está en la consulta pequeña.

El queso está en la cocina de la casa.

El cubano come el queso aquí en el parque pequeño.

Lecturas culturales

Una joven nerviosa

La pobre Patricia está muy enferma hoy.
No tiene energía. Está cansada. Tiene dolor de
garganta y tiene tos. Está de muy mal humor
porque mañana tiene que jugar en un partido
importante de fútbol. No quiere perder[1]
el partido pero no puede jugar
si está tan enferma y débil[2].
Pues, no hay más remedio para
Patricia. Tiene que ir a ver al
médico. Llega al consultorio.

[1]perder *to miss*
[2]débil *weak*

Reading Strategy

Visualizing As you are
reading, try to visualize (or
make a mental picture of)
exactly what it is you are
reading. Allow your mind to
freely develop an image.
This will help you to
remember what you read. It
may also help you identify
with the subject you are
reading about.

Málaga, España

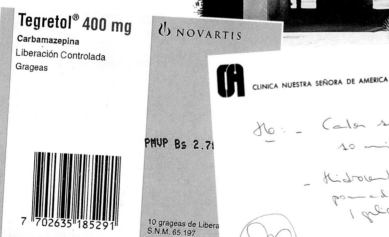

En el consultorio Patricia habla con el médico. Explica que tiene un partido importante que no quiere perder. El médico examina a Patricia. Ella abre la boca y el médico examina la garganta. Sí, está un poco roja pero no es nada serio. Su condición no es grave.

Habla Patricia:

—Doctor, no puedo guardar cama. Tengo que jugar fútbol mañana.

—Patricia, estás muy nerviosa. Tienes que estar tranquila. No hay problema. Aquí tienes una receta. Vas a tomar una pastilla tres veces al día—una pastilla con cada comida. Mañana vas a estar mucho mejor[3] y no vas a perder tu partido. Y, ¡buena suerte[4]!

[3]mucho mejor *much better*
[4]buena suerte *good luck*

Madrid, España

Pobre Patricia

Contesten.

1. ¿Quién está enferma?
2. ¿Cuáles son sus síntomas?
3. ¿Está de buen humor o de mal humor?
4. ¿Por qué está nerviosa?
5. ¿Cuál es el único remedio para Patricia?
6. ¿Con quién habla Patricia en el consultorio?
7. ¿Qué examina el médico?
8. ¿Cómo está la garganta?
9. ¿Cómo es su condición?
10. ¿Tiene que guardar cama Patricia?
11. ¿Qué tiene que tomar?
12. ¿Cuándo tiene que tomar las pastillas?
13. ¿Cómo va a estar mañana?

Lectura opcional ❶

La farmacia

En Estados Unidos si uno quiere o necesita antibióticos, es necesario tener una receta. Es necesario visitar al médico para un examen. El médico receta los medicamentos y el paciente lleva la receta a la farmacia. El farmacéutico no puede despachar medicamentos sin la receta de un médico.

En muchos países hispanos no es necesario tener una receta para comprar antibióticos. Uno puede explicar sus síntomas al farmacéutico y él o ella puede despachar los medicamentos. Pero hay una excepción. Los farmacéuticos no pueden despachar medicamentos que contienen sustancias controladas como un narcótico o un medicamento con alcohol.

Y hay otra cosa importante. El precio[1] de las medicinas en los países hispanos es mucho más bajo que el precio de las mismas medicinas en Estados Unidos.

Buenos Aires, Argentina

[1]precio *price*

¿Comprendes?

¿Sí o no? Digan que sí o que no.
1. El farmacéutico en Estados Unidos no puede despachar medicamentos si el cliente no tiene una receta de su médico.
2. En Latinoamérica el médico despacha los medicamentos.
3. En Latinoamérica es necesario ir a una clínica por los antibióticos.
4. El farmacéutico en Latinoamérica puede despachar antibióticos sin una receta del médico.
5. El farmacéutico en Latinoamérica no puede vender medicamentos que contienen o llevan una droga o alcohol sin una receta.
6. Los medicamentos cuestan más en los países hispanos que en Estados Unidos.

La Habana, Cuba

Lectura opcional ②

Una biografía— El doctor Antonio Gassett

El doctor Antonio Gassett es de La Habana, Cuba. Recibe su bachillerato en ciencias en la Universidad de Belén, en Cuba. Más tarde estudia en la Facultad de Medicina de la Universidad de La Habana. Poco después, sale de[1] Cuba por motivos políticos. Va a Boston donde trabaja de técnico de laboratorio en la Fundación de Retina de Boston.

Le interesa mucho el trabajo con los ojos y decide estudiar oftalmología. Estudia en Harvard y en la Universidad de la Florida.

Hoy el doctor Gassett es una persona famosa. Descubre un método para tratar la córnea. Con el tratamiento del doctor Gassett muchas personas ciegas—que no pueden ver—recobran la vista[2]. El doctor recibe muchos premios[3] por sus investigaciones y descubrimientos[4].

[1]sale de *he leaves*
[2]recobran la vista *regain sight*
[3]premios *prizes, awards*
[4]descubrimientos *discoveries*

¿Comprendes?

A Estudio de palabras Contesten.
1. The word **investigar** is a cognate of *investigate.* What does *to investigate* mean? In Spanish, **investigar** can mean both *to investigate* and *to do research.* Related words are: **las investigaciones, el investigador.** Use these words in a sentence.
2. In the reading, find a word related to each of the following: **tratar, descubrir.**

B Palabras sinónimas Busquen una expresión equivalente.
1. obtiene su bachillerato
2. por razones políticas
3. le fascina el trabajo
4. es una persona célebre, renombrada

LA SALUD Y EL MÉDICO

doscientos sesenta y tres 🔷 **263**

Conexiones
Las ciencias naturales

La nutrición

Good nutrition is very important. What we eat can determine if we will enjoy good health or have poor health. For this reason, it is most important to have a balanced diet and avoid the temptation to eat "junk food."

Read the following information about nutrition in Spanish. Before reading this selection, however, look at the following groups of related words. Often if you know the meaning of one word you can guess the meaning of several other words related to it.

varía, la variedad, la variación
activo, la actividad
los adolescentes, la adolescencia
proveen, la provisión, el proveedor
el consumo, consumir, el consumidor
elevar, la elevación, elevado

Comer bien

Es muy importante comer bien para mantener la salud. Cada día debemos[1] comer una variedad de vegetales, frutas, granos y cereales y carnes o pescado.

Calorías

El número de calorías que necesita o requiere una persona depende de su metabolismo, de su tamaño y de su nivel[2] de actividad física. Los adolescentes necesitan más calorías que los ancianos o viejos. Requieren más calorías porque son muy activos y están creciendo[3]. Una persona anciana de tamaño pequeño con un nivel bajo de actividad física requiere menos calorías.

[1]debemos *we should* [2]nivel *level* [3]creciendo *growing*

Proteínas

Las proteínas son especialmente importantes durante los períodos de crecimiento. Los adolescentes, por ejemplo, deben comer comestibles o alimentos ricos[4] en proteínas porque están creciendo.

Carbohidratos

Los carbohidratos son alimentos como los espaguetis, las papas y el arroz. Los carbohidratos proveen mucha energía.

Grasas

Las grasas o lípidos son otra fuente[5] importante de energía. Algunas carnes contienen mucha grasa. Pero es necesario controlar el consumo de lípidos o grasa porque en muchos individuos elevan el nivel de colesterol.

Vitaminas

Las vitaminas son indispensables para el funcionamiento del organismo o cuerpo. ¿Cuáles son algunas fuentes de las vitaminas que necesita el cuerpo humano?

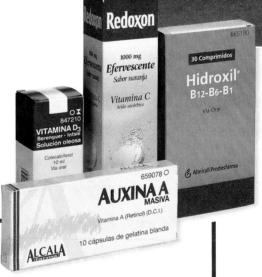

VITAMINAS Y MINERALES EN EL DEPORTE

Dr. Corominas, Catedrático de Fisiología y Biología Celular del Hospital Universitario

Estepona, España

VITAMINA	FUENTE
A	vegetales, leche, algunas frutas
B	carne, huevos, leche, cereales, vegetales verdes
C	frutas cítricas, tomates, lechuga
D	leche, huevos, pescado
E	aceites[6], vegetales, huevos, cereales

[4]ricos *rich*   [5]fuente *source*   [6]aceites *oils*

¿Comprendes?

La nutrición Contesten.
1. ¿Qué debemos comer cada día?
2. ¿De qué depende el número de calorías que requiere una persona?
3. ¿Quiénes requieren más calorías? ¿Por qué?
4. ¿Por qué necesitan los adolescentes alimentos ricos en proteínas?
5. ¿Qué proveen los carbohidratos?
6. ¿Por qué es necesario controlar el consumo de grasas o lípidos?

¡Te toca a ti!

Use what you have learned

HABLAR

1 Todos están enfermos.

✔ *Describe cold symptoms and minor ailments*

Work with a classmate. Choose one of the people in the illustrations. Describe him or her. Your partner will guess which person you're talking about and say what's the matter with the person. Take turns.

Paco   Gloria   Ana   David

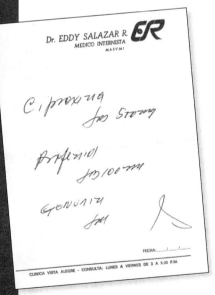

HABLAR

2 Una receta

✔ *Discuss a prescription with a pharmacist*

You are in a pharmacy in Spain or Latin America. Your classmate will be the pharmacist. Make up a conversation about your prescription. Explain why and how you have to take the medicine.

HABLAR

3 ¿Qué te pasa? ¿Qué tienes?

✔ *Explain an illness to a doctor*

With a partner, prepare a skit about a nervous person in a doctor's office. If you want, prepare the skit based on the story about **Una joven nerviosa.** Your skit can be about Patricia and her doctor.

HABLAR

4 Juego ¡Qué enfermo(a) estoy!

✔ *Talk about how you are feeling*

Work with a partner. Make gestures to indicate how you're feeling today. Your partner will ask you why you feel that way. Tell him or her. Be as creative and humorous as possible.

ESCRIBIR

5 ¡Por favor!

✔ *Write a note describing a minor illness*

You're supposed to take a Spanish test today but you're not feeling well. Write a note to your Spanish teacher explaining why you can't take the test, and mention some symptoms you have.

For more information about medical services in the Spanish-speaking world, go to the Glencoe Spanish Web site: spanish.glencoe.com

ESCRIBIR

6 El servicio en la comunidad

Your Spanish Club has a community service requirement. You have decided to work in the emergency room (**la sala de emergencia**) at your local hospital. You serve as a translator or interpreter for patients who speak only Spanish. Write a flyer for your Spanish Club. Tell about your experience with one or more patients. Give your feelings about the work you do and try to encourage other club members to volunteer their services, too.

Writing Strategy

Writing a personal essay In writing a personal essay, a writer has several options: to tell a story, describe something, or encourage someone to think a certain way or to do something. Whatever its purpose, a personal essay allows a writer to express a viewpoint about a subject he or she has experienced. Your essay will be much livelier if you allow your enthusiasm to be obvious; do so by choosing interesting details and vivid words to relay your message.

Vocabulario

1 Escojan.

1. Roberto está enfermo.
   a. No está bien.
   b. Está contento.
   c. Está nervioso.
2. Ella tiene fiebre.
   a. No tiene síntomas.
   b. Y tiene escalofríos.
   c. Está tranquila.
3. El muchacho tiene catarro.
   a. Está nervioso.
   b. Está resfriado.
   c. Tiene dolor de estómago.
4. ¿Por qué tiene que guardar cama?
   a. Porque no está de buen humor.
   b. Tiene tos.
   c. Tiene la gripe y tiene fiebre.

To review **Palabras 1**, turn to pages 242–243.

2 Identifiquen.

To review **Palabras 2**, turn to pages 246–247.

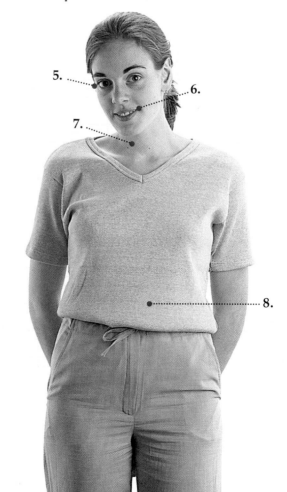

5. ......
6. ......
7. ......
8. ......

3 Expresen de otra manera.

    9. Tengo dolor de cabeza.

Estructura

4 Completen con **ser** o **estar**.

    10. Él ＿＿＿ rubio.

    11. Alicia ＿＿＿ enferma.

    12. El curso de historia ＿＿＿ muy interesante.

    13. Él ＿＿＿ de mal humor porque ＿＿＿ cansado.

    14. ¿Dónde ＿＿＿ la sala de consulta del médico?

    15. Madrid ＿＿＿ en España.

    16. El amigo de Teresa ＿＿＿ de Cuba.

    17. Ahora (él) ＿＿＿ en Nueva York.

To review ser and estar, turn to pages 250 and 253.

5 Completen.

  18–19. —Cuando tienes la gripe, ¿el médico ＿＿＿ da una receta?

        —Sí, ＿＿＿ da una receta para unos antibióticos.

    20. Sí, cuando tenemos la gripe, el médico siempre ＿＿＿ receta antibióticos.

To review object pronouns, turn to page 256.

Madrid, España

Tell all you can about this illustration.

Vocabulario

Describing minor health problems

la salud	el dolor
la fiebre	enfermo(a)
los escalofríos	cansado(a)
la gripe	estornudar
el catarro	estar resfriado(a)
la tos	toser
la energía	

Speaking with the doctor

¿Qué te pasa?	Me duele…
la consulta, el consultorio	Tengo dolor de…
el/la médico(a)	creer
el hospital	examinar
el síntoma	abrir la boca
la diagnosis	guardar cama
la alergia	recetar
la inyección	

How well do you know your vocabulary?

- Find as many cognates as you can in the list.
- Use five cognates to write several sentences.

Describing some emotions

contento(a)	nervioso(a)
triste	tranquilo(a)
de buen humor, de mal humor	

VIDEOTUR

Episodio 8

In this video episode, you will learn another facet of Alberto's personality. See page 499 for more information.

Identifying more parts of the body

la garganta	la boca
los ojos	el estómago

Speaking with a pharmacist

la farmacia
el/la farmacéutico(a)
la receta
el medicamento, la medicina
la aspirina
el antibiótico
la pastilla, la píldora, la tableta
la dosis
despachar, vender

Capítulo 9

El verano y el invierno

Objetivos

In this chapter you will learn to:

❖ describe summer and winter weather
❖ talk about summer activities and sports
❖ talk about winter sports
❖ discuss past actions and events
❖ refer to people and things already mentioned
❖ talk about resorts in the Hispanic world

Daniel Hernández *A Breath of Fresh Air*

El balneario

la plancha de vela

En el verano hace calor.
Hace buen tiempo.
Hace (Hay) sol.
El sol brilla en el cielo.

Hace mal tiempo.
A veces hay nubes.
A veces llueve.

el buceo

el mar

la ola

la playa

la toalla playera

el traje de baño, el bañador

los anteojos de sol, las gafas de sol

la loción bronceadora, la crema protectora

la arena

la tabla hawaiana

el esquí acuático

Adriana y sus amigos fueron a la playa
    el viernes.
Ellos pasaron el fin de semana en la playa.
Pedro practicó la plancha de vela.
Diego buceó.
Carlos tomó el sol.

Claudia esquió en el agua.

Alejandro practicó el surfing.

La natación

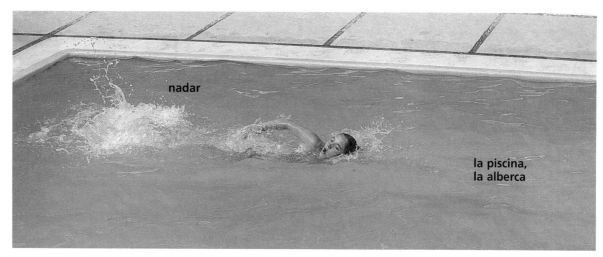

nadar

la piscina,
la alberca

Sandra fue a la piscina
Ella nadó en la piscina.

El tenis

la
raqueta

la pelota

la red

la cancha de tenis

el juego de tenis

Los amigos jugaron (al) tenis.
Jugaron tenis en una cancha al aire libre.
No jugaron en una cancha cubierta.

Jugaron singles, no dobles.
Un jugador golpeó la pelota.
La pelota pasó por encima de la red.

Vocabulario

¿Qué palabra necesito?

1 Historieta ¡A la playa!

Contesten con **sí.**

1. ¿Fue Isabel a la playa?
2. ¿Pasó el fin de semana allí?
3. ¿Nadó en el mar?
4. ¿Esquió en el agua?
5. ¿Buceó?
6. ¿Tomó el sol?
7. ¿Usó una crema protectora?

San Juan, Puerto Rico

Acapulco, México

2 Historieta El tiempo

Completen.

En el verano __1__ calor. Hay __2__. El sol brilla en el __3__. Pero no hace buen tiempo siempre. A veces hay __4__. Cuando hay __5__, el cielo está nublado. No me gusta cuando __6__ cuando estoy en la playa.

3 **¿Qué compró Claudia?** Contesten según las fotografías.

Claudia fue a la tienda. ¿Qué compró?

1.

2.

3.

4.

276 ✿ *doscientos setenta y seis*

CAPÍTULO 9

Cancún, México

4 **Historieta** **El balneario**

Completen.

1. Un balneario tiene ____.
2. El Mediterráneo es un ____ y el Caribe es un ____.
3. En un mar o en un océano hay ____.
4. En la playa la gente ____ y ____ el sol.
5. ____ da protección contra el sol.
6. Una persona lleva ____ y ____ cuando va a la playa.
7. Me gusta mucho ir a la playa en el ____ cuando hace ____ y hay mucho ____.
8. Si uno no vive cerca de la costa y no puede ir a la playa, puede nadar en ____.

5 **Historieta** **Un juego de tenis**

 Contesten.

1. ¿Dónde jugaron los tenistas al tenis?
2. ¿Jugaron singles o dobles?
3. ¿Cuántas personas hay en la cancha cuando juegan dobles?
4. ¿Golpearon los tenistas la pelota?
5. ¿La pelota tiene que pasar por encima de la red?

Estepona, España

6 **Vamos a la playa.** Work with a classmate. You are going to spend a day or two at the beach. Go to the store to buy some things you need for your beach trip. One of you will be the clerk and the other will be the shopper. Take turns.

7 **¿Dónde vamos a jugar tenis?** Call some friends (your classmates) to try to arrange a game of doubles. Decide where you're going to play, when, and with whom.

SPANISH Online

For more information about the popularity of tennis in the Spanish-speaking world, go to the Glencoe Spanish Web site: spanish.glencoe.com

El invierno

la esquiadora

el esquí

los guantes

el anorak

el bastón

la bota

El tiempo en el invierno

En el invierno hace frío.
Nieva.
Hay mucha nieve.
La temperatura baja a cinco grados
bajo cero.

La estación de esquí

Los esquiadores compraron los boletos en la ventanilla.

Ellos tomaron el telesilla para subir la montaña.

Bajaron la pista.
Esquiaron muy bien.
Bajaron la pista para expertos, no la pista para principiantes.

Nota You are familiar with the following expressions to talk about things that happen in the present. Look also at time expressions you use to talk about things that happened in the past.

EL PRESENTE
hoy
esta noche
esta tarde
esta mañana
este año
esta semana

EL PASADO
ayer
anoche
ayer por la tarde
ayer por la mañana
el año pasado
la semana pasada

¿Qué palabra necesito?

8 **¿Qué tiempo hace?** Describan el tiempo en la foto.

Villarrica, Chile

9 **Historieta En una estación de esquí**
Contesten según se indica.

1. ¿Cuándo son populares las estaciones de esquí? (en el invierno)
2. ¿Qué tipo de pistas hay en una estación de esquí? (para expertos y para principiantes)
3. ¿Dónde compraron los esquiadores los tickets para el telesquí? (en la ventanilla)
4. ¿Qué tomaron los esquiadores para subir la montaña? (el telesilla)
5. ¿Qué bajaron los esquiadores? (la pista)

10 **Me gusta esquiar.** Completen.

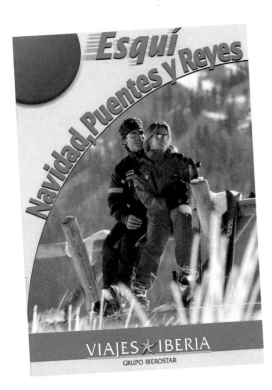

En el __1__ hace frío. A veces nieva. Cuando hay mucha __2__ me gusta ir a una __3__ de esquí. Llevo mis __4__, mis botas y los __5__ y voy a las montañas. Tomo el __6__ para subir la montaña. No soy un esquiador muy bueno. Siempre bajo una __7__ para principiantes.

11 **¡A esquiar!** You're at a ski resort in Chile and have to rent **(alquilar)** some equipment for a day on the slopes. Tell the clerk (your partner) what you need. Find out whether he or she has what you need and how much it all costs.

12 **En una estación de esquí** Have a conversation with a classmate. Tell as much as you can about what people do at a ski resort. Find out which one of you knows more about skiing. If skiing is a sport that is new to you, tell whether you think it would interest you.

13 **¿A qué ciudad?** With a classmate, look at the following weather map that appeared in a Spanish newspaper. You are in Madrid and want to take a side trip. Since you both have definite preferences regarding weather, use the map to help you make a decision. After you choose a city to go to, tell what you are going to do there.

Estructura

Pretérito de los verbos en -ar
Describing past actions

1. You use the preterite to express actions that began and ended at a definite time in the past.

> **Ayer María pasó el día en la playa.**
> **Yo, no. Pasé el día en la escuela.**

2. The preterite of regular **-ar** verbs is formed by dropping the infinitive ending **-ar** and adding the appropriate endings to the stem. Study the following forms.

INFINITIVE	hablar	tomar	nadar	ENDINGS
STEM	habl-	tom-	nad-	
yo	hablé	tomé	nadé	-é
tú	hablaste	tomaste	nadaste	-aste
él, ella, Ud.	habló	tomó	nadó	-ó
nosotros(as)	hablamos	tomamos	nadamos	-amos
vosotros(as)	hablasteis	tomasteis	nadasteis	-asteis
ellos, ellas, Uds.	hablaron	tomaron	nadaron	-aron

3. Note that verbs that end in **-car, -gar,** and **-zar** have a spelling change in the **yo** form.

c → qué   g → gué   z → cé

¿Marcaste un tanto?   Sí, marqué un tanto.
¿Llegaste a tiempo?   Sí, llegué a tiempo.
¿Jugaste (al) baloncesto?   Sí, jugué (al) baloncesto.
¿Empezaste a jugar?   Sí, empecé a jugar.

DEPORTES

* Basquet
* VoleyFutbol
* Handball
* Raquetball
* Pelota a mano
* Gimnasia deportiva

¿Cómo lo digo?

14 Historieta Una tarde en la playa

Contesten.

1. Ayer, ¿pasó Rubén la tarde en la playa?
2. ¿Tomó él mucho sol?
3. ¿Usó crema protectora?
4. ¿Nadó en el mar?
5. ¿Buceó?
6. ¿Esquió en el agua?

15 Historieta Un partido de tenis

Contesten según se indica.

1. ¿Qué compraron los amigos? (una raqueta)
2. ¿A qué jugaron los jóvenes? (tenis)
3. ¿Jugaron en una cancha cubierta? (no, al aire libre)
4. ¿Golpearon la pelota? (sí)
5. ¿Jugaron singles o dobles? (dobles)
6. ¿Quiénes marcaron el primer tanto? (Alicia y José)
7. ¿Quiénes ganaron el partido? (ellos)

San Juan, Puerto Rico

MERIDIANO TELEVISIÓN

MAÑANA
06:00 Golf Boomme Valley Classic 2 Ronda
07:30 Formula 1 Gran Premio de Luxemburgo (En Vivo)
10:00 Máxima Velocidad
11:00 Mundo Marcial
11:30 Basket Nacional: Cocodrilos vs Tanqueros (En Vivo)
TARDE
01:30 Formula 1 Gran Premio de Luxemburgo
04:00 Fútbol Nacional: Caracas F.C. vs Minerven (En Vivo)
06:00 Supergolazo
06:30 Revista Semanal
NOCHE
07:00 Tenis Copa Davis USA vs Italia
09:00 Retrospectiva de Golf
09:30 Revista Semanal
10:00 Tercer Tiempo
10:30 Noticiero Meridiano
11:30 Wheelies

NOTA: Esta programación puede estar sujeta a cambios por motivos de fuerza mayor.

16 Historieta En casa

Contesten personalmente.

1. Anoche, ¿a qué hora llegaste a casa?
2. ¿Preparaste la comida?
3. ¿Estudiaste?
4. ¿Miraste la televisión?
5. ¿Escuchaste CDs?
6. ¿Hablaste por teléfono?
7. ¿Con quién hablaste?

17 Historieta Yo llegué al estadio.

Cambien **nosotros** a **yo.**

Ayer nosotros llegamos al estadio y empezamos a jugar fútbol. Jugamos muy bien. No tocamos el balón con las manos. Lo lanzamos con el pie o con la cabeza. Marcamos tres tantos.

Estructura

 18 **El baloncesto**

Formen preguntas según el modelo.

—**¿Jugó Pablo?**
—**A ver, Pablo, ¿jugaste?**

1. ¿Jugó Pablo al baloncesto?
2. ¿Dribló con el balón?
3. ¿Pasó el balón a un amigo?
4. ¿Tiró el balón?
5. ¿Encestó?
6. ¿Marcó un tanto?

19 **Historieta** **Una fiesta**

Sigan el modelo.

hablar ⟶
Mis amigos y yo hablamos
durante la fiesta.

1. bailar
2. cantar
3. tomar un refresco
4. tomar fotos
5. escuchar música

Valdesquí, España

20 **Historieta** **En una estación de esquí**

Completen.

El fin de semana pasado José, algunos amigos y yo __1__ (esquiar). __2__ (Llegar) a la estación de esquí el viernes por la noche. Luego nosotros __3__ (pasar) dos días en las pistas.

José __4__ (comprar) un pase para el telesquí. Todos nosotros __5__ (tomar) el telesquí para subir la montaña. Pero todos nosotros __6__ (bajar) una pista diferente. José __7__ (bajar) la pista para expertos porque él esquía muy bien. Pero yo, no. Yo __8__ (tomar) la pista para principiantes. Y yo __9__ (bajar) con mucho cuidado.

21 Pasaron el fin de semana en la playa. Look at the illustration. Work with a classmate, asking and answering questions about what these friends did at the beach in Acapulco.

22 Pasé un día en una estación de esquí. You went on a skiing trip in the Sierra Nevada, Granada, Spain. You had a great time. Call your friend (a classmate) to tell him or her about your trip. Your friend has never been skiing so he or she will have a few questions for you.

GRANADA

SIERRA NEVADA

UN POCO MÁS

*For more practice using words from **Palabras 1** and **2** and the preterite, do Activity 9 on page H10 at the end of this book.*

Estructura

Pronombres—lo, la, los, las
Referring to items already mentioned

1. The following sentences each have a direct object. The direct object is the word in the sentence that receives the action of the verb. The direct object can be either a noun or a pronoun.

Ella compró el bañador.	Ella lo compró.
Compró los anteojos de sol.	Los compró en la misma tienda.
¿Compró loción bronceadora?	Sí, la compró.
¿Compró las toallas en la misma tienda?	No, no las compró en la misma tienda.
¿Invitaste a Juan a la fiesta?	Sí, lo invité.
¿Invitaste a Elena?	Sí, la invité.

2. Note that **lo, los, la,** and **las** are direct object pronouns. They must agree with the noun they replace. They can replace either a person or a thing. The direct object pronoun comes right before the verb.

Ella compró el regalo.	Ella lo compró.
Invitó a Juan.	Lo invitó.
No miré la fotografía.	No la miré.
No miré a Julia.	No la miré.

¿Cómo lo digo?

23 **¿Dónde está?** Sigan el modelo.

¿El bañador?

Aquí lo tienes.

1. ¿El traje de baño?
2. ¿El tubo de crema?
3. ¿La pelota?
4. ¿La crema protectora?
5. ¿Los anteojos de sol?
6. ¿Los boletos?
7. ¿Los esquís acuáticos?
8. ¿Las toallas playeras?
9. ¿Las raquetas?
10. ¿Las tablas hawaianas?

24 **De compras** Sigan el modelo.

—¿Cuándo compraste los bastones?
—Los compré ayer.
—¿Dónde los compraste?
—Los compré en la tienda Padín.
—¿Cuánto te costaron?
—Me costaron ciento cinco pesos.

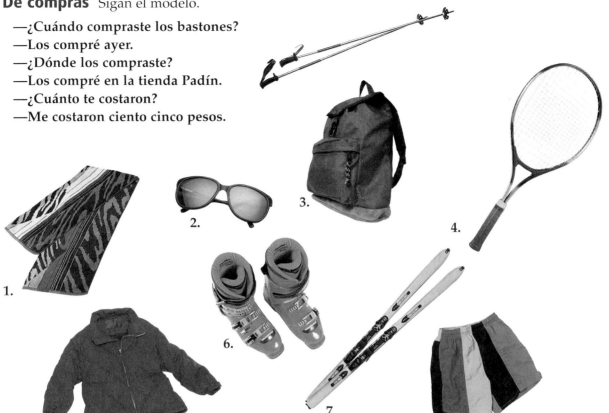

1.

2.

3.

4.

5.

6.

7.

8.

25 **Historieta** **Un regalo que le gustó**
Completen.

   Yo compré un regalo para Teresa. __1__ compré en la tienda de departamentos Corte Inglés. Compré unos anteojos de sol. A Teresa le gustaron mucho. Ella __2__ llevó el otro día cuando fue a la piscina. Ella tiene algunas fotografías con sus anteojos de sol. Su amigo Miguel __3__ tomó.

Madrid, España

26 Historieta Una fiesta Contesten.

1. ¿Invitaste a Juan a la fiesta?
2. ¿Invitaste a Alejandra?
3. ¿Compraste los refrescos?
4. ¿Preparaste la ensalada?
5. ¿Tomó Pepe las fotografías de la fiesta?

Ir y ser en el pretérito
Describing past actions

1. The verbs **ir** and **ser** are irregular in the preterite tense. Note that they have identical forms.

INFINITIVE	ir	ser
yo	fui	fui
tú	fuiste	fuiste
él, ella, Ud.	fue	fue
nosotros(as)	fuimos	fuimos
vosotros(as)	*fuisteis*	*fuisteis*
ellos, ellas, Uds.	fueron	fueron

2. The context in which each verb is used in the sentence will clarify the meaning. The verb **ser** is not used very often in the preterite.

> **El Sr. Martínez fue profesor de español.**
> **Él fue a España.**
> **Mi abuela fue médica.**
> **Mi abuela fue al consultorio de la médica.**

¿Cómo lo digo?

27 **¿Y tú?** Contesten personalmente.

1. Ayer, ¿fuiste a la escuela?
2. ¿Fuiste a la playa?
3. ¿Fuiste a la piscina?
4. ¿Fuiste al campo de fútbol?
5. ¿Fuiste a la cancha de tenis?
6. ¿Fuiste a las montañas?
7. ¿Fuiste a casa?
8. ¿Fuiste a la tienda?

28 **¿Quién fue y cómo?** Contesten personalmente.

1. ¿Fuiste a la escuela ayer?
2. ¿Fue tu amigo también?
3. ¿Fueron juntos?
4. ¿Fueron en carro?
5. ¿Fue también la hermana de tu amigo?
6. ¿Fue ella en carro o a pie?

29 **Anteayer** Work with a classmate. Ask whether he or she went to one of the places below the day before yesterday **(anteayer).** Your partner will respond. Take turns asking and answering the questions.

1.

2.

3.

4.

5.

Andas bien. ¡Adelante!

¡A la playa!

Gloria ¿Adónde fuiste ayer?

Paula Pues, fui a la playa. Y no puedes imaginar lo que me pasó.

Gloria ¿Qué te pasó?

Paula Llegué a la playa sin mi traje de baño.

Gloria ¿Sin tu traje de baño?

Paula Sí, ¡sin mi traje de baño! Lo dejé en casa.

Gloria ¡Fuiste a la playa y dejaste tu traje de baño en casa! ¡Muy inteligente, Paula!

Paula Ah, pero lo pasé muy bien. Fui a nadar.

Gloria ¿Nadaste? ¿Sin traje de baño?

Paula Querer es poder. Fui al agua en mi blue jean.

¿Comprendes?

Contesten.

1. ¿Adónde fue Paula ayer?
2. ¿Llegó a la playa con su traje de baño?
3. ¿Dónde dejó su traje de baño?
4. Pero, ¿lo pasó bien en la playa?
5. ¿Nadó?
6. ¿Qué llevó cuando fue al agua?

Vamos a hablar más

A **¿Qué tiempo hace?** Work with a classmate. One of you lives in tropical San Juan, Puerto Rico. The other lives in Buffalo, New York. Describe the winter weather where you live.

B **Fuimos de vacaciones.** Work with a classmate. Take turns telling one another what you did last summer. You may wish to use the following words.

jugar · nadar · tomar · hablar · bailar · ir · esquiar · mirar · estudiar · comprar · invitar

Pronunciación

La consonante g

The consonant **g** has two sounds, hard and soft. You will study the soft sound in Chapter 10. **G** in combination with **a, o, u, (ga, go, gu)** is pronounced somewhat like the *g* in the English word *go.* To maintain this hard **g** sound with **e** or **i**, a **u** is placed after the **g: gue, gui.**

Repeat the following.

ga	gue	gui	go	gu
gafa	Rodríguez	guitarra	goma	agua
amiga	guerrilla	guía	estómago	guante
garganta			tengo	
paga			juego	
gato				

Repeat the following sentences.

El gato no juega en el agua.
Juego béisbol con el guante de mi amigo
  Rodríguez.
No tengo la guitarra de Gómez.

Lecturas culturales

Reading Strategy

Summarizing When reading an informative passage, we try to remember what we read. Summarizing helps us to do this. The easiest way to summarize is to begin to read for the general sense and take notes on what you are reading. It is best to write a summarizing statement for each paragraph and then one for the entire passage.

Paraísos del mundo hispano

¿Viajar[1] por el mundo hispano y no pasar unos días en un balneario? ¡Qué lástima[2]! En los países de habla española hay playas fantásticas. España, Puerto Rico, Cuba, México, Uruguay— todos son países famosos por sus playas.

En el verano cuando hace calor y un sol bonito brilla en el cielo, ¡qué estupendo es pasar un día en la playa! Y en lugares (sitios) como México, Puerto Rico y Venezuela, el verano es eterno. Podemos ir a la playa durante todos los meses del año.

Muchas personas toman sus vacaciones en una playa donde pueden disfrutar de[3] su tiempo libre. En la playa nadan o toman el sol. Vuelven a casa muy tostaditos o bronceados. Pero, ¡cuidado! Es necesario usar una crema protectora porque el sol es muy fuerte[4] en las playas tropicales.

[1]Viajar *To travel*
[2]lástima *pity*
[3]disfrutar de *enjoy*
[4]fuerte *strong*

Marbella, España

Cancún, México

La playa de Varadero, Cuba

Playa de Guajataca, Puerto Rico

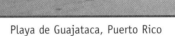
Pocitos, Uruguay

¿Comprendes?

A La palabra, por favor.

Den la palabra apropiada.

1. un lugar que tiene playas donde la gente puede nadar
2. una cosa triste y desagradable
3. maravillosas, estupendas
4. célebres
5. lindo, hermoso
6. de y para siempre
7. regresan a casa

B En la playa Contesten.

1. ¿Qué hay en los países de habla española?
2. ¿Cuándo es estupendo pasar un día en la playa?
3. ¿Cómo disfruta de su tiempo la gente que va a la playa?
4. ¿Cómo es el sol en las playas tropicales?

Lectura opcional 1

Estaciones inversas

Es el mes de julio. En España es el verano y la gente va a la playa a nadar. Y en la Argentina y Chile la gente va a las montañas a esquiar. ¿Cómo es que esquían en julio? Pues, el mes de julio es invierno. En el hemisferio sur las estaciones son inversas de las estaciones del hemisferio norte.

Sitges, España

Los Andes, Chile

¿Comprendes?

A **¿A esquiar o a nadar?** Contesten.
1. ¿Qué mes es?
2. ¿Qué estación es en España?
3. ¿Adónde va la gente?
4. ¿Qué estación es en Argentina y Chile?
5. ¿Adónde va la gente?
6. En julio, ¿dónde nada la gente?
7. En julio, ¿dónde esquía la gente?

B **¿Qué estación es?** Explica por qué es invierno en julio en Chile y Argentina.

Lectura opcional ②

«Snowboarding» en Chile

El «snowboarding»

¿Qué es el «snowboarding» o «el surf de nieve»? Es un deporte como el surfing—pero no sobre el agua. Practican el «snowboarding» sobre la nieve. Hay dos tipos o modalidades de surf de nieve—las carreras[1] y las exhibiciones.

Para practicar el «snowboarding», necesitas una tabla, un casco[2], guantes y rodilleras[3].

Sobre el «snowboard»—que es un tipo de tabla—el aficionado[4] hace unas piruetas y movimientos difíciles. Hay competencias de «snowboarding» en los Juegos Olímpicos.

[1]carreras *races*
[2]casco *helmet*
[3]rodilleras *kneepads*
[4]aficionado *fan*

¿Comprendes?

¿Sí o no? Digan que sí o que no.
1. El «snowboarding» es como el surfing sobre el agua, pero los aficionados lo practican en la nieve.
2. Hay solamente un tipo de surf de nieve.
3. El «snowboard» es un tipo de tabla, similar a una tabla hawaiana.
4. El aficionado de «snowboarding» hace unas piruetas en el aire.
5. Hay competencias de «snowboarding» en la Copa mundial.

Las Leñas, Argentina

Conexiones
Las ciencias sociales

El clima

We often talk about the weather, especially when on vacation. When planning a vacation trip, it's a good idea to take into account the climate of the area we are going to visit. When we talk about weather or climate, we must remember, however, that there is a difference between the two. Weather is the condition of the atmosphere for a short period of time. Climate is the term used for the weather that prevails in a region over a long period of time. Let's read about weather and climate throughout the vast area of the Spanish-speaking world.

El Parque Nacional de los Glaciares, Argentina

El clima y el tiempo

El clima y el tiempo son dos cosas muy diferentes. El tiempo es la condición de la atmósfera durante un período breve o corto. El tiempo puede cambiar[1] frecuentemente. Puede cambiar varias veces en un solo día.

El clima es el término que usamos para el tiempo que prevalece[2] en una zona por un período largo. El clima es el tiempo que hace cada año en el mismo lugar.

Zonas climáticas

En el mundo de habla española hay muchas zonas climáticas. Mucha gente cree que toda la América Latina tiene un clima tropical, pero es erróneo. El clima de Latinoamérica varía de una región a otra.

[1]cambiar *change*
[2]prevalece *prevails*

La vegetación tropical, Costa Rica

El río Santiago Cayapas, Ecuador

El Amazonas

Toda la zona o cuenca amazónica es una región tropical. Hace mucho calor y llueve mucho durante todo el año.

Los Andes

En los Andes, aún en las regiones cerca de la línea ecuatorial, el clima no es tropical. En las zonas montañosas el clima depende de la elevación. En los picos andinos, por ejemplo, hace frío.

Clima templado

Algunas partes de Argentina, Uruguay y Chile tienen un clima templado. España también tiene un clima templado. En una región de clima templado hay cuatro estaciones: el verano, el otoño, el invierno y la primavera. Y el tiempo cambia con cada estación. ¡Y una cosa importante! Las estaciones en la América del Sur son inversas de las de la América del Norte.

Los picos andinos cerca de Cuzco, Perú

Una aldea en las montañas, Ecuador

¿Comprendes?

¿Sabes? Contesten en inglés.

1. What's the difference between weather and climate?
2. What is an erroneous idea that many people have about Latin America?
3. How can it be cold in some areas that are actually on the equator?
4. What is a characteristic of a tropical area?
5. What is a characteristic of a region with a temperate climate?

¡Te toca a ti!

Use what you have learned

1 ¿El mar o la montaña?
✔ *Talk about summer or winter vacations*

Work with a classmate. Tell him or her where you like to go on vacation. Tell what you do there and some of the reasons why you enjoy it so much. Take turns.

2 ¡Unas vacaciones maravillosas!
✔ *Talk about different vacation activities*

Work with a classmate. Pretend you each have a million dollars. Take turns describing your millionaire's dream vacation.

3 El esquí
✔ *Talk about skiing*

You are at a café near the slopes of Bariloche in Argentina. You meet an Argentine skier (your partner). Find out as much as you can about each other's skiing habits and abilities.

San Carlos de Bariloche, Argentina

ESCRIBIR

4 Una tarjeta postal

✔ *Write about a summer or winter vacation destination*

Look at these postcards. Choose one. Pretend you spent a week there. Write the postcard to a friend.

Bariloche, Argentina

Cancún, México

ESCRIBIR

5 Irene y José Luis durante un día de julio

It's a typical July day. But Irene is in Santiago de Chile and José Luis is in Santiago de Compostela in Spain. The days are quite different in these two places. Write a comparison between a July day in Santiago de Chile and in Santiago de Compostela. Explain why the days are so different.

Because of the type of weather, Irene's activities on this day are probably different from those of José Luis. Explain what each one is doing. Are they wearing the same clothing or not?

Not everything is different, however. What are Irene and José Luis both doing on this July day in two different places in spite of the different weather?

Writing Strategy

Comparing and contrasting
Before you begin to write a comparison of people, places, or things, you must be aware of how they are alike and different. When you compare, you are emphasizing similarities; when you contrast, you are emphasizing differences. Making a diagram or a list of similarities and differences is a good way to organize your details before you begin to write.

Vocabulario

1 Identifiquen.

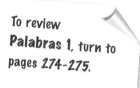

1.

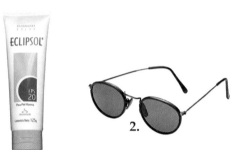

2.

3.

4.

5.

To review **Palabras 1**, turn to pages 274-275.

2 Contesten.

6. ¿Qué tiempo hace en el verano?

3 Completen.

7. La esquiadora lleva un _____ cuando hace frío y nieva mucho.

8. Para esquiar es necesario tener (uno necesita) _____ y bastones.

9. Los esquiadores tomaron el _____ para subir la montaña.

10. Los esquiadores que no esquían bien bajan la _____ para principiantes.

To review **Palabras 2**, turn to pages 278-279.

Estructura

4 **Completen con el pretérito.**

11. Él _____ en el mar. (nadar)
12. Sus amigos _____ en la piscina. (nadar)
13. Y tú, ¿_____ en el agua? (esquiar)
14. No. Yo _____ el sol. (tomar)
15. Nosotros _____ toda la tarde en la playa. (pasar)
16. Y ustedes, ¿_____ a la playa también? (ir)

5 **Escriban en el pretérito.**

17. Juego al fútbol.
18. Sí, empiezo a jugar.

6 **Escriban con un pronombre.**

19. No tengo *mis anteojos de sol.*
20. Compré *la loción bronceadora* en la farmacia.
21. Tomás tomó *las fotografías.* Yo, no.
22. Invitamos *a José* a ir a la playa.
23. Ella compró *el bañador* en El Corte Inglés.

To review the preterite, turn to pages *282* and *288*.

To review direct object pronouns, turn to page *286*.

Cultura

7 **¿Sí o no?**

24. Un balneario es una estación de esquí.
25. Muchos países de habla española tienen playas fabulosas.

To review this cultural information, turn to page *292*.

Tell all you can about this illustration.

Describing the beach

el balneario	la arena	el mar
la playa	la ola	la piscina, la alberca

Describing summer weather

el verano	el cielo	Hace buen (mal) tiempo.
la nube	Hace (Hay) sol.	Llueve.
estar nublado	Hace calor.	El sol brilla.

Identifying beach gear

el traje de baño, el bañador	los anteojos (las gafas)	el esquí acuático
la loción bronceadora,	de sol	la plancha de vela
la crema protectora	la toalla playera	la tabla hawaiana

Describing summer and beach activities

la natación	nadar	esquiar en el agua	pasar el fin de semana
el buceo	tomar el sol	bucear	practicar el surfing

Describing a tennis game

el tenis	el/la tenista	la red	jugar (al) tenis
la cancha de tenis (al	la raqueta	singles	golpear la pelota
aire libre, cubierta)	la pelota	dobles	

Describing a ski resort

la estación de esquí	el ticket, el boleto	la pista	el/la principiante
la ventanilla, la	el/la esquiador(a)	el telesquí, el telesilla	
boletería	la montaña	el/la experto(a)	

Identifying ski gear

el esquí	el bastón	el guante
la bota	el anorak	

Describing winter activities

esquiar	tomar (subir en)	bajar
	el telesilla	la pista

Describing winter weather

el invierno	el grado	Hace frío.
la nieve	bajo cero	Nieva.
la temperatura		

Other useful expressions

ayer	por encima de

> ### How well do you know your vocabulary?
> - Choose one season—**el verano, el invierno**—from the list.
> - Have a classmate make up sentences that tell about that season.

VIDEOTUR

Episodio 9

In this video episode, you will join Claudia and Alberto in a ski shop. See page 500 for more information

Capítulo 10

Diversiones culturales

Objetivos

In this chapter you will learn to:

❖ discuss movies, museums, and theater
❖ discuss cultural events
❖ relate more past actions or events
❖ tell for whom something is done
❖ discuss some dating customs in the United States and compare them with those in Spanish-speaking countries
❖ talk about cultural activities that are popular in the Spanish-speaking world

Rufino Tamayo *Músicos*

Al cine

el cine

la taquilla, la boletería

la cola, la fila

Hay una cola delante de la taquilla.
Los amigos van a ver una película (un film).
Compran sus entradas (boletos).
Van a la sesión de las cuatro de la tarde.

En el cine

la pantalla

el film, la película

la fila

la butaca

Cine Apolo

LA CELESTINA
MENOR   2.73 CST
● 5:00PM   0.27 TAX
              3.00 TOT
004226   16:5

la entrada,
el boleto

El joven vio una película.
Vio una película americana.
No la vio en versión original (en inglés).
La vio doblada al español.
Si la película no está doblada, lleva subtítulos.

Luego salió del cine.
¡Ay! Perdió el autobús (la guagua, el camión).

Como perdió el autobús, el joven fue
    a la estación de metro.
Subió al metro en la estación Insurgentes.
Volvió a casa en el metro.

Nota The verb **salir** has several uses.
Note the following meanings the verb can convey.

Diego salió anoche.
Diego went out last night.
Diego left last night.

Diego salió con Sandra.
Diego went out with (dated) Sandra.

Todo salió muy bien.
Everything turned out fine.

¿Qué palabra necesito?

1 Historieta **Al cine** Contesten.

1. ¿Fue Eduardo al cine?
2. ¿Compró su entrada en la taquilla?
3. ¿Fue a la sesión de las ocho de la tarde?
4. ¿Tomó una butaca en una fila cerca de la pantalla?
5. ¿Vio la película en versión original o doblada?
6. ¿A qué hora salió del cine?
7. ¿Perdió el autobús?
8. ¿Volvió a casa en el metro?

Málaga, España

2 Historieta **En la taquilla**
Escojan.

1. La gente hace cola delante de ____.
   a. la pantalla   **b.** la fila   **c.** la taquilla
2. Compran ____ en la taquilla.
   a. butacas   **b.** películas   **c.** entradas
3. En el cine presentan o dan ____ americana.
   a. una entrada   **b.** una película   **c.** una novela
4. No es la versión original de la película. Está ____ al español.
   a. entrada   **b.** doblada   **c.** en fila
5. Los clientes entran en el cine y toman ____.
   a. una pantalla   **b.** una entrada   **c.** una butaca
6. Proyectan la película en ____.
   a. la pantalla   **b.** la butaca   **c.** la taquilla

Una taquilla, España

3 **Lo mismo** Den un sinónimo.

1. la película
2. el autobús
3. la boletería
4. la entrada

4 **Vamos al cine.** Work with a classmate. Pretend you and your partner are making plans to go out tonight to a Spanish-language movie. Discuss your plans together.

La estación de metro en la Puerta del Sol, Madrid

5 **Una encuesta** Work in groups of four. Conduct a survey. Find out the answers to the following:

- ¿Eres muy aficionado(a) al cine o no?
- ¿Cuántas películas ves en una semana?
- ¿Ves las películas en el cine o las alquilas (rentas) en una tienda de videos?

Compile the information and report the results of your survey to the class.

En el museo

el mural

el cuadro

la estatua

la escultora

el artista

Los turistas fueron al museo.
Vieron una exposición de arte.

En el teatro

el teatro

el escenario

la actriz

el actor

el telón

la escena

El autor escribió la obra.
Escribió una obra teatral.
García Lorca escribió la obra
Bodas de Sangre.

Los actores dieron una representación
   de *Bodas de Sangre*.
Los actores entraron en escena.
El público vio el espectáculo.
Les gustó mucho (el espectáculo).
Todos aplaudieron. Los actores
   recibieron aplausos.

Después de la función, el público
   salió del teatro.

¿Qué palabra necesito?

6 Historieta En el museo

Contesten según se indica.

1. ¿Adónde fueron los turistas? (al museo)
2. ¿Qué vieron? (una exposición de arte)
3. ¿Vieron unos cuadros de Botero, el artista colombiano? (sí)
4. ¿Qué más vieron de Botero? (unas estatuas en bronce)
5. ¿Les gustó la obra de Botero? (sí, mucho)

7 ¿Qué es? Identifiquen.

1.

2.

3.

4.

5.

6.

7.

8.

9.

8 **Historieta** **Una noche en Buenos Aires**
Contesten según se indica.

1. ¿Quiénes salieron anoche?
   (Susana y sus amigos)
2. ¿Adónde fueron?
   (al Teatro Colón)
3. ¿Qué vieron? (una obra
   de García Lorca)
4. ¿Quién escribió la obra?
   (García Lorca)
5. ¿Le gustó la representación
   al público? (sí, mucho)
6. ¿Quiénes recibieron aplausos?
   (los actores)
7. ¿A qué hora salieron del teatro
   Susana y sus amigos? (a eso de
   las diez y media)
8. ¿Cómo volvieron a casa?
   (en taxi)

El Teatro Colón, Buenos Aires

9 **La palabra, por favor.**
Escojan.

1. El ____ escribió la obra.
   a. actor   **b.** autor   **c.** artista
2. Cuando empieza el espectáculo, levantan ____.
   a. la pantalla   **b.** el telón   **c.** el escenario
3. El ____ es magnífico y muy bonito. Es una
   obra de arte.
   a. autor   **b.** público   **c.** escenario
4. Los ____ actuaron muy bien.
   a. autores   **b.** actores   **c.** escenarios
5. Al público le gustó mucho la representación
   y todos ____.
   a. aplaudieron   **b.** salieron
   c. entraron en escena

10 **Me gusta ir al museo.** Work with a classmate.
One of you likes to go to museums and the other
one finds them boring but really likes the theater.
Discuss the reasons for your preferences.

El interior del Teatro Colón, Buenos Aires

Estructura

Pretérito de los verbos en -er e -ir
Telling what people did

1. You have already learned the preterite forms of regular **-ar** verbs. Study the preterite forms of regular **-er** and **-ir** verbs. Note that they also form the preterite by dropping the infinitive ending and adding the appropriate endings to the stem. The preterite endings of regular **-er** and **-ir** verbs are the same.

INFINITIVE	comer	volver	vivir	subir	ENDINGS
STEM	com-	volv-	viv-	sub-	
yo	comí	volví	viví	subí	-í
tú	comiste	volviste	viviste	subiste	-iste
él, ella, Ud.	comió	volvió	vivió	subió	-ió
nosotros(as)	comimos	volvimos	vivimos	subimos	-imos
vosotros(as)	comisteis	volvisteis	vivisteis	subisteis	-isteis
ellos, ellas, Uds.	comieron	volvieron	vivieron	subieron	-ieron

2. The preterite forms of the verbs **dar** and **ver** are the same as those of regular **-er** and **-ir** verbs.

INFINITIVE	dar	ver
yo	di	vi
tú	diste	viste
él, ella, Ud.	dio	vio
nosotros(as)	dimos	vimos
vosotros(as)	disteis	visteis
ellos, ellas, Uds.	dieron	vieron

3. Remember that the preterite is used to tell about an event that happened at a specific time in the past.

> **Ellos salieron anoche.**
> **Ayer no comí en casa. Comí en el restaurante.**
> **¿Viste una película la semana pasada?**

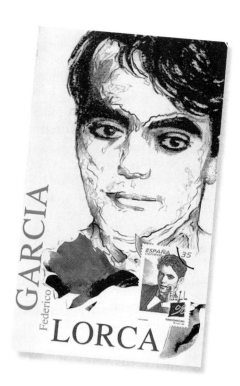

¿Cómo lo digo?

11 **Historieta** Una fiesta fabulosa
Contesten.

1. ¿Dio Carlos una fiesta?
2. ¿Dio la fiesta para celebrar el cumpleaños de Teresa?
3. ¿Escribió Carlos las invitaciones?
4. ¿Recibieron las invitaciones los amigos de Teresa?
5. ¿Vio Teresa a todos sus amigos en la fiesta?
6. ¿Le dieron regalos a Teresa?
7. ¿Recibió Teresa muchos regalos?
8. Durante la fiesta, ¿comieron todos?
9. ¿A qué hora salieron de la fiesta?
10. ¿Volvieron a casa muy tarde?

Málaga, España

12 En la escuela Contesten personalmente.

1. ¿A qué hora saliste de casa esta mañana?
2. ¿Perdiste el bus escolar o no?
3. ¿Aprendiste algo nuevo en la clase de español?
4. ¿Escribiste una composición en la clase de inglés?
5. ¿Comprendiste la nueva ecuación en la clase de álgebra?
6. ¿Viste un video en la clase de español?
7. ¿A qué hora saliste de la escuela?
8. ¿A qué hora volviste a casa?

El Teatro Ayacucho, Caracas, Venezuela

13 Al cine

Sigan el modelo.

> **ir al cine** ⟶
> —**¿Fuiste al cine?**
> —**Sí, fui al cine.**

1. ver una película en versión original
2. comprender la película en versión original
3. aplaudir
4. perder el autobús
5. volver a casa un poco tarde

Estructura

14 **Historieta** **Al cine y al restaurante**
Contesten.

1. ¿Salieron tú y tus amigos anoche?
2. ¿Vieron una película?
3. ¿Qué vieron?
4. ¿A qué hora salieron del cine?
5. ¿Fueron a un restaurante?
6. ¿Qué comiste?
7. Y tus amigos, ¿qué comieron?
8. ¿A qué hora volviste a casa?

15 **Historieta** **En la clase de español**
Completen.

—Ayer en la clase de español, ¿ __1__ (aprender) tú una palabra nueva?

—¿Una? __2__ (Aprender) muchas.

—¿Les __3__ (dar) un examen el profesor?

—Sí, nos __4__ (dar) un examen.

—¿ __5__ (Salir) ustedes bien en el examen?

—Pues, yo __6__ (salir) bien pero otros no __7__ (salir) muy bien.

—Entonces tú __8__ (recibir) una nota buena, ¿no?

Caracas, Venezuela

16 **Ayer** Work in groups of four. Find out what you all did yesterday. Ask each other lots of questions and tabulate your answers. What did most of you do? Use the following words.

volver salir ver estudiar
tomar ir escribir comer
comprar mirar nadar

*For more practice using words from **Palabras 1** and **2** and the preterite, do Activity 10 on page H11 at the end of this book.*

Complementos le, les

Telling what you do for others

1. You have already learned the direct object pronouns **lo, la, los,** and **las.** Now you will learn the indirect object pronouns **le** and **les.** Observe the difference between a direct object and an indirect object in the following sentences.

le   **a Carmen**

Juan <u>lanzó la pelota</u>. Juan <u>lanzó la pelota</u> .

In the preceding sentences, **la pelota** is the direct object because it is the direct receiver of the action of the verb **lanzó** *(threw)*. **Carmen** is the indirect object because it indicates "to whom" the ball was thrown.

2. The indirect object pronoun **le** is both masculine and feminine. **Les** is used for both the feminine and masculine plural. **Le** and **les** are often used along with a noun phrase—**a Juan, a sus amigos.**

> **María le dio un regalo a Juan.**
> **María les dio un regalo a sus amigos.**
>
> **Juan le dio un regalo a María.**
> **Juan les dio un regalo a sus amigas.**

3. Since **le** and **les** can refer to more than one person, they are often clarified as follows:

Le hablé $\begin{cases} \textbf{a él.} \\ \textbf{a ella.} \\ \textbf{a Ud.} \end{cases}$ **Les hablé** $\begin{cases} \textbf{a ellos.} \\ \textbf{a ellas.} \\ \textbf{a Uds.} \end{cases}$

¿Cómo lo digo?

Madrid, España

17 **¿Qué o a quién?** Indiquen el complemento directo y el indirecto.

1. Carlos recibió la carta.
2. Les vendimos la casa a ellos.
3. Vimos a Isabel ayer.
4. Le hablamos a Tomás.
5. ¿Quién tiene el periódico?
   Tomás lo tiene.
6. El profesor nos explicó la lección.
7. Ella le dio los apuntes a su profesor.
8. Ellos vieron la película en el cine.

18 Historieta Pobre Eugenio

Contesten según la foto.

1. ¿Qué le duele?
2. ¿Qué más le duele?
3. ¿Quién le examina la garganta?
4. ¿Quién le da la diagnosis?
5. ¿Qué le da la médica?
6. ¿Quién le da los medicamentos?

19 Sí que le hablé. Contesten.

1. ¿Le hablaste a Rafael?
2. ¿Le hablaste por teléfono?
3. ¿Le diste las noticias?
4. ¿Y él les dio las noticias a sus padres?
5. ¿Les escribió a sus padres?
6. ¿Les escribió en inglés o en español?

20 Historieta Tiene que tener la dirección.

Completen.

—¿ __1__ hablaste a Juan ayer?

—Sí, __2__ hablé por teléfono y __3__ hablé a Sandra también.

  __4__ hablé a los dos.

—¿ __5__ diste la dirección de Maricarmen?

—No, porque Adriana __6__ dio la dirección. Y __7__ dio su

  número de teléfono también.

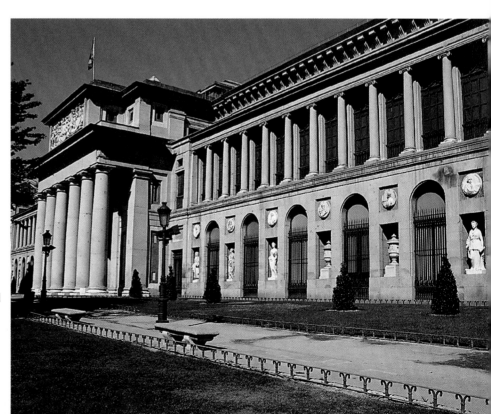

El Museo del Prado, Madrid

21 **Historieta** **Juan es aficionado al arte.**
Contesten.

1. ¿A Juan le interesa el arte?
2. ¿Le gusta ir a los museos?
3. ¿Le encantan las exposiciones de arte?
4. ¿Le gusta mucho la obra de Velázquez?
5. ¿Le gustan también los cuadros de Goya?
6. A sus amigos, ¿les interesa también el arte?
7. ¿Les gustan las obras de los muralistas mexicanos?

La fragua de Vulcano
de Diego Velázquez

22 **Regalos para todos** Work in pairs. Tell what each of the following
people is like. Then tell what you buy or give to each one as a gift.

    mi mamá
    mi hermano
    mi profesor(a) de español
    mi papá
    mis abuelos
    mi amigo(a)

Andas bien. ¡Adelante!

¿Saliste?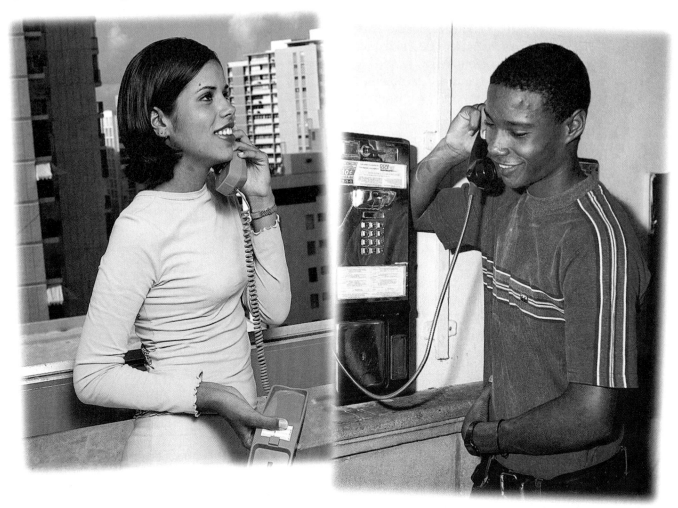

Paco Hola, Julia. Te llamé por teléfono anoche y no contestaste.

Julia ¿Ah, sí? ¿A qué hora me llamaste?

Paco A las siete y pico.

Julia Ay, no volví a casa hasta las ocho y media.

Paco ¿Adónde fuiste?

Julia Pues, fui al cine con Felipe.

Paco ¿Ustedes fueron al cine y tú volviste a casa a las ocho y media? ¿Cómo puede ser?

Julia Pues, fuimos a la sesión de las cinco. Y después del cine comimos en Pizza Perfecta.

¿Comprendes?

Contesten.

1. ¿A quién telefoneó Paco anoche?
2. ¿Ella contestó?
3. ¿A qué hora la llamó Paco?
4. ¿A qué hora volvió Julia a casa?
5. ¿Adónde fue?
6. ¿Con quién fue?
7. ¿A qué sesión fueron?
8. ¿Dónde comieron?

Vamos a hablar más

A **El viernes pasado y el viernes que viene** Get together with a group of classmates. Tell one another what you did last Friday night. Then tell what you're going to do next Friday night.

B **Un viaje escolar** The Spanish Club is going on a field trip. It's just in the planning stages. You may go to a museum that's showing the works of an Hispanic artist, a Spanish-language movie, a play in Spanish, or a Mexican or Spanish restaurant. Your Spanish teacher wants some input from you. With your classmates, discuss where you want to go and why.

C **¿Por qué volviste tan tarde?** You got home really late last night. One of your parents (your partner) wants to know why. He or she will ask a lot of questions. You'd better have some good answers!

Pronunciación

Las consonantes j, g

The Spanish **j** sound does not exist in English. In Spain, the **j** sound is very guttural. It comes from the throat. In Latin America, the **j** sound is much softer. Repeat the following.

ja	je	ji	jo	ju
Jaime	Jesús	Jiménez	joven	jugar
hija	garaje	ají	viejo	junio
roja			trabajo	julio
			ojos	

G in combination with **e** or **i** (**ge, gi**) has the same sound as **j**. For this reason you must pay particular attention to the spelling of the words with **je, ji, ge,** and **gi**. Repeat the following.

ge	gi
general	biología
gente	alergia
generoso	original
Insurgentes	

Repeat the following sentences.

> **El hijo del viejo general José trabaja en junio en Gijón.**
> **El jugador juega en el gimnasio.**
> **El joven Jaime toma jugo de naranja.**

Lecturas culturales

Reading Strategy

Recognizing text organization Before you read a passage, try to figure out how the text is organized. If you can follow the organization of a text, you will understand the main ideas more quickly and be able to look for certain ideas and information more easily.

Dating

Algunas diferencias culturales son muy interesantes. Y las diferencias culturales pueden tener una influencia en la lengua que hablamos. Por ejemplo, *dating, boyfriend* y *girlfriend* son palabras que usamos mucho en inglés, ¿no? Y son palabras que no tienen equivalente en español. ¿Cómo es posible? Pues, vamos a hablar con Verónica. Ella es de Perú.

—Verónica, ¿saliste anoche?

—Sí, salí con un grupo de amigos de la escuela.

—¿Adónde fueron?

—Fuimos al cine. Vimos una película muy buena. Fue una película americana. La vimos en versión original con subtítulos en español.

—Verónica, ¿no sales a veces sola con un muchacho, con un amigo de la escuela?

—Pues, no mucho. Generalmente salimos en grupo. Pero es algo que está cambiando[1]. Está cambiando poco a poco[2]. Hoy en día una pareja[3] joven puede salir a solas. Podemos ir a un café, por ejemplo, a tomar un refresco. A veces vamos al cine o sólo damos un paseo[4] por el parque. Pero, para nosotros, es algo bastante nuevo.

[1]cambiando *changing*
[2]poco a poco *little by little*
[3]pareja *couple*
[4]damos un paseo *take a walk*

Buenos Aires, Argentina

Teatro Colón, Lima, Perú

Marbella, España

¿Comprendes?

A Dating Contesten.
1. ¿En qué lengua usamos las palabras *dating, boyfriend* y *girlfriend?*
2. ¿Tienen equivalente en español?
3. ¿Hay mucho *dating* entre los jóvenes de Latinoamérica y España?
4. ¿Ahora empiezan a salir en parejas?
5. Por lo general, ¿cómo salen?
6. ¿Con quién salió Verónica?
7. ¿Adónde fueron?
8. ¿Qué vieron?

B Aquí Contesten personalmente.
1. Donde tú vives, ¿salen los jóvenes con más frecuencia en grupos o en parejas?
2. Y tú, ¿sales a veces con sólo un(a) muchacho(a)?
3. ¿Adónde van?
4. ¿Pueden salir durante la semana?
5. ¿Qué noche salen?
6. ¿A qué hora tienes que estar en casa?

Lectura opcional ❶

La zarzuela

Hay un género teatral exclusivamente español. Es la zarzuela. La zarzuela es una obra dramática muy ligera. No es profunda. Generalmente tiene un argumento[1] gracioso.

La zarzuela es un tipo de opereta. A veces, durante la presentación, los actores hablan y a veces cantan.

[1]argumento *plot*

Una zarzuela,
Madrid, España

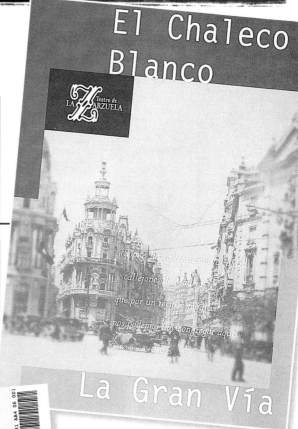

El Chaleco Blanco

La Gran Vía

¿Comprendes?

La zarzuela Digan que sí o que no.
1. La zarzuela es una novela española.
2. La zarzuela es un tipo de obra teatral.
3. En una zarzuela los actores no hablan, sólo bailan.
4. Una zarzuela es un tipo de opereta.
5. Los actores en una zarzuela hablan y cantan.
6. El tema o argumento de una zarzuela es siempre serio y profundo.

Lectura opcional ②

El Palacio de Bellas Artes, México

El baile

El Ballet Folklórico de México goza de fama mundial. El espectáculo que presenta el Ballet Folklórico todos los domingos y miércoles en el Palacio de Bellas Artes es uno de los shows más populares de la Ciudad de México. La compañía baila una variedad de danzas regionales de México. A veces la coreografía del Ballet Folklórico de México es muy graciosa y divertida.

Hay también el Ballet Folklórico Nacional de México. Esta compañía presenta un programa auténtico y clásico de danzas mexicanas regionales en el Teatro de la Ciudad.

El Ballet Folklórico, México

¿Comprendes?

Una comparación Expliquen la diferencia entre el Ballet Folklórico de México y el Ballet Folklórico Nacional de México.

Conexiones

Las bellas artes

La música

Music does not attempt to reproduce what we see in the world in such a tangible way as do painting and literature. Music is, and has been, however, an integral part of the daily lives of people in even the most primitive cultures.

First let's take a look at the many cognates that exist in the language of music. Then let's read some general information about music. Finally, let's take a look at some special music of the Hispanic world.

la danza

la orquesta sinfónica

la orquesta

la ópera

el coro

la banda

In addition, many names of musical instruments are cognates: **el piano, el órgano, el violín, la viola, la guitarra, la trompeta, el clarinete, el saxofón, la flauta, el trombón.**

Música y músicos

Instrumentos musicales

Clasificamos los instrumentos musicales en cuatro grupos. Son los instrumentos de cuerda, los instrumentos de viento, los instrumentos de metal y los instrumentos de percusión. Dividimos la orquesta en secciones de cuerda, viento, metal y percusión.

Una orquesta y una banda

¿Cuál es la diferencia entre una orquesta y una banda? En una banda no hay instrumentos de cuerda. No hay violines ni violas, por ejemplo.

La ópera

La ópera es una obra teatral. Pero en una ópera los actores no hablan. Cantan al acompañamiento de una orquesta.

La música popular

Además de[1] la música clásica hay muchas variaciones de música popular. De influencia afroamericana hay jazz y «blues». Hay «reggae» de Jamaica.

De las islas hispanohablantes de las Antillas hay salsa y merengue. Hay una relación íntima entre el canto (la canción) y la danza (el baile) en la música latinoamericana. Por ejemplo, en la lengua quechua del área andina, una sola palabra—taqui—significa «canción y baile».

Ejemplos de la música típica de Latinoamérica

Un instrumento muy popular entre los indios andinos es la flauta. El yaraví es una canción muy popular. En quechua esta palabra significa «lamento». Es una canción triste. A veces cantan un yaraví pero a veces sólo lo tocan con la flauta sin cantar.

Un instrumento popular de los indígenas de Guatemala es la marimba. Hay orquestas de marimba que van de un pueblo a otro para tocar en las fiestas locales.

La banda mariachi es un pequeño grupo de músicos ambulantes. Tocan guitarras, violines y trompetas. La música mariachi tiene su origen en Guadalajara, México, en el estado de Jalisco.

La salsa, el merengue y el mambo de Cuba, Puerto Rico y la República Dominicana son canciones y bailes.

El cante jondo es una canción triste y espontánea de los gitanos[2] andaluces. Es apasionada y emocional como lo es también el baile flamenco.

[1]Además de *In addition to*   [2]gitanos *gypsies*

Cuzco, Perú

Guatemala

México

¿Comprendes?

A ¿Cuáles son? Identifiquen.
1. algunos instrumentos de cuerda
2. algunos instrumentos de viento
3. algunos instrumentos de metal

B Distintos tipos de música Expliquen la diferencia entre una orquesta y una banda.

C ¿Sabes? Contesten.
1. ¿Qué es una ópera?
2. ¿Cuáles son algunos tipos de música popular?
3. ¿Entre qué hay una relación íntima en la música latinoamericana?

Murcia, España

¡Te toca a ti!

Use what you have learned

HABLAR

1

Diversiones
✔ *Discuss movies, plays, and museums*

Work with a classmate. Pretend you're on vacation in Cancún, México. You meet a Mexican teenager (your partner) who's interested in what you do for fun in your free time **(cuando tienes tiempo libre).** Tell him or her about your leisure activities. Then your partner will tell you what he or she does.

HABLAR

2

Una visita al museo
✔ *Ask and answer questions about a museum visit*

Work in groups of three or four. Several of you spent the day at a museum last Saturday. Other friends have some questions. Describe your museum visit and be sure to answer all their questions.

ESCRIBIR

3

Información, por favor.
✔ *Write for information about cultural events*

You're going to spend a month in the Spanish-speaking city of your choice. Write a letter or an e-mail to the tourist office **(la oficina de turismo)** asking for information about cultural events during your stay. Be sure to mention your age, what kind of cultural activities you like, and the dates of your stay.

ESCRIBIR
4 Un anuncio

✔ *Make a poster for a play*

Prepare a poster in Spanish for your school play. Give all the necessary information to advertise **el espectáculo.**

ESCRIBIR
5 Un reportaje

Your local newspaper has asked you to write an article to attract Spanish-speaking readers to a cultural event taking place in your hometown. You can write about a real or fictitious event. You have seen the event and you really liked it. Tell why as you try to convince or persuade your readers to go see it.

Vocabulario

1 Completen.

1. Si mucha gente quiere ver la película, hay una ____ delante de la taquilla.
2. Un boleto para ir al cine es una ____.
3. Hay una ____ a las cuatro y otra a las siete de la tarde.
4. No, la película no está ____, pero no hay problema porque lleva subtítulos.
5. Él perdió el autobús y tomó el ____. El ____ es un tren subterráneo.

To review **Palabras 1**, turn to pages 306–307.

2 Identifiquen.

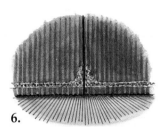

6.

7.

8.

9.

To review **Palabras 2**, turn to pages 310–311.

10.

Estructura

3 **Escojan.**

11. Yo ____ una hamburguesa con papas fritas.
    a. comió   **b.** comí   **c.** comimos
12. Ellos ____ del cine.
    a. volvimos   **b.** volvió   **c.** volvieron
13. ¿Cuándo ____ (tú) en Bogotá?
    a. vivió   **b.** viviste   **c.** volvisteis
14. Los actores ____ muchos aplausos.
    a. recibieron   **b.** recibió   **c.** recibiste
15. Él lo ____ en la escuela.
    a. vi   **b.** vieron   **c.** vio

To review the preterite, turn to page 314.

4 **Completen con un pronombre.**

16. María ____ dio un regalo a su amigo Felipe.
17. Ella ____ devolvió el balón a la otra jugadora.
18. A los amigos ____ gustó mucho la película.

To review **le** and **les**, turn to page 317.

Cultura

5 **Contesten.**

19. ¿Cuáles son dos palabras inglesas que no tienen equivalente en español?
20. Por lo general, ¿cómo salen los jóvenes en los países hispanos?

To review this cultural information, turn to page 322.

Los amigos salen juntos.

Tell all you can about this illustration.

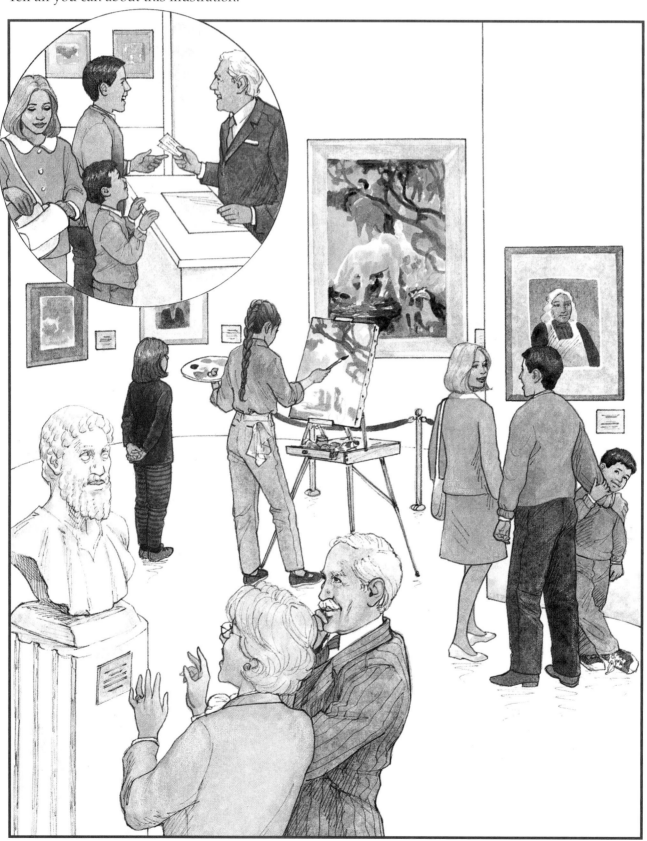

Discussing a movie theater

el cine	la butaca	con subtítulos
la taquilla, la boletería	la fila	doblado(a)
la entrada, el boleto	la pantalla	
la sesión	la película, el film	
la cola	en versión original	

Describing a museum visit

el museo	la estatua
la exposición	el/la artista
el mural	el/la escultor(a)
el cuadro	

Describing a play

el teatro	el telón	la representación
la escena	el actor	la obra teatral
el escenario	la actriz	el público

Describing cultural events and activities

una diversión cultural	entrar en escena
ver una película (un espectáculo)	aplaudir
dar una representación	salir del teatro

How well do you know your vocabulary?

- Choose the name of a cultural event or an artistic profession.
- Have a classmate tell you his or her favorite in the category you chose.

Discussing transportation

perder el autobús (la guagua, el camión)
la estación de metro

Other useful expressions

el/la joven
delante de
luego

Episodio 10

In this video episode, you will join Vicky and Alejandra as they discuss the meaning of "culture." See page 501 for more information.

Capítulo 11

Un viaje en avión

Objetivos

In this chapter you will learn to:

- ❖ check in for a flight
- ❖ talk about some services on board the plane
- ❖ get through the airport after deplaning
- ❖ tell what you or others are currently doing
- ❖ tell what you know and whom you know
- ❖ discuss the importance of air travel in South America

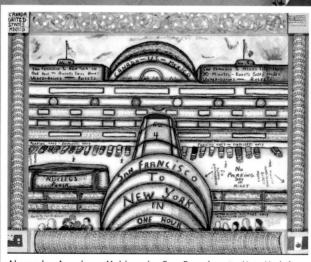

Alexander Aramburo Maldonado *San Francisco to New York in one hour*

Vocabulario

Antes del vuelo

el aeropuerto

el maletero, la maletera

el taxi

¿Me permite ver su pasaporte, por favor? ¿Y su boleto?

el agente

la agente

el billete, el boleto

el pasaporte

el mostrador

la pantalla de salidas y llegadas

La agente revisa el pasaporte y el boleto.

el número del vuelo

la puerta de salida

la tarjeta de embarque

el destino

la sección de no fumar

el número del asiento

el control de seguridad

el equipaje de mano

Los pasajeros están pasando
por el control de seguridad.

el talón

las maletas

el equipaje

la báscula

Clarita hace un viaje en avión.
Hace un viaje a la América del Sur.
Toma un vuelo a Lima.
Clarita está facturando su equipaje.
Pone sus maletas en la báscula.
El agente pone un talón en cada maleta.

14

8:30

la puerta de salida,
la sala de salida

Los pasajeros están esperando en la puerta de
salida.
El avión sale de la puerta número catorce.
El vuelo sale a tiempo.
No sale tarde. No sale con una demora.

Vocabulario

¿Qué palabra necesito?

1 **Historieta** **En el aeropuerto**

Contesten.

1. ¿Hace Lupe un viaje a la América del Sur?
2. ¿Está en el aeropuerto?
3. ¿Está hablando con la agente de la línea aérea?
4. ¿Dónde pone sus maletas?
5. ¿Está facturando su equipaje a Bogotá?
6. ¿Pone la agente un talón en cada maleta?
7. ¿Revisa la agente su boleto?
8. ¿Tiene Lupe su tarjeta de embarque?
9. ¿De qué puerta va a salir su vuelo?

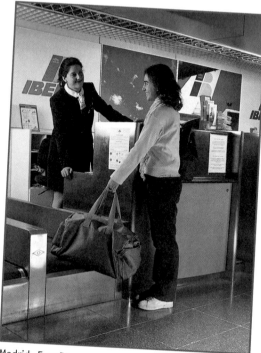

Madrid, España

2 **La tarjeta de embarque**

Den la información siguiente.

1. el nombre de la línea aérea
2. el número del vuelo
3. el destino del vuelo
4. la hora de embarque
5. la fecha del vuelo, el día que sale

3 **¿Dónde está su asiento?** Completen según la tarjeta de embarque.

1. ¿Cuál es la letra del asiento que tiene el pasajero?
2. ¿En qué fila está el asiento?
3. ¿De qué puerta sale el avión?
4. ¿Tiene que conservar el pasajero la tarjeta durante el vuelo?
5. ¿Está su asiento en la sección de fumar o de no fumar?

4 **Historieta** **Antes de la salida** Escojan.

1. ____ indica el asiento que tiene el pasajero a bordo del avión.
   a. El talón   **b.** La tarjeta de embarque   **c.** El boleto
2. Bogotá es ____ del vuelo.
   a. el número   **b.** la ciudad   **c.** el destino
3. Inspeccionan el equipaje de mano de los pasajeros en ____.
   a. el mostrador de la línea aérea   **b.** el control de seguridad
   c. la puerta de salida
4. El vuelo para Bogotá sale ____ número cinco.
   a. del mostrador   **b.** del control   **c.** de la puerta
5. Los pasajeros están ____ por el control de seguridad.
   a. saliendo   **b.** facturando   **c.** pasando

5 **En el aeropuerto** Work with a classmate. You're checking in at the airport for your flight to Quito, Ecuador. Have a conversation with the airline agent (your partner) at the ticket counter.

6 **Un vuelo** Work with a classmate. Look at the following photograph. You are a passenger on this flight. Tell as much as you can about your experience at the airport.

 *For more practice using words from **Palabras 1**, do Activity 11 on page H12 at the end of this book.*

Después del vuelo

Cuando los pasajeros desembarcan, tienen que pasar por el control de pasaportes.
Tienen que pasar por el control de pasaportes cuando llegan de un país extranjero.

el reclamo de equipaje

Los pasajeros están reclamando (recogiendo) sus maletas.

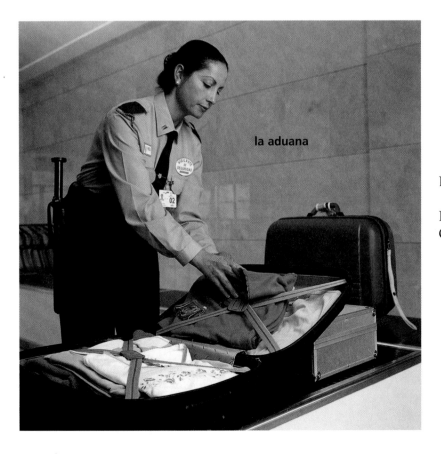

la aduana

La agente de aduana está abriendo las maletas.
Está inspeccionando el equipaje.
Quiere saber lo que está en las maletas.

El vuelo

Un avión está despegando.

Otro avión está aterrizando.

La tripulación

el comandante, el piloto

la copiloto

el asistente de vuelo

la asistente de vuelo

La tripulación trabaja a bordo del avión.
Los asistentes de vuelo les dan la bienvenida
a los pasajeros.

Vocabulario

¿Qué palabra necesito?

7 Historieta La llegada

Contesten.

1. Cuando el avión aterriza, ¿abordan o desembarcan los pasajeros?
2. ¿Tienen que pasar por el control de pasaportes cuando llegan a un país extranjero?
3. ¿Van los pasajeros al reclamo de equipaje?
4. ¿Reclaman su equipaje?
5. ¿Tienen que pasar por la aduana?
6. ¿Abre las maletas el agente?

Málaga, España

8 ¿Sí o no? Digan que sí o que no.

1. El avión aterriza cuando sale.
2. El avión despega cuando llega a su destino.
3. Un vuelo internacional es un vuelo que va a un país extranjero.
4. Los agentes de la línea aérea que trabajan en el mostrador en el aeropuerto son miembros de la tripulación.
5. La tripulación consiste en los empleados que trabajan a bordo del avión.

9 Pareo Busquen una palabra relacionada.

1. asistir   a. la llegada
2. controlar   b. la salida
3. reclamar   c. el asistente, la asistente
4. inspeccionar   d. el despegue
5. despegar   e. el aterrizaje
6. aterrizar   f. el control
7. salir   g. la inspección
8. llegar   h. el reclamo
9. embarcar   i. el vuelo
10. volar   j. el embarque

10 **¿Qué tenemos que hacer?** You're on a flight to Caracas. The person seated next to you (your partner) has never flown before. He or she is confused as to what you have to do when you get off the plane. Be as helpful as possible in answering his or her questions.

11 **Un trabajo** Work with a classmate. You got a part-time job working at the airport because you can speak Spanish. You are called upon to help the Spanish-speaking passengers. In just one hour, the following situations need your attention. Help each of the following passengers.

- A person is leaving on flight 125 for Chicago. He doesn't know if it's leaving on time. Help him out.
- Another passenger is confused. He doesn't know his flight number to New York. Let him know what it is. Be extra helpful and let him know what time his flight leaves.
- Another passenger is in a real hurry. She's changing **(cambiar)** flights and wants to know what gate to go to for her flight to Los Angeles. Tell her.
- A young woman missed her flight and has to change her ticket. Go with her to the airline counter and explain to her what the agent says she has to do.

★Lan Chile

Nombre del Pasajero

RUIZ/CARMEN

Desde	Hacia	Vuelo N°
LPB	SCL	LA961

Clase	Fecha	Hora de Salida
Y	26JAN	1245

Hora de Embarque	Puerta	Asiento
1145	P	9A

Maletas	Peso
2	18

12 **Una tarjeta de embarque** This is a boarding card for a flight you are about to take. Tell a classmate (your partner) all you can about your flight based on the information on the card.

Punta Arenas, Chile

Estructura

Hacer, poner, traer, salir en el presente
Telling what people do

1. The verbs **hacer** *(to do, to make)*, **poner** *(to put)*, **traer** *(to bring)*, and **salir** *(to leave, to go out)* have an irregular **yo** form. The **yo** form has a **g.** All other forms are the same as those of a regular **-er** or **-ir** verb.

INFINITIVE	hacer	poner	traer	salir
yo	hago	pongo	traigo	salgo
tú	haces	pones	traes	sales
él, ella, Ud.	hace	pone	trae	sale
nosotros(as)	hacemos	ponemos	traemos	salimos
vosotros(as)	hacéis	ponéis	traéis	salís
ellos, ellas, Uds.	hacen	ponen	traen	salen

2. The verb **venir** *(to come)* also has an irregular **yo** form. Note that in addition it has a stem change **e → ie** in all forms except **nosotros** and **vosotros**.

> VENIR **vengo vienes viene venimos** *venís* **vienen**

¿Te acuerdas?

The verb **tener** also has a **g** in the **yo** form: **tengo**

3. The verb **hacer** means *to do* or *to make*. The question **¿Qué haces?** or **¿Qué hace usted?** means *What are you doing?* or *What do you do?* In Spanish, you will almost always answer these questions with a different verb.

> **¿Qué haces? Trabajo en el aeropuerto.**

4. The verb **hacer** is used in many idiomatic expressions. An idiomatic expression is one that does not translate directly from one language to another. The expression **hacer un viaje** *(to take a trip)* is an idiomatic expression because in Spanish the verb **hacer** is used, whereas in English we use the verb *to take*. Another idiomatic expression is **hacer la maleta** which means *to pack a suitcase*.

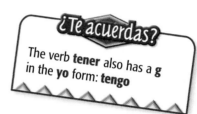

¿Cómo lo digo?

13 **Historieta** **Un viaje en avión** Contesten.

1. ¿Haces un viaje?
2. ¿Haces un viaje a Europa?
3. ¿Haces un viaje a España?
4. ¿Sales para el aeropuerto?
5. ¿Sales en coche o en taxi?
6. ¿Traes equipaje?
7. ¿Pones el equipaje en la maletera del taxi?
8. En el aeropuerto, ¿pones el equipaje en la báscula?
9. ¿En qué vuelo sales?
10. ¿Sales de la puerta de salida número ocho?

Hoyo de Manzanares, Madrid, España

14 **Historieta** **Al aeropuerto** Sigan el modelo.

Ellos hacen un viaje...

Ellos hacen un viaje y nosotros también hacemos un viaje.

1. Ellos salen para el aeropuerto.
2. Ellos salen en taxi.
3. Ellos traen mucho equipaje.
4. Ellos ponen las maletas en la maletera.
5. Ellos salen a las seis.
6. Ellos vienen solos.

15 **Historieta** **Un viaje a Marbella**
Completen.

Yo __1__ (hacer) un viaje a
Marbella. Marbella __2__ (estar) en
la Costa del Sol en el sur de España.
Mi amiga Sandra __3__ (hacer) el
viaje también. Nosotros __4__ (hacer)
el viaje en avión hasta Málaga y
luego __5__ (ir) a tomar el autobús
a Marbella.

—¡Ay, ay, Sandra! Pero tú
   __6__ (traer) mucho equipaje.

—No, yo no __7__ (traer) mucho.

Marbella, España

   __8__ (Tener) sólo dos maletas.

Tú exageras. Tú también __9__ (venir) con mucho equipaje.

—¡Oye! ¿A qué hora __10__ (salir) nuestro vuelo?

—No __11__ (salir) hasta las seis y media. Nosotros __12__ (tener)
   mucho tiempo.

16 **¿Adónde vas y qué haces?** Work with a classmate. Ask one
another about places you go to and what activities you do there.
Following are suggestions for places you may want to find out about:
**la escuela, el mercado, la tienda, el museo, las montañas, la playa,
el supermercado, una exposición de arte, el aeropuerto, el café,
la piscina, el cine.**

17 **¿Qué haces cuando… ?** Work with a classmate. Find out what he
or she does under the following weather conditions. Take turns
asking and answering questions.

nieva

llueve

hace buen tiempo

hay mucho sol

hace mal tiempo

hace frío

hace calor

El presente progresivo
Describing an action in progress

1. The present progressive is used in Spanish to express an action that is presently going on—an action in progress. The present progressive is formed by using the present tense of the verb **estar** and the present participle—*speaking, doing.* To form the present participle of most verbs in Spanish you drop the ending of the infinitive and add **-ando** to the stem of **-ar** verbs and **-iendo** to the stem of **-er** and **-ir** verbs. Study the following forms of the present participle.

INFINITIVE	hablar	llegar	comer	hacer	salir
STEM	habl-	lleg-	com-	hac-	sal-
PARTICIPLE	hablando	llegando	comiendo	haciendo	saliendo

2. Note that the verbs **leer** and **traer** have a **y** in the present participle.

   leyendo   **trayendo**

3. Study the following examples of the present progressive.

   ¿Qué está haciendo Isabel?
   Ahora está esperando el avión.
   Ella está mirando y leyendo su tarjeta de embarque.
   Y yo estoy buscando mi boleto.

¿Cómo lo digo?

18 **Historieta** **En el aeropuerto**
Contesten según se indica.

1. ¿Adónde están llegando los pasajeros? (al aeropuerto)
2. ¿Cómo están llegando? (en taxi)
3. ¿Adónde están viajando? (a Europa)
4. ¿Cómo están haciendo el viaje? (en avión)
5. ¿Dónde están facturando el equipaje? (en el mostrador de la línea aérea)
6. ¿Qué está mirando el agente? (los boletos y los pasaportes)
7. ¿De qué puerta están saliendo los pasajeros para Madrid? (número siete)
8. ¿Qué están abordando? (el avión)

• Tarjeta Iberia Plus Platino

La Tarjeta Iberia Plus Platino es el mayor reconocimiento de Iberia a su confianza. Una distinción exclusiva al acumular 7.000 Puntos Aéreos Básicos¹ en un año² para que disfrute de servicios de prestigio que le llevarán a lo más alto: crédito personal de hasta 1.500 puntos, servicio especial de limusina**, máxima franquicia de equipaje, etc.

** En aquellos aeropuertos donde exista este servicio, en utilización de puntos, para vuelos intercontinentales, en Gran Clase o Business Class.
¹ Puntos Aéreos Básicos son aquellos publicados en tablas sin tener en cuenta las promociones y ofertas.
Para titulares residentes fuera de España:
Tarjeta Iberia Plus Platino   6.500 Puntos Aéreos Básicos
² Periodo comprendido entre el 1 de abril del año en curso al 31 de marzo del siguiente año.

IBERIA plus

19 **¿Qué estás haciendo?** Formen oraciones según el modelo.

Estoy viajando.
No estoy viajando. ◄ viajar ►

1. comer
2. hablar
3. estudiar
4. bailar
5. escribir
6. aprender
7. trabajar
8. hacer un viaje
9. leer
10. salir para España

Saber y conocer en el presente
Telling what and whom you know

1. The verbs **saber** and **conocer** both mean *to know*. Note that like many Spanish verbs they have an irregular **yo** form in the present tense. All other forms are regular.

INFINITIVE	saber	conocer
yo	sé	conozco
tú	sabes	conoces
él, ella, Ud.	sabe	conoce
nosotros(as)	sabemos	conocemos
vosotros(as)	sabéis	conocéis
ellos, ellas, Uds.	saben	conocen

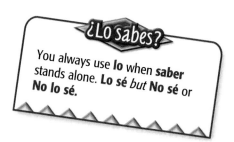

¿Lo sabes?

You always use **lo** when **saber** stands alone. **Lo sé** but **No sé** or **No lo sé.**

2. The verb **saber** means *to know a fact* or *to have information about something*. It also means *to know how to do something*.

> Yo sé el número de nuestro vuelo.
> Pero no sabemos a qué hora sale.
> Yo sé esquiar y jugar tenis.

3. The verb **conocer** means *to know* in the sense of *to be acquainted with*. It is used to talk about people and complex or abstract concepts rather than simple facts.

> Yo conozco a Luis.
> Teodoro conoce muy bien la literatura mexicana.

¿Cómo lo digo?

20 **Mi vuelo** Contesten.

1. ¿Sabes el número de tu vuelo?
2. ¿Sabes a qué hora sale?
3. ¿Sabes de qué puerta va a salir?
4. ¿Sabes la hora de tu llegada a Cancún?
5. ¿Conoces al comandante del vuelo?
6. ¿Conoces a mucha gente en Cancún?

21 **Historieta** Adela Del Olmo

Completen con **saber** o **conocer**.

La bahía de Panamá

PEPITA   Sandra, ¿ __1__ tú a Adela Del Olmo?

SANDRA   Claro que __2__ a Adela. Ella y yo somos muy buenas amigas.

PEPITA   ¿ __3__ tú que ella va a Panamá?

SANDRA   ¿Ella va a Panamá? No, yo no __4__ nada de su viaje. ¿Cuándo va a salir?

PEPITA   Pues, ella no __5__ exactamente qué día va a salir. Pero __6__ que va a salir en junio. Ella va a hacer su reservación mañana. Yo __7__ que ella quiere tomar un vuelo directo.

SANDRA   ¿Adela __8__ Panamá?

PEPITA   Creo que sí. Pero yo no __9__ definitivamente. Pero yo __10__ que ella __11__ a mucha gente en Panamá.

SANDRA   ¿Cómo es que ella __12__ a mucha gente allí?

PEPITA   Pues, tú __13__ que ella tiene parientes en Panamá, ¿no?

SANDRA   Ay, sí, es verdad. Yo __14__ que tiene familia en Panamá porque yo __15__ a su tía Lola. Y __16__ que ella es de Panamá.

22 **Juego** **Lo/La conozco muy bien.** Work with a classmate.

Think of someone in the class whom you know quite well. Tell your partner some things you know about this person. Don't say who it is. Your partner will guess. Take turns.

Andas bien. ¡Adelante!

Está saliendo nuestro vuelo.

Señores pasajeros. Su atención, por favor. La compañía de aviación anuncia la salida de su vuelo ciento seis con destino a Santafé de Bogotá. Embarque inmediato por la puerta de salida número seis.

Antonio ¡Chist, Luisa! Están anunciando la salida de nuestro vuelo.

Luisa Sí, lo sé. ¡Y Dios mío! Antonio, ¿sabes dónde está Fernando?

Antonio Sí, tú conoces a Fernando. Llegó tarde otra vez. Todavía está facturando su equipaje.

Luisa Hablando de equipaje, ¿tienes los talones para nuestras maletas?

Antonio Sí, aquí están. Los tengo con los boletos.

Luisa ¿De qué puerta sale nuestro vuelo?

Antonio De la puerta número seis. Primero tenemos que pasar por el control de seguridad.

Luisa ¡Vamos ya! No vamos a esperar a Fernando. Él puede perder el vuelo si quiere. Pero yo, no.

¿Comprendes?

Contesten.

1. ¿Está Fernando con Antonio y Luisa?
2. ¿Sabe Antonio dónde está Fernando?
3. ¿Qué está haciendo Fernando?
4. ¿Siempre llega tarde?
5. ¿Qué va a perder?

Vamos a hablar más

A **Un billete para Madrid** Work with a classmate. You want to fly from Mexico City to Madrid. Call the airline to get a reservation. Your partner will be the reservation agent. Before you call, think about all the information you will need to give or get from the agent: date of departure, departure time, arrival time in Madrid, flight number, price.

B **Antonio, Antonio** Work with a classmate. You both know Antonio. He's a great guy, but he'll never get to the airport on time. He's always late. Have a conversation about Antonio. Tell some things you know about him that always make him late.

Pronunciación

La consonante r

When a word begins with an **r** (initial position), the **r** is trilled in Spanish. Within a word, **rr** is also trilled. The Spanish trilled **r** sound does not exist in English. Repeat the following.

ra	re	ri	ro	ru
rápido	reclama	Ricardo	Roberto	Rubén
raqueta	recoger	rico	rojo	rubio
párrafo	corre	perrito	perro	
		aterrizar	catarro	

The sound for a single **r** within a word (medial position) does not exist in English either. It is trilled less than the initial **r** or **rr**. Repeat the following.

ra	re	ri	ro	ru
demora	arena	Clarita	maletero	Perú
verano		consultorio	número	Aruba
para			miro	

Repeat the following sentences.

El mesero recoge los refrescos.
El perrito de Rubén corre en la arena.
El maletero corre rápido por el aeropuerto.
El avión para Puerto Rico aterriza con una demora de una hora.
El rico tiene una raqueta en el carro.

Lecturas culturales

El avión en la América del Sur

El avión es un medio de transporte muy importante en la América del Sur. ¿Por qué? Pues, vamos a mirar un mapa del continente sudamericano. Van a ver que es un continente inmenso. Por consiguiente[1], toma mucho tiempo viajar de una ciudad a otra, sobre todo por tierra.

En la mayoría de los casos es imposible viajar de un lugar a otro por tierra. ¿Por qué? Porque es imposible cruzar[2] los picos de los Andes o la selva (jungla) tropical del río Amazonas. Por eso, a todas horas del día y de la noche, los aviones de muchas líneas aéreas están sobrevolando[3] el continente. Hay vuelos nacionales que enlazan[4] una ciudad con otra en el mismo país. Y hay vuelos internacionales que enlazan un país con otro.

[1]Por consiguiente *Consequently*
[2]cruzar *to cross*
[3]sobrevolando *flying over*
[4]enlazan *connect*

Reading Strategy

Identifying the main idea When reading, it is important to identify the main idea the author is expressing. Each paragraph usually discusses a different idea. The main idea is often found in the first or second sentence of a paragraph. Go through the reading quickly to find the main idea in each paragraph. Do not read every word. Once you know the main idea of the passage, go back and read it again more carefully.

El río Amazonas

Los Andes, Chile

La selva amazónica
cerca de Iquitos, Perú

La carretera panamericana
en Ecuador

¿Comprendes?

A **¿Sí o no?** Digan que sí o que no.
1. El continente sudamericano es muy pequeño.
2. El tren es un medio de transporte importante en la América del Sur.
3. En muchas partes de la América del Sur, es difícil viajar por tierra.
4. Los picos andinos son muy altos.
5. Las selvas tropicales están en los picos andinos.

B **Análisis** Contesten.
1. ¿Por qué es el avión un medio de transporte importante en la América del Sur?
2. ¿Por qué es imposible viajar por tierra de una ciudad a otra en muchas partes de la América del Sur?
3. ¿Cuál es la diferencia entre un vuelo nacional y un vuelo internacional?
4. ¿Cuál es la idea principal de esta lectura?

Lectura opcional 1

El aeropuerto JFK
en Nueva York

Distancias y tiempo de vuelo

Nueva York a Madrid

Los vuelos entre Estados Unidos y Europa son muy largos, ¿no? El Atlántico es un océano grande. Para cruzar el océano Atlántico toma mucho tiempo. Pero los vuelos dentro de la América del Sur pueden ser muy largos también. Vamos a hacer algunas comparaciones.

Susana Rogers está abordando un jet en el aeropuerto internacional de John F. Kennedy en Nueva York. Va a ir a Madrid. Es un vuelo sin escala[1] y después de unas siete horas, el avión va a aterrizar en el aeropuerto de Barajas en Madrid.

Caracas a Buenos Aires

A la misma hora que Susana está abordando el vuelo para Madrid, José Dávila está saliendo de Caracas, Venezuela. Él va a Buenos Aires, Argentina. Su vuelo es también un vuelo sin escala. ¿Sabe usted cuánto tiempo va a tomar? José va a llegar a Ezeiza, el aeropuerto de Buenos Aires, después de un vuelo de unas siete horas. Como ven ustedes, hay muy poca diferencia entre el vuelo que cruza el océano de Nueva York a Madrid y el vuelo de Caracas a Buenos Aires.

[1]sin escala *nonstop*

El aeropuerto en
Caracas, Venezuela

¿Comprendes?

¿Lo sabes? Busquen la siguiente información.
1. el nombre de un océano
2. el nombre de un país
3. el nombre de una ciudad norteamericana
4. el nombre de una ciudad sudamericana
5. la duración del vuelo entre Nueva York y Madrid
6. la duración del vuelo entre Caracas y Buenos Aires

Lectura opcional ②

Las líneas de Nazca

Un vuelo muy interesante es el vuelo en una avioneta de un solo motor sobre las figuras o líneas de Nazca. ¿Qué son las figuras de Nazca? En el desierto entre Nazca y Palpa en el Perú, hay toda una serie de figuras o dibujos misteriosos en la arena. Hay figuras de aves[1], peces[2] y otros animales. Hay también figuras geométricas—rectángulos, triángulos y líneas paralelas.

El origen de las figuras de Nazca es un misterio. No sabemos de dónde vienen. Pero sabemos que tienen unos tres o cuatro mil años de edad. Y son tan[3] grandes y cubren[4] un área tan grande que para ver las figuras bien es necesario tomar un avión. La avioneta para Nazca sale todos los días de Jorge Chávez, el aeropuerto internacional de Lima.

[1]aves *birds*   [3]tan *so*
[2]peces *fish*   [4]cubren *cover*

¿Comprendes?

Nazca Contesten.
1. ¿Sobre qué vuela la avioneta?
2. ¿Cuántos motores tiene la avioneta?
3. ¿Dónde están las figuras o líneas de Nazca?
4. ¿Están en un desierto las figuras?
5. ¿Es un misterio el origen de las figuras o sabemos de dónde vienen?
6. ¿Qué tipo de figuras o líneas hay?
7. ¿Cuántos años tienen?
8. ¿Cubren un área muy grande las líneas?
9. ¿De dónde salen los aviones para ver las líneas?

Conexiones

Las matemáticas

Las finanzas

When we travel we have to take into account how much the trip will cost. A wise traveler has some idea of an affordable travel budget. Can the budget afford a luxury hotel or is it better to stay in an inexpensive hostel? Some travel ads, like this one below, suggest that people can travel now and pay later. Before making a decision, one must consider the financial impact. When are the payments due? What is the interest rate?

Here is some important information about everyday finances that may come in handy when traveling to a Spanish-speaking country.

la tarjeta de crédito

el cheque de viajero

el dinero en efectivo

Las finanzas

Si vamos a hacer un viaje, es necesario saber cuánto va a costar. Es una buena idea preparar un presupuesto[1]. El presupuesto nos permite saber cuánto dinero tenemos y cuánto podemos gastar[2]. El presupuesto tiene que incluir los siguientes gastos[3]:

Cuando viajamos, podemos pagar nuestras cuentas o facturas con una tarjeta de crédito, cheques de viajero o (dinero) en efectivo.

En un país extranjero no vamos a pagar con dólares. Vamos a usar la moneda nacional—pesos o soles, por ejemplo. Tenemos que cambiar dinero. En México es necesario cambiar dólares en pesos. Antes de cambiar dinero, es importante saber el tipo de cambio[4].

Si decidimos pagar a plazos[5], es necesario pagar un pronto[6] (un pie, un enganche). Luego hay que hacer un pago cada mes—una mensualidad. Antes de decidir pagar algo a plazos, es necesario saber la tasa de interés[7] que tenemos que pagar. Todos debemos ser consumidores inteligentes porque la tasa de interés puede ser muy alta.

[1]presupuesto *budget* [4]tipo de cambio *exchange rate* [6]pronto *down payment*
[2]gastar *to spend* [5]pagar a plazos *to pay in installments* [7]tasa de interés *interest rate*
[3]gastos *expenses*

precio del vuelo
transporte local
hotel
comidas y refrescos
entradas
— museos, teatros

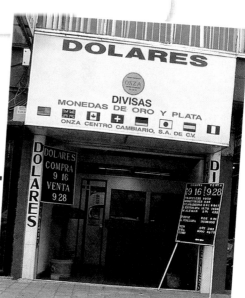

Guanajuato, México

¿Comprendes?

La palabra, por favor. Completen.
1. El ____ nos indica cuánto dinero tenemos y cuánto podemos gastar en varias categorías.
2. El dinero que tenemos que pagar es un ____.
3. Los ____ no pueden exceder la cantidad de dinero que tenemos.
4. Podemos pagar nuestras ____ con una tarjeta de crédito, ____ o ____.
5. En un país ____, no vamos a pagar con dólares.
6. En México tenemos que ____ dólares en pesos mexicanos. En España tenemos que ____ dólares en euros.
7. Antes de cambiar dinero es necesario saber el ____.
8. Si uno decide comprar algo a plazos, es necesario pagar un ____ al principio.
9. Un pago mensual es una ____.
10. Si vamos a comprar algo a plazos, es siempre necesario saber la ____ que puede ser bastante alta.

¡Te toca a ti!

Use what you have learned

1

¿Adónde vas?
✔ *Talk about a plane trip*

You just got to the airport and unexpectedly ran into a friend (your partner). Exchange information about the trip and flight each of you is about to take.

2

¿Vas a hacer un viaje?
✔ *Plan a plane trip to a Spanish-speaking destination*

Go to a travel agency in your community. Get some travel brochures and plan a plane trip. Tell all about your trip.

SPANISH Online

For more information about travel agencies and tours in the Spanish-speaking world, go to the Glencoe Spanish Web site: spanish.glencoe.com

PONCE
PUERTO RICO, U.S.A

Bariloche *en verano*

Cabalgatas

HOTEL ★★★★★
PANAMERICANO
BARILOCHE
ARGENTINA

MADRID

3 Un viaje en avión

✔ *Write about airport activities and services aboard the plane*

You have a Venezuelan pen pal who is going to visit you this winter. This will be his or her first flight. Write your pen pal a letter and explain all the things he or she is going to experience before, during, and after the flight.

4 Un concurso

In order to win an all-expense-paid trip to the Spanish-speaking country of your choice, you have to write an essay in Spanish and send it to the company sponsoring the trip. Read the following essay questions and then write your answers. You really want to go, so be sure to plan your answers carefully and check your work.

¿A qué país quiere usted viajar?
¿Cómo quiere usted viajar?
¿Por qué quiere usted ir allí?
¿Qué quiere usted hacer allí?
¿Qué quiere aprender?

Writing Strategy

Answering an essay question
When writing an answer to an essay question, first read the question carefully to look for clues to determine how your answer should be structured. Then begin by restating the essay question in a single statement in your introduction. Next, support the statement in the body of the answer with facts, details, and reasons. Finally, close with a conclusion that summarizes your answer.

Vocabulario

1 Identifiquen.

To review **Palabras 1**, turn to pages 336-337.

2 ¿Sí o no?

To review **Palabras 2**, turn to pages 340-341.

8. Cuándo los pasajeros desembarcan de un vuelo, tienen que pasar por el control de seguridad.

9. Después de un vuelo, los pasajeros reclaman su equipaje.

10. A veces un(a) agente de aduana inspecciona el equipaje de los pasajeros cuando desembarcan de un vuelo internacional (cuando llegan de un país extranjero).

Estructura

3 Contesten.

11. Cuando haces un viaje, ¿pones tu ropa en una maleta o en una mochila?

12. ¿Traes mucho equipaje cuando haces un viaje largo?

13. ¿Vienen ustedes a la fiesta de Marta?

14. ¿Sale el vuelo para Madrid del aeropuerto internacional?

To review **hacer, poner, traer, salir,** turn to page 344.

4 Escriban según el modelo.

El avión aterriza ahora. ⟶
El avión está aterrizando ahora.

15. Ellas hacen sus maletas ahora.

16. Su vuelo llega ahora.

17. No como nada.

18. ¿Qué lees?

To review the present progressive, turn to page 347.

5 Completen con **saber** o **conocer.**

19. Yo no ____ a qué hora sale nuestro vuelo.

20. Ellos ____ muchas ciudades de España.

21. Yo ____ al amigo de Maricarmen. Es un tipo muy simpático.

22. ¿Tú ____ dónde vive (él)?

To review **saber** and **conocer,** turn to page 348.

Cultura

6 ¿Sí o no?

23. El continente sudamericano es bastante pequeño.

24. Es imposible cruzar los picos altos de los Andes por tierra.

25. Hay muchas selvas tropicales en los picos andinos donde hace mucho frío.

To review this cultural information, turn to page 352.

Tell all you can about this illustration.

Getting around an airport—Departure

el aeropuerto
el taxi
la línea aérea
el avión
el mostrador
el/la agente
el billete, el boleto
el pasaporte
la pantalla de salidas y
    llegadas
la tarjeta de embarque
el número del asiento

el número del vuelo
el destino
la puerta de salida,
    la sala de salida
la sección de no fumar
la báscula
el talón
la maleta
el/la maletero(a)
el/la pasajero(a)
el equipaje (de mano)
el control de seguridad

Getting around an airport—Arrival

el control de pasaportes
la aduana
el reclamo de equipaje

Identifying airline personnel

el/la agente
la tripulación
el/la comandante,
    el/la piloto

el/la copiloto
el asistente de vuelo
la asistente de vuelo

How well do you know your vocabulary?
- Choose a word from the list.
- Have a classmate give a related word: **el viaje, viajar.**

Describing airport activities

hacer un viaje
dar la bienvenida
salir a tiempo
    tarde
    con una demora
revisar el boleto
pasar por el control
    de seguridad
tomar un vuclo

facturar el equipaje
abrir las maletas
inspeccionar
abordar
desembarcar
despegar
aterrizar
reclamar (recoger)
    el equipaje

VIDEOTUR

Episodio 11

In this video episode, you will join Julián and Francisco as they discuss Julián's travel plans. See page 502 for more information.

Other useful expressions

el país
extranjero(a)
permitir
venir

poner
saber
conocer

Conversación

El pobre Juanito

Anita	Juanito fue a Navacerrada a esquiar.
Antonio	Ah, sí. ¿Qué tal lo pasó?
Anita	Muy bien. Pasó un fin de semana estupendo. Pero, ¿sabes dónde está ahora?
Antonio	No sé. No tengo idea.
Anita	Pues, está en la consulta del médico.
Antonio	¿Qué tiene? ¿Qué le pasó?
Anita	No sé. Le duele mucho el estómago y no sabe si tiene fiebre.
Antonio	Pues, tú conoces a Juanito. Siempre está haciendo cosas que no debe hacer. ¿Qué comió?

¿Comprendes?

El pobre Juanito Contesten.

1. ¿Adónde fue Juanito?
2. ¿Por qué fue a Navacerrada?
3. ¿Qué tal fue el fin de semana?
4. ¿Dónde está Juanito ahora?
5. ¿Por qué? ¿Qué tiene?
6. ¿Qué está haciendo siempre Juanito?
7. ¿Comió algo malo Juanito?

CLINICA MEDICA ARABIAL

HOMEOPATIA — OXIGENOTERAPIA
— HOMOTOXICOLOGIA
— HOMEOSINIATRIA
TERAPIAS BIOLOGICAS — MESOTERAPIA
— ACUPUNTURA
— NEURALTERAPIA
— MEDICINA ESTETICA
— FITOTERAPIA

C/. Arabial, 118 - 1.º D
Teléfono 42 13 5   GRANADA

RECUERDE:

«PORQUE HAY OTROS CAMINOS PARA SU CURACION, NO DEJE DE CONSULTARNOS CUALQUIERA QUE SEA SU PROBLEMA».

CLINICA MEDICA ARABIAL

SE RUEGA PEDIR CITA AL TELEFONO 42 13 57

Estructura

Ser y estar

1. The verbs **ser** and **estar** both mean *to be*. **Ser** is used to tell where someone or something is from. It is also used to describe an inherent trait or characteristic.

> **Roberto es de Los Ángeles.**
> **Roberto es inteligente y guapo.**

2. **Estar** is used to tell where someone or something is located. It is also used to describe a temporary condition or state.

> **Ahora Roberto está en Madrid.**
> **Madrid está en España.**
> **Roberto está muy contento en Madrid.**

3. **Estar** is used with a present participle to form the progressive tense.

> **Estamos estudiando y aprendiendo mucho.**

1 **Historieta Roberto** Completen con la forma apropiada de **ser** o **estar.**

Roberto __1__ de Caracas. Él __2__ muy simpático. __3__ muy gracioso también. Ahora él __4__ en Nueva York. __5__ estudiando en la universidad. Roberto __6__ muy contento en Nueva York.

Nueva York __7__ en el noreste de Estados Unidos. Nueva York __8__ muy grande. __9__ muy interesante también. A Roberto le gusta mucho.

Hoy Roberto __10__ de mal humor. No __11__ muy contento. La nota que recibió en un curso no __12__ muy buena y Roberto __13__ muy inteligente.

Nueva York

Verbos irregulares en el presente

The following verbs all have an irregular **yo** form in the present tense. All other forms are regular.

HACER	**yo hago**	TRAER	**yo traigo**	SABER	**yo sé**
PONER	**yo pongo**	SALIR	**yo salgo**	CONOCER	**yo conozco**

 2 Entrevista Contesten personalmente.

1. ¿Haces un viaje a Madrid?
2. ¿A qué hora sales para el aeropuerto?
3. ¿Pones las maletas en la maletera del carro?
4. ¿Traes mucho equipaje?

5. ¿Sabes a qué hora sale tu vuelo?
6. ¿Sabes el número del vuelo?
7. ¿Conoces Madrid?
8. ¿Sabes hablar español?

Los pronombres de complemento

1. The object pronouns **me, te,** and **nos** can function as either direct or indirect object pronouns. Note that the object pronouns in Spanish precede the conjugated verb.

> **¿Te vio Juan?   Sí, Juan me vio y me dio el libro.**

2. **Lo, los, la,** and **las** function as direct object pronouns only. They can replace persons or things.

Pablo compró el boleto.	**Pablo lo compró.**
Pablo compró los boletos.	**Pablo los compró.**
Elena compró la raqueta.	**Elena la compró.**
Elena compró las raquetas.	**Elena las compró.**
Yo vi a los muchachos.	**Yo los vi.**

3. **Le** and **les** function as indirect object pronouns only.

> **Yo le escribí una carta (a él, a ella, a usted).**
> **Yo les escribí una carta (a ellos, a ellas, a ustedes).**

Chacaltaya, una estación de esquí en Bolivia

3 ¡A esquiar! Cambien los sustantivos a pronombres.

1. Llevo *los esquís* a la cancha.
2. También llevo *las botas.*
3. Compro *el boleto* en la taquilla.
4. Veo a *mi hermana* en el telesquí.
5. Doy *el boleto* a mi hermana.
6. Ella da *los esquís* a los muchachos.

Literary Companion

You may wish to read the adaptation of «La camisa de Margarita» by Ricardo Palma. You will find this literary selection on pages 478–483.

 El pretérito

1. The preterite is used to express an event that started and ended in the past. Review the forms of the preterite of regular verbs.

INFINITIVE	mirar	comer	vivir
yo	miré	comí	viví
tú	miraste	comiste	viviste
él, ella, Ud.	miró	comió	vivió
nosotros(as)	miramos	comimos	vivimos
vosotros(as)	mirasteis	comisteis	vivisteis
ellos, ellas, Uds.	miraron	comieron	vivieron

2. The forms of **ir** and **ser** in the preterite are identical. The meaning is made clear by the context of the sentence.

fui   fuiste   fue   fuimos   *fuisteis*   fueron

4 ¿Qué hicieron todos? Contesten.

1. ¿Fuiste al museo ayer?
   ¿Viste una exposición de arte?
   ¿Tomaste un refresco en la cafetería del museo?

2. ¿Salieron ustedes anoche?
   ¿Fueron al cine?
   ¿Tomaron el metro?

3. ¿Esquió Roberto?
   ¿Subió la pista en el telesilla?
   ¿Bajó la pista para expertos?

4. ¿Pasaron tus amigos el fin de semana en la playa?
   ¿Te escribieron una tarjeta postal?
   ¿Nadaron y tomaron el sol en la playa?

5 Deportes The Latin American exchange student (your partner) at your school asks you what sports you played last year. Tell him or her and say which one you liked most and why. Then ask the exchange student the same questions.

6 Diversiones Work with a classmate. Discuss what you each do when you have free time. Do you like to do the same activities?

Una expedición a los países andinos

Bolivia es un país sudamericano. ¿De dónde o de qué origen es el nombre Bolivia? Antes de[1] llegar los conquistadores españoles, ¿qué país es el centro de la civilización de los famosos incas? Y, ¿de qué origen es el nombre de otro país de los Andes, Ecuador? ¿Cómo contestas?

- "Bolivia" es del nombre del gran héroe y libertador latinoamericano, Simón Bolívar. Es la contestación correcta.

- Perú es el centro de la civilización incaica—de los incas. Una vez más, una respuesta correcta.

- Ecuador recibe su nombre de la línea del ecuador, de la línea ecuatorial que divide el mundo en dos hemisferios: el hemisferio norte y el hemisferio sur.

Hay otros datos de la región andina que son muy interesantes. La UNESCO de las Naciones Unidas declara los siguientes sitios Patrimonio Mundial de la Humanidad.

Entérate Perú

Machu Picchu Las famosas ruinas de los incas están en un pico estrecho[2] de los majestuosos Andes. En Machu Picchu hay torres de vigilancia, acueductos, casas, observatorios y un reloj solar[3]. El reloj solar marca las estaciones del año. En quechua, la lengua de los incas, Machu Picchu significa "montaña vieja". En la época en que llegan los españoles, los incas no tienen una forma escrita[4] de su lengua. Interpretan mensajes[5] y números con cuerdas de muchos colores con nudos[6].

Muchos aspectos de la historia de Machu Picchu son un misterio. Pero algo está muy claro; en la época en que construyen los incas la fabulosa ciudad no tienen cemento, no tienen ruedas y no tienen caballos ni bestias de carga ni carritos.

Cuzco Por mucho tiempo Cuzco es la capital de los incas y es el centro de un sistema de caminos que une Sudamérica. Cuando llega Francisco Pizarra a Cuzco y conquista la ciudad, los españoles transforman los templos y palacios de los incas en iglesias y magníficas casas.

Arequipa Arequipa es "la Ciudad Blanca." Es una ciudad blanca porque construyen las casas y los otros edificios de una piedra volcánica que hay en Arequipa. La piedra tiene un color blanco brillante.

Machu Picchu

[1]antes de: *before*
[2]estrecho: *narrow*
[3]reloj solar: *solar clock*
[4]escrita: *written*
[5]mensajes: *messages*
[6]cuerdas… con nudos: *cords… with knots*

Entérate Bolivia

Potosí Durante una parte de la época colonial Potosí es la ciudad más grande de las Américas a causa de la explotación de plata[1] en la región. Hoy Potosí es la ciudad más alta[2] del mundo.

Sucre La ciudad colonial de Sucre es muy importante porque es en Sucre donde acuñan monedas[3] de plata. Los españoles envían[4] las monedas a España. El dinero que envían a España tiene mucha importancia en la economía de España y Europa en el siglo XVII.

[1]plata: *silver*
[2]más alta: *highest*
[3]acuñan monedas: *they mint coins*
[4]envían: *send*

Potosí

Las Islas Galápagos

Entérate Ecuador

Parque Nacional Sangay En el parque hay tres volcanes. El parque lleva el nombre de uno de los volcanes—el volcán Sangay. De todos los volcanes del mundo el Sangay es activo durante más tiempo que cualquier otro[1]. Varias comunidades indígenas viven en el parque que está en la lista de Patrimonios en Peligro[2]. ¿Por qué está en peligro? A causa de la construcción de una carretera moderna y la caza[3] ilegal.

Quito Cerca del volcán Pichincha, la bella ciudad de Quito tiene iglesias coloniales decoradas de pan de oro[4]. El barrio antiguo de la ciudad con sus calles estrechas de piedra y casas con balcones y patios refleja la influencia española.

Las Islas Galápagos Galápagos son las tortugas[5] gigantes que habitan el archipiélago de las Galápagos a unos mil kilómetros de la costa ecuatoriana. En el pasado naturalistas como Charles Darwin estudian las especies de flora y fauna del archipiélago. Algunas son únicas en el mundo.

---

[1]cualquier otro: *any other*
[2]peligro: *danger*
[3]caza: *hunting*
[4]pan de oro: *gold leaf*
[5]tortugas: *turtles*

Calendario de fiestas

Carnaval, Oruro, Bolivia, febrero
Declarado Obra Maestra por la UNESCO el carnaval de Oruro, Bolivia, es una fiesta muy alegre. Hay danzantes en las calles que llevan trajes y máscaras vistosas[1] de muchos colores.

Pachamama Raymi, todo el país, Perú, 1° de agosto
Pachamama es la diosa de la Tierra de los indígenas peruanos. El 1° de agosto marca el comienzo del año andino y los indígenas

Carnaval, Oruro, Bolivia

hacen tributo[2] a su diosa con una ceremonia de ofrenda[3] que llaman[4] "Pago de la Tierra".

Tradiciones ancestrales, Amazonia, Ecuador
En la comunidad indichuris y la comunidad de los quechuas—poblaciones indígenas—habitan shamanes que practican sus tradiciones ancestrales. A veces dejan a los visitantes participar en los rituales.

---

[1]vistosas: *colorful*
[2]hacen tributo: *pay tribute*
[3]ofrenda: *offering*
[4]llaman: *they call*

música

El sonido andino

En todo el mundo goza de cierta popularidad la música andina. Pero hay muchos que no son familiares con los instrumentos musicales de los Andes. Unos son de origen puro andino y datan de miles de años. Otros son de origen europeo pero adaptados a los distintos ritmos y tonos andinos. ¡A tocar la zampoña!

La zampoña

La zampoña Es un instrumento de tubos de caña de tamaños diferentes. La nota musical varía según el tamaño del tubo.

La quena Es un instrumento de viento. Es de caña, madera[1] o hueso[2]. El tamaño del instrumento varía de una región a otra.

El charango

El charango Es como la guitarra, pero el instrumento es más pequeño que la guitarra y tiene catorce cuerdas[3].

---

[1]madera: *wood*
[2]hueso: *bone*
[3]cuerdas: *strings*

mi cocina

Ceviche

Ingredientes

2 libras de pescado y mariscos mixtos, incluyendo un pescado de carne firme, almejas[1], camarones[2]

1 cebolla grande en rebanadas[3] finas

$^1/_2$ taza de perejil[4] picado

chiles serranos al gusto

jugo[5] de limón para cubrir

Preparación

Combinar todos los ingredientes y refrigerar durante dos horas. El resultado es un platillo delicioso. Delicioso para una fiesta.

---

[1]almejas: *clams*

[2]camarones: *shrimp*

[3]rebanadas: *slices*

[4]perejil: *parsley*

[5]jugo: *juice*

Gente andina

Ceviche

¿Te apetecen papas fritas coloreadas?

En las montañas de Perú y Bolivia, la gente cultiva papas nativas, pero no son las mismas papas que comes tú. Son de varios colores. Son rojas, azules, amarillas y blancas. Además de ser coloreadas, tienen mucha variedad de textura, sabor y olor. Los pueblos indígenas llevan miles de años cultivando miles de variedades de papas. Hay hasta cientos de variedades en una sola parcela de cultivo.

Muchas papas están adaptadas a florecer[1] en las regiones muy altas de los Andes. Mucha gente cree[2] que la papa es de Irlanda. Pero no es verdad. La papa es un producto de las Américas, gracias a las comunidades indígenas. Hoy la papa es uno de los alimentos[3] básicos del mundo entero.

---

[1]florecer: *bloom*   [2]cree: *believe*   [3]alimentos: *foods*

¡La gente!

Si viajas[1] por los Andes vas a ver a gente de muchas etnias y culturas. Tienes que tratar[2] de asistir a unos ritos ancestrales de curanderos[3] y shamanes. Los curanderos curan a sus pacientes con hierbas medicinales.

Si vas a la selva tropical[4] es posible ver de lejos[5] a comunidades indígenas que no tienen contacto con otras personas. Ellos viven como sus antepasados o ancestros desde hace ya cientos de años.

¿Vas a comprar artesanía? ¿Por qué no visitas un mercado indígena de colores y olores[6] exóticos? Si tienes hambre cuando estás en el mercado, puedes[7] comer algo en uno de los puestos de comida[8]. Si estás en una de las ciudades como La Paz, Lima o Quito, puedes comer en un restaurante elegante o ir de compras en una tienda bonita.

---

[1]viajas: *you travel*   [5]de lejos: *from a distance*

[2]tratar: *try*   [6]olores: *smells*

[3]curanderos: *healers*   [7]puedes: *you can*

[4]selva tropical: *rainforest*   [8]puestos de comida: *food stands*

el mundo salvaje

Entérate de detalles[2] interesantes

El Salar de Uyuni

Lugares sorprendentes

- **El Salar de Uyuni** es el fondo de un mar desaparecido en Bolivia. Aquí hay hoteles construidos de bloques de sal.
- **La línea ecuatorial** pasa por Ecuador. Así, puedes estar de pie en dos hemisferios al mismo tiempo—con un pie en el hemisferio sur y el otro en el hemisferio norte.
- **El lago Titicaca** en Bolivia es el lago navegable más alto del mundo.
- **Las Islas Galápagos** son de origen volcánico y tienen una intensa actividad sísmica y volcánica con varias erupciones al año.

Flora fascinante

- En la región amazónica de Ecuador, hay un sinnúmero de **plantas,** muchas de ellas desconocidas[1].
- En muchas partes de la cordillera de los Andes hay miles de especies de **orquídeas**.
- Muchas **especies de árboles** en la región amazónica están en peligro[2] de extinción. A causa de la deforestación bosques[3] enteros de miles de años de edad ya no existen.

Orquídeas

Fauna fenomenal

- ¿Cuál es el animal más típico de los Andes? Es **la llama,** el amigo de toda la población andina. La llama es un medio de transporte importante.
- El clima del altiplano de Bolivia no permite sobrevivir[4] muchas especies de aves. Pero aquí viven miles de **flamencos rosados**[5].
- Según los científicos, hay más de 4,200 especies de **mariposas**[6] en Perú. Pero hasta ahora sólo 3,700 especies son conocidas.

Flamencos

---

[1]desconocidas: *unknown*
[2]peligro: *danger*
[3]bosques: *forests*
[4]permite sobrevivir: *enable to survive*
[5]flamencos rosados: *pink flamingos*
[6]mariposas: *butterflies*

SUCESOS

Mario Vargas Llosa

- El escritor peruano **Mario Vargas Llosa** es considerado uno de los grandes novelistas latinoamericanos por sus obras como *La ciudad de los perros.* Él pasa mucho tiempo en París pero aquí está en su Perú natal donde escribe su autógrafo para una de sus aficionados.

- ¿Qué es **un sombrero de jipijapa?** La traducción en inglés es "Panama hat," pero no es de Panamá. ¡Es de Ecuador!

- El conductor **Miguel Harth-Bedoya** es de Perú. Va a Nueva York donde estudia en la famosa Juilliard School of Music. Ahora es el director musical de una orquesta sinfónica norteamericana.

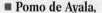

Miguel Harth-Bedoya

- **Pomo de Ayala,** de madre indígena y padre español, capta perfectamente el cultivo de papas en los Andes. ¿Toma una fotografía? No, de ninguna manera. Él pinta una escena del cultivo de papas en el año 1580. Pomo de Ayala es un conocido cronista peruano (1534–1615).

Capítulo 12

Una gira

Objetivos

In this chapter you will learn to:

❖ describe your personal grooming habits
❖ talk about your daily routine
❖ tell some things you do for yourself
❖ talk about a backpacking trip

Susana González-Pagliere *Southern Lake*

Vocabulario

La rutina

Hola. Yo me llamo José. ¿Y tú? ¿Cómo te llamas?

El muchacho se llama José.

José se acuesta.
Se acuesta a las once de la noche.
Él se duerme enseguida.

La muchacha se despierta temprano.
Se levanta enseguida.

El muchacho se lava la cara.

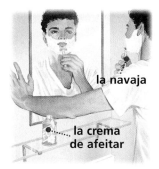

El muchacho se afeita.
Se afeita con la navaja.

El muchacho toma una ducha.
El muchacho se lava el pelo.

La muchacha se baña.

El muchacho se cepilla (se lava) los dientes.

La muchacha se maquilla.
Se pone el maquillaje.

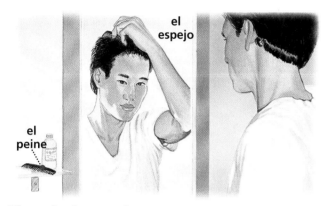

El muchacho se peina.
Se mira en el espejo cuando se peina.

Ella se pone la ropa.

La muchacha se sienta a la mesa.
Toma el desayuno.
Se desayuna.

¿Qué palabra necesito?

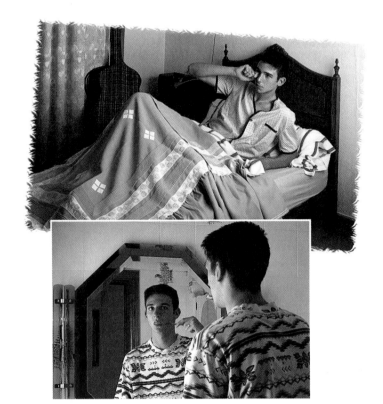

1 Historieta Un día en la vida de…

 Contesten según se indica.

1. ¿Cómo se llama el joven? (Paco)
2. ¿A qué hora se despierta?
   (a las seis y media)
3. ¿Cuándo se levanta? (enseguida)
4. ¿Adónde va? (al cuarto de baño)
5. ¿Qué hace? (se lava la cara y
   se cepilla los dientes)
6. Luego, ¿adónde va? (a la cocina)
7. ¿Se sienta a la mesa? (sí)
8. ¿Qué toma? (el desayuno)

2 ¿Qué hace el muchacho o la muchacha? Describan.

1.

2.

3.

4.

5.

6.

3 Historieta Las actividades de Sarita
Completen.

Sarita __1__ por la mañana. Ella __2__ la cara y las manos. Ella __3__ los dientes. Ella __4__ el pelo. Ella __5__ la ropa—un blue jean y una camiseta. Ella __6__ en la cocina. Ella __7__ a la mesa.

Málaga, España

4 Entrevista
Contesten personalmente.

1. ¿Cómo te llamas?
2. ¿A qué hora tomas el desayuno?
3. ¿Tomas el desayuno en la cocina o en el comedor?
4. ¿Te gusta tomar un desayuno grande?
5. ¿Qué comes en el desayuno?
6. ¿Te gustan los cereales?

5 La rutina
Work with a classmate. Each of you will choose one family member and tell each other about that person's daily activities.

- mi gato
- papá
- mi prima
- mi hermana
- mamá
- mi perro
- mi primo
- mi hermano

*For more practice using words from **Palabras 1**, do Activity 12 on page H13 at the end of this book.*

Una gira

Los amigos están viajando por España.
Están haciendo un viaje económico.
Lo están pasando muy bien.
 Se divierten mucho.
Duermen en el saco de dormir.

el saco de dormir

¿Qué ponen o llevan en la mochila?

una botella de
agua mineral

el champú

un cepillo

un cepillo de dientes

un rollo de
papel higiénico

un tubo
de pasta (crema) dentífrica

una barra (una pastilla)
de jabón

Los amigos dan una caminata.
Algunos van a pie.
Y otros van en bicicleta.

Pasan la noche en un albergue para jóvenes.
Y a veces pasan la noche en un hostal o en
una pensión.

Vocabulario

¿Qué palabra necesito?

6 **¿Qué pierde Pepe de la mochila?** Identifiquen.

7 **Historieta** **Una gira** Contesten.

1. ¿Hacen los jóvenes un viaje de lujo o un viaje económico?
2. ¿Por dónde están viajando?
3. ¿En qué llevan sus cosas?
4. ¿Cuáles son algunas cosas que ponen en la mochila?
5. ¿Cómo van de un lugar (sitio) a otro?
6. ¿En qué duermen a veces?
7. ¿Dónde pasan la noche de vez en cuando (a veces)?
8. ¿Se divierten?

380 ✧ *trescientos ochenta*

CAPÍTULO 12

8 **Historieta** **En el cuarto de baño** Completen.

1. El muchacho va a tomar una ducha. Necesita ____.
2. La muchacha quiere peinarse pero, ¿dónde está ____?
3. El muchacho va a afeitarse. Necesita ____.
4. Juanito quiere lavarse los dientes. ¿Dónde está ____?
5. No hay pasta dentífrica. Tengo que comprar otro ____.
6. No hay más jabón. Tengo que comprar otra ____.
7. Siempre uso ____ para lavarme el pelo.

9 **En la farmacia** You're a clerk in a drugstore. A classmate is a Spanish-speaking customer who wants to buy the following toiletries. Have a conversation.

Estructura

Verbos reflexivos
Telling what people do for themselves

1. Compare the following pairs of sentences.

Mariana baña al perro.

Mariana cepilla al perro.

Mariana se baña.

Mariana se cepilla.

In the sentences above the illustrations, Mariana performs the action. The dog receives the action. In the sentences below the drawings, Mariana both performs and receives the action of the verb. For this reason, the pronoun **se** must be used. **Se** refers back to Mariana in these sentences and is called a "reflexive pronoun." It indicates that the action of the verb is reflected back to the subject.

2. Study the forms of a reflexive verb.

INFINITIVE	lavarse	levantarse
yo	me lavo	me levanto
tú	te lavas	te levantas
él, ella, Ud.	se lava	se levanta
nosotros(as)	nos lavamos	nos levantamos
vosotros(as)	os laváis	os levantáis
ellos, ellas, Uds.	se lavan	se levantan

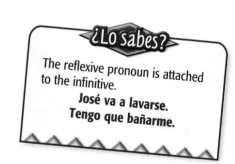

¿Lo sabes?

The reflexive pronoun is attached to the infinitive.

José va a lavarse.
Tengo que bañarme.

3. In the negative form, **no** is placed before the reflexive pronoun.

¿No te lavas las manos?
La familia Martínez no se desayuna en el comedor.

4. In Spanish when you refer to parts of the body and articles of clothing, you often use the definite article, not the possessive adjective.

> **Él se lava la cara.**
> **Me lavo los dientes.**
> **Me pongo la camisa.**

¿Cómo lo digo?

10 **Historieta Teresa** Contesten.

1. ¿A qué hora se levanta Teresa?
2. ¿Se baña por la mañana o por la noche?
3. ¿Se desayuna en casa?
4. ¿Se lava los dientes después del desayuno?
5. ¿Se pone una chaqueta si sale cuando hace frío?

11 **El aseo** Contesten personalmente.

1. ¿A qué hora te levantas? ¿Y a qué hora te levantaste esta mañana?
2. ¿Te bañas por la mañana o tomas una ducha? Y esta mañana, ¿te bañaste o tomaste una ducha?
3. ¿Te cepillas los dientes con frecuencia? ¿Cuántas veces te cepillaste los dientes hoy?
4. ¿Te desayunas en casa o en la escuela? Y esta mañana, ¿dónde te desayunaste?
5. ¿Te afeitas o no? Y hoy, ¿te afeitaste?
6. ¿Te peinas con frecuencia? ¿Te miras en el espejo cuando te peinas? ¿Cuántas veces te peinaste hoy?

Estructura

12 **¿Qué hace?** Sigan el modelo.

—¿Se lava los dientes?
—Sí, se lava los dientes.

1.

2.

3.

4.

5.

6.

13 **¿Y ustedes?** Sigan el modelo.

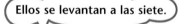

Ellos se levantan a las siete.

Nos levantamos a las siete también.

Ah, sí. ¿Y a qué hora se levantan Uds.?

1. Ellos se levantan a las seis y media.
2. Ellos se bañan a las siete menos cuarto.
3. Ellos se desayunan a las siete y media.

14 **Nombres** Contesten.

1. ¿Cómo te llamas?
2. Y tu hermano(a), ¿cómo se llama?
3. ¿Cómo se llama tu profesor(a) de español?
4. ¿Y cómo se llaman tus abuelos?
5. Una vez más, ¿cómo te llamas?

15 **¿Qué hacen todos?** Completen según las fotos.

1. Yo
   Él
   Tú
   Usted

2. Nosotros
   Ellos
   Ustedes
   Él y yo

16 **Me desayuno y luego...** Work in groups of three or four. Tell the order of your daily activities from morning to night. Do you all do everything in the same order? Does anyone do things really differently? What's the most common routine? What's the weirdest routine?

17 *Juego* **Me pongo...** Describe some clothing you're putting on. A classmate will guess where you are going or what you are going to do.

Estructura

Verbos reflexivos de cambio radical
Telling what people do for themselves

1. The reflexive verbs **acostarse (o → ue)** and **(divertirse e → ie)** are stem-changing verbs. Study the following forms.

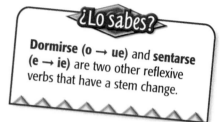

¿Lo sabes?

Dormirse (o → ue) and **sentarse (e → ie)** are two other reflexive verbs that have a stem change.

INFINITIVE	acostarse	divertirse
yo	me acuesto	me divierto
tú	te acuestas	te diviertes
él, ella, Ud.	se acuesta	se divierte
nosotros(as)	nos acostamos	nos divertimos
vosotros(as)	os acostáis	os divertís
ellos, ellas, Uds.	se acuestan	se divierten

2. Many verbs in Spanish can be used with a reflexive pronoun. Often the reflexive pronoun gives a different meaning to the verb. Study the following examples.

María pone la blusa en la mochila.	*Mary puts the blouse in the backpack.*
María se pone la blusa.	*Mary puts on her blouse.*
María duerme ocho horas.	*Mary sleeps eight hours.*
María se duerme enseguida.	*Mary falls asleep immediately.*
María llama a Carlos.	*Mary calls Carlos.*
Ella se llama María.	*She calls herself Mary. (Her name is Mary.)*
María divierte a sus amigos.	*Mary amuses her friends.*
María se divierte.	*Mary amuses herself. (Mary has a good time.)*

¿Cómo lo digo?

 18 **¿Cómo lo haces tú?**

Contesten personalmente.

1. ¿Duermes en una cama o en un saco de dormir?
2. Cuando te acuestas, ¿te duermes enseguida?
3. Y cuando te despiertas, ¿te levantas enseguida?
4. ¿Te sientas a la mesa para tomar el desayuno?
5. ¿Te diviertes en la escuela?

Cataluña, España

19 **Historieta** **Duermo ocho horas.** Completen.

Cuando yo __1__ (acostarse), yo __2__ (dormirse) enseguida. Cada noche yo __3__ (dormir) ocho horas. Yo __4__ (acostarse) a las once y __5__ (levantarse) a las siete de la mañana. Cuando yo __6__ (despertarse), __7__ (levantarse) enseguida. Pero cuando mi hermana __8__ (despertarse), ella no __9__ (levantarse) enseguida. Y mi hermano, cuando él __10__ (acostarse), no __11__ (dormirse) enseguida. Él pasa horas escuchando música en la cama. Así él __12__ (dormir) solamente unas seis horas.

20 **¿Lo está pasando bien? ¿Se divierte?** Choose an illustration below and describe it. A classmate will tell which one you're describing and let you know whether he or she thinks the people are having fun. Take turns.

1.

2.

3.

4.

21 **Juego** **¿Qué tengo?** You have something you have to use every day for part of your daily routine. Tell a classmate what it is. He or she will then guess what you do with it.

—**Tengo una navaja.**
—**Ah, te afeitas.**

Andas bien. ¡Adelante!

¿A qué hora te despertaste?

Timoteo Maripaz, ¿a qué hora te despertaste esta mañana?

Maripaz Esta mañana me levanté un poco tarde.

Timoteo ¿Te levantaste tarde? ¿Por qué?

Maripaz Porque anoche me acosté muy tarde.

Timoteo ¿Por qué te acostaste tan tarde? ¿Saliste?

Maripaz No, no salí. Pasé la noche estudiando. Hoy tengo un examen de álgebra. Estudié hasta la medianoche.

Timoteo ¿Estudiaste hasta la medianoche?

Maripaz Sí, y por lo general me despierto a las seis pero esta mañana no me desperté hasta las seis y media.

Timoteo ¿Llegaste tarde a la escuela?

Maripaz No, afortunadamente llegué a tiempo porque la clase de álgebra es mi primera clase.

¿Comprendes?

Contesten.

1. Esta mañana, ¿se levantó tarde o temprano Maripaz?
2. ¿Por qué se levantó tarde?
3. ¿Salió ella anoche?
4. ¿Cómo pasó la noche?
5. ¿Hasta qué hora estudió?
6. Por lo general, ¿a qué hora se despierta ella?
7. ¿A qué hora se despertó esta mañana?
8. ¿Llegó tarde a la escuela?
9. ¿Cuál es la primera clase de Maripaz?

Vamos a hablar más

A **Me acosté muy tarde.** You got to bed really late last night and you're feeling tired. Tell a classmate why. Then he or she will ask you some questions about what you're doing today and how things are.

B **Vamos a dar una caminata.** You're planning to backpack through a Spanish-speaking country. Work with a classmate. Decide what country you want to go to. Then decide what you are going to take with you, how long you'll be away, how much money you'll need, and how you plan to get around.

Pronunciación

La h, la y, la ll

The **h** in Spanish is silent. It is never pronounced. Repeat the following.

hijo	**hotel**	**higiénico**
hermano	**hace**	**hostal**

Y in Spanish can be either a vowel or a consonant. As a vowel, it is pronounced exactly the same as the vowel **i.** Repeat the following.

Juan y María
el jabón y el champú

Y is a consonant when it begins a word or a syllable. As a consonant, **y** is pronounced similarly to the *y* in the English word *yo-yo.* This sound has several variations throughout the Spanish-speaking world. Repeat the following.

ya	**desayuno**	**ayuda**	**playa**

The **ll** is pronounced as a single consonant in Spanish. In many areas of the Spanish-speaking world, it is pronounced the same as the **y.** It too has several variations. Repeat the following.

llama	**botella**	**cepillo**	**toalla**
llega	**pastilla**	**rollo**	**lluvia**

Repeat the following sentences.

La hermana habla hoy con su hermano en el hotel.
Está lloviendo cuando ella llega a la calle Hidalgo.
El hombre lleva una botella de agua a la playa hermosa.

Lecturas culturales

Del norte de España 🔄 🎧

¡Hola! Me llamo Iván Orama. Soy de San Juan, Puerto Rico. Pero ahora no estoy en Puerto Rico. Estoy en España donde un grupo de amigos de nuestro colegio estamos pasando el verano. Es una experiencia fabulosa. Nos divertimos mucho. ¿Me permites describir un día típico?

Esta mañana nos despertamos temprano. Todos nos levantamos enseguida. Con la mochila en la espalda[1] salimos de la pensión. Fuimos a una cafetería donde nos desayunamos. Yo tomé un jugo de china o, como lo llaman aquí en España, un zumo de naranja. Marta comió churros, una cosa típica española. Y los otros, no sé lo que comieron.

Cuando salimos del café, fuimos en nuestras bicicletas en dirección a Santiago de Compostela. Estamos siguiendo[2] más o menos el Camino[3] de Santiago.

[1]en la espalda *on our backs*
[2]siguiendo *following*
[3]Camino *Way, Route*

El lago Enol en el Parque Nacional de Covadonga, España

Reading Strategy

Skimming There are several ways to read an article or a passage—each one with its own purpose. Skimming means reading quickly in order to find out the general idea of a passage. To skim means to read without paying careful attention to small details, noting only information about the main theme or topic. Sometimes a reader will skim a passage only to decide whether it's interesting enough to then read it in detail.

El otro día pasamos un día estupendo en San Sebastián. Nos sentamos en la playa y nos bañamos en el mar Cantábrico. Te aseguro[4] que el agua del Cantábrico está mucho más fría que el agua del Caribe en nuestro Puerto Rico.

El lunes dimos una caminata por los Picos de Europa. Fue increíble. Los picos son tan altos que aún[5] en julio están cubiertos de nieve.

No sabemos cuándo vamos a llegar a Santiago. Pero lo estamos pasando muy bien. Nos divertimos mucho.

[4]Te aseguro *I assure you*
[5]aún *even*

San Sebastián, España

¿Comprendes?

A Un día con los amigos Contesten.

1. ¿Cómo se llama el muchacho?
2. ¿De dónde es?
3. ¿Dónde está ahora?
4. ¿Con quiénes está?
5. ¿Qué están haciendo?
6. ¿Cuándo se levantaron esta mañana?
7. ¿Adónde fueron cuando salieron de la pensión?
8. ¿Qué comió Marta en el desayuno?

B Más sobre la caminata Escojan.

1. Cuando salieron del café, fueron ____.
   a. al albergue juvenil
   b. a San Sebastián
   c. hacia Santiago de Compostela

2. Pasaron el otro día ____.
   a. en la playa
   b. en el Camino de Santiago
   c. en el Cantábrico

3. Hay una playa bonita en ____.
   a. Santiago de Compostela
   b. los Picos de Europa
   c. San Sebastián

4. El agua del mar está fría en ____.
   a. el mar Cantábrico
   b. el mar Caribe
   c. los Picos de Europa

5. Los Picos de Europa están cubiertos de nieve porque ____.
   a. están cerca del mar Cantábrico
   b. son muy altos y allí hace mucho frío
   c. son increíbles

C La ruta Dibujen un mapa de la ruta de los jóvenes.

Lectura opcional

El Camino de Santiago

Durante la Edad Media[1] hay tres peregrinaciones[2] famosas—la peregrinación a Jerusalén en Israel, la peregrinación a Roma y la peregrinación a Santiago de Compostela.

Santiago de Compostela está en Galicia, una región pintoresca en el noroeste de España. Galicia se parece más a[3] Irlanda que al resto de España. Llueve mucho en Galicia y todo es muy verde.

El Camino de Santiago es el camino que tomaron los peregrinos de la Edad Media. El camino empieza en los Pirineos, en el pueblo de Roncesvalles y termina en Santiago. Atraviesa o cruza todo el norte de España. ¿Por qué quieren ir a Santiago los peregrinos? Porque creen que allí está enterrado[4] el apóstol Santiago.

[1]Edad Media *Middle Ages*
[2]peregrinaciones *pilgrimages*
[3]se parece más a *looks more like*
[4]enterrado *buried*

Galicia, España

La catedral en Santiago de Compostela

Los peregrinos viajan a pie (caminan) de un pueblo a otro. Cada día cubren un trecho[5] (tramo) fijo. Al final de cada trecho hay un hostal donde los peregrinos pueden pasar la noche. En el siglo XI hay hostales que pueden alojar[6] a unos mil peregrinos.

Una vez más el Camino de Santiago es muy popular. Hoy día muchos turistas toman la misma ruta. Pero no van a pie. Van en carro. Y muchos jóvenes van en bicicleta.

[5]trecho *stretch*
[6]alojar *lodge, accommodate*

Hostal de los Reyes Católicos, Santiago de Compostela

¿Comprendes?

A Santiago de Compostela
Contesten.
1. ¿Dónde está Santiago de Compostela?
2. ¿En qué parte de España está Galicia?
3. ¿Por qué se parece mucho a Irlanda?
4. ¿Quién está enterrado en la catedral en Santiago de Compostela?

B ¿Qué sabes? Describan lo que aprendieron del Camino de Santiago.

Conexiones
Las ciencias naturales

La ecología

Ecology is a subject of great interest to young people around the world. No one wants to wake up each morning and breathe polluted air. No one wants to hike along a river bank that is loaded with debris or swim in a contaminated ocean. As people travel around the world, they are appalled by the destruction they see done to the environment. We are all aware that urgent and dramatic steps must be taken to avert future ecological disasters.

Santiago, Chile

La ecología

El término «ecología» significa el equilibrio entre los seres vivientes—los seres humanos—y la naturaleza[1]. Hoy en día hay grandes problemas ecológicos en casi todas partes del mundo.

La contaminación del aire

La contaminación del medio ambiente[2] es el problema número uno. La contaminación de todos los tipos es la plaga de nuestros tiempos.

El aire que respiramos[3] está contaminado. Está contaminado principalmente por las emisiones de gases que escapan de los automóviles y camiones. Está contaminado también por el humo[4] que emiten las chimeneas de las fábricas[5] que queman[6] sustancias químicas.

[1]naturaleza *nature*
[2]medio ambiente *environment*
[3]respiramos *we breathe*
[4]humo *smoke*
[5]fábricas *factories*
[6]queman *burn*

Caracas, Venezuela

El agua

Nuestras aguas están contaminadas también. Buques petroleros derraman[7] cantidades de petróleo cada año en nuestros mares y océanos. En las zonas industriales las fábricas echan los desechos[8] industriales en los ríos. Muchos de los desechos son tóxicos. Los ríos contaminados son portadores[9] de enfermedades serias.

El reciclaje

Hoy en día hay grandes campañas de reciclaje. El reciclaje consiste en recoger los desechos—papel, vidrio[10], metal—para transformar y poder utilizar estos productos de nuevo (una vez más).

[7]Buques petroleros derraman *Oil tankers spill*
[8]desechos *wastes*
[9]portadores *carriers*
[10]vidrio *glass*

Río de la Plata, Buenos Aires

¿Comprendes?

A En español, por favor.
Busquen las palabras equivalentes en español.
1. ecology
2. ecological problems
3. air pollution
4. toxic wastes
5. recycling

B Para discutir Contesten.
1. ¿Está contaminado el aire donde ustedes viven?
2. ¿Hay mucha industria donde viven?
3. ¿Hay muchas fábricas?
4. ¿Hay muchos automóviles y camiones?
5. ¿Escapan gases de los automóviles?
6. ¿Hay campañas de reciclaje donde viven?

SPANISH Online

For more information about environmental issues in the Spanish-speaking world, go to the Glencoe Spanish Web site: spanish.glencoe.com

Use what you have learned

1 HABLAR

Mi familia

✔ *Compare your family's routine to someone else's*

Work with a classmate. Talk about some of the family's habits in your respective homes. Compare them.

2 HABLAR

Una gira

✔ *Talk about a backpacking trip*

Work with a classmate. The two of you plan to backpack around Spain next summer. Discuss all the things you plan or want to do.

3 Hay una diferencia.

✔ *Talk about your weekday and weekend routines*

Most people like a change of pace on the weekend. Talk with a classmate about things that students do or don't do during the week. Your partner will say how that differs on the weekend and why. Take turns.

> Durante la semana los alumnos se despiertan muy temprano.

> Durante los fines de semana los alumnos se despiertan más tarde.

4 Un día típico

✔ *Write about your daily routine*

Your Colombian pen pal is curious about your daily routine. Send him or her an e-mail describing all the activities you do on a typical day from the time you wake up to the time you go to bed.

5 Un trabajo de verano

You are working abroad this summer. You are going to help take care of two small children in Seville, Spain. The children's mother gives you many instructions about the children's routine and activities. Since you probably will not remember all she is telling you, you jot down notes. Take your notes and organize them to describe each child's day. Then write down your responsibilities—what it is you have to do.

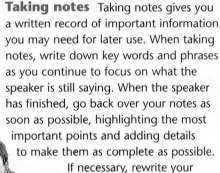

Writing Strategy

Taking notes Taking notes gives you a written record of important information you may need for later use. When taking notes, write down key words and phrases as you continue to focus on what the speaker is still saying. When the speaker has finished, go back over your notes as soon as possible, highlighting the most important points and adding details to make them as complete as possible. If necessary, rewrite your notes, organizing them so they will be of utmost use to you.

Vocabulario

1 **Pareen.**

a.

b.

c.

d.

To review **Palabras 1**, turn to pages 374–375.

1. _____ Se afeita.
2. _____ Se acuesta.

3. _____ Se peina.
4. _____ Se levanta.

2 **Identifiquen.**

3 **Completen.**

8. Lo están pasando muy bien. _____ mucho.
9. No duermen en una cama. Duermen en un _____.
10. Un _____ es un tipo de hotel económico donde un cuarto no cuesta mucho.

To review **Palabras 2**, turn to pages 378–379.

4 **Identifiquen.**

11.

12.

13.

Estructura

5 Completen en el presente.

14–15. Cuando yo ____, ____ la cara enseguida.
(levantarse, lavarse)

16. ¿A qué hora ____ ustedes? (acostarse)

17. ¿Tu hermano ____? (afeitarse)

18. Nosotros ____ mucho. (divertirse)

19–20. Cuando tú ____, ¿____ enseguida?
(acostarse, dormirse)

6 Completen cuando necesario.

21. Yo ____ pongo mi chaqueta en la maleta porque
____ pongo la chaqueta cuando hace frío.

22. Ella ____ duerme enseguida y luego ____ duerme
ocho horas sin problema.

To review reflexive verbs, turn to pages 382 and 386.

Cultura

7 Den la(s) palabra(s).

23. *orange juice* en España y Puerto Rico

24. una cosa típica que comen los españoles en
el desayuno

25. el mar que baña las costas de Puerto Rico

To review this cultural information, turn to page 390.

San Juan, Puerto Rico

Tell all you can about this illustration.

Vocabulario

Stating daily activities

la rutina	tomar una ducha	cepillarse	dormirse(ue)
despertarse(ie)	afeitarse	peinarse	llamarse
levantarse	ponerse la ropa	sentarse(ie)	divertirse(ie)
lavarse	mirarse	desayunarse	
bañarse	maquillarse	acostarse(ue)	

Identifying articles for grooming and hygiene

la navaja	el maquillaje	un rollo de papel
la crema de afeitar	una barra (una	higiénico
el cepillo	pastilla) de jabón	el champú
el peine	un tubo de pasta	
el cepillo de dientes	(crema) dentífrica	
el espejo		

Identifying more parts of the body

la cara
los dientes
el pelo

Identifying more breakfast foods

una botella de agua	el cereal
mineral	el pan tostado
un vaso de jugo de	
naranja	

Describing backpacking

una gira	el hostal
la mochila	la pensión
el saco de dormir	dar una caminata
el albergue para	ir en bicicleta
jóvenes	

Other useful expressions

el lugar
de vez en cuando

How well do you know your vocabulary?
- Choose an expression from the list that describes something you do as part of your daily routine.
- Ask a classmate to give words related to that particular daily activity.

VIDEOTUR

Episodio 12

In this video episode, you will join Claudia and Alejandra on a hike. See page 503 for more information.

Capítulo 13

Un viaje en tren

Objetivos

In this chapter you will learn to:

❖ use expressions related to train travel
❖ purchase a train ticket and request information about arrival, departure, etc.
❖ talk about more past events or activities
❖ tell what people say
❖ discuss an interesting train trip in Spain and in Peru

Casimiro Castro *Álbum del ferrocarril mexicano*

En la estación de ferrocarril

el tablero de llegadas

el tablero de salidas

el quiosco

la sala de espera

HORARIOS
MADRID ALMERIA GRANADA

el horario

Un billete para Madrid, por favor.

¿En primera o en segunda?

En segunda—de ida y vuelta.

la ventanilla

el billete de ida y vuelta

el billete sencillo

el vagón, el coche

el tren

el mozo, el maletero

la bolsa

el equipaje

la maleta

la vía

el andén

La señora hizo un viaje.
Hizo el viaje en tren.
Tomó el tren porque no quiso ir en carro.
Subió al tren.

El mozo vino con el equipaje.
El mozo puso el equipaje en el tren.
Los mozos ayudaron a los pasajeros
   con su equipaje.

El tren salió del andén número dos.
Algunos amigos estuvieron en el andén.

Vocabulario

¿Qué palabra necesito?

1 Historieta En la estación de ferrocarril

Contesten según se indica.

1. ¿Cómo vino la señora a la estación? (en taxi)
2. ¿Dónde puso sus maletas? (en la maletera del taxi)
3. En la estación, ¿adónde fue? (a la ventanilla)
4. ¿Qué compró? (un billete)
5. ¿Qué tipo de billete compró? (de ida y vuelta)
6. ¿En qué clase? (segunda)
7. ¿Dónde puso su billete? (en su bolsa)
8. ¿Qué consultó? (el horario)
9. ¿Adónde fue? (al andén)
10. ¿De qué andén salió el tren? (del número dos)
11. ¿Por qué hizo la señora el viaje en tren? (no quiso ir en coche)

Atocha, una estación de ferrocarril en Madrid

En la estación de Atocha

2 Historieta Antes de abordar el tren

Escojan.

1. ¿Dónde espera la gente el tren?
   a. en la ventanilla   b. en la sala de espera
   c. en el quiosco
2. ¿Dónde venden o despachan los billetes?
   a. en la ventanilla   b. en el equipaje
   c. en el quiosco
3. ¿Qué venden en el quiosco?
   a. boletos   b. maletas
   c. periódicos y revistas
4. ¿Qué consulta el pasajero para verificar la hora de salida del tren?
   a. la llegada   b. la vía   c. el horario
5. ¿Quién ayuda a los pasajeros con el equipaje?
   a. el mozo   b. el tablero   c. el andén
6. ¿De dónde sale el tren?
   a. de la ventanilla   b. del andén
   c. del tablero

3 **Historieta** **El billete del tren** Contesten.

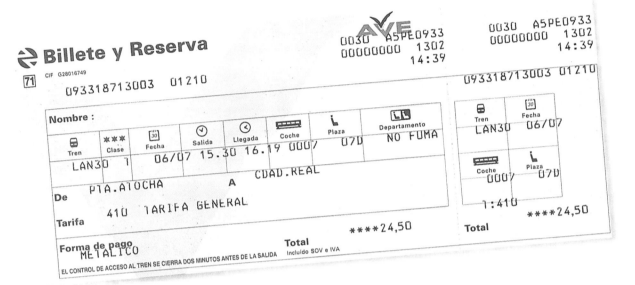

Billete y Reserva

1. ¿De qué estación sale el tren?
2. ¿Adónde va el tren?
3. ¿Cuál es la fecha del billete?
4. ¿A qué hora sale el tren?
5. ¿Está el asiento en la sección de fumar o de no fumar?
6. ¿Qué clase de billete es?
7. ¿Con qué pagó el/la pasajero(a)?

4 **RENFE (Red Nacional de Ferrocarriles Españoles)**
You're in Spain and you want to visit one of the cities on the map.
A classmate will be the ticket agent. Get yourself a ticket and ask the
agent any questions you have about your train trip.

En el tren

el asiento, la plaza

libre

el revisor

el pasillo

ocupado

el coche-comedor, el coche-cafetería

el coche-cama

la litera

MADRID Puerta de Atocha CADIZ	LLANO	
NUMERO DE TREN	9220	41 (1)
DIAS DE CIRCULACION	LMXJVSD	LMXJVSD
MADRID Puerta de Atocha	10:05	16:05
CIUDAD REAL	11:06	17:06
PUERTOLLANO	11:23	17:23
CORDOBA	12:12	18:11
SEVILLA Santa Justa	13:19	19:26
JEREZ DE LA FRONTERA	14:16	20:23
EL PUERTO DE STA. MARIA	14:27	20:36
SAN FERNANDO DE CADIZ	14:41	20:50
CADIZ	14:55	21:05

El tren salió a tiempo.
No salió tarde.
No salió con retraso
   (con una demora).

bajar(se) del tren

Los pasajeros van a bajar en la próxima
   parada (estación).
Van a transbordar en la próxima parada.

transbordar

¿Qué palabra necesito?

5 Historieta En el tren
Contesten.

1. Cuando llegó el tren a la estación, ¿subieron los pasajeros a bordo?
2. ¿El tren salió tarde?
3. ¿Con cuántos minutos de demora salió?
4. ¿Vino el revisor?
5. ¿Revisó él los boletos?

Santiago, Chile

Madrid, España

6 Historieta El tren
Contesten según la foto.

1. ¿Tiene el tren compartimientos?
2. ¿Tiene el coche o vagón un pasillo?
3. ¿Cuántos asientos hay a cada lado del pasillo?
4. ¿Hay asientos libres o están todos ocupados?
5. ¿Está completo el tren?
6. ¿Hay pasajeros de pie en el pasillo?

7 Historieta Un viaje en tren Completen.

1. Entre Granada y Málaga el tren local hace muchas ____.
2. No hay un tren directo a Benidorm. Es necesario cambiar de tren. Los pasajeros tienen que ____.
3. Los pasajeros que van a Benidorm tienen que ____ en la próxima ____ o ____.
4. ¿Cómo lo sabes? El ____ nos informó que nuestro tren no es directo.

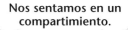

8 **¿Qué tienes que hacer?**

Work with a classmate. You are spending a month in Madrid and your Spanish hosts are taking you to San Sebastián. You're trying to pack your bags and their child (your partner) has a lot of questions. Answer his or her questions and try to be patient. The child has never taken a train trip before.

¿Dónde nos sentamos en el tren?

Nos sentamos en un compartimiento.

Madrid

San Sebastián

9 **De Santiago a Puerto Montt** You're planning a trip from Santiago de Chile to Puerto Montt. A classmate will be your travel agent. Get as much information as you can about the trip from Santiago to Puerto Montt. It gets rather cold and windy there and it rains a lot. You may want to find out if there are frequent delays. The following are some words and expressions you may want to use with the travel agent: **la demora, la tarifa, reservar, el número de paradas, el horario, el boleto de ida y vuelta, primera (segunda) clase.**

UN POCO MÁS

*For more practice using words from **Palabras 2**, do Activity 13 on page H14 at the end of this book.*

Estructura

Hacer, querer y venir en el pretérito
Relating more past actions

1. The verbs **hacer, querer,** and **venir** are irregular in the preterite. Note that they all have an **i** in the stem and the endings for the **yo, él, ella,** and **usted** forms are different from the endings of regular verbs.

INFINITIVE	hacer	querer	venir
yo	hice	quise	vine
tú	hiciste	quisiste	viniste
él, ella, Ud.	hizo	quiso	vino
nosotros(as)	hicimos	quisimos	vinimos
vosotros(as)	*hicisteis*	*quisisteis*	*vinisteis*
ellos, ellas, Uds.	hicieron	quisieron	vinieron

2. The verb **querer** has several special meanings in the preterite.

| **Quise ayudar.** | *I tried to help.* |
| **No quise ir en carro.** | *I refused to go by car.* |

SPANISH Online

For more information about travel in Peru and other areas of the Spanish-speaking world, go to the Glencoe Spanish Web site:
spanish.glencoe.com

¿Cómo lo digo?

10 **Historieta** **¿Cómo viniste?**
Contesten.

1. ¿Viniste a la estación en taxi?
2. ¿Viniste en un taxi público o privado?
3. ¿Hiciste el viaje en tren?
4. ¿Hiciste el viaje en el tren local?
5. ¿Lo hiciste en tren porque no quisiste ir en carro?

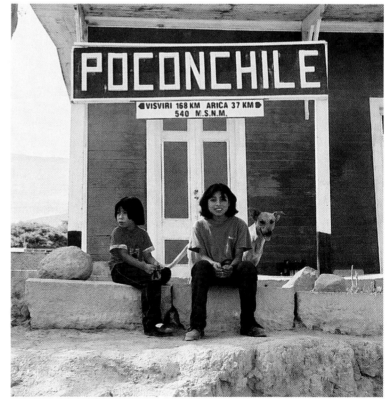

Poconchile, Chile

11 **No quisieron.** Completen.

1. —Ellos no __1__ (querer) hacer el viaje.

   —¿No lo __2__ (querer) hacer?

   —No, de ninguna manera.

   —Pues, ¿qué pasó entonces? ¿Lo __3__ (hacer) o no lo __4__ (hacer)?

   —No lo __5__ (hacer).

2. —¿Por qué no __6__ (venir) ustedes esta mañana?

   —Nosotros no __7__ (venir) porque no __8__ (hacer) las reservaciones.

3. —Carlos no __9__ (querer) hacer la cama.

   —Entonces, ¿quién la __10__ (hacer)?

   —Pues, la __11__ (hacer) yo.

   —¡Qué absurdo! ¿Tú la __12__ (hacer) porque él no la __13__ (querer) hacer?

12 **¡Rebelde!** A friend of yours (your classmate) is in trouble with his or her parents because he or she didn't help to get ready for their trip. Find out what your friend didn't do and why. Use the model as a guide.

¿Hiciste la maleta?

No.

¿Por qué no hiciste la maleta?

No hice la maleta porque no quise.

hacer la maleta
reservar un taxi
comprar los billetes
llamar a los parientes
hacer las reservaciones

13 **¿Qué hiciste durante el fin de semana?** With a classmate, take turns asking each other what you and other friends did over the weekend.

Estructura

Verbos irregulares en el pretérito
Describing more past actions

1. The verbs **estar, andar,** and **tener** are irregular in the preterite. They all have a **u** in the stem. Study the following forms.

INFINITIVE	estar	andar	tener
yo	estuve	anduve	tuve
tú	estuviste	anduviste	tuviste
él, ella, Ud.	estuvo	anduvo	tuvo
nosotros(as)	estuvimos	anduvimos	tuvimos
vosotros(as)	*estuvisteis*	*anduvisteis*	*tuvisteis*
ellos, ellas, Uds.	estuvieron	anduvieron	tuvieron

2. The verb **andar** means *to go,* but not to a specific place. The verb **ir** is used with a specific place.

Fueron a Toledo.
They went to Toledo.

Anduvieron por las plazas pintorescas de Toledo.
They wandered through (walked around) the picturesque squares of Toledo.

Vista de Toledo de El Greco

3. The verbs **poder, poner,** and **saber** are also irregular in the preterite. Like the verbs **estar, andar,** and **tener,** they all have a **u** in the stem. Study the following forms.

INFINITIVE	poder	poner	saber
yo	pude	puse	supe
tú	pudiste	pusiste	supiste
él, ella, Ud.	pudo	puso	supo
nosotros(as)	pudimos	pusimos	supimos
vosotros(as)	pudisteis	pusisteis	supisteis
ellos, ellas, Uds.	pudieron	pusieron	supieron

4. Like **querer,** the verbs **poder** and **saber** have special meanings in the preterite.

Pude parar.	*(After trying hard) I managed to stop.*
No pude parar.	*(I tried but) I couldn't stop.*
Yo lo supe ayer.	*I found it out (learned it) yesterday.*

¿Cómo lo digo?

14 **Historieta** **¿Dónde está mi tarjeta de identidad estudiantil?**
Contesten según se indica.

1. ¿Estuviste ayer en la estación de ferrocarril? (sí)
2. ¿Tuviste que tomar el tren a Toledo? (sí)
3. ¿Pudiste comprar un billete de precio reducido? (no)
4. ¿Tuviste que presentar tu tarjeta de identidad estudiantil? (sí)
5. ¿Dónde la pusiste? (no sé)
6. ¿La perdiste? (sí, creo)
7. ¿Cuándo supiste que la perdiste? (cuando llegué a la estación)

Toledo, España

15 **Historieta** **En el mercado**
Completen.

El otro día yo __1__ (estar) en
el mercado de Chichicastenango,
en Guatemala. Ramón __2__ (estar)
allí también. Nosotros __3__ (andar)
por el mercado pero no __4__ (poder)
comprar nada. No es que no __5__
(querer) comprar nada, es que no
__6__ (poder) porque __7__ (ir) al
mercado sin un quetzal.

Chichicastenango, Guatemala

Decir en el presente y en el pretérito
Telling what people say

1. The verb **decir** *(to say)* is irregular in the present and preterite tenses.
Study the following forms.

	Presente	**Pretérito**
yo	digo	dije
tú	dices	dijiste
él, ella, Ud.	dice	dijo
nosotros(as)	decimos	dijimos
vosotros(as)	*decís*	*dijisteis*
ellos, ellas, Uds.	dicen	dijeron

¿Cómo lo digo?

16 ¿Qué dices? Sigan el modelo.

¿Qué dices de la clase de español?

Pues, yo digo que es fantástica. Estoy aprendiendo mucho.

1. ¿Qué dices de la clase de matemáticas?
2. ¿Qué dices de la clase de inglés?
3. ¿Qué dices de la clase de biología?

4. ¿Qué dices de la clase de educación física?
5. ¿Qué dices de la clase de historia?

17 ¿Qué dicen todos? Completen con la forma apropiada del presente de **decir.**

Yo __1__ que quiero ir en tren pero Elena me __2__ que prefiere tomar el avión. Ella y Tomás también __3__ que no hay mucha diferencia entre la tarifa del avión y la tarifa del tren.

—¿Qué __4__ tú?

—Yo __5__ que es mejor ir en tren.

—Bien. Tú y yo __6__ la misma cosa. Estamos de acuerdo.

18 ¿Qué dijeron todos? Contesten.

1. ¿Dijiste tú que quieres ir?
2. ¿Dijeron ustedes que es mejor ir en tren?
3. ¿Dije yo que sí?

4. ¿Dijo Elena que ella tiene los boletos?
5. ¿Dijimos la misma cosa?

Andas bien. ¡Adelante!

Conversación

En la ventanilla

Pasajera	Un billete para Madrid, por favor.
Agente	¿Sencillo o de ida y vuelta?
Pasajera	Sencillo, por favor.
Agente	¿Para cuándo, señorita?
Pasajera	Para hoy.
Agente	¿En qué clase, primera o segunda?
Pasajera	En segunda. ¿Tiene usted una tarifa reducida para estudiantes?
Agente	Sí. ¿Tiene usted su tarjeta de identidad estudiantil?
Pasajera	Sí, aquí la tiene usted.
Agente	Con el descuento son veintidós euros.
Pasajera	¿A qué hora sale el próximo tren?
Agente	Sale a las veinte y diez del andén número ocho.
Pasajera	Gracias.

¿Comprendes?

Contesten.

1. ¿Dónde está la señorita?
2. ¿Adónde va?
3. ¿Qué tipo de billete quiere?
4. ¿Para cuándo lo quiere?
5. ¿En qué clase quiere viajar?
6. ¿Es alumna la señorita?
7. ¿Hay una tarifa reducida para estudiantes?
8. ¿Qué tiene la señorita?
9. ¿Cuánto cuesta el billete con el descuento estudiantil?
10. ¿A qué hora sale el tren?
11. ¿De qué andén sale?

Vamos a hablar más

A El horario Look at the train schedule. With a classmate, ask and answer as many questions as you can about it.

B Vamos a Barcelona. You and a classmate are spending a semester in Spain. You will be going to Barcelona for a couple of days. One of you is going to fly and the other is going to take the train. Compare your trips: time, cost, and what you have to do the day of departure.

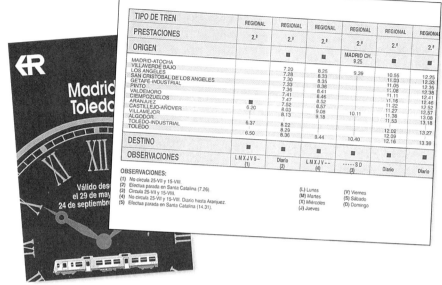

TIPO DE TREN	REGIONAL	REGIONAL	REGIONAL	REGIONAL	REGIONAL	REGIONAL
PRESTACIONES	2.ª	2.ª	2.ª	2.ª	2.ª	2.ª
ORIGEN						
MADRID-ATOCHA			MADRID CH. 9.25			
VILLAVERDE BAJO	7.20	8.25		10.55	12.25	
LOS ANGELES	7.28	8.33	9.39	11.03	12.33	
SAN CRISTOBAL DE LOS ANGELES	7.30	8.35		11.05	12.35	
GETAFE-INDUSTRIAL	7.33	8.38		11.08	12.38	
PINTO	7.36	8.41		11.11	12.41	
VALDEMORO	7.41	8.46		11.16	12.46	
CIEMPOZUELOS	7.47	8.52		11.22	12.52	
ARANJUEZ	7.52	8.57		11.27	12.57	
CASTILLEJO-AÑOVER	6.20	8.03	9.08	10.11	11.38	13.08
VILLAMEJOR	8.13	9.18		11.53	13.18	
ALGODOR	6.37	8.22				
TOLEDO-INDUSTRIAL	8.29			12.02	13.27	
TOLEDO	6.50	8.36	9.44	10.40	12.09	13.39
					12.16	
DESTINO						
OBSERVACIONES	L M X J V S - (1)	Diario (2)	L M X J V - - (4)	- - - - - S D (3)	Diario	Diario

OBSERVACIONES:
(1) No circula 25-VII y 15-VIII
(2) Efectúa parada en Santa Catalina (7.26).
(3) Circula 25-VII y 15-VIII.
(4) No circula 25-VII y 15-VIII. Diario hasta Aranjuez.
(5) Efectúa parada en Santa Catalina (14.31).

(L) Lunes   (V) Viernes
(M) Martes   (S) Sábado
(X) Miércoles   (D) Domingo
(J) Jueves

Pronunciación

La consonante ñ y la combinación ch

The **ñ** is a separate letter of the Spanish alphabet. The mark over it is called a **tilde**. Note that it is pronounced similarly to the *ny* in the English word *canyon*. Repeat the following.

señor	otoño	España
señora	pequeño	cumpleaños
año		

Ch is pronounced much like the *ch* in the English word *church*. Repeat the following.

coche	chaqueta
chocolate	muchacho

Repeat the following sentences.

El señor español compra un coche cada año en el otoño.
El muchacho chileno duerme en una cama pequeña en el coche-cama.
El muchacho pequeño lleva una chaqueta color chocolate.

Lecturas culturales

En el AVE

José Luis y su hermana, Maripaz, pasan dos días en Sevilla. Vinieron a visitar a sus abuelos. El viaje que hicieron de Madrid, donde viven, fue fantástico. Tomaron el tren y llegaron a Sevilla en sólo dos horas y quince minutos. Salieron de Atocha en Madrid a las 17:00 y bajaron del tren en Sevilla a las 19:15. ¿Es posible recorrer el trayecto[1] Madrid–Sevilla en dos horas quince minutos? Es una distancia de 538 kilómetros. ¡Es increíble!

[1]recorrer el trayecto *cover the route*

Reading Strategy

Interpretation of images Reading passages sometimes use images as a symbol to create an impression. Many times these images are animals. If you are able to identify an image, it is helpful to stop for a moment and think about the qualities and characteristics of the particular symbol the author is using in his or her imagery. Then when you have finished reading, go back and think about how the image and the topic of the reading are alike.

A bordo del AVE

Plaza de España, Sevilla

Sí, es increíble, pero es verdad. El tren español de alta velocidad es uno de los trenes más rápidos del mundo. Viaja a 250 kilómetros por hora. El tren se llama el AVE. ¿Por qué el AVE? Porque el tren vuela como un ave o pájaro.

José Luis y Maripaz tomaron el AVE. Según ellos, el viaje fue fantástico. ¿Por qué? Primero la velocidad. Pero el tren es también muy cómodo[2]. Lleva ocho coches en tres clases. Los pasajeros pueden escuchar música estereofónica o mirar tres canales de video. El tren también dispone de[3] teléfono por si acaso[4] un pasajero quiere o necesita hacer una llamada telefónica.

[2]cómodo *comfortable*
[3]dispone de *has available*
[4]por si acaso *in case*

Torre del Oro, Sevilla

¿Comprendes?

A Una visita a los abuelos
Contesten.
1. ¿Quiénes hicieron un viaje de Madrid a Sevilla?
2. ¿Quiénes vinieron a Sevilla, José Luis y su hermana o sus abuelos?
3. ¿Cómo hicieron el viaje?
4. ¿Qué tal fue el viaje?
5. ¿Cuánto tiempo tardó el viaje?
6. ¿A qué hora salieron de Madrid?
7. ¿A qué hora llegaron a Sevilla?

B Información Busquen la información.
1. uno de los trenes más rápidos del mundo
2. el nombre del tren
3. el número de coches que lleva el tren
4. el número de clases que tiene
5. algunas comodidades que el tren ofrece a los pasajeros

Plaza de España, Sevilla

Lectura opcional

De Cuzco a Machu Picchu

Un viaje muy interesante en tren es el viaje de Cuzco a Machu Picchu en el Perú. Cada día a las siete de la mañana, un tren de vía estrecha[1] sale de la estación de San Pedro en Cuzco y llega a Machu Picchu a las diez y media. Cuzco está a unos 3.500 metros sobre el nivel del mar. El tren tiene que bajar a 2.300 metros para llegar a Machu Picchu. Tiene que bajar 1.200 metros y en el viaje de regreso tiene que subir 1.200 metros.

Pero, ¿quiénes toman el tren para ir a Machu Picchu? Es un tren que lleva a muchos turistas que quieren ir a ver las famosas ruinas de los incas. Machu Picchu es una ciudad entera, totalmente aislada[2] en un pico andino al borde de[3] un cañón. Un dato histórico increíble es que los españoles no

[1]de vía estrecha *narrow gauge*
[2]aislada *isolated*
[3]al borde de *on the edge of*

La Plaza de Armas, Cuzco

El valle del Urubamba, Perú

Machu Picchu

descubrieron a Machu Picchu durante su conquista de Perú. Los historiadores creen que Machu Picchu fue el último refugio de los nobles incas al escaparse[4] de los españoles.

Machu Picchu fue descubierto por Hiram Bingham, el explorador y senador de Estados Unidos, en 1911. ¿Cómo llegó Bingham a Machu Picchu en 1911? ¡A pie! Y aún hoy hay sólo dos maneras de ir a Machu Picchu—a pie o en el tren que sale a las siete y media de Cuzco.

[4]al escaparse *upon escaping*

¿Comprendes?

¿Sí o no? Digan que sí o que no.
1. Machu Picchu está a una altura más elevada que Cuzco.
2. El tren que va de Machu Picchu a Cuzco tiene que subir 1.200 metros.
3. El viaje de Cuzco a Machu Picchu toma tres horas y media.
4. Hay muy pocos turistas en el tren a Machu Picchu.
5. En Machu Picchu hay ruinas famosas de los incas.
6. Machu Picchu fue una ciudad de los incas.
7. Los españoles descubrieron la ciudad de Machu Picchu durante su conquista de Perú.
8. Hiram Bingham fue un senador de Estados Unidos.
9. Él también fue a Machu Picchu en tren.

Conexiones

Las matemáticas

Conversiones aritméticas

When traveling through many of the Spanish-speaking countries, you will need to make some mathematical conversions. For example, train as well as plane schedules and hours for formal events, radio, and television are given using the twenty-four-hour clock. The metric system rather than the English system is used for weights and measures. Let's take a look at some of the conversions that must be made.

La hora

Cuando lees el horario para el tren o un anuncio para un programa cultural, dan la hora usando las 24 horas. La una (1:00) es la una de la mañana y las doce (12:00) es el mediodía. Las trece (13:00), una hora después del mediodía, es la una de la tarde y las veinticuatro horas (00:00) es la medianoche.

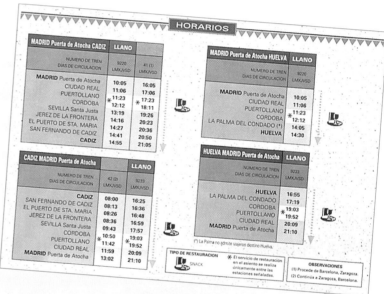

Nuestros amigos José Luis y Maripaz salieron de Madrid a las 17:00 y llegaron a Sevilla a las 19:15. Es decir que salieron de Madrid a las 5:00 de la tarde y llegaron a las 7:15 de la tarde.

El sistema métrico—pesos y medidas[1]

Pesos

Las medidas tradicionales para peso en los Estados Unidos son la onza, la libra y la tonelada. En el sistema métrico decimal, las medidas para peso están basadas en el kilogramo, o kilo.

[1]pesos y medidas *weights and measures*

Hay mil gramos en un kilo. El kilo es igual a 2,2 libras. Una libra estadounidense es un poco menos de medio kilo.

Líquidos

Las medidas para líquidos en Estados Unidos son la pinta, el cuarto y el galón. En el sistema métrico es el litro. Un litro contiene un poco más que un cuarto.

Distancia y altura

Para medir la distancia y la altura en Estados Unidos usamos la pulgada, el pie, la yarda y la milla. El sistema métrico usa el metro. El metro es un poco más que una yarda. Un kilómetro (mil metros) es 0,621 millas—un poco más que media milla.

¿Comprendes?

A La hora Read the schedule on page 424 and give the arrival and departure times of the trains using our system of telling time.

B El sistema métrico Contesten según las fotografías.
1. ¿Cuánto cuesta un litro de gasolina?
2. ¿Cuál es el límite de velocidad?
3. ¿Cuánto cuesta un litro de leche?
4. ¿Cuánto cuesta un kilo de carne?

UN VIAJE EN TREN

¡Te toca a ti!

Use what you have learned

HABLAR

1 El tren, el bus o el avión

✔ *Discuss train, bus, and plane travel*

Work in groups of three or four. Discuss the advantages **(las ventajas)** and the disadvantages **(las desventajas)** of bus, train, and air travel. In your discussion, include such things as speed, price, location of stations, and anything else you consider important.

HABLAR

2 Y ahora, ¿qué hacemos?

✔ *Discuss what to do if you miss your train*

You and a classmate are on a bus on the way to the Atocha station in Madrid. There's an awful traffic jam **(un tapón, un atasco).** You know you are going to miss your train. Discuss your predicament with one another and figure out what you can do.

La estación de ferrocarril, Málaga

3 En la estación de ferrocarril
✔ *Talk about activities at a train station*

With a classmate look at the photograph and talk about it.

4 ¡Una experiencia!
✔ *Write about an interesting train trip in Spain*

You took the AVE from Madrid to Sevilla. Write home and tell all about it.

5 Un viaje excelente

Write about a trip you took to a place you love. The place can be real or imaginary. Describe how and where you went and when. Then describe what the weather is like in that place and what clothing you need there. Continue writing about what you saw and how you got to each place you visited. In your description of the place, try to make your readers understand what it is about the place that you think is so great.

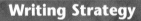

Writing Strategy

Writing a descriptive paragraph Your overall goal in writing a descriptive paragraph is to enable the reader to visualize your scene. To achieve this you must select and organize details that create an impression. Using a greater number of specific nouns and vivid adjectives will make your writing livelier.

Vocabulario

1 Completen.

To review **Palabras 1**, turn to pages 404–405.

1. Elena va de Madrid a Córdoba y va a volver a Madrid. Quiere un billete ____.
2. Los pasajeros esperan el tren en el andén o en la ____.
3. El ____ de llegadas indica a qué hora llegan los trenes a la estación.
4. Venden periódicos y revistas en el ____ en la estación de ferrocarril.
5. Un tren tiene varios vagones o ____.

2 ¿Sí o no?

To review **Palabras 2**, turn to pages 408–409.

6. El revisor trabaja en la estación de ferrocarril.
7. Una litera es un tipo de cama donde puede dormir un pasajero en un tren.
8. El tren que salió a tiempo salió con una demora.
9. Los pasajeros que van de Cuzco a Machu Picchu bajan del tren en Cuzco.

Estructura

3 Escriban en el pretérito.

    10. Los turistas andan por la plaza principal.
    11. Él hace la cama por la mañana.
    12. Lo pongo en la maleta.
    13. ¿Quién lo sabe?
    14. No estamos en la capital.

To review the preterite, turn to pages 412, 414, and 415.

4 Completen con **decir**.

    15–16. Yo lo _____ ahora y lo _____ ayer.
    17–18. Ellos lo _____ ahora y lo _____ ayer.

To review **decir**, turn to page 416.

Cultura

5 Contesten.

    19. ¿Qué es el AVE?
    20. ¿A qué ciudad de Andalucía fueron José Luis y su hermana?

To review this cultural information, turn to page 420.

UN VIAJE EN TREN

Tell all you can about this illustration.

Getting around a train station

la estación de
  ferrocarril
la ventanilla
el billete, el boleto sencillo
  de ida y vuelta
la sala de espera
el mozo, el maletero
el equipaje
la maleta
la bolsa

el tablero de llegadas,
  de salidas
el horario
el quiosco
el tren
el andén
la vía
en segunda (clase)
en primera (clase)

Describing activities at a train station

bajar(se) del tren
subir al tren
transbordar
salir a tiempo
  con retraso, con una demora

On board the train

el coche, el vagón
el pasillo
el compartimiento
el asiento, la plaza
  libre
  ocupado(a)
  reservado(a)
completo(a)
el coche-cama
el coche-comedor, el coche-cafetería
la litera
el revisor
la parada
en la próxima parada

VIDEOTUR

Episodio 13

In this video episode, you will join
Claudia and Francisco in an unusual train
experience. See page 504 for more
information.

How well do you know your vocabulary?

- Choose five words from the vocabulary list.
- Use the words in original sentences to tell a story.

En el restaurante

Objetivos

In this chapter you will learn to:

❖ order food or a beverage at a restaurant
❖ identify eating utensils and dishes
❖ identify more foods
❖ make a reservation at a restaurant
❖ talk about present and past events
❖ describe some cuisines of the Hispanic world

Hernán Miranda *Interiores con mesa*

En el restaurante

El mesero pone la mesa.

el camarero,
el mesero

Tengo hambre.

Tengo hambre y quiero comer.

Tengo sed.

Tengo sed y quiero beber algo.

.... el vaso

la sal

la pimienta ....

la taza

el platillo

el plato

la cuchara ....

el tenedor ....

la cucharita ....

la servilleta ....

el cuchillo

el mantel

La señorita pide el menú.

freír

el cocinero

El cocinero fríe las papas.
Está friendo las papas.

El mesero le sirve la comida.

la tarjeta
de crédito

la cuenta

el dinero

la propina

La señorita pide la cuenta.
El servicio no está incluido.
Ella deja una propina.

Vocabulario

¿Qué palabra necesito?

1 **¿Qué necesitas?** Contesten según el modelo.

> **¿Para tomar leche?** →
> **Para tomar leche necesito un vaso.**

1. ¿Para tomar agua?
2. ¿Para tomar café?
3. ¿Para comer la ensalada?
4. ¿Para comer el postre?
5. ¿Para cortar la carne?

2 **Historieta** **En el restaurante**
Contesten.

1. ¿Cuántas personas hay en la mesa?
2. ¿Tiene hambre María?
3. ¿Pide María el menú?
4. ¿Le trae el menú el mesero?
5. ¿Qué pide María?
6. ¿El mesero le sirve?
7. ¿El mesero le sirve bien?
8. Después de la comida, ¿le pide la cuenta al mesero?
9. ¿Le trae la cuenta el mesero?
10. ¿Paga con su tarjeta de crédito María?
11. ¿María le da (deja) una propina al mesero?
12. Después de la comida, ¿tiene hambre María?

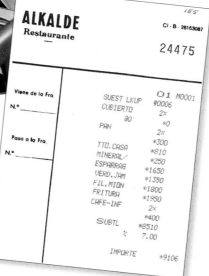

3 Palabras relacionadas Pareen las palabras relacionadas.

1. la mesa   a. el servicio
2. la cocina   b. la bebida
3. servir   c. el cocinero
4. freír   d. la comida
5. comer   e. el mesero
6. beber   f. frito

Alcalá de Henares, España

4 Historieta El mesero pone la mesa. Completen.

1. Para comer, los clientes necesitan ____, ____, ____ y ____.
2. Dos condimentos son la ____ y la ____.
3. El mesero cubre la mesa con ____.
4. En la mesa el mesero pone una ____ para cada cliente.
5. El niño pide un ____ de leche y sus padres piden una ____ de café.
6. Ellos tienen ____ y piden una botella de agua mineral.

5 En el restaurante Look at the advertisement for a restaurant in Santiago de Chile. Tell as much as you can about the restaurant based on the information in the advertisement. A classmate will tell whether he or she wants to go to the restaurant and why.

Aquí está Coco

El sabor de los mejores pescados y mariscos del Pacífico Sur, preparados como usted quiera, en un ambiente agradable e informal.

Más alimentos o comestibles

la carne

la carne de res, el biftec

la ternera

el cerdo

el cordero

el pescado

los mariscos

los camarones

las almejas

la langosta

el arroz

la alcachofa

el ajo

la berenjena

el maíz

los guisantes

el aceite

La joven pidió un biftec.
El mesero sirvió el biftec.
La comida está rica, deliciosa.

¡Diga!

Quisiera reservar una mesa, por favor.

Sí, señor. ¿Para cuándo?

Para esta noche a las nueve y media.

¿Cuántas personas?

Cuatro.

¿A nombre de quién, por favor?

A nombre de Julio Amaral.

Conforme, señor.

Vocabulario

¿Qué palabra necesito?

6 **¿Te gusta(n) o no te gusta(n)?** Contesten según los dibujos.

1.

2.

3.

4.

5.

6.

Barcelona, España

7 **Historieta** **Cenó en el restaurante.**
Contesten.

1. ¿Fue Victoria al restaurante anoche?
2. ¿Quién le sirvió?
3. ¿Pidió Victoria un biftec?
4. ¿Pidió también una ensalada?
5. ¿Le sirvió el mesero una ensalada de lechuga y tomate?
6. ¿Le sirvió una comida deliciosa o una comida mala?

SPANISH
Online

For more information about varieties of food in the Spanish-speaking world, go to the Glencoe Spanish Web site: spanish.glencoe.com

8 **¿Qué te gusta?** Contesten personalmente.

1. ¿Te gusta la ensalada?
2. ¿Te gusta la ensalada con aceite y vinagre?
3. ¿Te gusta el biftec?
4. ¿Te gusta el sándwich de jamón y queso?
   ¿Te gusta más con pan tostado?
5. ¿Te gusta la tortilla de queso?
6. ¿Te gustan los huevos con jamón?

9 **Una reservación** You call a restaurant in Buenos Aires. The headwaiter (a classmate) answers. Make a reservation for yourself and a group of friends.

10 **¿Qué recomienda usted?** Here's a menu from a very famous restaurant in Madrid. In fact, it's the oldest restaurant in the city, dating from 1725. There are many items on the menu that you will be able to recognize. A classmate will be the server. Ask what he or she recommends and then order.

C A R T A
I.V.A. 7% INCLUIDO

RESTAURANT
3ª Categoría

ENTRADAS
Jugos de tomate, naranja	2,60
Pimientos asados con bacalao	6,40
Lomo ibérico de bellota	15,00
Jamón ibérico de bellota	16,50
Surtido ibérico de bellota	14,10
Melón con jamón	13,00
Queso (manchego)	5,80
Ensalada riojana	6,20
Ensalada de lechuga y tomate	3,10
ENSALADA BOTIN (con pollo y jamón)	7,90
Ensalada de rape y langostinos	17,00
Ensalada de endivias con perdiz	13,00
Morcilla de Burgos	4,80
Croquetas de pollo y jamón	5,80
Manitas de cochinillo rebozadas	5,20
Salmón ahumado	13,20

SOPAS
Sopa al cuarto de hora (de pescados)	10,60
SOPA DE AJO CON HUEVO	3,80
Caldo de ave	3,20
Gazpacho	5,30

HUEVOS
Revuelto de la casa (morcilla y patatas)	5,50
Huevos revueltos con espárragos trigueros	6,60
Huevos revueltos con salmón ahumado	7,00
Tortilla de gambas	7,00

VERDURAS
Espárragos con mahonesa	8,90
Menestra de verduras salteadas con jamón ibérico	7,80
Alcachofas salteadas con jamón ibérico	5,90
Judías verdes con jamón ibérico	5,90
Setas a la segoviana	6,40
Patatas fritas	2,40
Patatas asadas	2,40

PESCADOS
(según mercado)
Angulas	15,70
ALMEJAS BOTIN	24,00
Langostinos con mahonesa	17,00
Gambas al ajillo	17,00
Gambas a la plancha	18,00
Cazuela de pescados	17,40
Rape en salsa	20,00
Merluza al horno o frita	16,00
Lenguado frito, al horno o a la plancha (pieza)	10,00
Calamares fritos	10,10
CHIPIRONES EN SU TINTA (arroz blanco)	

ASADOS Y PARRILLAS
COCHINILLO ASADO	15,40
CORDERO ASADO	16,00
Pollo asado 1/2	6,30
Pollo en cacerola 1/2	8,40
Perdiz estofada (pieza)	16,40
Filete de ternera a la plancha	12,00
Escalope de ternera	12,00
Ternera asada con guisantes	12,00
Solomillo a la plancha	17,00
SOLOMILLO BOTIN (al champiñón)	17,00
"Entrecotte" de cebón a la plancha	16,00

POSTRES
Cuajada	4,30
Tarta helada	4,40
Tarta de la casa (crema y bizcocho)	4,50
Tarta de chocolate	4,70
Tarta de frambuesa	5,30
Pastel ruso (crema de praliné)	5,20
Flan de la casa	2,70
Flan de la casa con nata	4,50
Helado de chocolate o caramelo	3,40
Helado de vainilla con salsa de chocolate	3,50
Surtido de buñuelos	5,70
Hojaldre de crema	4,80
Piña natural al dry-sack	4,00
Fresón con nata	5,10
Sorbete de limón	3,80
Melón	4,20
Bartolillos (sábados y domingos)	4,70

MENU DE LA CASA
(Primavera - Verano)

Precio: 26,00 €

Gazpacho campero
Cochinillo asado
Helado

HORAS DE SERVICIO: ALMUERZO, de 1:00 A 4:00 - CENA, de 8:00 A 12:00

HAY HOJAS DE RECLAMACION

ABIERTO TODOS LOS DIAS

Estructura

Verbos con el cambio e → i en el presente
Describing more present activities

1. The verbs **pedir, servir, repetir, freír, seguir** *(to follow)*, and **vestirse** *(to get dressed)* are stem-changing verbs. The **e** of the infinitive stem changes to **i** in all forms of the present tense except the **nosotros** and **vosotros** forms. Study the following forms. Note the spelling of **seguir.**

INFINITIVE	pedir	servir	seguir	vestirse
yo	pido	sirvo	sigo	me visto
tú	pides	sirves	sigues	te vistes
él, ella, Ud.	pide	sirve	sigue	se viste
nosotros(as)	pedimos	servimos	seguimos	nos vestimos
vosotros(as)	*pedís*	*servís*	*seguís*	*os vestís*
ellos, ellas, Uds.	piden	sirven	siguen	se visten

¿Cómo lo digo?

11 **Lo que yo pido** Digan si piden lo siguiente o no.

1.

2.

3.

4.

5.

6.

12 **Lo que pedimos en el restaurante**
Sigan el modelo.

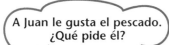 A Juan le gusta el pescado. ¿Qué pide él?

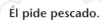 Él pide pescado.

1. A Teresa le gustan los mariscos. ¿Qué pide ella?
2. A Carlos le gusta el biftec. ¿Qué pide él?
3. A mis amigos les gustan las legumbres. ¿Qué piden ellos?
4. A mis padres les gusta mucho la ensalada. ¿Qué piden ellos?
5. Nos gusta el postre. ¿Qué pedimos?
6. Nos gustan las tortillas. ¿Qué pedimos?
7. ¿Qué pides cuando tienes sed?
8. ¿Qué pides cuando tienes hambre?

13 **Historieta Vamos al restaurante.** Completen.

Cuando mi amiga y yo __1__ (ir) al restaurante, nosotros __2__ (pedir) casi siempre una hamburguesa. Yo la __3__ (pedir) con lechuga y tomate y ella la __4__ (pedir) con queso. A mi amiga le __5__ (gustar) mucho las papas fritas. Ella __6__ (decir) que le __7__ (gustar) más cuando el cocinero las __8__ (freír) en aceite de oliva.

Marbella, España

14 **Entrevista** Contesten personalmente.

1. Cuando vas a un restaurante, ¿qué pides?
2. ¿Pides papas? Si no pides papas, ¿pides arroz?
3. ¿Qué más pides con la carne y las papas o el arroz?
4. ¿Quién te sirve en el restaurante?
5. Si te sirve bien, ¿qué le dejas?

15 **¿Por qué no pides... ?** You're in a restaurant with a friend (a classmate). You are hungry and thirsty, but you don't know what to order. Your friend will suggest something. Then you decide.

UN POCO MÁS

*For more practice using words from **Palabras 2** and the verb **pedir**, do Activity 14 on page H15 at the end of this book.*

Estructura

Verbos con el cambio e → i, o → u en el pretérito
Describing more activities in the past

1. The verbs **pedir, repetir, freír, servir,** and **vestirse** have a stem change in the preterite. The **e** of the infinitive stem changes to **i** in the **él** and **ellos** forms.

INFINITIVE	pedir	repetir	vestirse
yo	pedí	repetí	me vestí
tú	pediste	repetiste	te vestiste
él, ella, Ud.	pidió	repitió	se vistió
nosotros(as)	pedimos	repetimos	nos vestimos
vosotros(as)	*pedisteis*	*repetisteis*	*os vestisteis*
ellos, ellas, Uds.	pidieron	repitieron	se vistieron

2. The verbs **preferir, divertirse,** and **dormir** also have a stem change in the preterite. The **e** in **preferir** and **divertirse** changes to **i** and the **o** in **dormir** changes to **u** in the **él** and **ellos** forms.

INFINITIVE	preferir	divertirse	dormir
yo	preferí	me divertí	dormí
tú	preferiste	te divertiste	dormiste
él, ella, Ud.	prefirió	se divirtió	durmió
nosotros(as)	preferimos	nos divertimos	dormimos
vosotros(as)	*preferisteis*	*os divertisteis*	*dormisteis*
ellos, ellas, Uds.	prefirieron	se divirtieron	durmieron

¿Cómo lo digo?

16 **Historieta Servicio bueno o malo** Contesten según se indica.

1. ¿Qué pediste en el restaurante? (una ensalada)
2. ¿Cómo la pediste? (sin aceite y vinagre)
3. ¿Cuántas veces repetiste «sin aceite y vinagre»? (dos veces)
4. Y, ¿cómo sirvió el mesero la ensalada? (con aceite y vinagre)
5. ¿Qué hiciste? (pedí otra ensalada)
6. ¿Qué pidió tu amigo? (puré de papas)
7. ¿Y qué pasó? (el cocinero frió las papas)
8. ¿Qué sirvió el mesero? (papas fritas)
9. ¿Pidieron ustedes una bebida? (sí)
10. ¿Qué pidieron para beber? (una limonada)
11. ¿Qué sirvió el mesero? (un té)
12. ¿Le dieron ustedes una propina al mesero? (no)

17 **Historieta** Preparando la comida
Completen con el pretérito.

Anoche mi hermano y yo __1__ (preparar) la comida para la familia. Yo __2__ (freír) el pescado. Mi hermano __3__ (freír) las papas. Mamá __4__ (poner) la mesa. Y papá __5__ (servir) la comida. Todos nosotros __6__ (comer) muy bien. A todos nos __7__ (gustar) mucho el pescado. Mi hermano y mi papá __8__ (repetir) el pescado. Luego yo __9__ (servir) el postre, un sorbete. Después de la comida mi hermano tomó una siesta. Él __10__ (dormir) media hora. Yo no __11__ (dormir). No me gusta dormir inmediatamente después de comer.

Valparaíso, Chile

18 **Lo siento mucho.** You're in a restaurant and you're fed up with the waiter. He hasn't done a thing right. Call over the manager (a classmate) and tell him or her all that happened. He or she will apologize and say something to try to make you happy.

Andas bien. ¡Adelante!

En el restaurante

Teresa ¿Tiene usted una mesa para dos personas?

Mesero Sí, señorita. Por aquí, por favor.

Teresa ¿Es posible tener un menú en inglés?

Mesero Sí, ¡cómo no!

Paco Teresa, no necesito un menú en inglés. Lo puedo leer en español.
(El mesero les da un menú en inglés.)

Paco No sé por qué ella me pidió un menú en inglés.

Mesero No hay problema. Le traigo uno en español.

Paco Gracias.

Teresa Pues, Paco, ¿qué vas a pedir?

Paco Para mí, la especialidad de la casa.

Teresa Yo también pido la especialidad de la casa.

¿Comprendes?

Completen.

1. ¿Para cuántas personas quiere la mesa Teresa?
2. ¿Tiene el mesero una mesa libre?
3. ¿Qué tipo de menú pide Teresa?
4. ¿Necesita un menú en inglés Paco?
5. ¿Sabe él por qué ella le pidió un menú en inglés?
6. ¿Qué va a pedir Paco?
7. Y Teresa, ¿qué pide ella?

Vamos a hablar más

A **Fuimos al restaurante.** You and your parents went to a restaurant last night. A classmate will ask you questions about your experience. Answer him or her.

B **Preferencias** Work with a classmate and discuss whether you prefer to eat at home or in a restaurant. Give reasons for your preferences.

Pronunciación

La consonante x

An **x** between two vowels is pronounced much like the English *x* but a bit softer. It's like a **gs: examen → eg-samen.** Repeat the following.

> exacto   examen
> éxito   próximo

When **x** is followed by a consonant, it is often pronounced like an **s.** Repeat the following.

> extremo   explicar   exclamar

Repeat the following sentence.

> **El extranjero exclama que baja en la próxima parada.**

Lecturas culturales

La comida mexicana

Reading Strategy

Thinking while reading
Good readers always think while reading. They think about what the passage might be about after reading the title and looking at the visuals. They predict, create visual images, compare, and check for understanding; they continually think while the author is explaining.

Es muy difícil decir lo que es la comida hispana porque la comida varía mucho de una región hispana a otra.

Aquí en Estados Unidos la comida mexicana es muy popular. Hay muchos restaurantes mexicanos. Algunos sirven comida típicamente mexicana y otros sirven variaciones que vienen del suroeste de Estados Unidos donde vive mucha gente de ascendencia mexicana.

La base de muchos platos mexicanos es la tortilla. La tortilla es un tipo de panqueque. Puede ser de harina[1] de maíz o de trigo[2]. Con las tortillas, los mexicanos preparan tostadas, tacos, enchiladas, etc. Rellenan[3] las tortillas de pollo, carne de res o frijoles y queso.

[1]harina *flour*
[2]trigo *wheat*
[3]Rellenan *They fill*

San Miguel de Allende, México

El cultivo del maíz
de Diego Rivera

SECRETARIA DE EDUCACION, CULTURA
Y RECREACION

MUSEO CASA
"DIEGO RIVERA"
GUANAJUATO, GTO.
COOPERACION N$ 5.00

¿Comprendes?

La comida mexicana Contesten.

1. ¿Varía mucho la cocina hispana de una región a otra?
2. ¿Dónde es popular la comida mexicana?
3. ¿De dónde vienen muchas variaciones de la cocina mexicana?
4. ¿Qué sirve de base para muchos platos mexicanos?
5. ¿Qué es una tortilla? ¿De qué puede ser?
6. ¿De qué rellenan las tortillas?

Lectura opcional ①

Málaga, España

La comida española

En España, como en México, hay tortillas también. Pero hay una gran diferencia entre una tortilla mexicana y una tortilla española. La tortilla española no es de maíz. El cocinero español prepara la tortilla con huevos. La tortilla española, que es muy típica, lleva patatas (papas) y cebollas[1].

La cocina española es muy buena y muy variada. Como España es un país que tiene mucha costa, muchos platos españoles llevan marisco y pescado. Y los cocineros preparan muchos platos con aceite de oliva.

[1]cebollas *onions*

Málaga, España

¿Comprendes?

La cocina española Contesten.
1. ¿Cuál es la diferencia entre una tortilla española y una tortilla mexicana?
2. ¿Qué lleva la típica tortilla española?
3. ¿Por qué llevan marisco y pescado muchos platos españoles?
4. ¿Qué usan muchos cocineros españoles para preparar una comida?

Lectura opcional 2

La comida del Caribe

Humacao, Puerto Rico

En el Caribe, en Puerto Rico, Cuba y la República Dominicana, la gente come muchos mariscos y pescado. Es natural porque Puerto Rico, Cuba y la República Dominicana son islas. Pero la carne favorita de la región es el puerco o el lechón[1]. No hay nada más delicioso que un buen lechón asado[2]. Sirven el lechón con arroz, frijoles (habichuelas) y tostones. Para hacer tostones el cocinero corta en rebanadas[3] un plátano, una banana grande, verde y dura. Luego fríe las rebanadas en manteca[4].

[1]lechón *suckling pig*   [3]rebanadas *slices*
[2]asado *roast*   [4]manteca *lard*

¿Comprendes?

¿Lo sabes? Busquen la información.
1. algunos países de la región del Caribe
2. por qué come la gente muchos mariscos y pescado en la región del Caribe
3. una carne favorita de los puertorriqueños, cubanos y dominicanos
4. lo que sirven con el lechón asado
5. lo que son tostones

Conexiones

Las humanidades

El lenguaje

As we already know, Spanish is a language that is spoken in many areas of the world. In spite of the fact that the Spanish-speaking world covers a large area of the globe, it is possible to understand a speaker of Spanish regardless of where he or she is from. Although there are regional differences, these differences do not cause serious comprehension problems.

However, pronunciation does change from area to area. For example, people from San Juan, Puerto Rico; Buenos Aires, Argentina; and Madrid, Spain have pronunciations that are quite different from one another. However, the same is true of English. People from New York, Memphis, and London also have a distinct pronunciation, but they can all understand one another.

The use of certain words also changes from one area to another. This is particularly true in the case of words for foods. Let's look at some regional differences with regard to vocabulary.

Regionalismos

Comestibles

En España son patatas y en todas partes de Latinoamérica son papas.

En casi todas partes es el maíz, pero en México es el maíz o el elote y en Chile es el choclo.

En España son cacahuetes; en muchas partes de Latinoamérica son cacahuates, pero en el Caribe son maní.

En muchas partes es jugo de naranja, pero en Puerto Rico es jugo de china y en España es zumo de naranja.

Las judías verdes tienen muchos nombres. Además de judías verdes son habichuelas tiernas, chauchas, vainitas, ejotes y porotos.

Cosas que no son comestibles

Tomamos el autobús en España, el camión en México y la guagua en el Caribe y en las Islas Canarias.

En España todos duermen en el dormitorio o en la habitación. En México duermen en la recámara y en muchas partes en el cuarto o en el cuarto de dormir.

En España sacas un billete en la ventanilla y en Latinoamérica compras un boleto en la ventanilla o en la boletería.

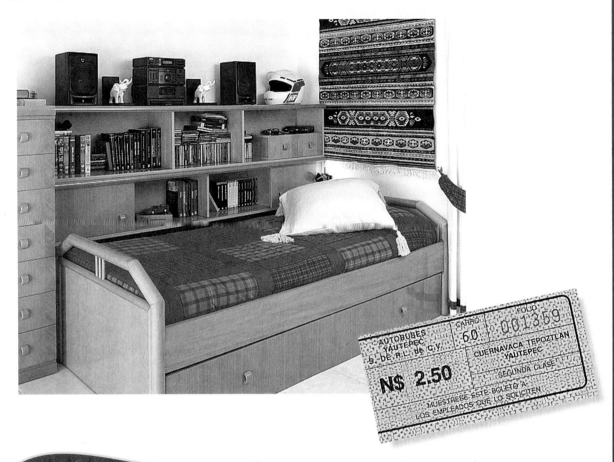

¿Comprendes?

A Hispanohablantes If any of your classmates are heritage speakers of Spanish, ask them to compare the way they say things. Have them share this information with you.

B El inglés There are variations in the use of English words. Discuss the following terms and where they might be heard.

1. bag, sack
2. soda, pop
3. elevator, lift
4. line, queue
5. pram, baby carriage
6. truck, lorry
7. traffic circle, rotary, roundabout
8. subway, underground

Use what you have learned

1 Vamos a un restaurante

✔ *Order food and beverages at a restaurant*

Pretend your Spanish class is at a restaurant. The restaurant serves food from Spain or Latin America. All the waiters and waitresses are Spanish speaking. Order your meal in Spanish and speak together in Spanish during your meal.

2 Una comida hispana

✔ *Describe a meal from some area of the Spanish-speaking world*

Work with a classmate. You have learned about some Hispanic cuisines. Talk about a meal or dish that you want to try **(probar).**

3 La comida

✔ *Talk about categories of food*

Mention a food category, such as meat, seafood, fruit, vegetable. Your partner will give the name of a food that belongs in that category. Take several turns each. Try to use as much as possible of the food vocabulary you've learned.

ESCRIBIR

4 El menú

✔ *Plan a menu*

Write out the menu for several meals in Spanish. You can plan meals for **el desayuno, el almuerzo,** and **la cena.**

35° Aniversario

La Estancia

ASADOR CRIOLLO

Lechón al Asador	$ 14,00
Chivito «La Estancia»	$ 15,00
Asado al Asador	$ 11,00

COCINA

Costilla de Cerdo con puré de manzana	$ 10,00
Costilla de Cerdo a la Riojana	$ 12,00
Lomo a la Pimienta con papas a la crema	$ 16,00
Lomo al Champignon	$ 17,00
Milanesa de Lomo	$ 6,50
Milanesa de Lomo a la Napolitana	$ 9,50
Milanesa de Pollo	$ 6,00
Milanesa de Pollo a la Napolitana	$ 9,00
Suprema de Pollo «La Estancia»	$ 10,50
Suprema de Pollo a la Maryland	$ 10,00
1/2 Pollo deshuesado a la Parrilla	$ 10,00

BIFES

Bife de costilla con Lomo con guarnición de papas fritas	$ 8,50
Bife de Chorizo	$ 7,50
Bife especial «La Estancia»	$ 14,50
Bife de Lomo especial «La Estancia».	$ 15,00
Costillas de Cerdo	$ 8,00
Chorizos (c/u)	$ 2,50
Salchicha Criolla (c/u)	$ 3,00
Morcillas (c/u)	$ 2,50
Matambrito Tiernizado	$ 10,00
Bife Aniversario con Lomo	$ 17,00
Mollejas porción	$ 11,00
Longaniza (c/u)	$ 4,00
Riñones porción	$ 5,00
Chinchulines de Ternera porción	$ 5,00
Chinchulines de Cordero porción	$ 9,00
Ubre porción	$ 4,50

Writing Strategy

Writing a letter of complaint When you write a letter of complaint, you must clearly identify the problem and suggest solutions; you should use a businesslike tone. You might be angry when you write a letter of complaint. But to be effective, you must control your emotions since your goal is to get the problem corrected. Your tone of voice is reflected in writing as much as it is in speech; your results will be better if you address the situation calmly and reasonably.In addition, it is important that the letter be addressed to the person who has the most authority.

ESCRIBIR

5 ¡Qué desastre!

Pretend you went to a restaurant where you had a very bad experience. The waiter didn't serve you what you ordered nor the way you ordered it. Write a letter to the management complaining about the food and the service.

Vocabulario

1 Identifiquen.

To review
Palabras 1, turn to
pages 434–435.

2 Identifiquen.

6.

7.

8.

To review
Palabras 2, turn to
pages 438–439.

9.

10.

3 **¿Sí o no?** Indiquen si la persona contesta bien.

11. —¿Para cuándo quiere usted la reservación?
   —Para cuatro.

12. —¿A nombre de quién, por favor?
   —Conforme, señor Pereda.

Estructura

4 **Completen con el presente.**

13. El mesero les ____ a los clientes en el restaurante. (servir)
14. Yo siempre ____ la misma cosa, un biftec. (pedir)
15. Ellas ____ elegantemente para ir al restaurante. (vestirse)
16. Nosotros no lo ____. (repetir)
17. El cocinero ____ las papas. (freír)

To review the present of stem-changing verbs, turn to page 442.

5 **Sigan el modelo.**

Él lo pidió. ⟶
Y yo lo pedí, también.

18. Ellos se divirtieron.
    Y yo ____, también.
19. Yo dormí bien.
    Y él ____ bien, también.
20. Tú lo repetiste.
    Y nosotros lo ____, también.
21. Ellos lo prefirieron.
    Y su amigo lo ____, también.
22. Nos vestimos.
    Y ellos ____, también.

To review the preterite of stem-changing verbs, turn to page 444.

Cultura

6 **Contesten.**

23. ¿Cuál es la base de muchas comidas mexicanas?
24. ¿Qué es una tortilla mexicana?
25. ¿De qué rellenan las tortillas para hacer tacos y enchiladas?

To review this cultural information, turn to page 448.

Tell all you can about this illustration.

Vocabulario

Getting along at a restaurant

el restaurante
la mesa
el/la mesero(a),
　el/la camarero(a)
el/la cocinero(a)

el menú
la cuenta
la tarjeta de crédito
la propina
el dinero

Identifying a place setting

el vaso
la taza
el platillo
el plato
el tenedor
el cuchillo

la cucharita
la cuchara
el mantel
la servilleta

How well do you know your vocabulary?

- Choose a food category from the list, for example, **la carne.**
- Have classmates choose the names of foods that belong to that category.

Describing some restaurant activities

poner la mesa
pedir
servir
freír

repetir
reservar
tener hambre
tener sed

Identifying more foods

la carne
la carne de res,
　el biftec
la ternera
el cerdo

el cordero
el pescado
los mariscos
los camarones
las almejas

la langosta
el ajo
la berenjena
la alcachofa
el arroz

el maíz
la sal
la pimienta
el aceite
el vinagre

Describing food

rico(a), delicioso(a)

VIDEOTUR

Episodio 14

In this video episode, you will join Vicky and Alberto as they help out at his father's restaurant. See page 505 for more information.

Conversación

El viaje en tren

Alberto ¿Te gustó el viaje que hiciste en tren?

María Sí, bastante. Dormí bien en la litera.

Alberto ¿Te desayunaste en el tren?

María No, porque llegamos a Madrid a las seis y media.

Alberto Y, ¿a qué hora salieron de San Sebastián?

María Salimos de San Sebastián a las veinte cuarenta.

¿Comprendes?

Los pasajeros Contesten.

1. ¿A María le gustó el viaje que hizo en tren?
2. ¿Cómo durmió en la litera?
3. ¿Se desayunó en el tren?
4. ¿A qué hora llegaron a Madrid?
5. ¿A qué hora salieron de San Sebastián?

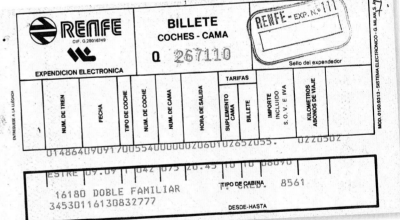

Estructura

Verbos irregulares en el pretérito

1. Review the preterite forms of the following irregular verbs.

HACER	hice	hiciste	hizo	hicimos	*hicisteis*	hicieron
QUERER	quise	quisiste	quiso	quisimos	*quisisteis*	quisieron
VENIR	vine	viniste	vino	vinimos	*vinisteis*	vinieron
ANDAR	anduve	anduviste	anduvo	anduvimos	*anduvisteis*	anduvieron
ESTAR	estuve	estuviste	estuvo	estuvimos	*estuvisteis*	estuvieron
TENER	tuve	tuviste	tuvo	tuvimos	*tuvisteis*	tuvieron
PODER	pude	pudiste	pudo	pudimos	*pudisteis*	pudieron
PONER	puse	pusiste	puso	pusimos	*pusisteis*	pusieron
SABER	supe	supiste	supo	supimos	*supisteis*	supieron

1 **Historieta** **En la estación de ferrocarril**

Completen con el pretérito.

El otro día yo __1__ (tener) que ir a Toledo. Carlos __2__ (ir) también. Nosotros __3__ (estar) en la estación de ferrocarril. Carlos __4__ (hacer) cola en la ventanilla. Él me __5__ (dar) mi billete y yo lo __6__ (poner) en mi bolsa. Nosotros __7__ (estar) en el andén. Cuando __8__ (venir) el tren, yo no __9__ (poder) hallar mi billete. No sé dónde lo __10__ (poner). No sé dónde está.

Verbos de cambio radical

1. Some verbs have a stem change in both the present and preterite tenses. Verbs like **pedir (i, i)** change the **e** to **i** in both the present and preterite.

PRESENT	pido	pides	pide	pedimos	*pedís*	piden
PRETERITE	pedí	pediste	pidió	pedimos	*pedisteis*	pidieron

2. Verbs like **preferir (ie, i)** change the **e** to **ie** in the present; they change **e** to **i** in the preterite.

PRESENT	prefiero	prefieres	prefiere	preferimos	*preferís*	prefieren
PRETERITE	preferí	preferiste	prefirió	preferimos	*preferisteis*	prefirieron

3. Verbs like **dormir (ue, u)** change the **o** to **ue** in the present; they change **o** to **u** in the preterite.

PRESENT	duermo	duermes	duerme	dormimos	*dormís*	duermen
PRETERITE	dormí	dormiste	durmió	dormimos	*dormisteis*	durmieron

2 **Información** Completen con el presente.

1. Yo te ____ el café y tú me ____ el postre. Nosotros nos ____. (servir)
2. Tú lo ____ y yo lo ____. Nosotros dos lo ____. (preferir)
3. Ellos lo ____ y yo lo ____. Todos nosotros lo ____. (repetir)
4. Él ____ enseguida y yo ____ enseguida. Todos ____ enseguida. (dormirse)

3 **Información** Completen con el pretérito.

1. Yo pedí un biftec y usted ____ un biftec también.
2. Yo freí el biftec y usted también lo ____.
3. Nosotros les servimos a todos los clientes y ustedes también les ____ a todos.
4. Seguimos trabajando en el comedor hasta las once y ustedes también ____ trabajando hasta las once.

4 **Historieta En un restaurante mexicano**

Contesten.

1. ¿Quién pidió tacos, tú o tu amigo(a)?
2. ¿Quién pidió enchiladas?
3. ¿Sirvieron las enchiladas con mucho queso?
4. ¿Pediste arroz y frijoles también?
5. ¿Frió el cocinero los frijoles?
6. ¿Sirvió el mesero la ensalada con la comida?
7. Después de comer, ¿dormiste?
8. Y tu amigo(a), ¿durmió él/ella también?

Comida mexicana en el restaurante
«La Fonda», San Miguel de Allende

 ## Verbos reflexivos

The subject of a reflexive verb both performs and receives the action of the verb. Each subject has its corresponding reflexive pronoun.

INFINITIVE	levantarse	acostarse
yo	me levanto	me acuesto
tú	te levantas	te acuestas
él, ella, Ud.	se levanta	se acuesta
nosotros(as)	nos levantamos	nos acostamos
vosotros(as)	*os levantáis*	*os acostáis*
ellos, ellas, Uds.	se levantan	se acuestan

5 **¿Y tú?**
Contesten personalmente.

1. ¿A qué hora te acuestas?
2. ¿Te duermes enseguida?
3. Y, ¿a qué hora te despiertas?
4. ¿Te levantas enseguida?
5. ¿Cuántas horas duermes?

6 **¿Y ellos?** Escriban las respuestas de Actividad 5, cambiando **yo** a **mis hermanos.**

7 **Un día típico** Work with a classmate. Compare a typical day in your life with a typical day in your partner's life.

8 **Comidas** Work with a classmate. Ask your partner about the meals he or she ate yesterday. Which meals did he or she eat, at what time, and what foods? Your partner will answer and tell you what he or she liked and didn't like to eat. Take turns.

Tapas, Estepona, España

Literary Companion

You may wish to read the adaptation of *El Quijote* by Miguel de Cervantes Saavedra. You will find this literary selection on pages 484–489.

Entérate España

Trovadores de hoy

Si te encuentras con un grupo de chicos que llevan traje[1] medieval, medias[2] y capa[3] negra con lazos[4] de colores, no son actores de una obra[5] de Shakespeare. Son universitarios que forman parte de grupos musicales que se llaman La Tuna. La Tuna, en sus comienzos ya hace siete siglos, es un grupo de trovadores universitarios que probablemente cantan para ganar el dinero que necesitan para pagar el viaje de vuelta a casa cuando llegan las vacaciones. Algunas cosas no cambian nunca.

[1]traje: *clothes, suit*   [3]capa: *cape*   [5]obra: *work*
[2]medias: *stockings*   [4]lazos: *ribbons*

Obras maestras[1] de la historia

España es el país del mundo que más ciudades tiene con el título "Ciudades Patrimonio de la Humanidad," una distinción de la UNESCO. Son 11 las ciudades españolas que no tienen precio[2]. Hacemos un breve recorrido[3] por algunas de ellas:

Alcalá de Henares: Lugar de nacimiento de Cervantes.

Ávila: Una ciudad completamente amurallada[4].

Córdoba: Cuenta con más de 2,000 años de historia.

Salamanca: Sinónimo de universidad con sus catedrales y palacios.

Santiago de Compostela: Miles de peregrinos[5] viajaron aquí a través del Camino de Santiago.

Segovia: Una calle principal pasa por debajo de un acueducto[6] romano.

Toledo: El Greco pintó aquí.

¡A comer como Hemingway!

¿Sabes que en el corazón del viejo Madrid, se encuentra el restaurante más antiguo del mundo, que una vez fue el sitio favorito de Ernest Hemingway? Entérate de la historia de Casa Botín:

■ *El Libro Guinness de los Records* proclama a Casa Botín, fundado en 1725, el restaurante más antiguo del mundo. Además, afirma que un adolescente con el nombre de Goya trabajó allí como lavaplatos[1].

■ Al principio, Casa Botín sirve de posada donde los comerciantes terminan su viaje, cenan y duermen.

■ Ernest Hemingway lo nombra en su libro *The Sun Also Rises.*

■ Tiene cuatro plantas[2].

■ La especialidad es el cochinillo asado[3].

■ A eso de la medianoche, La Tuna normalmente llega para tocar y bailar.

Ernest Hemingway

[1]lavaplatos: *dishwasher*
[2]plantas: *floors*
[3]cochinillo asado: *roast suckling pig*

[1]obras maestras: *masterpieces*
[2]no tienen precio: *priceless*
[3]breve recorrido: *short journey*
[4]amurallada: *walled*
[5]peregrinos: *pilgrims*
[6]acueducto: *aquaduct*

Ávila

Córdoba

Santiago

Segovia

Toledo

Un éxito[1] a pedir de boca[2]

Teresa Barrenechea encuentra la receta[3] de su fama: una pizca[4] de sabor y bastante nostalgia

De joven en Bilbao, Teresa Barrenechea se cuela[5] en las sociedades gastronómicas privadas donde solamente los socios[6] se reúnen a cocinar. Cada vez que la descubren, la mandan a casa. Sin embargo, Barrenechea es hoy una de los jefes de cocina más respetados de España y Estados Unidos. En su restaurante en Manhattan, dice que "la gente ahora sabe que las enchiladas no son españolas." ¿Y qué ocurre cuando Barrenechea regresa a Bilbao? La dejan entrar en los clubes de cocina.

[1]éxito: *success*

[2]a pedir de boca: *just right, exactly as one wishes*

[3]receta: *recipe*

[4]pizca: *pinch of*

[5]se cuela: *slips into*

[6]socios: *members*

Calendario de fiestas

Marzo: Valencia

Las Fallas son monumentos satíricos, hechos con materiales combustibles como el cartón[1] y la madera[2]. Se montan[3] unas 300 en las plazas de la ciudad. En la noche del 19 de marzo, festividad de San José, se queman[4].

Abril: Sevilla

Se construye una "ciudad" de casetas[5] adornadas con farolillos[6] de papel para celebrar la Feria de Abril. Mucha gente llega en carrozas tiradas por caballos[7], se visten en trajes tradicionales y bailan las sevillanas, un baile tradicional.

Octubre: Zaragoza

El día 12 de ocubre, para celebrar las Fiestas del Pilar, miles de zaragozanos recorren las calles en un desfile[8]—llamado la ofrenda de flores[9]—en el que llevan todo tipo de flores a la catedral. A la vez, bailan la jota, un típico baile folklórico.

[1]cartón: *cardboard*

[2]madera: *wood*

[3]se montan: *are set up*

[4]se queman: *they're burned*

[5]casetas: *tents*

[6]farolillos: *little lanterns*

[7]carrozas tiradas por caballos: *horse-drawn carriages*

[8]desfile: *parade*

[9]ofrenda de flores: *flower offering*

mi**cocina**

El plato más típico de la cocina española, sin ninguna duda, es la paella. Se originó como el plato tradicional de la provincia de Valencia, tomando su nombre de la sartén[1] ancha con dos asas[2]—llamada "paellera"—en la que se prepara. Actualmente, aparte de[3] la paella valenciana, existen muchas clases de paella, como la paella marinera que se hace con mariscos. Cada cocinero añade ingredientes distintos, como las aceitunas[4], los guisantes, el pimiento[5] y las gambas[6]. Sin embargo, hay quien dice que la paella valenciana es la más auténtica. He aquí los ingredientes del sabroso plato tradicional.

Paella valenciana

Ingredientes (*para 6 personas*)

    1 pollo
    200 gramos de judías verdes
    200 gramos de judías blancas
    400 gramos de arroz
    100 gramos de tomate
    1 diente de ajo
    1½ litros de agua
    sal y pimenta
    azafrán[7]
    aceite de oliva
    24 caracoles[8]

[1]sartén: *pan*

[2]asas: *handles*

[3]aparte de: *aside from*

[4]aceitunas: *olives*

[5]pimiento: *pepper*

[6]gambas: *shrimp*

[7]azafrán: *saffron*

[8]caracoles: *snails*

Paella marinera

¡ACCIÓN!

People EN ESPAÑOL

Anthony Hopkins y Antonio Banderas

Un festival de película[1]

Cada año durante los últimos días del mes de septiembre, la ciudad de San Sebastián recibe una dosis de "glamour." Se celebra el Festival Internacional de Cine. Cuando empieza el festival, el público espera ansioso la llegada de las estrellas. Actores, actrices y directores famosos asisten para ver las proyecciones de las películas del momento. Más de una docena[2] de filmes de distintas nacionalidades compiten por el máximo premio, la Concha de Oro[3]. Además, hay ruedas de prensa[4] y retrospectivas. Y...las palomitas de maíz[5].

[1]de película: *awesome, incredible, fantastic*
[2]docena: *dozen*
[3]Concha de Oro: *Golden Shell*
[4]ruedas de prensa: *press conferences*
[5]palomitas de maíz: *popcorn*

EN EL SET

Banderas

Antonio Banderas, actor: Ha actuado en más de 69 filmes en español e inglés, entre ellos *Evita* y *Spy Kids*. Hizo su debut en Broadway en un musical.

Cruz

Penélope Cruz, actriz: Actuó en una película española ganadora[1] del Óscar. Trasciende las fronteras[2] de España, ya que es una estrella de Hollywood.

Almodóvar

Pedro Almodóvar, cineasta[3]: Una de sus películas en español ganó el Óscar a la mejor película extranjera[4]. Otra ganó el Óscar al mejor guión[5] original.

Bardem

Javier Bardem, actor: Es muy conocido en España y América Latina. Fue candidato al Óscar al mejor actor protagonista.

[1]ganadora: *winner*
[2]trasciende las fronteras: *transcends the borders*
[3]cineasta: *filmmaker*
[4]extranjera: *foreign*
[5]guión: *script*

466

Un museo de sueño[1]

He aquí unas obras maestras de unos pintores españoles. ¿Adivinas[2] el nombre del artista que pintó cada cuadro[3]?

[1]de sueño: *a dream*
[2]adivinas: *can you guess*
[3]cuadro: *painting*

1

2

3

4

Respuestas:
1. Joan Miró
2. El Greco (Domeníkos Theotocópoulos)
3. Francisco de Goya
4. Pablo Picasso

Lo mejor del año

música

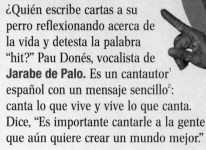

Jarabe de Palo

Paco de Lucia

¿Quién escribe cartas a su perro reflexionando acerca de la vida y detesta la palabra "hit?" Pau Donés, vocalista de **Jarabe de Palo.** Es un cantautor[1] español con un mensaje sencillo[2]: canta lo que vive y vive lo que canta. Dice, "Es importante cantarle a la gente que aún quiere crear un mundo mejor."

Cuando toca la guitarra **Paco de Lucía,** quizá el más popular de los guitarristas flamencos, el público suele[3] dar palmas[4], gritar "¡Óle!" e incluso bailar. Nació en Cádiz, y en su niñez está rodeado[5] del cante y del baile flamencos. Ha intervenido[6] en algunas películas, entre ellas *Carmen* de Carlos Saura. Se venden sus discos mundialmente.

Con su disco *Muchas flores*, **Rosario Flores,** ha logrado[7] un Grammy como el "Mejor Álbum de Cantante Pop." Además, fue protagonista de la película española del cineasta Almodóvar que ganó el Óscar al mejor guión. Dice, "Crecí en una familia llena de amor, alegría, comida, flores, gente, guitarras, baile y cante."

Rosario Flores ha logrado un Grammy como el "Mejor Álbum de Cantante Pop."

[1]cantautor: *singer/songwriter*
[2]mensaje sencillo: *simple message*
[3]suele: *usually*
[4]dar palmas: *claps*
[5]rodeado: *surrounded*
[6]intervenido: *appeared*
[7]logrado: *captured*

Atletas que destacan

Arantxa Sánchez Vicario La mejor tenista española de todos los tiempos, nació en Barcelona. Fue la primera jugadora de España en ganar el Abierto de Estados Unidos de América. Tiene tres títulos más de Grand Slam en singles.

David Beckham Cuando el centrocampista[1] inglés se unió al Real Madrid, pasó a ser uno de sus jugadores más famosos. Dice el futbolista[2], "Formar parte del Real Madrid es un sueño hecho realidad[3]."

Sergio García Llamado "El Niño," es el mejor jugador de golf español, siguiendo los pasos[4] de Seve Ballesteros y José María Olazábal. Empezó a jugar a los 3 años. Se hizo profesional en 1999, batiendo[5] el record del jugador más joven en disputar[6] un PGA (terminó en segundo lugar; Tiger Woods ganó).

[1]centrocampista: *midfielder*
[2]futbolista: *soccer player*
[3]sueño hecho realidad: *a dream come true*
[4]siguiendo los pasos: *following in the footsteps*
[5]batiendo: *breaking*
[6]disputar: *playing in*

Sánchez Vicario

Beckham

García

SUCESOS

100,000 personas se comieron la paella más grande del mundo en España.

El ingenioso hidalgo Don Quijote de la Mancha, de Miguel de Cervantes, fue elegido como el mejor libro de ficción de todos los tiempos, en un sondeo[1] realizado entre los autores más prestigiosos del mundo.

El escritor **José Jiménez Lozano** recibió de manos del Rey **Don Juan Carlos de España** el Premio Cervantes, considerado como el Nóbel de la literatura en castellano. La ceremonia tuvo lugar en Alcalá de Henares.

[1]sondeo: *opinion poll*

467

Literary Companion

These literary selections develop reading and cultural skills and introduce students to Hispanic literature.

Biblioteca,
Universidad
de México ▶

Versos sencillos José Martí

Vocabulario

una rosa

una flor

el corazón

El señor da la mano.

Actividad

¿Sí o no? Digan que sí o que no.

1. Una rosa es una flor bonita.
2. El corazón es un órgano vital.
3. Damos la mano a un amigo.

La Habana, Cuba

INTRODUCCIÓN   José Martí (1853–1895) es cubano. Es un hombre muy famoso. Es poeta y es también un héroe. Durante toda la vida Martí lucha[1] por la independencia de Cuba.

Estudia en Madrid y en Zaragoza en España. José Martí admira mucho a la España artística y humana. Pero ataca la España política porque su país, Cuba, en aquel entonces[2] es una colonia de España.

Martí pasa mucho tiempo en varias repúblicas hispanoamericanas—México, Guatemala, Venezuela y Honduras. «De América soy hijo»—proclama Martí. Pasa también unos catorce años en Estados Unidos. Publica *Versos sencillos* en Nueva York en 1891.

Versos sencillos es una colección de poemas (poesías).

[1]lucha *fights*
[2]en aquel entonces *at that time*

Versos sencillos

Cultivo una rosa blanca,
en julio como en enero
para el amigo sincero
que me da su mano franca.

Y para el cruel que me arranca°
el corazón con que vivo,
cardo ni ortiga° cultivo
cultivo la rosa blanca.

arranca *pulls out*
cardo ni ortiga *thistle nor nettle*

¿Comprendes?

En inglés, por favor.   Contesten.
1. Is the theme of this short poem gardening, friendship, or roses?
2. What two types of people does the poet speak about?
3. In your own words, explain how the poet tells us that he treats all people equally.
4. How does the poet express "all the time"?

«Una moneda de oro» Francisco Monterde

Vocabulario

la luna

el parque

el dedo

el suelo

una moneda de oro

Es temprano por la noche (8:30).
Hay una moneda en el suelo.

La moneda refleja la luz de la luna.
Un señor halla la moneda.

la luz

La señora enciende la luz.

el agujero

el bolsillo

Ella cose el bolsillo porque
tiene un agujero.

el
chaleco

La señora cuelga el chaleco
en la silla.

el mantel

El señor esconde la moneda.
Mete la moneda debajo del mantel.

El señor levanta el mantel.
Debajo del mantel hay dinero.
El señor está muy alegre.

un juguete

Es la Navidad.
El señor recoge el juguete.
La niña está dormida.

Actividades

A **¿Sabes la palabra?** Escojan.

1. El ____ de diciembre es la Navidad.
   a. veinticinco **b.** veinticuatro
2. Los niños reciben ____ para la Navidad.
   a. sillas **b.** juguetes
3. Ella tiene que coser el bolsillo porque tiene ____.
   a. un agujero **b.** una moneda
4. El señor no pierde la moneda. ____ la moneda.
   a. Busca **b.** Halla

5. La señora cuelga ____ en la silla.
   a. el chaleco **b.** el mantel
6. El señor mete la moneda debajo del mantel. Él ____ la moneda.
   a. recoge **b.** esconde
7. En la mano hay cinco ____.
   a. monedas **b.** dedos

B **La moneda** Contesten.

1. ¿Dónde está el señor? (en el parque)
2. ¿Qué parte del día es? (la noche)
3. ¿Qué halla el señor? (una moneda)
4. ¿Recoge la moneda? (sí)
5. ¿De qué es la moneda? (de oro)
6. ¿Qué refleja la moneda? (la luna)

INTRODUCCIÓN   Francisco Monterde es de México. Nace en 1894. Es poeta, dramaturgo y novelista. Es también cuentista. Publica una colección de cuentos[1] en 1943. Sus cuentos presentan un estudio serio de la historia de México.

Aquí tenemos el cuento «Una moneda de oro». Es un cuento sencillo[2] y tierno[3]. El autor habla de una pobre familia mexicana del campo.

[1] cuentos *stories*   [2] sencillo *simple*   [3] tierno *tender*

«Una moneda de oro»

1

Es una Navidad alegre para el pobre. El pobre es Andrés. No tiene dinero y no tiene trabajo desde el otoño.

Es temprano por la noche. Andrés pasa por el parque. En el suelo ve una moneda que refleja la luz de la luna. —¿Es una moneda de oro?—pregunta Andrés. —Pesa° mucho. ¡Imposible! No puede ser una moneda de oro. Es sólo una medalla.

Pesa *It weighs*

Andrés sale del parque y examina la moneda. No, no es una medalla. Es realmente una moneda de oro. Andrés acaricia° la moneda. ¡Es muy agradable su contacto!

acaricia *caresses*

2

Con la moneda entre los dedos, mete la mano derecha en el bolsillo de su pantalón. No, no puede meter la moneda en el bolsillo. Tiene miedo° de perder la moneda. Examina el bolsillo. No, no tiene agujeros. No hay problema. Puede meter la moneda en el bolsillo. No va a perder la moneda.

Tiene miedo *He is afraid*

Andrés va a casa a pie. Anda rápido. La moneda de oro salta° en el bolsillo. El pobre Andrés está muy contento.

salta *jumps around*

Luego tiene una duda. ¿Es falsa la moneda? Andrés tiene una idea. Va a entrar en una tienda. Va a comprar algo. Y va a pagar con la moneda. Si el dependiente acepta la moneda, es buena, ¿no? Y si no acepta la moneda, ¿qué? Andrés reflexiona. No, no va a ir a la tienda. Prefiere ir a casa con la moneda. Su mujer va a estar muy contenta.

3

Su casa es una casa humilde. Tiene sólo dos piezas o cuartos. Cuando llega a casa, su mujer no está. No está porque cada día tiene que ir a entregar° la ropa que cose para ganar unos pesos.

Andrés enciende una luz. Pone la moneda en la mesa. En unos momentos oye° a su mujer y a su hija. Ellas vuelven a casa. Esconde la moneda debajo del mantel.

La niña entra. Andrés toma la niña en sus brazos. Luego llega su mujer. Tiene una expresión triste y melancólica. —¿Tienes trabajo?—pregunta ella. —Hoy no puedo comprar pan. No me pagan cuando entrego la costura°.

Andrés no contesta. Levanta el mantel. Su mujer ve la moneda. Toma la moneda en las manos. —¿Quién te da la moneda?

—Nadie°—Andrés habla con su mujer. Explica como halla la moneda en el parque.

La niña toma la moneda y empieza a jugar con la moneda. Andrés tiene miedo. No quiere perder la moneda. Puede irse por° un agujero.

Andrés toma la moneda y pone la moneda en uno de los bolsillos de su chaleco. —¿Qué compramos con la moneda?—pregunta Andrés.

—No compramos nada. Tenemos que pagar mucho—suspira su mujer. Debemos° mucho.

—Es verdad—contesta Andrés. —Pero hoy es Nochebuena°. Tenemos que celebrar.

—No—contesta su mujer. —Primero tenemos que pagar el dinero que debemos.

entregar *return, deliver*

oye *he hears*

costura *sewing*

Nadie *No one*

irse por *slip through*

Debemos *We owe*
Nochebuena *Christmas Eve*

Una casa humilde, México

Andrés está un poco malhumorado. Se quita° el chaleco y el saco. Cuelga el chaleco y el saco en la silla.

—Bueno, Andrés. Si quieres, puedes ir a comprar algo. Pero tenemos que guardar lo demás°.

Andrés acepta. Se pone° el chaleco y el saco y sale de casa.

4

En la calle Andrés ve a su amigo Pedro.

—¿Adónde vas? ¿Quieres ir a tomar algo?

Andrés acepta. Los amigos pasan un rato en un café pequeño. Beben y hablan. Y luego Andrés sale. Va a la tienda. Sólo va a comprar comida para esta noche. Y un juguete para la niña.

Andrés compra primero los alimentos. El paquete está listo°. Andrés busca la moneda. Busca en el chaleco. No está. Busca en el saco. No está. Busca en su pantalón. La moneda no está en ninguno de sus bolsillos. El pobre Andrés está lleno de terror. Tiene que salir de la tienda sin la comida.

Una vez más está en la calle. Vuelve a casa. Llega a la puerta. No quiere entrar. Pero tiene que entrar. Entra y ve a la niña dormida con la cabeza entre los brazos sobre la mesa. Su mujer está cosiendo a su lado.

—La moneda…

—¿Qué?

—No tengo la moneda.

—¿Cómo?

La niña sobresalta°. Abre los ojos. Baja los brazos y bajo la mesa Andrés y su mujer oyen el retintín° de la moneda de oro.

¡Qué contentos están Andrés y su mujer! Recogen la moneda que la niña había escamoteado° del chaleco cuando estaba colgado en la silla.

Se quita He takes off

guardar lo demás keep the rest
Se pone He puts on

listo ready

sobresalta jumps up
retintín jingle

había escamoteado had secretly taken out

¿Comprendes?

A Comprensión Contesten.
1. ¿Quién es el pobre?
2. ¿Por qué no tiene dinero?
3. ¿Por dónde pasa Andrés?
4. ¿Qué ve en el suelo?
5. ¿Es una moneda de oro o es una medalla?

B Andrés y la moneda Escojan.
1. ¿Por qué no debe Andrés meter la moneda en el bolsillo de su pantalón?
   a. Porque el bolsillo tiene un agujero.
   b. Porque puede perder la moneda.

2. Cuando Andrés examina el bolsillo, ¿qué decide?
   a. Puede meter la moneda en el bolsillo porque no tiene agujero.
   b. Va a perder la moneda.
   c. La moneda de oro es sólo una medalla.
3. ¿Cómo va Andrés a casa?
   a. Salta.
   b. A pie y rápido.
   c. Con miedo.
4. ¿Qué duda tiene Andrés?
   a. Si tiene que comprar algo.
   b. Si la moneda es falsa o no.
   c. Si su pantalón tiene un agujero.
5. Si compra algo en una tienda, ¿por qué quiere pagar con la moneda?
   a. Si el dependiente acepta la moneda, no es falsa.
   b. Porque la moneda es falsa y Andrés no quiere la moneda.
   c. Porque no tiene dinero.
6. ¿Qué decide Andrés?
   a. Decide que la moneda es falsa.
   b. Decide que no necesita nada.
   c. Decide que no va a la tienda. Prefiere ir a casa.

Una vista del campo, México

La Navidad, México

C ¿Sí o no? Digan que sí o que no.
1. La casa de Andrés es muy humilde.
2. La casa tiene cuatro piezas.
3. Cuando llega Andrés, su mujer cose.
4. Su mujer cose para ganar dinero.
5. Su mujer y su hija vuelven a casa.
6. Andrés toma a su mujer en sus brazos.
7. Su mujer está muy contenta.
8. Hoy ella compra pan.
9. Cuando Andrés levanta el mantel, su mujer ve la moneda.
10. La niña empieza a jugar con la moneda.
11. Andrés quiere comprar algo para celebrar la Navidad.
12. Su mujer quiere comprar mucho.
13. Por fin Andrés puede ir a la tienda a comprar algo.

D Andrés sale. Contesten.
1. ¿A quién ve Andrés en la calle?
2. ¿Adónde van los dos?
3. Luego, ¿adónde va Andrés?
4. ¿Qué va a comprar?
5. ¿Qué busca Andrés?
6. ¿Qué no puede hallar?
7. ¿Qué ve cuando entra en la casa?
8. ¿Dónde está la moneda?

«*La camisa de Margarita*» Ricardo Palma

Vocabulario

Es un galán.
Es un señor muy elegante.
Es soltero. No tiene esposa.
  No está casado.

Los jóvenes están enamorados.
El joven le echa flores a la señorita.
La joven le flecha el corazón al joven.
Los jóvenes tienen una sonrisita.

el cuello

el vestido
de novia

una cadena de diamantes (brillantes)

El sacerdote habla con los recién casados.
Están en la iglesia.

el **suegro** el padre del marido o de la mujer
el **sacerdote** un padre (religioso) católico
el **pobretón** un muchacho pobre que no tiene dinero
el **chisme** la historieta, un rumor
los **muebles** la silla, la mesa, la cama, etc., son muebles
altivo arrogante
con mucha plata que tiene mucho dinero, rico

Nota In this story you will come across the following words that describe money used in Peru in the eighteenth century. From the context of the reading you will be able to tell which were of little value and which were of great value. It is not necessary for you to learn these words: **un ochavo, un real, un maravedí, un duro, un morlaco.**

Actividades

A **Los jóvenes** Contesten según los dibujos.

1. ¿Es un tipo galán el joven?
2. ¿Es un poco altivo?
3. ¿Es soltero?
4. ¿Tiene esposa?
5. ¿Está enamorado el joven?
6. ¿Qué le echa a la señorita?
7. ¿Qué tiene en la cara?
8. ¿Tiene la señorita una cadena de diamantes en el cuello?

B **El galán** Expresen de otra manera.

1. Él no tiene mujer. No está casado.
2. Es un señor elegante.
3. Es un tipo muy arrogante.
4. No es un joven que tiene mucho dinero.
5. No sé si es verdad. Es un rumor.

INTRODUCCIÓN   Ricardo Palma es uno de los hombres más famosos de letras peruanas de todos los tiempos. Él da origen a un nuevo género literario—la tradición. La tradición es una anécdota histórica.

   Ricardo Palma publica sus *Tradiciones peruanas* en diez tomos de 1872 a 1910. Las tradiciones presentan la historia de Perú desde la época precolombina hasta la guerra con Chile (1879–1883). Las tradiciones más interesantes y más famosas son las tradiciones que describen la época colonial. «La camisa de Margarita» es un ejemplo de una tradición de la época colonial.

«La camisa de Margarita»

1

   Cuando las señoras viejas de Lima quieren describir algo que cuesta mucho, ¿qué dicen? Dicen: —¡Qué! Si esto es más caro que la camisa de Margarita Pareja.

   Margarita Pareja es por los años 1765 la hija mimada° de don Raimundo Pareja, un colector importante del Callao. La muchacha es una de estas limeñitas que es tan bella que puede cautivar° al mismo diablo°. Tiene unos ojos negros cargados° de dinamita que hacen explosión sobre el alma° de los galanes limeños.

   Llega de España un arrogante joven llamado don Luis de Alcázar. Don Luis tiene en Lima un tío aragonés, don Honorato. Don Honorato es solterón y es muy rico. Si el tío es rico, no lo es el joven. No tiene ni un centavo.

mimada *spoiled*

cautivar *captivate, charm*

diablo *devil*

cargados *charged*

alma *soul*

2

   En la procesión de Santa Rosa, Alcázar conoce a la linda Margarita. La muchacha le flecha el corazón. El joven le echa flores. Ella no le contesta ni sí ni no. Pero con sonrisitas y otras armas del arsenal femenino le da a entender al joven que es plato muy de su gusto.

   Los enamorados olvidan° que existe la aritmética. Don Luis no considera su presente condición económica un obstáculo. Va al padre de Margarita y le pide su mano°. Al padre de Margarita, don Raimundo, no le gusta nada la petición del joven arrogante. Le dice que Margarita es demasiado joven para tomar marido.

olvidan *forget*

le pide su mano *asks for her hand*

Pero la edad de su hija no es la verdadera razón. Don Raimundo no quiere ser suegro de un pobretón. Les dice la verdad a algunos de sus amigos. Uno de ellos va con el chisme al tío aragonés. El tío, que es un tipo muy altivo, se pone° furioso.

se pone *becomes*

—¡Cómo! ¡Desairar° a mi sobrino! No hay más gallardo en todo Lima. Ese don Raimundo va a ver…

Desairar *To snub*

3

Y la pobre Margarita se pone muy enferma. Pierde peso° y tiene ataques nerviosos. Sufre mucho. Su padre se alarma y llama a varios médicos y curanderos. Todos declaran que la única medicina que va a salvar a la joven no se vende en la farmacia. El padre tiene que permitir a la muchacha casarse° con el varón de su gusto.

peso *weight*

casarse *to marry*

Don Raimundo va a la casa de don Honorato. Le dice: —Usted tiene que permitir a su sobrino casarse con mi hija. Porque si no, la muchacha va a morir.

—No puede ser—contesta de la manera más desagradable el tío. —Mi sobrino es un pobretón. Lo que usted debe buscar para su hija es un hombre con mucha plata.

El diálogo entre los dos es muy borrascoso°.

—Pero, tío, no es cristiano matar° a quien no tiene la culpa°—dice don Luis.

borrascoso *stormy*
matar *kill*
culpa *blame*

Iglesia de San Francisco, Lima, Perú

—¿Tú quieres casarte con esa joven?

—Sí, de todo corazón, tío y señor.

—Pues bien, muchacho. Si tú quieres, consiento. Pero con una condición. Don Raimundo me tiene que jurar° que no va a regalar un ochavo a su hija. Y no le va a dejar un real en la herencia—. Aquí empieza otra disputa.

jurar *to swear*

—Pero, hombre, mi hija tiene veinte mil duros de dote°.

—Renunciamos a la dote. La niña va a venir a casa de su marido con nada más que la ropa que lleva o tiene puesta°.

—Entonces me permite regalar a mi hija los muebles° y el ajuar (vestido) de novia.

—Ni un alfiler°.

—Usted no es razonable, don Honorato. Mi hija necesita llevar una camisa para reemplazar la puesta.

—Bien, usted le puede regalar la camisa de novia y se acaba°.

Al día siguiente don Raimundo y don Honorato van a la Iglesia de San Francisco a oír misa°. En el momento que el sacerdote eleva la Hostia, dice el padre de Margarita: —Juro no dar a mi hija más que la camisa de novia.

Y don Raimundo cumple con° su promesa. Ni en la vida ni en la muerte le da después a su hija un maravedí.

Los encajes° de Flandes que adornan la camisa de la novia cuestan dos mil setecientos duros. El cordoncillo que ajusta al cuello es una cadena de brillantes que tienen un valor de treinta mil morlacos.

Los recién casados hacen creer al tío aragonés que la camisa no vale° nada. Porque don Honorato es tan testarudo°, que a saber el valor real de la camisa, le hace al sobrino divorciarse.

Ahora sabemos por qué es muy merecida° la fama que tiene la camisa nupcial de Margarita Pareja.

dote *dowry*

tiene puesta *has on*

muebles *furniture*

alfiler *pin*

se acaba *that's it*

oír misa *to hear mass*

cumple con *fulfills*

encajes *lace*

vale *is worth*

testarudo *hard-headed*

merecida *deserved*

Palacio arzobispal, Lima

¿Comprendes?

A Margarita Pareja Contesten.

1. ¿Quiénes dicen: —¡Qué! ¡Si esto es más caro que la camisa de Margarita Pareja?
2. ¿Quién es Margarita Pareja?
3. ¿Cómo es Margarita?
4. ¿Quién llega a Perú?
5. ¿De dónde viene?
6. ¿Quién es?
7. ¿Cómo es el tío?
8. ¿Cómo es el sobrino?

B Don Luis Completen.

1. Don Luis conoce a Margarita en ____.
2. Margarita le ____. Y don Luis le ____.
3. Don Luis no considera su condición económica ____
4. Don Luis va al padre de Margarita y ____.
5. Al padre no le gusta nada ____.
6. No le gusta la petición porque ____.
7. Cuando el tío sabe lo que dice don Raimundo, él se pone ____.

Palacio arzobispal, Lima

C En español, por favor.

Contesten en español.

1. What happens to Margarita?
2. What medicine does she need?
3. Why does the young man's uncle say his nephew cannot marry Margarita?
4. Under what condition does the uncle consent?

D En tus propias palabras

In your own words in English, explain the ending of this story. What does Margarita's father do?

Plaza de Armas, Lima

El Quijote Miguel de Cervantes Saavedra

Vocabulario

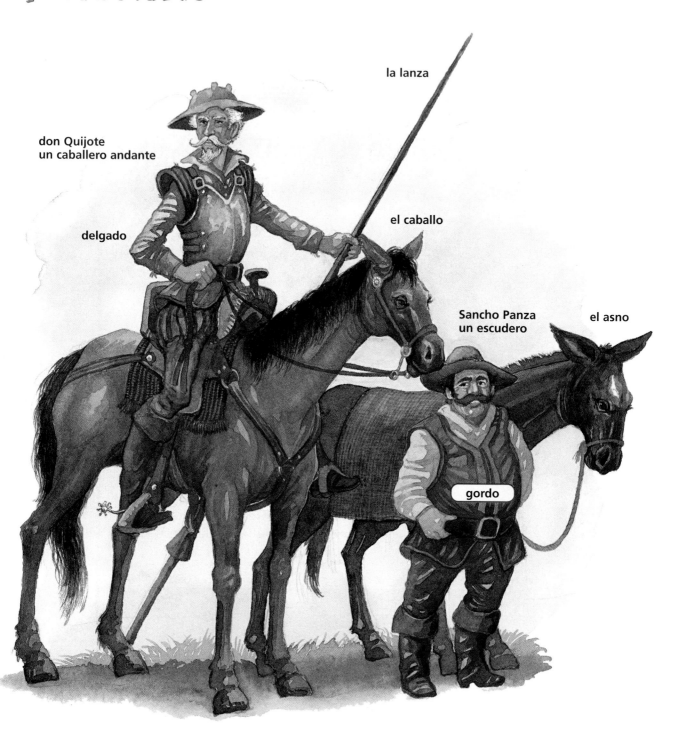

la lanza

don Quijote
un caballero andante

delgado

el caballo

Sancho Panza
un escudero

el asno

gordo

el aspa

el campo

el molino de viento

un(a) vecino(a) una persona que vive cerca, en la misma calle, por ejemplo
sabio(a) inteligente, astuto(a)
espantoso horrible, terrible
a toda prisa muy rápido
de nuevo otra vez
socorrer ayudar, dar auxilio o ayuda
no les hizo caso no les prestó atención

Actividades

A **Don Quijote y Sancho Panza** Contesten.

1. ¿Es don Quijote delgado o gordo?
2. ¿Quién es gordo?
3. ¿Quién es un caballero andante?
4. ¿Quién es su escudero?
5. ¿Quién tiene una lanza?
6. ¿Quién tiene un caballo?
7. Y Sancho Panza, ¿qué tiene él?
8. ¿Tiene aspas un molino de viento?

B **¿Cómo son?** Describan a don Quijote y a Sancho Panza.

C **¿Cómo se dice?** Expresen de otra manera.

1. Ellos viven en *una región rural.*
2. Fue una aventura *horrible.*
3. Él salió *rápido.*
4. No le *prestó atención* a su vecino.
5. Él es un señor *inteligente y astuto.*
6. Él lo hizo *otra vez.*
7. Trató pero no pudo *ayudar* a su vecino.

INTRODUCCIÓN La obra más famosa de todas las letras hispanas es la novela *El ingenioso hidalgo don Quijote de la Mancha* de Miguel de Cervantes Saavedra.

Los dos personajes principales de la novela son don Quijote y Sancho Panza. Don Quijote, un hombre alto y delgado, es un caballero andante. Es un idealista que quiere conquistar todos los males[1] del mundo. Su escudero, Sancho Panza, es un hombre bajo y gordo. Él es un realista puro. Siempre trata de desviar[2] a don Quijote de sus ilusiones y aventuras.

[1]males *evils*

[2]trata de desviar *tries to dissuade*

El Quijote

1

Un día, don Quijote salió de su pueblo en la región de la Mancha. Un idealista sin par°, don Quijote salió en busca de aventuras para conquistar los males del mundo. Es el trabajo de un verdadero caballero andante. Pero después de unos pocos días, don Quijote volvió a casa porque hizo su primera expedición sin escudero. No hay caballero andante sin escudero— sobre todo un caballero andante de la categoría de don Quijote.

Cuando volvió a su pueblo, empezó a buscar un escudero. Por fin encontró a un vecino, Sancho Panza, un hombre bajo y gordo. Salió por segunda vez, esta vez acompañado de su escudero. Don Quijote montó a su caballo, Rocinante, y Sancho lo siguió° montado en su asno.

> sin par *without equal*

> siguió *followed*

2

Los dos hicieron muchas expediciones por la región de la Mancha. El idealista don Quijote hizo muchas cosas que no quiso hacer el realista Sancho Panza. Más de una vez Sancho le dijo: —Pero, don Quijote, noble caballero y fiel compañero. Vuestra Merced° está loco. ¿Por qué no dejamos° con estas tonterías°? ¿Por qué no volvemos a casa? Yo quiero comer. Y quiero dormir en mi cama.

Don Quijote no les hizo mucho caso a los consejos° de Sancho. Uno de los episodios más famosos de nuestro estimado caballero es el episodio de los molinos de viento.

> Vuestra Merced *Your Highness*

> no dejamos con *put an end to*

> tonterías *foolish things*

> consejos *advice*

3

Del buen suceso que el valeroso don Quijote tuvo en la espantable y jamás imaginada aventura de los molinos de viento.

En esto descubrieron treinta o cuarenta molinos de viento que hay en aquel campo; y así como° don Quijote los vio, dijo a su escudero: —¡Sancho! ¡Mira! ¿Tú ves lo que veo yo?

—No, Vuestra Merced. No veo nada.

—Amigo Sancho, ¿no ves allí unos treinta o más gigantes que vienen hacia nosotros a hacer batalla?

—¿Qué gigantes?

—Aquellos que allí ves, de los brazos largos.

—Don Quijote. No son gigantes. Son simples molinos de viento. Y lo que en ellos parecen° brazos son aspas.

—Bien parece, Sancho, que tú no sabes nada de aventuras. Ellos son gigantes. Y si tienes miedo…

—¡Don Quijote! ¿Adónde va Vuestra Merced?

así como *as soon as*

parecen *appear to be*

Molinos de viento, La Mancha, España

¿Adónde fue don Quijote? Él fue a hacer batalla con los terribles gigantes. Gigantes como éstos no deben ni pueden existir en el mundo. En nombre de Dulcinea, la dama de sus pensamientos°, don Quijote los atacó. Puso su lanza en el aspa de uno de los molinos. En el mismo instante vino un viento fuerte. El viento movió el aspa. El viento la revolvió con tanta furia que hizo pedazos° de la lanza de don Quijote y levantó a don Quijote en el aire.

A toda prisa el pobre Sancho fue a socorrer a su caballero andante. Lo encontró° en el suelo muy mal herido°.

—Don Quijote, no le dije a Vuestra Merced que no vio gigantes. Vio simples molinos de viento. No puedo comprender por qué los atacó.

—Sancho, tú no sabes lo que dices. Son cosas de guerra° que tú no comprendes. Tú sabes que tengo un enemigo. Mi enemigo es el horrible pero sabio monstruo Frestón. Te dije las cosas malas que él hace. Y ahora convirtió a los gigantes en molinos de viento.

—Yo no sé lo que hizo vuestro enemigo, Frestón. Pero yo sé lo que le hizo el molino de viento.

Sancho levantó a don Quijote del suelo. Don Quijote subió de nuevo sobre Rocinante. Habló más de la pasada aventura pero Sancho no le hizo caso. Siguieron el camino hacia Puerto Lápice en busca de otras jamás imaginadas aventuras.

dama de sus pensamientos *lady of his dreams*

pedazos *pieces*

encontró *found*
herido *wounded*

guerra *war*

Plaza de España, Madrid

¿Comprendes?

A Don Quijote y Sancho Panza Escojan.

1. Don Quijote es ____.
   a. un realista
   b. un idealista
   c. un escudero
2. Don Quijote salió de su pueblo ____.
   a. en busca de la Mancha
   b. en busca de un escudero
   c. en busca de aventuras
3. Don Quijote volvió a casa para ____.
   a. comenzar su primera expedición
   b. buscar un escudero
   c. ver a Dulcinea

4. Sancho Panza es ____.
   a. un caballero andante también
   b. un idealista sin par
   c. un vecino de don Quijote
5. Sancho Panza tiene ____.
   a. un asno
   b. un caballo
   c. una lanza

B ¿Sí o no? Digan que sí o que no.

1. Don Quijote y Sancho Panza hicieron sólo dos expediciones.
2. Sancho le dice a don Quijote que está loco.
3. Don Quijote siempre quiere volver a casa.
4. Un episodio famoso del *Quijote* es el episodio de los molinos de viento.

C Los molinos de viento Completen.

1. Don Quijote ve unos treinta o cuarenta ____.
2. Sancho no ve ____.
3. Según don Quijote, los ____ quieren hacer ____.
4. Según don Quijote, los ____ que ve tienen ____ largos.
5. Según Sancho, no son gigantes. Don Quijote ve unos ____ y no tienen brazos. Tienen ____.

D La batalla Contesten.

1. ¿Contra quiénes fue don Quijote a hacer batalla?
2. ¿En dónde puso su lanza?
3. ¿Qué hizo mover al aspa?
4. ¿Revolvió rápidamente el aspa?
5. ¿Adónde levantó a don Quijote?
6. ¿Dónde encontró Sancho a don Quijote?
7. ¿Quién convirtió a los gigantes en molinos de viento?
8. Cuando Sancho levantó a don Quijote del suelo, ¿volvieron a casa?
9. Después de este episodio, ¿admite don Quijote que los gigantes son molinos de viento?

Video Companion

Using video in the classroom

The use of video in the classroom can be a wonderful asset to the World Languages teacher and a most beneficial learning tool for the language student. Video enables students to experience whatever it is they are learning in their textbook in a real-life setting. With each lesson, they are able to take a vicarious field trip. They see people interacting at home, at school, at the market, etc., in an authentic milieu. Students sitting in a classroom can see real people going about their real life in real places. They may experience the target culture in many countries. The cultural benefits are limitless.

Developing listening and viewing skills

In addition to its tremendous cultural value, video, when properly used, gives students much needed practice in developing good listening and viewing skills. Video allows students to look for numerous clues that are evident in a tone of voice, facial expressions, and gestures. Through video students can see and hear the diversity of the target culture and, as discerning viewers and listeners, compare and contrast the Spanish-speaking cultures to each other and to their own culture. Video introduces a dimension into classroom instruction that no other medium—teachers, overhead, text, audio CDs—can provide.

Reinforcing learned language

Video that is properly developed for classroom use has speakers reincorporate the language students have learned in a given lesson. In keeping with reality, however, speakers introduce some new words, expressions, and structures because students functioning in a real-life situation would not know every word native speakers use with them in a live conversation. The lively and interactive nature of video allows students to use their listening and viewing skills to comprehend new language in addition to seeing and hearing the language they have learned come to life.

Getting the most out of video

The intrinsic benefit of video is often lost when students are allowed to read the scripted material before viewing. In many cases, students will have come to understand language used by the speakers in the video by means of reading comprehension, thus negating the inherent benefits of video as a tool to develop listening and viewing skills. Because today's students are so accustomed to the medium of video as a tool for entertainment and learning, a well-written and well-produced video program will help them develop real-life language skills and confidence in those skills in an enjoyable way.

Videotur

¡Viva el mundo hispano!

Episodio 1

Julián y Francisco en Buenos Aires

Alberto y Claudia en El Caminito

Antes de mirar

Make an educated guess!

In the photos you see several of our new Spanish friends—Francisco and Julián and Alberto and Claudia. One of them is from Spain. What clue is there in one of the photos to let you know that he or she is from there?

Después de mirar

Expansión In the video you have just taken a tour of Argentina, Mexico, and Spain. What similarities did you notice among the three countries? What differences did you see? Choose a place in one of the countries that you would like to visit. Do some research to find out more about that place. Why do you find it interesting?

¡Viva el mundo hispano!

Episodio 2

Alberto y Claudia en la escuela

Alberto en la clase

Antes de mirar

Can you spot the following?

1. un muchacho
2. una alumna
3. una clase
4. un libro
5. una escuela

Después de mirar

Expansión *El Quijote* by Miguel de Cervantes de Saavedra is one of the most famous novels of all times. Do some research to find out about this author. When did he live? What jobs did he have? Did anything unusual happen to him during his lifetime? You may also want to research more about the story of don Quijote. It has been retold in other forms. Can you find out what musical was based on the story of don Quijote? Are you familiar with any of the music from this musical? What is one of the important themes of this story?

¡Viva el mundo hispano!

Episodio 3

El mercado al aire libre

Julián con un "look" nuevo

Antes de mirar

Make an educated guess!

1. What do you think would be sold in the market you see in the first photograph?

2. In the second photograph, does Julián look as though he is having a good time?

3. What do you think Vicky might be saying to Julián?

Después de mirar

Expansión After you view the video about weavers in Peru, do some research on some of the patterns the weavers use. Choose a pattern and duplicate it either by drawing it or creating it from colored construction paper.

¡Viva el mundo hispano!

Episodio 4

La clase de matemáticas

Francisco y Vicky después de las clases

Antes de mirar

Can you see the following? If so, give an adjective to describe each.

1. una pizarra
2. unos alumnos
3. una sala de clase
4. un profesor
5. una mochila

Después de mirar

Expansión When you first met Francisco in the video, you may remember that he was wearing a shirt that said **Danza flamenco Madrid.** Flamenco is one of the traditional forms of music from Spain. Do some research to find more information about flamenco music.

VIDEOTUR

¡Viva el mundo hispano!

Episodio 5

Julián en el parque

Alejandra saluda a Julián

Antes de mirar

Invent the following.

1. el nombre de la revista que Julián lee
2. el nombre del café
3. lo que Alejandra toma
4. lo que Julián toma

Después de mirar

Expansión As you can imagine from what you saw in the video, café life is an important part of Spanish culture. Do you have any cafés near where you live? If you do, do you and your friends go there often? If not, do you think you might enjoy them based on what you viewed in the video?

¡Viva el mundo hispano!

Episodio 6

Francisco y Claudia en la estancia

Dentro de la casa de la tía de Claudia

Antes de mirar

Can you see the following? If so, describe each.

1. una casa
2. unos amigos
3. una madre
4. una fiesta
5. una mochila

Después de mirar

Expansión   In the video you visited San Lorenzo de Escorial and saw a festival called **La Romería.** Do some research on the Internet about the monastery at **El Escorial** or about **La Romería.** Write a travel guide for someone who might visit these places.

¡Viva el mundo hispano!

Episodio 7

Alberto y Julián afuera de la escuela

Alberto habla con Julián.

Antes de mirar

Answer the questions.

1. ¿Dónde están los amigos?
2. ¿Quién lee?
3. ¿Quién escribe?

Después de mirar

Expansión In the video you hear about a game called **pato.** From what you learned does it remind you of any other sport you are familiar with? Do some research on the Internet to find out the countries it is played in, what the rules of the game are, and who some of its most famous players are. Discuss with a friend the skills you need to participate and whether or not you think this is a sport you would enjoy.

VIDEOTUR

¡Viva el mundo hispano!

Episodio 8

Vicky llama al «médico».

Alberto tiene una condición muy grave.

Antes de mirar

Answer the questions.

1. ¿Dónde está Alberto?
2. ¿Cómo está Alberto?
3. ¿Quién llega para ayudar?
4. ¿Qué le duele a Alberto?
5. ¿Qué piensas? ¿Está muy enfermo Alberto o no?

Después de mirar

Expansión   In the video you travel to the rainforest in Costa Rica. Do some research on Costa Rica to find out more about the jungle and the conservation of the rainforest there. Why do you think Costa Rica is so important for scientists and conservationists like Luis Poveda?

¡Viva el mundo hispano!

Episodio 9

Alberto y Claudia van de compras.

Ellos miran el escaparate de la tienda.

Antes de mirar

Answer the questions.

1. ¿Dónde están Alberto y Claudia?
2. ¿Qué tipo de tienda es?
3. ¿Qué hay en el escaparate?
4. ¿Es ropa para el invierno y para el verano?
5. ¿Para qué pueden usar este tipo de ropa?

Después de mirar

Expansión You are going on a short vacation. Do some research on the Internet to find out more about beaches to visit in Puerto Rico. Choose a beach you like. Discuss how you will get there and what you will do there. Tell what you might eat on this vacation to Puerto Rico.

¡Viva el mundo hispano!

Episodio 10

Alejandra y Vicky en la Plaza de San Telmo

Vicky y Alejandra hablan mientras escuchan una orquesta típica.

Antes de mirar

Can you spot the following?

1. un artista
2. una orquesta
3. unas pinturas
4. un museo

Después de mirar

Expansión   In the video you see a very colorful event known as the **charreada.** Carmen mentions in the video that **Un charro no se hace. Un charro se nace.** What do you think this means? Why do you think she says this? Do some research on the Internet to find out more about this very popular cultural event in Mexico.

¡Viva el mundo hispano!

Episodio 11

Julián y Francisco hablan de algo importante.

Francisco y Julián llegan al aeropuerto.

Antes de mirar

Let's invent!

Make up a conversation that Julián and Francisco might be having. Take clues from the photographs to finish the dialogue.

Julián: Francisco, voy de vacación.

Francisco: ¿Ah, sí? ¿Adónde vas?

Después de mirar

Expansión   In the video you see a form of art that is famous in Venezuela. Do some research on the Internet to find other forms of art that are typical of Venezuela. **El arte murano** originated in Italy. What are the origins of the other art forms you found out about?

¡Viva el mundo hispano!

Episodio 12

Claudia y Alejandra en camino

Alejandra y Claudia descansan un poco.

Antes de mirar

Let's invent!

1. ¿Dónde están las amigas?
2. ¿Qué llevan?
3. ¿Qué tiempo hace?
4. ¿A quién llama Alejandra?
5. ¿Se divierten Alejandra y Claudia?

Después de mirar

Expansión In the video you see the Inca trail. Do some research on the Internet to find out more about the Incas. We already know that they built the beautiful **pueblo** of Macchu Picchu. What else did they build or invent?

¡Viva el mundo hispano!

Episodio 13

Francisco y Claudia leen un libro.

«Una mujer misteriosa» en la estación de ferrocarril

Antes de mirar

Let's invent!

1. ¿Dónde están Francisco y Claudia?

2. ¿Qué tipo de libro leen?

3. ¿Hacen un viaje?

4. ¿Adónde van?

5. ¿Quién es el otro señor con «la mujer misteriosa»?

Después de mirar

Expansión As you can see from the video, train travel is very popular in some Spanish-speaking countries. Do you think it is as popular where you live? What is your favorite means of transportation for long trips? Why? Survey your friends to find out their preferred means of travel. Share your results with the class.

VIDEOTUR

¡Viva el mundo hispano!

Episodio 14

Alberto en el restaurante de su tío

Vicky y Alberto con cara de sorpresa

Antes de mirar

Can you spot the following?

1. un camarero
2. un cliente
3. las papas
4. una propina
5. un vaso de agua

Después de mirar

Expansión Are there many Hispanic restaurants in your community? Are they representative of a variety of different Spanish-speaking countries? Which ones are they? Do you have a favorite? Look at the menus of the different restaurants in your community or do research on the Internet to find some menus of Hispanic restaurants in this country. Are the foods very different? If any of the Hispanic restaurants in your community are run by a family, speak with one of the family members about the history of their business. Try to do this in Spanish if possible.

Handbook

Cristina

Sara   **Alejandro / Eduardo**

Isabel   **Alberto**

Alumno A Now answer your partner's questions based on the pictures below.

Alumno A Ask your partner the following questions. Correct answers are in parentheses.

1. ¿Cómo es Antonio, rubio o moreno? (*Antonio es moreno.*)

2. ¿Cómo es Fernando, gracioso o serio? (*Fernando es gracioso.*)

3. ¿Cómo es María, alta o baja? (*María es baja.*)

4. ¿Cómo es Ricardo, ambicioso o perezoso? (*Ricardo es perezoso.*)

5. ¿Cómo es Elena, cómica o seria? (*Elena es seria.*)

6. ¿Cómo es Ana, alta o baja? (*Ana es alta.*)

Alumno B Answer your partner's questions based on the pictures below.

Ana / María   **Ricardo**

Elena   **Fernando**

Antonio

Alumno B Ask your partner the following questions. Correct answers are in parentheses.

1. ¿Cómo es Alejandro, alto o bajo? (*Alejandro es alto.*)

2. ¿Cómo es Isabel, ambiciosa o perezosa? (*Isabel es perezosa.*)

3. ¿Cómo es Sara, graciosa o seria? (*Sara es graciosa.*)

4. ¿Cómo es Cristina, rubia o morena? (*Cristina es rubia.*)

5. ¿Cómo es Eduardo, alto o bajo? (*Eduardo es bajo.*)

6. ¿Cómo es Alberto, ambicioso o perezoso? (*Alberto es ambicioso.*)

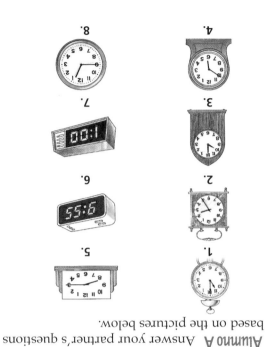

Alumno A Ask your partner **¿Qué hora es?**
Correct answers are in parentheses.

1. ¿Qué hora es? (*Son las dos.*)

2. ¿Qué hora es? (*Son las tres y cinco.*)

3. ¿Qué hora es? (*Son las cuatro y veinticinco.*)

4. ¿Qué hora es? (*Son las cinco menos veinte.*)

5. ¿Qué hora es? (*Son las seis y media.*)

6. ¿Qué hora es? (*Es la una.*)

7. ¿Qué hora es? (*Son las siete menos cuarto.*)

8. ¿Qué hora es? (*Es la una y diez.*)

Alumno A Answer your partner's questions based on the pictures below.

Alumno B Answer your partner's questions based on the pictures below.

1.

5.

2.

6.

3.

7.

4.

8.

Alumno B Ask your partner **¿Qué hora es?**
Correct answers are in parentheses.

1. ¿Qué hora es? (*Son las once.*)

2. ¿Qué hora es? (*Son las dos y veinticinco.*)

3. ¿Qué hora es? (*Son las diez.*)

4. ¿Qué hora es? (*Son las seis menos diez.*)

5. ¿Qué hora es? (*Son las ocho y cuarto.*)

6. ¿Qué hora es? (*Son las diez menos cinco.*)

7. ¿Qué hora es? (*Es la una.*)

8. ¿Qué hora es? (*Es la una menos cuarto.*)

Alumno A Answer your partner's questions based on the pictures below.

Alumno A Ask your partner the following questions. Correct answers are in parentheses.

1. ¿Buscas una gorra? (Sí, busco una gorra.)

2. ¿Necesitas un disquete? (No, no necesito un disquete.)

3. ¿Buscas un bolígrafo? (No, no busco un bolígrafo.)

4. ¿Compras una camisa? (Sí, compro una camisa.)

5. ¿Llevas un traje? (No, no llevo un traje.)

6. ¿Necesitas una mochila? (Sí, necesito una mochila.)

7. ¿Compras una falda? (No, no compro una falda.)

8. ¿Buscas pantalones? (Sí, busco pantalones.)

Alumno B Answer your partner's questions based on the pictures below.

Alumno B Ask your partner the following questions. Correct answers are in parentheses.

1. ¿Buscas una falda? (Sí, busco una falda.)

2. ¿Necesitas una calculadora?
(Sí, necesito una calculadora.)

3. ¿Llevas un traje? (No, no llevo un traje.)

4. ¿Buscas una mochila?
(No, no busco una mochila.)

5. ¿Compras un bolígrafo?
(Sí, compro un bolígrafo.)

6. ¿Buscas un libro? (No, no busco un libro.)

7. ¿Necesitas un par de tenis?
(Sí, necesito un par de tenis.)

8. ¿Compras una camisa?
(No, no compro una camisa.)

Activity 4

Alumno A Ask your partner the following questions. Correct answers are in parentheses.

1. ¿Cómo llegan a la escuela Antonio y Ernesto?
(Antonio y Ernesto llegan a pie.)

2. ¿Cómo llegan a la escuela Alicia y Pepe? (Alicia y Pepe llegan en el bus escolar.)

3. ¿Cómo llegan a la escuela José y Sara?
(José y Sara llegan en carro/coche.)

4. ¿Cómo llegan a la escuela Anita y Paco? (Anita y Paco llegan a pie.)

5. ¿Cómo llegan a la escuela Conchita y Beatriz?
(Conchita y Beatriz llegan en carro/coche.)

Alumno A Answer your partner's questions based on the pictures below.

Lupe
Rodolfo

Juan
Elena
Marisol
Vicente

Pedro
Silvia
Ana
Pablo

Alumno B Answer your partner's questions based on the pictures below.

José
Conchita
Sara
Beatriz

Antonio
Anita
Ernesto
Paco

Alicia
Pepe

Alumno B Ask your partner the following questions. Correct answers are in parentheses.

1. ¿Cómo llegan a la escuela Lupe y Rodolfo?
(Lupe y Rodolfo llegan en carro/coche.)

2. ¿Cómo llegan a la escuela Silvia y Pedro? (Silvia y Pedro llegan en el bus escolar.)

3. ¿Cómo llegan a la escuela Elena y Marisol?
(Elena y Marisol llegan a pie.)

4. ¿Cómo llegan a la escuela Ana y Pablo? (Ana y Pablo llegan en el bus escolar.)

5. ¿Cómo llegan a la escuela Vicente y Juan?
(Vicente y Juan llegan a pie.)

Alumno A Answer your partner's questions based on the pictures below.

Alumno A Ask your partner the following questions. Correct answers are in parentheses.

1. ¿Comes pan dulce? (Sí, como pan dulce.)
2. ¿Comes pollo? (No, no como pollo.)
3. ¿Comes sopa? (Sí, como sopa.)
4. ¿Comes pescado? (No, no como pescado.)
5. ¿Comes un bocadillo? (Sí, como un bocadillo.)
6. ¿Comes mariscos? (Sí, como mariscos.)
7. ¿Comes queso? (No, no como queso.)
8. ¿Comes jamón? (Sí, como jamón.)

Alumno B Answer your partner's questions based on the pictures below.

Alumno B Ask your partner the following questions. Correct answers are in parentheses.

1. ¿Comes sopa? (No, no como sopa.)
2. ¿Comes pollo? (Sí, como pollo.)
3. ¿Comes pescado? (Sí, como pescado.)
4. ¿Comes huevos? (Sí, como huevos.)
5. ¿Comes un bocadillo?
   (No, no como un bocadillo.)
6. ¿Comes una tortilla? (Sí, como una tortilla.)
7. ¿Comes queso? (Sí, como queso.)
8. ¿Comes mariscos? (No, no como mariscos.)

Alumno A Ask your partner the following questions. Correct answers are in parentheses.

1. ¿Cuántos años tiene Armando?
   (Armando tiene catorce años.)

2. ¿Cuántos años tienen Paco y José?
   (Paco y José tienen diecisiete años.)

3. ¿Cuántos años tienes tú?
   (Yo tengo _____ años.)

4. ¿Cuántos años tiene el profesor de ciencias? (El profesor de ciencias tiene treinta y seis años.)

5. ¿Cuántos años tienen Susana y Gabriela?
   (Susana y Gabriela tienen veintidós años.)

6. ¿Cuántos años tiene Pepe?
   (Pepe tiene ocho años.)

Alumno A Use the chart below to answer your partner's questions. Reminder: **tú** is you.

Sofía	15 años
Los abuelos	75 años
Pedro y Alicia	16
Tú	?
Teresa	9 años
Juan y Norma	13 años

Alumno B Use the chart below to answer your partner's questions. Reminder: **tú** is you.

Armando	14 años
Paco y José	17 años
Tú	?
El profesor de ciencias	36 años
Susana y Gabriela	22 años
Pepe	8 años

Alumno B Ask your partner the following questions. Correct answers are in parentheses.

1. ¿Cuántos años tiene Sofía?
   (Sofía tiene quince años.)

2. ¿Cuántos años tienen los abuelos?
   (Los abuelos tienen setenta y cinco años.)

3. ¿Cuántos años tienen Pedro y Alicia?
   (Pedro y Alicia tienen dieciséis años.)

4. ¿Cuántos años tienes tú?
   (Yo tengo _____ años.)

5. ¿Cuántos años tiene Teresa?
   (Teresa tiene nueve años.)

6. ¿Cuántos años tienen Juan y Norma?
   (Juan y Norma tienen trece años.)

Alumno A Ask your partner the following questions. Correct answers are in parentheses.

1. ¿Qué juega Antonio?
(Antonio juega al baloncesto.)

2. ¿Qué quiere el portero?
(El portero quiere bloquear el balón.)

3. ¿Qué prefieren Luisa y Carlos?
(Luisa y Carlos prefieren el fútbol.)

4. ¿Prefieres ser espectador(a) o jugador(a)? (Yo prefiero ser _____.)

5. ¿Qué devuelve el cátcher?
(El cátcher devuelve la pelota.)

Alumno A Use the chart below to answer your partner's questions. Reminder: **tú** is you.

Tomás y Sara	el fútbol
Marco	ser espectador
Los jugadores	marcar muchos tantos
Tú	?
Marta	el béisbol

Alumno B Use the chart below to answer your partner's questions. Reminder: **tú** is you.

Antonio	el baloncesto
El portero	bloquear el balón
Luisa y Carlos	el fútbol
Tú	?
El cátcher	la pelota

Alumno B Ask your partner the following questions. Correct answers are in parentheses.

1. ¿Qué juega Marta? (Marta juega al béisbol.)

2. ¿Prefieres ser espectador(a) o jugador(a)? (Yo prefiero ser _____.)

3. ¿Qué quieren los jugadores?
(Los jugadores quieren marcar muchos tantos.)

4. ¿Qué prefiere Marco?
(Marco prefiere ser espectador.)

5. ¿Qué juegan Tomás y Sara?
(Tomás y Sara juegan al fútbol.)

Activity 8

Ernesto

Juana

Beatriz

Silvia

Alberto

Alumno A Answer your partner's questions based on the pictures below.

Alumno A Ask your partner the following questions. Correct answers are in parentheses.

1. ¿Cómo está Sara, triste o contenta?
(*Sara está triste.*)

2. ¿Cómo es Fernando, ambicioso o perezoso?
(*Fernando es ambicioso.*)

3. ¿Cómo está Paco, contento o enfermo? (*Paco está enfermo.*)

4. ¿Cómo está Elena, de buen humor o de mal humor? (*Elena está de buen humor.*)

5. ¿Cómo es Isabel, ambiciosa o perezosa? (*Isabel es perezosa.*)

Alumno B Answer your partner's questions based on the pictures below.

Isabel

Fernando

Elena

Sara

Paco

Alumno B Ask your partner the following questions. Correct answers are in parentheses.

1. ¿Cómo es Silvia, rubia o morena?
(*Silvia es morena.*)

2. ¿Cómo está Ernesto, contento o nervioso?
(*Ernesto está nervioso.*)

3. ¿Cómo está Beatriz, contenta o cansada?
(*Beatriz está cansada.*)

4. ¿Cómo es Alberto, gracioso o serio?
(*Alberto es serio.*)

5. ¿Cómo es Juana, ambiciosa o perezosa? (*Juana es ambiciosa.*)

Alumno A Ask your partner the following questions. Correct answers are in parentheses.

1. ¿Qué jugaron Roberto y Ernesto?
   (Roberto y Ernesto jugaron tenis.)

2. ¿Jugaron singles o dobles?
   (Jugaron singles.)

3. ¿Quién buceó? *(Juan buceó.)*

4. ¿Quién esquió en el agua?
   (Claudia esquió en el agua.)

5. ¿Nadó Sandra o practicó el surfing?
   (Sandra nadó.)

6. ¿Los jóvenes pasaron el día en la playa o en la estación de esquí?
   (Los jóvenes pasaron el día en la playa.)

Alumno A Answer your partner's questions based on the pictures below.

Susana / Manuel

María / Patricio / Teresa / Armando

Tomás / Alicia

Alumno B Answer your partner's questions based on the pictures below.

Claudia

Juan

Roberto / Ernesto

Sandra

Alumno B Ask your partner the following questions. Correct answers are in parentheses.

1. ¿Patricio y Teresa tomaron el telesilla o compraron boletos?
   (Patricio y Teresa tomaron el telesilla.)

2. ¿Qué compró Susana en la ventanilla? *(Susana compró boletos en la ventanilla.)*

3. ¿Quiénes bajaron la pista?
   (Tomás y Alicia bajaron la pista.)

4. ¿Esquiaron en el agua o en la nieve? *(Esquiaron en la nieve.)*

5. ¿Tomó el telesilla Armando?
   (Sí, Armando tomó el telesilla.)

6. ¿Los jóvenes pasaron el día en la playa o en la estación de esquí? *(Los jóvenes pasaron el día en la estación de esquí.)*

Activity 10   CAPÍTULO 10, Palabras 1, 2, Estructura, pages 306–307, 310–311, 314

Alumno A Answer your partner's questions based on the picture below.

Alumno A Ask your partner the following questions. Correct answers are in parentheses.

1. ¿Adónde fueron los turistas?
 (*Los turistas fueron al museo.*)

2. ¿Qué vieron los turistas?
 (*Los turistas vieron una exposición de arte.*)

3. ¿Qué miraron los niños?
 (*Los niños miraron un mural.*)

Alumno B Answer your partner's questions based on the picture below.

Alumno B Ask your partner the following questions. Correct answers are in parentheses.

1. ¿Adónde fue el joven? (*El joven fue al cine.*)

2. ¿Qué vio el joven? (*El joven vio una película.*)

3. ¿Lleva subtítulos la película?
 (*No, la película no lleva subtítulos.*)

Alumno A Ask your partner the following questions about his or her airplane ticket. Correct answers are in parentheses.

Alumno A Answer your partner's questions based on your plane ticket below.

1. ¿Cuál es el nombre de la línea aérea? *(Lan Chile)*

2. ¿Cuál es el número del vuelo? *(doscientos)*

3. ¿Cuál es el destino del vuelo? *(Santiago)*

4. ¿Cuál es la fecha del vuelo? *(el veintiocho de julio)*

5. ¿Cuántas maletas tiene el/la pasajero(a)? *(dos)*

6. ¿Cuál es la hora de salida? *(las diez y media)*

Mexicana			
Vuelo 4	Destino Guadalajara	Puerta 8	Clase C
Fecha 13 abril	Hora de salida 06:30	Asiento 28A	
Maletas 2	Peso 18	Nombre del pasajero _____	

Alumno B Ask your partner the following questions about his or her airplane ticket. Correct answers are in parentheses.

Alumno B Answer your partner's questions based on your plane ticket below.

1. ¿Cuál es el nombre de la línea aérea? *(Mexicana)*

2. ¿Cuál es el número del vuelo? *(cuatro)*

3. ¿De qué puerta sale el vuelo? *(ocho)*

4. ¿Cuál es la fecha del vuelo? *(el trece de abril)*

5. ¿Cuál es el destino del vuelo? *(Guadalajara)*

6. ¿Cuál es la hora de salida? *(las seis y media)*

Lan Chile			
Vuelo 200	Destino Santiago	Puerta 15	Clase C
Fecha 28 julio	Hora de salida 10:30	Asiento 48B	
Maletas 2	Peso 20	Nombre del pasajero _____	

Activity 12

CAPÍTULO 12, Palabras 1, pages 374–375

Irene

Juana

Pepe

Gabriela

Faviola

Alumno A Answer your partner's questions based on the pictures below.

Alumno A Ask your partner the following questions. Correct answers are in parentheses.

1. ¿Quién se lava la cara? (*Francisco se lava la cara.*)

2. ¿Se baña un muchacho o una muchacha? (*Una muchacha se baña.*)

3. ¿Quién se despierta? (*Paco se despierta.*)

4. ¿Se afeita un muchacho o una muchacha? (*Un muchacho se afeita.*)

5. ¿Quién se sienta? (*Graciela se sienta.*)

Alumno B Answer your partner's questions based on the pictures below.

Graciela

Felipe

Paco

Adela

Francisco

Alumno B Ask your partner the following questions. Correct answers are in parentheses.

1. ¿Quién se cepilla los dientes?
   (*Gabriela se cepilla los dientes.*)

2. ¿Quién se peina? (*Pepe se peina.*)

3. ¿Se duerme un muchacho o una muchacha?
   (*Una muchacha se duerme.*)

4. ¿Quién se maquilla? (*Irene se maquilla.*)

5. ¿Se pone la ropa un muchacho o una
   muchacha? (*Una muchacha se pone la ropa.*)

Susana y Pedro

Señor Rivas

Alberto

Alumno A Answer your partner's questions based on the pictures below.

Alumno A Ask your partner the following questions. Correct answers are in parentheses.

1. ¿Quién es el revisor?
   (El señor Martínez es el revisor.)

2. ¿El revisor está en el coche-cama o en el pasillo? (El revisor está en el pasillo.)

3. ¿Están Pablo y Ramona en el coche-comedor o en sus asientos?
   (Están en sus asientos.)

4. ¿Luis y Antonia van a bajar o van a subir? (Luis y Antonia van a bajar.)

Alumno B Answer your partner's questions based on the pictures below.

Ramona   Pablo   Señor Martínez

Luis y Antonia

Alumno B Ask your partner the following questions. Correct answers are in parentheses.

1. ¿Dónde comen Susana y Pedro?
   (Susana y Pedro comen en el coche-comedor/coche-cafetería.)

2. ¿Alberto sube al tren o baja del tren? (Alberto baja del tren.)

3. ¿El señor Rivas compra un billete o transborda? (El señor Rivas transborda.)

4. ¿El señor Rivas va a subir al tren o va a la sala de espera?
   (El señor Rivas va a subir al tren.)

Paco y Mercedes   Antonio

(Los muchachos piden pollo.)
4. ¿Qué piden los muchachos?

(José pide una ensalada.)
3. ¿Quién pide una ensalada?

Los turistas   Norma

(Marta y Teresa piden la langosta.)
2. ¿Qué piden Marta y Teresa?

(Juanita pide el pescado.)
1. ¿Quién pide el pescado?

Alumno A Answer your partner's questions based on the pictures below.

Alumno A Ask your partner the following questions. Correct answers are in parentheses.

Alumno B Answer your partner's questions based on the pictures below.

Marta y Teresa   José

Juanita   Los muchachos

Alumno B Ask your partner the following questions. Correct answers are in parentheses.

1. ¿Quién pide las almejas?
   (*Antonio pide las almejas.*)

2. ¿Qué piden Paco y Mercedes?
   (*Paco y Mercedes piden la carne.*)

3. ¿Qué piden los turistas?
   (*Los turistas piden el maíz.*)

4. ¿Quién pide los camarones?
   (*Norma pide los camarones.*)

Study Tips

For students and parents/guardians

This guide is designed to help you as students achieve success as you embark on the adventure of learning another language and to enable your parents or guardians to help you in this exciting journey. There are many ways to learn new information. You may find some of these suggestions more useful than others, depending upon which style of learning works best for you. Before you begin, it is important to understand how we acquire language.

Receptive Skills

Each day of your life you receive a great deal of information through the use of language. In order to get this information, it is necessary to understand the language being used. It is necessary to understand the language in two different ways. First you must be able to understand what people are saying when they speak to you. This is referred to as oral or listening comprehension. Oral comprehension or listening comprehension is the ability to understand the spoken language.

You must also be able to understand what you read. This is referred to as reading comprehension. Reading comprehension is the ability to understand the written language.

Listening comprehension and reading comprehension are called the *receptive skills.* They are receptive skills because as you listen to what someone else says or read what someone else has written you receive information without having to produce any language yourself.

It is usually very easy to understand your native language. It is a bit more problematic to understand a second language that is new to you. As a beginner, you are still learning the sounds of the new language, and you recognize only a few words. Throughout **¡Buen viaje!** we will give you hints or suggestions to help you understand when people are speaking to you in Spanish or when you are reading in Spanish.

Hints for Listening Comprehension

When you are listening to a person speaking Spanish, don't try to understand every word. It is not necessary to understand everything to get the idea of what someone is saying. Listen for the general message. If some details escape you, it doesn't matter. Also, never try to translate what people are saying in Spanish into English. It takes a great deal of experience and expertise to be a translator. Trying to translate will hinder your ability to understand.

Hints for Reading Comprehension
Just as you will not always understand every word you hear in a conversation, you will not necessarily understand every word you encounter in a reading selection, either. In **¡Buen viaje!,** we have used only words you know or can easily figure out in the reading selections. This will make reading comprehension much easier for you. However, if at some time you wish to read a newspaper or magazine article in Spanish, you will most certainly come across some unfamiliar words. Do not stop reading. Continue to read to get the "gist" of the selection. Try to guess the meanings of words you do not know.

Productive Skills

There are two productive skills in language. These two skills are speaking and writing. They are called productive skills because it is you who has to produce the language when you say or write something. When you speak or write, you have control over the language and which words you use. If you don't know how to say something, you don't have to say it. With the receptive skills, on the other hand, someone else produces the language that you listen to or read, and you have no control over the words they use.

There's no doubt that you can easily speak your native language. You can write, too, even though you may sometimes make errors in spelling or punctuation. In Spanish, there's not a lot you can say or write as a beginner. You can only talk or write about those topics you have learned in Spanish class.

Hints for Speaking
Try to be as accurate as possible when speaking. Try not to make mistakes. However, if you do, it's not the end of the world. Spanish speakers will understand you. You're not expected to speak a language perfectly after a limited time. You have probably spoken with people from other countries who do not speak English perfectly, but you can understand them. Remember:

❖ Keep talking! Don't become inhibited for fear of making a mistake.
❖ Say what you know how to say. Don't try to branch out in the early stages and attempt to talk about topics or situations you have not yet learned in Spanish.

Hints for Writing
There are many activities throughout each chapter of ¡Buen viaje! that will help you to speak and write in Spanish. When you have to write something on your own, however, without the guidance or assistance of an activity in your book, be sure to choose a topic for which you know the vocabulary in Spanish. Never attempt to write about a topic you have not yet studied in Spanish. Write down the topic you are going to write about. Then think of the words you know that are related to the topic. Be sure to include some action words (verbs) that you will need.

From your list of words, write as many sentences as you can. Read them and organize them into a logical order. Fill in any gaps. Then proof your paragraph(s) to see if you made any errors. Correct any that you find.

When writing on your own, be careful not to rely heavily, if at all, on a bilingual dictionary. It's not that bilingual dictionaries are bad, but when you look up a word you will very often find that there are several translations for the same word.

As a beginning language student, you do not know which translation to choose; the chances are great that you will pick the wrong one.

As a final hint, never prepare your paragraph(s) in English and attempt to translate word for word. Always write from scratch in Spanish.

Capítulo 1

Vocabulario
PALABRAS 1 y 2 *(pages 14–21)*

1. Repeat each new word in the **Palabras** section as many times as possible. The more you use a word, the more apt you are to remember it and keep it as part of your active vocabulary.
2. Read the words as you look at the illustrations.
3. If you're the type of learner who has to write something down in order to remember it, copy each word once or twice.
4. Do these activities diligently. They provide you with the opportunity to use your new words many times.
5. This may sound strange, but it's a good idea to read these activities aloud at home or when using the CD-ROM.
6. When doing the vocabulary activities by yourself or for homework, try to do each item orally before writing the answer.
7. After doing any activity that says **Historieta,** read all the answers aloud. Each time you do this, you will be telling a story in Spanish. It's an excellent way to keep using the material you are learning.

Classroom Suggestion Listen to what your classmates say when they respond in class. Do not tune them out. Paying attention to them allows you additional opportunities to hear your new words. The more you hear them, the more likely you are to learn them.

Study Tips

Estructura

Los adjetivos y los artículos *(pages 22–24)*
Pay particular attention to the final sound of many of the nouns and adjectives that you are learning. Remember that the vowel **o** is associated with masculine and the vowel **a** is associated with feminine.

El verbo ser *(pages 25–27)*

1. **Ser** is the first verb you are learning in Spanish. Throughout your study of Spanish, you will continue to learn many more verbs. The form of a verb in Spanish changes according to the subject. At this point you know three verb forms:

soy	when talking about yourself
eres	when talking to someone
él/ella es	when talking about someone

   Get off to a good start! Learn these three simple forms and remember them.

2. As you do the more open-ended activities, don't try to use words you don't know in Spanish. For example, you may want to talk about someone who is very outgoing, but you don't know a Spanish equivalent for *outgoing*. Give the message using what you do know. For example, you can say: **Juan no es tímido.** You can also say: **¿Es tímida María? No, no. María no es tímida.** Using **no** with a word you know enables you to convey the meaning you wish even though you do not know the precise word.

Classroom Suggestion   Listen to your classmates as they respond to the structure activities. Remember, the more you hear a form, the more readily you will be able to use it.

3. After doing any activity that says **Historieta,** read all the answers aloud. Each time you do this, you will be telling a story in Spanish. It's an excellent way to keep using the material you are learning.

Lectura cultural

El Quijote *(pages 30–31)*

1. Always read the Reading Strategy at the beginning of the **Lectura cultural.** Practice these strategies and try applying them to other selections you read in Spanish. The Reading Strategy on page 30 talks about cognates and how they help you guess the meanings of words you do not know. For example, you read: **El Quijote es una novela muy famosa.** Even if you had never seen the word **famosa,** you could guess its meaning because it is a cognate of the English word *famous.*

2. Let's take a look at another way to guess meaning. You read: **El Quijote es una novela famosa, muy conocida.** You don't know the meaning of **conocida.** However, when you come across a word or expression followed by a comma and then another word (in apposition), the word in apposition almost always clarifies the previous word and has the same or similar meaning. Which of the following do you think **conocida** means? *Talented, creative? Famous, well-known? Good, interesting?*

   Hopefully you chose *famous, well-known.* Think about how and why you arrived at this correct answer.

Hints for Writing   As you complete your first chapter in Spanish, you are able to write a description of a person. At this point, you cannot tell what the person does because you don't have the necessary vocabulary. So avoid this. However, you are able to tell what he or she is like. Write down the words you know in order to write your description. Do not think of words in English. Try to think only of the words you know in Spanish. Begin to write your description. Remember what you learned about **o, a.** Be sure to use the **o** ending when describing a boy and the **a** ending as you describe a girl.

Vocabulario *(page 40)*
As you complete the chapter, look at the reference vocabulary list. If there are several words you don't remember, go back to the **Palabras 1** and **Palabras 2** sections and review. If there are only one or two, you can choose to look them up in the dictionaries beginning on page H34 at the end of this book.

Capítulo 2

Get off to a good start! Do your Spanish homework diligently and study for a short period of time each day. Do not skip some days and then try to cram. It doesn't work when studying a foreign language.

In each lesson of **¡Buen viaje!** you will learn a very manageable amount of new material. Since Spanish is a romance language, much of the new material will involve word endings. Study each small set of new endings on a daily basis, and you'll have no problem. Don't wait until you have lots of them and try to cram them in all at once.

Vocabulario
PALABRAS 1 y 2 *(pages 44–51)*
1. In Chapter 1 you learned that adjectives describing something masculine end in **o** and those describing something feminine end in **a**. In Chapter 2, you have seven new words that reinforce the same concept. They are **cuánto, pequeño, poco, mucho, aburrido, duro, mismo.**
   Es una clase aburrida.
   Es un curso aburrido.

Hint for Pronouncing New Words   Imitate the pronunciation of your teacher, the CDs, or the CD-ROM to the best of your ability. Try to acquire the best pronunciation possible. However, don't be worried if you have a slight American accent.

There are three levels of pronunciation.
- **Near-native**   Try to pronounce like a native. Strive for a near-native pronunciation.
- **Accented but comprehensible**   Many people have an accent when they speak a foreign language. You can tell they are not native speakers, but in spite of their accent, you can understand them. If you have such an accent, don't be concerned.
- **Very accented and incomprehensible**   Some people have such a strong accent that it's impossible to understand what they're saying. If you have such a strong accent, it will be necessary to repeat and imitate more carefully.

Always remember to listen carefully, repeating as accurately as possible, and you'll succeed in acquiring acceptable pronunciation.

Hint for Speaking   Listen to your teacher pronounce new words or phrases and then repeat them several times. Once you know how to pronounce the words, read the words in your book. If you try to read a word in Spanish before ever hearing it, you will probably mispronounce it. Always try to listen, repeat, and then read.

2. The vocabulary in **Palabras 2** should be very easy to recognize and learn because many words are cognates. A cognate is a word that looks alike in both English and Spanish and has the same meaning in both languages. In the early lessons of **¡Buen viaje!** we have used many cognates to help you acquire a substantial vocabulary quickly and easily. However, be careful with the pronunciation of cognates. Even though they look alike and mean the same thing in both languages, they can be pronounced very differently.

Study Tips

Estructura

Sustantivos, artículos y adjetivos en el plural
(pages 52–53)

When studying a new grammar or structure point try to simplify the rule to make it easy for you to remember. When it comes to adjectives, remember:

adjectives that end in **o** have four forms:

> **-o, -os, -a, -as**

adjectives that end in **e** and most adjectives that end in a consonant have two forms:

> **-e, -es**   consonant, **-es**

Presente de ser en el plural *(pages 54–57)*

1. In this lesson, you learn two new verb forms:

   somos   when talking about yourself and someone else

   son   when talking about or to two or more people

2. Go over all forms of the verb **ser** until you feel confident that you know them.

3. Do each activity aloud and then write the answers.

Lectura cultural

El español en Estados Unidos
(pages 62–63)

1. Read the Reading Strategy at the beginning of the **Lectura cultural.** Look at the title of the reading on page 62. It lets you know immediately the general topic you'll be reading about.

2. Read the two subtitles or heads in the passage. They give you a more specific idea of what you'll be reading. Without having read the reading selection, you now have some understanding of what the reading is about. This will make comprehension much easier.

3. After looking at the title and subtitles, you may very quickly skim the reading. Rather than trying to remember all the information, look at the comprehension questions that follow it. Then go back to the reading and look for the specific factual information called for.

·············· **Capítulo 3** ··················

Vocabulario

PALABRAS 1 y 2 *(pages 76–83)*

1. Look at each photo or illustration carefully.

2. Read each isolated word or sentence aloud.

3. When learning another language it is sometimes necessary to guess. In doing so, you may come up with the right answer. For example, suppose you're not quite sure what **compra** means. If someone goes to a store, looks for something he or she needs, finds out how much it costs and then pays for it, you could possibly figure out that **compra** means *buys.*

4. It is strongly recommended that you not translate the vocabulary into English.

5. It is very important to know your question or interrogative words. Activity 4 on page 79 and Activity 8 on page 82 will help you do this. The answer in parenthesis in Activity 8 on page 82 tells you the meaning of the question word in the sentence.

QUESTION	ANSWER
Qué	a thing
Quién	a person
Dónde	location
Cuándo	time

6. After you have practiced your new words in the **Palabras 1** and **2** sections, cover up the words. Look at the photo or illustration and see how much you can say about it.

Hint for Speaking   Whenever possible, read all the answers aloud to any activity labeled **Historieta.** Every time you do, you'll be telling a story on your own with the guidance of the activity in the text. This is an easy and useful way to get yourself speaking lots of Spanish.

Estructura

Presente de los verbos en -ar en el singular
(pages 84–86)

1. As you already know, the verb ending indicates who performs the action of the verb.

    -o   yourself
    -as   to a friend
    -a   about someone

2. The verb endings will be presented to you in very manageable segments. You now know three endings for an **-ar** verb. They are:

    -o
    -as
    -a

    Be sure to learn these three simple endings and how to use them. Learning just three is very easy. You will continue to learn more endings. Do not wait until you have lots of endings. Learn them step by step and you will have no problem.

Hint   Note that the structure activities in your book build from easy to more complex. For example, in Activity 14 on page 85 you use only **-a.** In Activity 15, you hear **-as** and respond always with **-o.** Activity 18 on page 86 makes you use and manipulate all three endings.

3. Do all the activities aloud before writing the answers.
4. Read all the answers to any activity labeled **Historieta** as a story.

Conversación *(page 88)*

This conversation should be very easy for you. You have already learned all the Spanish used in the conversation. When practicing this conversation with a classmate, feel free to make as many changes as you want, as long as they make sense. For example you can change **camisa** to another article of clothing you know.

Lectura cultural

Un alumno madrileño *(pages 90–91)*

1. Look at the photos on pages 90 and 91. Based on these photos, what do you think the reading is about?
    ❖ schools and students
    ❖ shopping for clothing
    ❖ planning a meal

2. Skim the reading selection and look for the important information such as:
    ❖ Who's the story about?
    ❖ Where does he live and go to school?
    ❖ What does he wear to school?

3. Factual recall is an important reading skill. First, find the facts in the reading and then commit them to memory. Activity B on page 91 tells you what factual information to look for.

Vocabulario *(page 100)*

As you complete the chapter, look at the reference vocabulary list. If there are several words you don't remember, go back to the **Palabras 1** and **Palabras 2** sections and review. If there are only one or two, you can choose to look them up in the dictionaries beginning on page H34 at the end of this book.

Capítulo 4

Vocabulario

PALABRAS 1 y 2 *(pages 104–111)*

1. Notice how one sentence can clarify the meaning of another.

    Los alumnos llegan a la escuela a eso de las ocho menos cuarto.
    No llegan a las ocho menos cuarto en punto.
    Llegan a las ocho menos veinte o a las ocho menos diez.

Study Tips

2. Notice how the way in which a word is used in several sentences helps to clarify meaning.

> **Los alumnos llegan a la escuela.**
> **¿A qué hora llegan?**
> **Llegan a las ocho menos cuarto.**
> **Algunos alumnos van a la escuela a pie.**
> **Otros alumnos van en carro.**

Which word do you think means *arrive?* Which one means *go?*

Hint If you're the type of learner who has to write something before you can remember, copy the words in the **Palabras** section once or twice. Use the following learning sequence: listen, repeat, read, write.

3. Activity 1 on page 106 once again helps you to respond correctly to the question or interrogative words.

4. After you have learned the new words in **Palabras 2**, look at each illustration, cover up the sentences, and say as much as you can about the illustration. If you can describe the illustration, you know your vocabulary. If you cannot describe it, you have to study some more.

Hint Read or say aloud all the answers to the **Historieta** activities to give you practice telling coherent stories in Spanish.

Estructura
Presente de los verbos en -ar en el plural
(pages 112–115)

1. You will now learn two more verb endings. Be sure to remember them and how to use them.

-amos	when talking about yourself and someone else
-an	when talking about two or more people
	when talking to two or more people

2. It's always a good idea to review something you already know that's related to something new that you are learning.

-o	when talking about yourself
-a	when talking about one person
-amos	when talking about yourself and someone
-an	when talking about more than one person

Hint Be diligent in doing your Spanish homework. Work for at least a brief period of time each day. This enables you to learn everything in small doses. Do not let things pile up.

Presente de los verbos ir, dar, estar
(pages 116–117)

1. We always try to group material together to make it as easy as possible for you to learn. With these three new verbs you have to learn only one new form—when talking about yourself.

> **voy   doy   estoy**

2. All other forms are the same as a regular **-ar** verb. You are therefore reviewing the same endings.

3. Recall—What is the **yo** form of the irregular verb **ser? Soy, ¿no?** Notice the similarity.

> **soy   voy   doy   estoy**

Conversación *(page 120)*

1. Pay careful attention when you listen to the conversation on the CD-ROM or when other students are repeating it in class. The more you hear spoken Spanish, the easier it will be for you to understand.

2. In this conversation there are two very common expressions. **Oye** is used to get a friend's attention. **Pues** has no specific meaning, but it is frequently used before answering a question.

Lectura cultural
Escuelas del mundo hispano *(pages 122–123)*

As you read this selection, concentrate on some differences between schools in the United States and in the Spanish-speaking world.

Capítulo 5

Vocabulario

PALABRAS 1 y 2 *(pages 142–149)*

1. It can be fun to study with a classmate. You can do the following.
   - ❖ Ask one another questions in Spanish about the illustrations.
   - ❖ Have a contest. See who can give more Spanish words describing the illustrations in a three-minute period.
   - ❖ Tell your friend which of the items you would order if you were at a café.
2. When doing the activities that follow each **Palabras** section, read aloud all the answers to each **Historieta** activity. By doing this you will be telling a story in Spanish. Always remember, the more you practice speaking Spanish, the better you'll be able to communicate.
3. In class, pay attention to the responses of the other students in class. Don't turn them off. The more you hear the new words used, the easier it will be for you to remember them.

Estructura

Presente de los verbos en -er e -ir
(pages 150–153)

1. Note the similarities in **-er, -ir** verb endings and those of the **-ar** verbs. The vowel **-a** is **-e** in most forms of the **-er** and **-ir** verbs.
2. Pay particular attention to the **nosotros** form, since it is the only one that is different.

comemos	**vivimos**
aprendemos	**escribimos**

Hint   The more you practice speaking Spanish, the better. When doing your homework, go over all the activities aloud. Don't just do your Spanish homework silently.

Conversación *(page 154)*

1. Listen carefully to the conversation. You can listen to your teacher or use the CD-ROM.

Listen more than once. Each time you'll pick up some more information.

2. Read the conversation several times aloud.
3. Try to answer the questions that follow without looking up the answers in the conversation.

Lectura cultural

En un café en Madrid *(pages 156–157)*

1. Based on the Reading Strategy, guess the meaning of the words **inmediatamente** and **cenan.**
2. Read the selection fast to get the general idea.
3. Read it a second time to get more details.
4. Making comparisons while reading is an important reading comprehension skill. In this reading, you learned about a cultural difference that's quite interesting. What is it? You may want to share this information with family or friends who don't know any Spanish.

¡Te toca a ti! *(pages 162–163)*

In Activity 6 on page 163, you're going to write about a restaurant in Spanish.

1. Make a mental picture of the restaurant.
2. Write words you know in Spanish to describe a restaurant and restaurant activities.
3. List items that people may order.
4. Put these words into sentences. Your first paragraph will describe the restaurant. Your second paragraph will tell what your "characters" order. To finish your article, tell who paid for the meal.

Capítulo 6

Vocabulario

PALABRAS 1 y 2 *(pages 170–177)*

1. In **Palabras 1,** remember to listen to the words and repeat them orally before reading them.

Hint   If you're the type of learner who has to write something in order to remember it, copy the words in the **Palabras** section once or twice. Use the following learning sequence: listen, repeat, read, write.

2. After you have learned the new words in **Palabras 2,** look at each illustration, cover up the sentences, and say as much as you can about the illustration. If you can describe the illustration, you know your vocabulary. If you cannot describe it, you have to study some more.

Hint   Read or say aloud all the answers to the **Historieta** activities to give you practice in telling coherent stories in Spanish.

Estructura

Presente de tener *(pages 178–180)*

1. Familiarize yourself with the forms of **tener** as you read the verb chart.
2. Do the activities that follow the explanation diligently. They give you the practice you need to learn and retain the verb forms. To help you, they build from easy to more difficult.
3. Do the activities orally and in writing.
4. After doing all the activities, reread the grammar explanation. See if you can give the forms of the verb **tener** on your own without reading them.

Tener que, Ir a *(pages 181–182)*

Review   Once again, review all the verbs you know so that you will be able to use the correct infinitive form.

-AR	-ER	-IR	IRREGULAR
necesitar	leer	escribir	ser
buscar	comer	recibir	tener
mirar	beber	vivir	ir
comprar	vender	subir	dar
pagar	comprender	cumplir	estar
usar, calzar	aprender		ver
llevar			
hablar			
trabajar			
llegar			

-AR *(cont'd)*

estudiar
enseñar
mirar
escuchar
prestar
tomar
sacar
bailar
cantar
preparar
desear
invitar

Conversación *(page 186)*

1. This conversation should be very easy for you. You have already learned all the Spanish that is used in the conversation. When practicing this conversation with a classmate, feel free to make as many changes as you want, as long as they make sense.
2. In this conversation, you hear Tadeo ask **¿Verdad? ¿Verdad?** is used a great deal by speakers to get confirmation of what they said.
3. **Hombre** is often used as a "flavor" word when speaking to a male rather than using his name.

Lectura cultural

La familia hispana *(pages 188–189)*

1. As you read each paragraph, draw a mental picture of what you're reading. To help you draw your mental picture, look at the photographs, too.

¡Te toca a ti! *(pages 194–195)*

In Activity 5 on page 195, you are going to write about your house or a house of your dreams.

1. Picture the house.
2. In Spanish, think of or write a list of words you can use to identify parts of the house.
3. Think about or write a list of words you know in Spanish to describe a house or rooms of a house.

4. Organize your story. Divide the house into parts, such as living area, sleeping area, first floor, second floor. You may even want to make a drawing of your house. Write a few sentences about each area.
5. Put the sentences in a logical order.
6. Add a few sentences to describe the area around your house.

Vocabulario *(page 198)*

As you complete the chapter, look at the reference vocabulary list. If there are several words you don't remember, go back to the **Palabras 1** and **Palabras 2** sections and review. If there are only one or two, you can choose to look them up in the dictionaries beginning on page H34 at the end of this book.

Capítulo 7

Vocabulario
PALABRAS 1 y 2 *(pages 202–209)*
1. Look at each photo or illustration carefully.
2. Read the labels. What does each word refer to?
3. The words are then used in a meaningful context in a complete sentence. Repeat the sentence aloud as you look at the illustration.
4. To help you learn vocabulary, work with a friend or classmate. Have a contest. See who can say the most about each illustration or photo.
5. To review the vocabulary and see how much of it you know, cover the words and sentences and say as much as you can about each photo or illustration.
6. Do the activities that follow both orally and in writing.

Estructura
Verbos de cambio radical *(pages 210–214)*
1. Always simplify a grammatical rule to bare essentials to be able to hold onto it.

a. These verbs take the same endings as any regular verb belonging to that conjugation.
b. The stem change **ie** or **ue** takes place in all forms except **nosotros** (and **vosotros**).

Interesar, aburrir, gustar *(pages 215–217)*
1. Note that **mí** and **ti** are used after prepositions. All other forms are the same as the subject: **para él, ella, usted, ellos, ellas, ustedes, nosotros(as)**

Conversación *(page 218)*
1. Intonation is the melody of a language. Intonation is produced by the rise and fall of the voice. Each language has its own intonation patterns. English intonation is very different from Spanish intonation. Pay special attention to the rise and fall of the speakers' voices as you listen to the conversations on the CD or CD-ROM.
2. Try to imitate the speakers' intonation as accurately as possible. If you do, you'll sound much more like a heritage Spanish speaker. Don't be inhibited. Pretend you are acting while you imitate the intonation.

Lectura cultural
El fútbol *(pages 220–221)*
1. Scan the reading. Get a general idea of what the **Liga española** is and what the **Copa mundial** is.
2. Read the passage a second time and look for the answer to the following question. Why can't the team members of **el Real Madrid** de Casero and da Silva play together on the same team during the **Copa mundial?**

Vocabulario *(page 230)*
Look at each word and see if you can use it in a short sentence.

Study Tips

Capítulo 8

Vocabulario
PALABRAS 1 y 2 *(pages 242–249)*

1. Whenever you have a chance to review previously learned material, do so. As you do **Palabras 1,** think of all the parts of the body you have learned in Spanish.
2. After studying the vocabulary, cover up the print and say as much about each photo or illustration as you can.

Estructura
Ser y estar *(pages 250–255)*

1. Keep the grammatical rule simple. Remember:

Characteristic	**ser**
Condition	**estar**
Place of origin	**ser**
Location, permanent or temporary	**estar**

2. As you do the practice activities, very quickly say why you used **ser** or **estar.** This will help you remember the rule.

Lectura cultural
Una joven nerviosa *(pages 260–261)*

1. As you read this selection, visualize Patricia's appearance and demeanor.
2. As you read, look for the following information.
   - ❖ What's wrong with Patricia
   - ❖ Why she's upset
   - ❖ What the doctor does
   - ❖ What the doctor tells Patricia

Capítulo 9

Vocabulario
PALABRAS 1 y 2 *(pages 274–281)*

1. For **Palabras 1,** after going over the new vocabulary, review immediately. Sit back for a moment and say aloud or to yourself five words or expressions associated with the beach.
2. Pretend you are on the beach. Think of three things you would like to do while on the beach. Start your sentences with **Quiero...**
3. After completing each activity on pages 276 and 277, read all the answers aloud or silently. You're not only reading a story with words you know; you're also having another opportunity to use your new words.
4. In **Palabras 2,** when learning the winter weather expressions, review the summer expressions on pages 274 and 275.
5. As you do the activities on pages 280 and 281, work with a classmate. Take turns asking and answering the questions orally. Then write your answers individually. Correct each other's work.

Estructura
Pretérito de los verbos en -ar *(pages 282–285)*

1. So far, all the verb endings you have learned are for the present tense. Be sure you are very familiar with these present tense endings that you have already learned because you are now about to learn a new set of endings.
2. The endings in this lesson are used with regular **-ar** verbs to express a past action. Compare present and past tense endings.

	PRESENT	PAST
yo	**-o**	**-é**
tú	**-as**	**-aste**
él, ella, Ud.	**-a**	**-ó**
nosotros	**-amos**	**-amos**
vosotros	*-áis*	*-asteis*
ellos, ellas, Uds.	**-an**	**-aron**

3. Go over all the practice activities very diligently. Do each activity aloud. Then write the answers. Then read your written answers. If you find any errors, correct them.
4. The more you practice using the endings, the easier it will be to remember them.
5. After doing the practice activities, see if you can give the correct verb ending for each subject without looking them up.

Pronombres lo, la, los, las *(pages 286–288)*
A direct object pronoun answers the question *whom* or *what*.

Whom did you see?	I saw my friend.
What did you buy?	I bought a gift.

Conversación *(page 290)*
1. As you listen to or read the conversation find out Paula's predicament and what she did about it.
2. Try to answer the questions without looking up the answers.

Lectura cultural

Paraísos del mundo hispano *(pages 292–293)*
Look at the photographs as you read this selection. They will help you visualize what you are reading about.

················ # Capítulo 10 ················

Vocabulario
PALABRAS 1 y 2 *(pages 306–313)*
1. Remember to listen to the words and repeat them orally before reading them.
2. After you have gone over the new vocabulary, see how many words you remember. Think of seven words about a movie. Think of five words about a play.
3. Go over each activity orally before you write the answers.

Estructura
Pretérito de los verbos en -er e -ir
(pages 314–316)
1. Remember that the verb ending in Spanish indicates not only who performed the action of the verb but also when he or she preformed the action. The tense of a verb indicates when the action was performed.
2. In this lesson you are learning the endings for the past tense (preterite) of **-er** and **-ir** verbs.

3. **Review** Contrast the endings for the past tense of **-ar** verbs and **-er, -ir** verbs.

-AR	-ER, -IR
-é	-í
-aste	-iste
-ó	-ió
-amos	-imos
-asteis	*-isteis*
-aron	-ieron

4. Do all the activities that follow the grammatical explanation diligently. We suggest you first do the activities aloud, even by yourself, and then write the answers. Practice using the verb endings is very important. The more practice you get, the better.
5. It is important to keep the verb endings straight without mixing up one group with another.

Complementos le, les *(pages 317–319)*
Here's an easy way to tell the difference between a direct object and an indirect object. A direct object answers the question *whom* or *what*.

What did Juan throw?	The ball.
Whom did Juan see?	His friend.

An indirect object answers the question to (for) whom or to (for) what.

Lectura cultural
Dating *(pages 322–323)*
1. When reading, it helps to understand the passage when you have some idea of the information you are looking for. First, read the title. It tells you what the reading selection is about.
2. As you read, look for the following.
   ❖ Differences, if any, in dating customs in Latin America and the United States
   ❖ How dating customs are changing in Spain and Latin America

Study Tips

Capítulo 11

Vocabulario
PALABRAS 1 y 2 *(pages 336–343)*

1. Repeat each new word in the **Palabras** sections several times. Look at the photo or illustration as you pronounce the word.
2. Some of you may remember information more easily after writing it down. Try copying each vocabulary word once or twice.
3. You may want to do the activities aloud with a friend as a paired activity. Then, individually write the answers and check each other's work.
4. Listen carefully to what your classmates say when they respond in class. The more you hear people use the new words, the more likely you are to remember them.

Estructura
Hacer, poner, traer, salir en el presente
(pages 344–346)

1. Review the present tense of a regular **-er** and **-ir** verb.

COMER	VIVIR
como	**vivo**
comes	**vives**
come	**vive**
comemos	**vivimos**
coméis	*vivís*
comen	**viven**

2. Remember, the verbs **hacer, traer, poner,** and **salir** have the same endings as a regular verb except in the **yo** form. Concentrate on the **yo** form.

   hago   pongo   traigo   salgo

3. Two other **g** verbs are **tener** and **venir.**

   hago   pongo   traigo   salgo
   tengo   vengo

Saber y conocer en el presente
(pages 348–349)

1. Simplify the grammatical rule: just remember that **saber** means to know something simple,

and **conocer** means to know or be familiar with something complex.

2. When doing these activities, pay particular attention to the object of each verb to determine the use of **saber** or **conocer.**

Conversación *(page 350)*
Note that **chist** is used in some areas of the Spanish-speaking world to have someone be quiet. It's like *shh* in English.

Lectura cultural
El avión en la América del Sur
(pages 352–353)
To identify the main idea of this reading selection, look for the following information: two reasons why air travel is so important in South America.

Capítulo 12

Vocabulario
PALABRAS 1 y 2 *(pages 374–381)*

1. After learning the new vocabulary, cover up the print and tell what you see in each illustration.

Hint   If you are the type of learner who has to write something to remember it, write the new words on a separate sheet of paper.

Estructura
Verbos reflexivos *(pages 382–385)*

1. Remember that if a person is doing something to or for himself or herself, the verb in Spanish is a reflexive verb, and you must use the additional pronoun.
2. You have already learned all the verb endings that are used in these activities. The only new concept is the use of the reflexive pronoun. Pay particular attention to this pronoun as you do these activities.

Verbos reflexivos de cambio radical
(pages 386–387)

Review These reflexive verbs have the same stem change as verbs you have already learned.

    e → ie   empezar, comenzar, querer, perder, preferir

    o → ue   volver, devolver, poder

Lectura cultural

Del norte de España *(pages 390–391)*
1. Go to the map of Spain on page xxx. Look at the area of northern Spain from the Pyrenees to the city of Santiago de Compostela to familiarize yourself with the area you'll be reading about.
2. To review the past tense of verbs you have already learned, look for all the preterite forms in this reading. There are quite a few of them.

Capítulo 13

Vocabulario

PALABRAS 1 y 2 *(pages 404–411)*
1. Listen to the new words in **Palabras 1** and repeat them orally before reading them.
2. After learning the new words, match the following opposites.

la llegada	bajar de
de ida y vuelta	ocupado
subir a	la salida
libre	tarde
a tiempo	sencillo

3. Read the answers aloud to all the **Historieta** activities.

Estructura

El pretérito de los verbos irregulares *(pages 412–416)*
Note that these irregular verbs have the same endings in the preterite as regular verbs except in the **yo** and **él, ella, usted** forms.

	Regular	Irregular
yo	-í	-e
él, ella, Ud.	-ió	-o

Lectura cultural

En el AVE *(pages 420–421)*
1. Before reading this selection, look at the photo of the bird—**el ave, el pájaro.** What's the association of the bird with the train?
2. Scan the reading selection to get just the general idea.
3. Read the selection again and look for some more precise details about a trip on the **AVE.**

Capítulo 14

Vocabulario

PALABRAS 1 y 2 *(pages 434–441)*
1. Do some review as you learn this new vocabulary. Think of all the foods you have learned in Spanish. You may wish to refer back to Chapter 5.

Hint If you're the type of learner who has to write something before you can remember it, write the new words several times.

2. Activity 8 on page 441 reviews the use of **gustar.** You may review **interesar** and **gustar** on page 215.

Estructura

Verbos con el cambio e → i *(pages 442–443)*
1. You have already come across this type of stem change in the irregular verb **decir.**

    digo, dices, dice, decimos, *decís*, dicen

2. As with other stem-changing verbs you have learned so far **(e → ie, o → ue)**, these verbs take the same endings as any other verb that belongs to that conjugation.

Hint If you pronounce these verbs correctly, you will never have trouble spelling them. Remember **i** is pronounced like *ee* in English *see* and **e** is pronounced like the *a* in *ate*.

Lectura cultural

La comida mexicana *(pages 448–449)*
If you have ever been to a Mexican restaurant, think about what you ate there. It will help you visualize what you are reading about.

Verb Charts

REGULAR VERBS

INFINITIVO	hablar *to speak*	comer *to eat*	vivir *to live*
PRESENTE	hablo	como	vivo
	hablas	comes	vives
	habla	come	vive
	hablamos	comemos	vivimos
	habláis	*coméis*	*vivís*
	hablan	comen	viven
PRETÉRITO	hablé	comí	viví
	hablaste	comiste	viviste
	habló	comió	vivió
	hablamos	comimos	vivimos
	hablasteis	*comisteis*	*vivisteis*
	hablaron	comieron	vivieron

STEM-CHANGING VERBS
(-**ar** and -**er** verbs)

INFINITIVO	empezar (e → ie)[1] *to begin*	almorzar (o → ue)[2] *to eat lunch*	perder (e → ie)[3] *to lose*	volver (o → ue) *to return*
PRESENTE	empiezo	almuerzo	pierdo	vuelvo
	empiezas	almuerzas	pierdes	vuelves
	empieza	almuerza	pierde	vuelve
	empezamos	almorzamos	perdemos	volvemos
	empezáis	*almorzáis*	*perdéis*	*volvéis*
	empiezan	almuerzan	pierden	vuelven

[1] **Comenzar, sentar,** and **pensar** are similar.
[2] **Acostar, costar,** and **jugar (ue → ue)** are similar.
[3] **Defender** and **entender** are similar.

Verb Charts

STEM-CHANGING VERBS (-ir verbs)

INFINITIVO	preferir (e →ie, i) *to prefer*	dormir (o →ue, u)[1] *to sleep*	pedir (e →i, i)[2] *to ask for*
PRESENTE	prefiero	duermo	pido
	prefieres	duermes	pides
	prefiere	duerme	pide
	preferimos	dormimos	pedimos
	preferís	*dormís*	*pedís*
	prefieren	duermen	piden
PRETÉRITO	preferí	dormí	pedí
	preferiste	dormiste	pediste
	prefirió	durmió	pidió
	preferimos	dormimos	pedimos
	preferisteis	*dormisteis*	*pedisteis*
	prefirieron	durmieron	pidieron

IRREGULAR VERBS

INFINITIVO	andar *to walk*	dar *to give*	decir *to tell, to say*	estar *to be*
PRESENTE	*(regular)*	doy	digo	estoy
		das	dices	estás
		da	dice	está
		damos	decimos	estamos
		dais	*decís*	*estáis*
		dan	dicen	están
PRETÉRITO	anduve	di	dije	estuve
	anduviste	diste	dijiste	estuviste
	anduvo	dio	dijo	estuvo
	anduvimos	dimos	dijimos	estuvimos
	anduvisteis	*disteis*	*dijisteis*	*estuvisteis*
	anduvieron	dieron	dijeron	estuvieron

[1] **Morir** *is similar.*
[2] **Repetir** *and* **servir** *are similar.*

Verb Charts

IRREGULAR VERBS

INFINITIVO	hacer *to do*	ir *to go*	poder *to be able*	poner *to put*
PRESENTE	hago	voy	puedo	pongo
	haces	vas	puedes	pones
	hace	va	puede	pone
	hacemos	vamos	podemos	ponemos
	hacéis	*vais*	*podéis*	*ponéis*
	hacen	van	pueden	ponen
PRETÉRITO	hice	fui	pude	puse
	hiciste	fuiste	pudiste	pusiste
	hizo	fue	pudo	puso
	hicimos	fuimos	pudimos	pusimos
	hicisteis	*fuisteis*	*pudisteis*	*pusisteis*
	hicieron	fueron	pudieron	pusieron

INFINITIVO	querer *to want*	saber *to know*	salir *to leave*	ser *to be*
PRESENTE	quiero	sé	salgo	soy
	quieres	sabes	sales	eres
	quiere	sabe	sale	es
	queremos	sabemos	salimos	somos
	queréis	*sabéis*	*salís*	*sois*
	quieren	saben	salen	son
PRETÉRITO	quise	supe	(regular)	fui
	quisiste	supiste		fuiste
	quiso	supo		fue
	quisimos	supimos		fuimos
	quisisteis	*supisteis*		*fuisteis*
	quisieron	supieron		fueron

IRREGULAR VERBS

INFINITIVO	tener *to have*	traer *to bring*	venir *to come*	ver *to see*
PRESENTE	tengo	traigo	vengo	veo
	tienes	traes	vienes	ves
	tiene	trae	viene	ve
	tenemos	traemos	venimos	vemos
	tenéis	*traéis*	*venís*	*veis*
	tienen	traen	vienen	ven
PRETÉRITO	tuve	traje	vine	vi
	tuviste	trajiste	viniste	viste
	tuvo	trajo	vino	vio
	tuvimos	trajimos	vinimos	vimos
	tuvisteis	*trajisteis*	*vinisteis*	*visteis*
	tuvieron	trajeron	vinieron	vieron

VERBS WITH A SPELLING CHANGE IN THE PRETERITE
(-car, -gar, -zar)

INFINITIVO	practicar[1] *to practice*	llegar[2] *to arrive*	comenzar[3] *to begin*
PRETÉRITO	practiqué	llegué	comencé
	practicaste	llegaste	comenzaste
	practicó	llegó	comenzó
	practicamos	llegamos	comenzamos
	practicasteis	*llegasteis*	*comenzasteis*
	practicaron	llegaron	comenzaron

[1] **Buscar** and **sacar** are similar.
[2] **Jugar** and **pagar** are similar.
[3] **Empezar** and **almorzar** are similar.

Spanish-English Dictionary

*This Spanish-English Dictionary contains all productive and receptive vocabulary from the text. The numbers following each productive entry indicate the chapter and vocabulary section in which the word is introduced. For example, **3.2** means that the word was taught in **Capítulo 3, Palabras 2**. BV refers to the preliminary **Bienvenidos** lessons. If there is no number following an entry, this means that the word or expression is there for receptive purposes only.*

A

a at; to
  a bordo de aboard, on board, 11.2
  a eso de at about (time), 4.1
  a fines de at the end of
  a la española Spanish style
  a pie on foot, 4.1
  a plazos in installments
  a solas alone
  a tiempo on time, 11.1
  a veces sometimes, 7.1
  a ver let's see
abordar to get on, board
abril April, BV
abrir to open, 8.2
abstracto(a) abstract
la **abuela** grandmother, 6.1
el **abuelo** grandfather, 6.1
los **abuelos** grandparents, 6.1
abundante plentiful
aburrido(a) boring, 2.1
aburrir to bore
la **academia** academy, school
acariciar to caress
el **acceso** access
el **aceite** oil, 14.2
aceptar to accept
el **acompañamiento** accompaniment
acompañar to accompany
acordarse (ue) to remember
acostarse (ue) to go to bed, 12.1
el **acrílico** acrylic
la **actividad** activity
activo(a) active
el **actor** actor, 10.2
la **actriz** actress, 10.2

la **acuarela** watercolor
acuático(a): el esquí acuático water-skiing, 9.1
acuerdo: de acuerdo OK, all right
adaptar to adapt
además moreover; besides
¡Adiós! Good-bye! BV
adivinar to guess
admirar to admire
admitir to admit
la **adolescencia** adolescence
el/la **adolescente** adolescent, teenager
¿adónde? where?, 1.1
adorable adorable
adorar to adore
adornar to adorn
la **aduana** customs, 11.2
aérea: la línea aérea airlines
el **aeropuerto** airport, 11.1
afeitarse to shave, 12.1
  la crema de afeitar shaving cream, 12.1
aficionado(a) a fond of, 10.1
el/la **aficionado(a)** fan (sports)
afortunadamente fortunately
africano(a) African
afroamericano(a) African-American
el/la **agente** agent, 11.1
  el/la agente de aduana customs agent, 11.2
agosto August, BV
agradable pleasant
el **agua** (f.) water, 9.1
  el agua mineral mineral water, 12.2
  esquiar en el agua to water-ski, 9.1
el **agujero** hole
ahora now, 4.2
el **aire** air

  al aire libre outdoor (adj.)
el **ají** chili pepper
el **ajo** garlic, 14.2
el **ajuar de novia** trousseau
ajustar to adjust
al to the
  al aire libre outdoor (adj.)
  al contrario on the contrary
  al principio at the beginning
alarmarse to be alarmed
la **alberca** swimming pool, 9.1
el **albergue para jóvenes (juvenil)** youth hostel, 12.2
el **álbum** album
la **alcachofa** artichoke, 14.2
el **alcohol** alcohol
alegre happy
el **alemán** German, 2.2
la **alergia** allergy, 8.2
el **álgebra** algebra, 2.2
algo something, 5.2
  ¿Algo más? Anything else?, 5.2
algunos(as) some, 4.1
el **alimento** food, 14.2
allí there
almacenar to store
la **almeja** clam, 14.2
almorzar (ue) to eat lunch
el **almuerzo** lunch, 5.2
  tomar el almuerzo to have, eat lunch
la **alpargata** sandal
alquilar to rent
alrededor de around, 6.2
los **alrededores** outskirts
altivo arrogant, haughty
alto(a) tall, 1.1; high, 4.2
  en voz alta aloud
  la nota alta high grade, 4.2

la **altura** height

el/la **alumno(a)** student, 1.1

amarillo(a) yellow, 3.2

amazónico(a) Amazonian

ambicioso(a) hardworking, 1.1

ambulante itinerant

la **América Central** Central America

la **América del Norte** North America

la **América del Sur** South America

americano(a) American, 1.1

el/la **amigo(a)** friend, 1.1

el **análisis** analysis

analítico(a) analytical

analizar to analyze

anaranjado(a) orange, 3.2

anciano(a) old, 6.1

el/la **anciano(a)** old person

andaluz(a) Andalusian

andante: el caballero andante knight errant

andar to walk, to go to

el **andén** railway platform, 13.1

andino(a) Andean

la **anécdota** anecdote

el **animal** animal

anoche last night, 9.2

el **anorak** parka, 9.2

la **Antártida** Antarctic

anteayer the day before yesterday

los **anteojos de sol** sunglasses, 9.1

antes de before, 5.1

el **antibiótico** antibiotic, 8.2

la **antigüedad** antiquity

antiguo(a) old, ancient

anunciar to announce

el **anuncio** announcement

el **año** year, BV

cumplir... años to be . . . years old

el año pasado last year, 9.2

este año this year, 9.2

tener... años to be . . . years old, 6.1

el **apartamento** apartment, 6.2

la casa de apartamentos apartment house, 6.2

apasionado(a) passionate

la **apertura: la apertura de clases** beginning of the school year

aplaudir to applaud, 10.2

el **aplauso** applause, 10.2

recibir aplausos to receive applause, 10.2

aplicar to apply

el **apóstol** apostle

aprender to learn, 5.1

el **apunte: tomar apuntes** to take notes, 4.2

aquel that

en aquel entonces at that time

aquí here

Aquí tiene (tienes, tienen)... Here is (are) ...

por aquí right this way

aragonés(a) from Aragon (Spain)

el **árbol** tree

el **arco** arc

el **área** (f.) area

la **arena** sand, 9.1

argentino(a) Argentinian, 2.1

el **argumento** plot

la **aritmética** arithmetic, 2.2

el **arma** (f.) weapon

la **arqueología** archeology

arqueológico(a) archeological

el/la **arqueólogo(a)** archeologist

arrancar to pull out

arrogante arrogant

el **arroyo** stream, brook

el **arroz** rice, 5.2

el **arsenal** arsenal

el **arte** (f.) art, 2.2

las bellas artes fine arts

el **artefacto** artifact

el/la **artista** artist, 10.2

artístico(a) artistic

la **ascendencia** background

el **ascensor** elevator, 6.2

así so, 12

el **asiento** seat, 11.1

el número del asiento seat number, 11.1

la **asignatura** subject, discipline, 2.2

el/la **asistente de vuelo** flight attendant, 11.2

asistir to attend

el **asno** donkey

el **aspa** (f.) sail (of a windmill)

la **aspirina** aspirin, 8.2

astuto(a) astute

atacar to attack

el **ataque** attack

la **atención: prestar atención** to pay attention, 4.2

aterrizar to land, 11.2

atlético(a) athletic

la **atmósfera** atmosphere

atrapar to catch, 7.2

atrás behind, in the rear

atravesar (ie) to cross

el **atún** tuna, 5.2

aún even

austral former Argentine unit of currency

auténtico(a) authentic

el **autobús** bus, 10.1

perder el autobús (la guagua, el camión) to miss the bus, 10.1

el/la **autor(a)** author, 10.2

el **autorretrato** self-portrait

el **ave** (f.) bird

la **aventura** adventure

la **aviación** aviation

el **avión** airplane, 11.1

la **avioneta** small airplane

ayer yesterday, 9.2

ayer por la mañana yesterday morning, 9.2

ayer por la tarde yesterday afternoon, 9.2

ayudar to help, 13.1

azul blue, 3.2

B

el **bachillerato** bachelor's degree

la **bacteria** bacteria

la **bahía** bay

bailar to dance, 4.2

el **baile** dance

bajar to lower; to go down, 9.2; to get off, 13.2

bajar(se) del tren to get off the train, 13.2

bajo: bajo cero below zero, 9.2

bajo(a) short, 1.1; low, 4.2

la nota baja low grade, 4.2

la planta baja ground floor, 6.2

el **balneario** beach resort, 9.1

el **balón** ball, 7.1

tirar el balón to throw (kick) the ball, 7.2

el **baloncesto** basketball, 7.2

la **banana** banana

la **banda** music band

el **bando** team

el **bañador** bathing suit 9.1

bañarse to take a bath, 12.1

el **baño** bathroom, 6.2; bath

el cuarto de baño bathroom, 6.2

el traje de baño bathing suit, 9.1

barato(a) cheap, inexpensive, 3.2

la **barra: la barra de jabón** bar of soap, 12.2

basado(a) based (on)

basar to base

basarse to be based

la **báscula** scales, 11.1

la **base** base, 7.2; basis

básico(a) basic

el **básquetbol** basketball, 7.2

la cancha de básquetbol basketball court, 7.2

bastante enough, rather, quite, 1.1

el **bastón** ski pole, 9.2

la **batalla** battle

el **bate** bat, 7.2

el/la **bateador(a)** batter, 7.2

batear to hit (sports), 7.2

el **batú** Taíno Indian game

el **bautizo** baptism

el/la **bebé** baby

beber to drink, 5.1

la **bebida** beverage, drink

el **béisbol** baseball, 7.2

el campo de béisbol baseball field, 7.2

el juego de béisbol baseball game, 7.2

el/la jugador(a) de béisbol baseball player, 7.2

el/la **beisbolista** baseball player

bello(a) beautiful, pretty, 1.1

las bellas artes fine arts

la **berenjena** eggplant, 14.2

la **bicicleta** bicycle

ir en bicicleta to go by bike, 12.2

bien fine, well, BV

muy bien very well, BV

la **bienvenida: dar la bienvenida** to welcome, 11.2

el **biftec** steak, 14.2

bilingüe bilingual

el **billete** ticket, 11.1

el billete de ida y vuelta round-trip ticket, 13.1

el billete sencillo one-way ticket, 13.1

la **biografía** biography

la **biología** biology, 2.2

biológico(a) biological

el/la **biólogo(a)** biologist

blanco(a) white, 3.2

el **bloc** writing pad, 3.1

bloquear to stop, block, 7.1

el **blue jean** jeans, 3.2

la **blusa** blouse, 3.2

la **boca** mouth, 8.2

el **bocadillo** sandwich, 5.1

la **boletería** ticket window, 9.2

el **boleto** ticket, 9.2

el **bolígrafo** ballpoint pen, 3.1

la **bolsa** bag, 5.2; pocketbook, 13.1

el **bolsillo** pocket

bonito(a) pretty, 1.1

la **bota** boot, 9.2

el **bote** can, 5.2

la **botella: la botella de agua mineral** bottle of mineral water, 12.2

el **brazo** arm, 7.1

breve brief

brillante bright

brillar to shine, 9.1

el **bronce** bronze, 10.2

bronceado(a) tan

bronceador(a): la loción bronceadora suntan lotion, 9.1

bucear to dive; to swim underwater, 9.1

el **buceo** diving, underwater swimming, 9.1

buen good

estar de buen humor to be in a good mood, 8.1

Hace buen tiempo. The weather is nice., 9.1

bueno(a) good, 1.2

Buenas noches. Good evening., BV

Buenas tardes. Good afternoon., BV

Buenos días. Hello, Good morning., BV

sacar una nota buena to get a good grade, 4.2

el **bus** bus, 4.1

el bus escolar school bus, 4.1

busca: en busca de in search of

buscar to look for, 3.1

la **butaca** seat (theater), 10.1

C

el **caballero** knight

el caballero andante knight errant

el **caballete** easel

la **cabeza** head, 7.1

el **cacahuete (cacahuate)** peanut

cada each, every, 1.2

la **cadena** chain (necklace)

el **café** coffee, BV; café, 5.1

el café al aire libre outdoor café

el café con leche coffee with milk, 5.1

el café solo black coffee, 5.1

la **cafetería** cafeteria

la **caja** cash register, 3.1

los **calcetines** socks, 3.2

la **calculadora** calculator, 3.1

calcular to calculate

el **cálculo** calculus, 2.2

la **calle** street, 6.2

el **calor: Hace calor.** It's hot., 9.1

la **caloría** calorie

calzar to take, wear (shoe size), 3.2

la **cama** bed, 8.1

guardar la cama to stay in bed, 8.1

hacer la cama to make the bed

el/la **camarero(a)** waiter, waitress, 5.1

el **camarón** shrimp, 14.2

cambiar to change; exchange

cambiar de tren to change trains (transfer), 13.2

caminar to walk

la **caminata: dar una caminata** to take a hike, 12.2

el **camino** trail, path

el **camión** bus (Mex.), 10.1

la **camisa** shirt, 3.2

la **camiseta** T-shirt, undershirt, 3.2

la **campaña** campaign

el/la **campeón(a)** champion

el **campeonato** championship

el **campo** country; field

el **campo de béisbol** baseball field, 7.2

el **campo de fútbol** soccer field, 7.1

la **casa de campo** country home

el **canal** channel (TV)

la **canasta** basket, 7.2

el **canasto** basket, 7.2

la **cancha** court, 7.2

la **cancha cubierta** enclosed court, 9.1

la **cancha de básquetbol** basketball court, 7.2

la **cancha de tenis** tennis court, 9.1

la **canción** song

cansado(a) tired, 8.1

cantar to sing, 4.2

el **cante jondo** traditional flamenco singing

la **cantidad** amount

el **canto** singing

el **cañón** canyon

la **capital** capital

el/la **capitán** captain

el **capítulo** chapter

la **cara** face, 12.1

el **carbohidrato** carbohydrate

cardinal: los puntos cardinales cardinal points

el **cardo** thistle

el **Caribe** Caribbean

el **mar Caribe** Caribbean Sea

la **carne** meat, 5.2

la **carne de res** beef, 14.2

caro(a) expensive, 3.2

la **carpeta** folder, 3.1

el **carro** car, 4.1

en carro by car, 4.1

la **carta** letter, 6.2

la **casa** home, house, 6.2

en casa at home

la **casa de apartamentos (departamentos)** apartment house, 6.2

la **casa de campo** country home

la **casa privada (particular)** private house, 6.2

casado(a): estar casado(a) to be married

casi almost, practically

el **caso** case

el **catarro** cold (illness), 8.1

tener catarro to have a cold, 8.1

el/la **cátcher** catcher, 7.2

la **catedral** cathedral

la **categoría** category

católico(a) Catholic

catorce fourteen, BV

el **CD** compact disc (CD), 4.2

la **celebración** celebration

celebrar to celebrate

célebre famous

la **célula** cell

celular cellular

la **cena** dinner, 5.2

cenar to have dinner

el **centavo** penny

central central

el **centro** center

cepillarse to brush one's hair, 12.1

cepillarse los dientes to brush one's teeth, 12.1

el **cepillo** brush, 12.2

el cepillo de dientes toothbrush, 12.2

cerca de near, 6.2

el **cerdo** pig (pork), 14.2

el **cereal** cereal, 5.2

cero zero, BV

la **cesta** basket (jai alai)

el **cesto** basket, 7.2

el **chaleco** vest

el **chalet** chalet

el **champú** shampoo, 12.2

¡Chao! Good-bye!, BV

la **chaqueta** jacket, 3.2

la **chaucha** string bean

el **cheque de viajero** traveler's check

chileno(a) Chilean

la **chimenea** chimney

la **china** orange (fruit)

el **chisme** piece of gossip

¡chist! shh!

el **choclo** corn

el **chocolate: de chocolate** chocolate (adj.), 5.1

el **churro** (type of) doughnut

el **cielo** sky, 9.1

las **ciencias** science, 2.2

las ciencias naturales natural sciences

las ciencias sociales social sciences, 2.2

científico(a) scientific

el/la **científico(a)** scientist

cien(to) one hundred, 3.2

cinco five, BV

cincuenta fifty, 2.2

el **cine** movie theater, 10.1

el **círculo** circle

la **ciudad** city

el **clarinete** clarinet

¡**claro!** certainly!, of course!

la **clase** class (school) 2.1; class (ticket). 13.1

> la **apertura de clases** beginning of the school year

> la **sala de clase** classroom, 4.1

> el **salón de clase** classroom, 4.1

> **primera clase** first-class, 13.1

> **segunda clase** second-class, 13.1

clásico(a) classic

clasificar to classify

el/la **cliente** customer, 5.1

el **clima** climate

climático(a) climatic

la **clínica** clinic

el **club** club, 4.2

> el **Club de español** Spanish Club, 4.2

el **coche** car, 4.1; train car, 13.2

> **en coche** by car, 4.1

el **coche-cafetería** cafeteria (dining) car, 13.2

el **coche-cama** sleeping car, 13.2

el **coche-comedor** dining car, 13.2

la **cocina** kitchen, 6.2

el/la **cocinero(a)** cook, 14.1

la **coincidencia** coincidence

la **cola** line (queue), 10.1

> **hacer cola** to stand in line, 10.1

la **colección** collection

el **colector** collector

el **colegio** school, 1.1

el **colesterol** cholesterol

colgar (ue) to hang

colocar to put, place

colombiano(a) Colombian, 1.1

la **colonia** suburb, colony

el **color** color, 3.2

> **de color marrón** brown, 3.2

> ¿**De qué color es?** What color is it?, 3.2

el/la **comandante** captain, 11.2

el **comedor** dining room, 6.2

comenzar (ie) to begin

comer to eat, 5.1

el **comestible** food, 14.2

cómico(a) funny, 1.1

la **comida** food, meal, 5.2

como like; as; since, 1.2

¿**cómo?** how?, what?, 1.1

> ¿**Cómo está... ?** How is. . . ?, 8.1

> ¡**Cómo no!** Of course!

la **comodidad** comfort

compacto(a): el disco compacto compact disc, CD, 4.2

el/la **compañero(a)** friend, 1.2

la **compañía** company

la **comparación** comparison

comparar to compare

la **competencia** competition

la **competición** competition, contest

competir (i, i) to compete

completo(a) full (train), 13.2

la **composición** composition

la **compra: ir de compras** to go shopping, to shop, 5.2

comprar to buy, 3.1

comprender to understand, 5.1

la **computadora** computer

con with

> **con mucha plata** rich

> ¿**con quién?** with whom?

> **con retraso** with a delay, 13.2

> **con una demora** with a delay, 11.1

el **concierto** concert

el **conde** count

la **condición** condition

el **condimento** seasoning

el **condominio** condominium

conectar to connect

la **conferencia** lecture

Conforme. Agreed., Fine., 14.2

congelado(a): los productos congelados frozen food, 5.2

el **conjunto** set, collection

conocer to know, to be familiar with, 11.1

la **conquista** conquest

conquistar to conquer

consentir (ie, i) to allow, tolerate

conservar to save

considerar to consider

consistir (en) to consist of

la **consulta: la consulta del médico** doctor's office, 8.2

consultar to consult, 13.1

el **consultorio** medical office, 8.2

el/la **consumidor(a)** consumer

consumir to consume

el **consumo** consumption

el **contacto** touch

la **contaminación** pollution

contaminado(a) polluted

contaminar to pollute

contener to contain

contento(a) happy, 8.1

contestar to answer

el **continente** continent

continuar to continue, 7.2

contra against, 7.1

el **control** inspection, 11.1

> el **control de pasaportes** passport inspection, 11.1

> el **control de seguridad** security check, 11.1

controlar to control

conversar to talk, speak

convertir (ie, i) to convert, transform

la **copa: la Copa mundial** World Cup

copiar to copy

el/la **copiloto** copilot, 11.2

el **corazón** heart

la **corbata** tie, 3.2

el **cordero** lamb, 14.2

el **cordoncillo** piping (embroidery)

la **coreografía** choreography

la **córnea** cornea

el **coro** choir, chorus

el **correo: el correo electrónico** e-mail, electronic mail

Spanish-English Dictionary

correr to run, 7.2

cortar to cut

la **cortesía** courtesy, BV

corto(a) short, 3.2

  el **pantalón corto** shorts, 3.2

la **cosa** thing

coser to sew

la **costa** coast

costar (ue) to cost, 3.1

costarricense Costa Rican

la **costumbre** custom

la **costura** sewing

crear to create

el **crecimiento** growth

crédito: la tarjeta de crédito credit card, 14.1

creer to believe, 8.2; to think so

la **crema: la crema de afeitar** shaving cream, 12.1

  la **crema dentífrica** toothpaste, 12.2

  la **crema protectora** sunblock, 9.1

criollo(a) Creole

cristiano(a) Christian

cruzar to cross

el **cuaderno** notebook, 3.1

el **cuadro** painting, 10.2

¿cuál? which?, what?, BV

  ¿Cuál es la fecha de hoy? What is today's date?, BV

¿cuáles? which ones?, what?

cuando when, 4.2

¿cuándo? when?, 4.1

¿cuánto? how much?, 3.1

  ¿A cuánto está(n)... ? How much is (are) . . . ?, 5.2

  ¿Cuánto cuesta(n)... ? How much do(es) . . . cost?, 3.1

  ¿Cuánto es? How much does it cost?, 3.1

¿cuántos(as)? how many?, 2.1

cuarenta forty, 2.2

el **cuarto** room, bedroom 6.2; quarter

  el **cuarto de baño** bathroom, 6.2

  el **cuarto de dormir** bedroom

menos cuarto a quarter to (the hour)

y cuarto a quarter past (the hour)

cuarto(a) fourth, 6.2

cuatro four, BV

cuatrocientos(as) four hundred, 3.2

cubano(a) Cuban

cubanoamericano(a) Cuban-American

cubrir to cover

la **cuchara** tablespoon, 14.1

la **cucharita** teaspoon, 14.1

el **cuchillo** knife, 14.1

el **cuello** neck

la **cuenca** basin

la **cuenta** bill, check, 5.1

el/la **cuentista** short-story writer

el **cuento** story

la **cuerda** string (instrument)

el **cuerpo** body

¡cuidado! careful!

  con mucho cuidado very carefully

cultivar to cultivate

el **cumpleaños** birthday, 6.1

cumplir: cumplir... años to be . . . years old, 6.1

el/la **curandero(a)** folk healer

el **curso** course, class, 2.1

  el **curso obligatorio** required course

  el **curso opcional** elective course

D

la **dama** lady-in-waiting, woman

la **danza** dance

dar to give, 4.2

  dar a entender to imply that

  dar auxilio to help

  dar énfasis to emphasize

  dar la mano to shake hands

  dar un examen to give a test, 4.2

  dar una fiesta to give (throw) a party, 4.2

  dar una representación to put on a performance, 10.2

datar to date

los **datos** data, information

de of, from, for, BV

  de... a... from (time) to (time), 2.2

  de joven as a young person

  De nada. You're welcome., BV

  de ninguna manera by no means, 1.1

  de vez en cuando sometimes

debajo (de) under, below

deber must; should; to owe

decidir to decide

décimo(a) tenth, 6.2

decir to say, 13

  ¡Diga! Hello! (answering the telephone—Spain), 14.2

declarar to declare

el **dedo** finger

el **defecto** fault, flaw

definitivamente once and for all

dejar to leave (something), 14.1; to let, allow

del of the, from the

delante de in front of, 10.1

delantero(a) front

delgado(a) thin

delicioso(a) delicious

demás other, rest

demasiado too much

la **demora: con una demora** with a delay, 11.1

dentífrico(a): la pasta (crema) dentífrica toothpaste, 12.2

dentro de within

  dentro de poco soon

el **departamento** apartment, 6.2

  la **casa de departamentos** apartment house, 6.2

depender (de) to depend (on)

el/la **dependiente(a)** employee, 3.1

el **deporte** sport, 7.1

  el deporte de equipo team sport

  el deporte individual individual sport

  deportivo(a) (related to) sports, 6.2

  la emisión deportiva sports program (TV), 6.2

derecho(a) right, 7.1

derrotar to defeat

desagradable unpleasant

desamparado(a): los niños desamparados homeless children

desayunarse to eat breakfast, 12.1

el **desayuno** breakfast, 5.2

  tomar el desayuno to eat breakfast, 12.1

el/la **descendiente** descendant

describir to describe

descubrir to discover

el **descuento** discount

desde since

desear to want, wish, 3.2

  ¿Qué desea usted? May I help you? (in a store), 3.2

los **desechos** waste

desembarcar to disembark, 11.2

el **desierto** desert

despachar to sell, 8.2

despegar to take off (airplane), 11.2

despertarse (ie) to wake up, 12.1

después (de) after, 5.1; later

el **destino** destination, 11.1

  con destino a to

devolver (ue) to return (something), 7.2

el **día** day, BV

  Buenos días. Good morning., BV

  hoy (en) día nowadays, these days

  ¿Qué día es (hoy)? What day is it (today)?, BV

la **diagnosis** diagnosis, 8.2

el **diálogo** dialogue

el **diamante** diamond

dibujar to draw

el **dibujo** drawing

diciembre December, BV

diecinueve nineteen, BV

dieciocho eighteen, BV

dieciséis sixteen, B

diecisiete seventeen, BV

el **diente: cepillarse los dientes** to brush one's teeth, 12.1

  el cepillo de dientes toothbrush, 12.2

diez ten

la **diferencia** difference

diferente different

difícil difficult, 2.1

¡Diga! Hello! (telephone), 14.2

diminuto(a) tiny, minute

la **dinamita** dynamite

el **dinero** money, 14.1

  el dinero en efectivo cash

¡Dios mío! Gosh!

la **dirección** address; direction

  en dirección a toward

directo(a) direct

el/la **director(a)** director, principal

la **disciplina** subject area (school), 2.2

el **disco: el disco compacto** compact disc, CD, 4.2

discutir to discuss

el/la **diseñador(a)** designer

el **diseño** design

disfrutar to enjoy

la **disputa** quarrel, argument

el **disquete** diskette, 3.1

la **distancia** distance

la **diversión** amusement

divertido(a) fun, amusing

divertirse (ie, i) to enjoy oneself, 12.2

dividir to divide

la **división** division

divorciarse to get divorced

doblado(a) dubbed, 10.1

dobles doubles, 9.1

doce twelve, BV

la **docena** dozen

el/la **doctor(a)** doctor

el **dólar** dollar

doler (ue) to hurt, 8.2

  Me duele(n)... My ... hurt(s) me, 8.2

el **dolor** pain, ache, 8.1

  el dolor de cabeza headache, 8.1

  el dolor de estómago stomachache, 8.1

  el dolor de garganta sore throat, 8.1

  Tengo dolor de... I have a pain in my . . . , 8.2

doméstico(a) domestic

  la economía doméstica home economics, 2.2

el **domingo** Sunday, BV

dominicano(a) Dominican, 2.1

  la República Dominicana Dominican Republic

don courteous way of addressing a male

donde where, 1.2

¿dónde? where?, 1.2

dormido(a) asleep

dormir (ue, u) to sleep

  el saco de dormir sleeping bag, 12.2

dormirse (ue, u) to fall asleep, 12.1

el **dormitorio** bedroom, 6.2

dos two, BV

doscientos(as) two hundred, 3.2

la **dosis** dose, 8.2

el/la **dramaturgo(a)** playwright

driblar to dribble, 7.2

la **droga** drug

la **ducha** shower, 12.1

  tomar una ducha to take a shower, 12.1

la **duda** doubt

dulce: el pan dulce sweet roll, 5.1

la **duración** duration

durante during

duro(a) hard, difficult, 2.1

el **DVD** digital video disc (DVD), 4.2

E

echar to throw

echar (tomar) una siesta to take a nap

echarle flores to pay someone a compliment

la **ecología** ecology

ecológico(a) ecological

la **economía** economics; economy

la **economía doméstica** home economics, 2.2

económico(a) economical, 12.2

la **ecuación** equation

ecuatoriano(a) Ecuadorean, 2.1

la **edad** age

el **edificio** building

la **educación** education

la **educación física** physical education, 2.2

efectivo: en efectivo in cash

el **ejemplo: por ejemplo** for example

el **ejote** string beans

el the (m. sing.), 1.1

él he, 1.1

electrónico(a) electronic

el **correo electrónico** e-mail, electronic mail

la **elevación** elevation

elevado(a) elevated

elevar to elevate

ella she, 1.1

ellos(as) they, 2.1

el **elote** corn (Mex.)

embarcar to board, 11.2

embarque: la tarjeta de embarque boarding pass, 11.1

la **puerta de embarque** departure gate

la **emisión** program (TV), 6.2; emission

la **emisión deportiva** sports program, 6.2

emitir to emit

la **emoción** emotion

emocional emotional

empatado(a) tied (score), 7.1

El tanto queda empatado. The score is tied., 7.1

empezar (ie) to begin, 7.1

el/la **empleado(a)** employee, 3.1

en in; on

en aquel entonces at that time

en punto on the dot, sharp, 4.1

el/la **enamorado(a)** sweetheart, lover

encantador(a) charming

encantar to delight

encender (ie) to light

encestar to put in (make) a basket, 7.2

encima: por encima de above, 9.1

encontrar (ue) to find

el/la **enemigo(a)** enemy

la **energía** energy

enero January, BV

el **énfasis: dar énfasis** to emphasize

enfatizar to emphasize

la **enfermedad** illness

enfermo(a) sick, 8.1

el/la **enfermo(a)** sick person, 8.1

el **enganche** down payment

enlatado(a) canned

la **ensalada** salad, 5.1

enseguida right away, immediately, 5.1

enseñar to teach, 4.1

entero(a) entire, whole

enterrar (ie) to bury

el **entierro** burial

entonces then

en aquel entonces at that time

la **entrada** inning, 7.2; admission ticket, 10.1

entrar to enter, 4.1

entrar en escena to come (go) on stage, 10.2

entre between, 7.1

entregar to deliver

la **entrevista** interview

enviar to send

envuelto(a) wrapped

el **episodio** episode

la **época** period of time, epoch

el **equilibrio** equilibrium

el **equipaje** baggage, luggage, 11.1

el **equipaje de mano** carry-on luggage, 11.1

el **equipo** team, 7.1; equipment

el **deporte de equipo** team sport, 7.2

erróneo(a) wrong, erroneous

la **escala** stopover

la **escalera** stairway, 6.2

los **escalofríos** chills, 8.1

escamotear to secretly take

escapar to escape

la **escena** scene

entrar en escena to come (go) on stage, 10.2

el **escenario** scenery, set (theater), 10.2

escoger to choose

escolar (related to) school, 2.1

el **bus escolar** school bus, 4.1

el **horario escolar** school schedule

los **materiales escolares** school supplies, 3.1

la **vida escolar** school life

esconder to hide

escribir to write, 5.1

escuchar to listen (to), 4.2

el **escudero** squire, knight's attendant

la **escuela** school, 1.1

la **escuela intermedia** middle school

la **escuela primaria** elementary school

la **escuela secundaria** high school, 1.1

la **escuela superior** high school

el/la **escultor(a)** sculptor, 10.2

la **escultura** sculpture

esencialmente essentially

eso: **a eso de** at about (time), 4.1

el **espagueti** spaghetti

espantoso frightful

España Spain

español(a) Spanish (*adj.*)

el **español** Spanish, 2.2

la **espátula** palette knife, spatula

especial special

la **especialidad** specialty

especialmente especially

el **espectáculo** show, 10.2

ver un espectáculo to see a show, 10.2

el/la **espectador(a)** spectator, 7.1

el **espejo** mirror, 12.1

espera: la sala de espera waiting room, 13.1

esperar to wait (for), 11.1

espontáneo(a) spontaneous

la **esposa** wife, spouse, 6.1

el **esposo** husband, spouse, 6.1

el **esquí** skiing, 9.2; ski

el esquí acuático waterskiing, 9.1

el/la **esquiador(a)** skier, 9.2

esquiar to ski, 9.2

esquiar en el agua to water-ski, 9.1

la **estación** season, BV; resort; station, 10.1

la estación de esquí ski resort, 9.2

la estación de ferrocarril train station, 13.1

la estación de metro subway station, 10.1

el **estadio** stadium, 7.1

el **estado** state

Estados Unidos United States

estadounidense from the United States

estar to be, 4.1

estar resfriado(a) to have a cold, 8.1

la **estatua** statue, 10.2

el **este** east

estereofónico(a) stereo

el **estilo** style

estimado(a) esteemed

el **estómago** stomach, 8.1

estornudar to sneeze, 8.1

la **estrategia** strategy

la **estrella** star

la **estructura** structure

el/la **estudiante** student

estudiantil (relating to) student

estudiar to study, 4.1

el **estudio** study

estupendo(a) stupendous

eterno(a) eternal

étnico(a) ethnic

Europa Europe

exactamente exactly

exagerar to exaggerate

el **examen** test, exam, 4.2

examinar to examine, 8.2

la **excavación** excavation

excavar to dig, excavate

exceder to exceed

excelente excellent

la **excepción** exception

exclamar to exclaim

exclusivamente exclusively

la **exhibición** exhibition

existir to exist

el **éxito** success

la **expedición** expedition

la **experiencia** experience

el/la **experto(a)** expert, 9.2

explicar to explain, 4.2

el/la **explorador(a)** explorer

la **explosión** explosion

la **exposición (de arte)** (art) exhibition, 10.2

la **expresión: el modo de expresión** means of expression

extranjero(a) foreign

el país extranjero foreign country, 11.2

el/la **extranjero(a)** foreigner

extraordinario(a) extraordinary

F

la **fábrica** factory

fabuloso(a) fabulous

fácil easy, 2.1

la **factura** invoice

facturar el equipaje to check luggage, 11.1

la **Facultad** school (of a university)

la **faja** sash

la **falda** skirt, 3.2

la **fama** fame

la **familia** family, 6.1

familiar (related to the) family

famoso(a) famous, 1.2

fantástico(a) fantastic, 1.2

el/la **farmacéutico(a)** pharmacist, 8.2

la **farmacia** pharmacy, 8.2

fascinar to fascinate

febrero February, BV

la **fecha** date, BV

¿Cuál es la fecha de hoy? What is today's date?, BV

feo(a) ugly, 1.1

la **fiebre** fever, 8.1

tener fiebre to have a fever, 8.1

fiel faithful

la **fiesta** party

dar una fiesta to give (throw) a party, 4.2

la **figura** figure

figurativo(a) figurative

fijo(a) fixed

la **fila** line (queue); row (of seats), 10.1

el **film** film, 10.1

el **fin** end

el fin de semana weekend, BV

a fines de at the end of

el **final: al final (de)** at the end (of)

las **finanzas** finances

la **física** physics, 2.1

físico(a): la educación física physical education, 2.2

flaco(a) thin, 1.2

la **flauta** flute

flechar to become enamored of (to fall for)

la **flor** flower

formar to make up, to form

la **foto** photo

la **fotografía** photograph

el **francés** French, 2.2

franco(a) frank, candid, sincere

la **frase** phrase, sentence

frecuentemente frequently

freír (i, i) to fry, 14.1

fresco(a) fresh

el **frijol** bean, 5.2

el **frío: Hace frío.** It's cold., 9.2

frito(a) fried, 5.1

las papas fritas French fries, 5.1

el **frontón** wall (of a jai alai court)

la **fruta** fruit, 5.2

la **fuente** source

fuerte strong

fumar: la sección de (no) fumar (no) smoking area, 11.1

la **función** performance, 10.2

el **funcionamiento** functioning

la **fundación** foundation

fundar to found, establish

la **furia** fury

furioso(a) furious

el **fútbol** soccer, 7.1

el campo de fútbol soccer field, 7.1

el **futuro** future

G

las **gafas de sol** sunglasses, 9.1

el **galán** beau, heartthrob

gallardo(a) gallant, fine-looking

el **galón** gallon

ganar to win, 7.1; to earn

la **ganga** bargain

el **garaje** garage, 6.2

la **garganta** throat, 8.1

el **gas** gas

gastar to spend

el/la **gato(a)** cat, 6.1

general: en general generally

por lo general in general

generalmente usually, generally

el **género** genre

generoso(a) generous, 1.2

la **gente** people

la **geografía** geography, 2.2

la **geometría** geometry, 2.2

geométrico(a) geometric

el **gigante** giant

el **gimnasio** gymnasium

la **gira** tour, 12.2

el **gol: meter un gol** to score a goal, 7.1

el **golfo** gulf

golpear to hit, 9.2

la **goma: la goma de borrar** eraser, 3.1

gordo(a) fat, 1.2

la **gorra** cap, hat, 3.2

gozar to enjoy

Gracias Thank you., BV

gracioso(a) funny, 1.1

el **grado** degree (temperature), 9.2

la **gramática** grammar

el **gramo** gram

gran, grande big, large, great

las Grandes Ligas Major Leagues

el **grano** grain

la **grasa** fat

grave serious, grave

la **gripe** flu, 8.1

gris gray, 3.2

el **grupo** group

la **guagua** bus (P.R., Cuba), 10.1

el **guante** glove, 7.2

guapo(a) handsome, 1.1

guardar to guard, 7.1; to keep

guardar cama to stay in bed, 8.1

guatemalteco(a) Guatemalan

la **guerra** war

la **guerrilla** guerrilla

el/la **guía** tour guide

el **guisante** pea, 5.2

la **guitarra** guitar

gustar to like, to be pleasing

el **gusto** pleasure

Mucho gusto. Nice to meet you.

H

la **habichuela** bean, 5.2

la habichuela tierna string bean

la **habitación** bedroom

el/la **habitante** inhabitant

habla: los países de habla española Spanish-speaking countries

hablar to speak, talk, 3.1

hace: Hace buen tiempo. The weather is nice., 9.1

Hace calor. It's hot., 9.1

Hace frío. It's cold., 9.2

Hace mal tiempo. The weather is bad., 9.1

Hace sol. It's sunny., 9.1

hacer to do, to make

hacer caso to pay attention

hacer la cama to make the bed

hacer la maleta to pack one's suitcase

hacer un viaje to take a trip, 11.1

hacia toward

hallar to find

hambre: tener hambre to be hungry, 14.1

la **hamburguesa** hamburger, 5.1

hasta until, BV

¡Hasta luego! See you later!, BV

¡Hasta mañana! See you tomorrow!, BV

¡Hasta pronto! See you soon!, BV

hay there is, there are, BV

hay que one must

Hay sol. It's sunny., 9.1

No hay de qué. You're welcome., BV

hecho(a) made

helado(a): el té helado iced tea, 5.1

el **helado** ice cream, 5.1

el helado de chocolate chocolate ice cream, 5.1

el helado de vainilla vanilla ice cream, 5.1

el **hemisferio norte** northern hemisphere

el **hemisferio sur** southern hemisphere

la **herencia** inheritance

la **hermana** sister, 6.1

el **hermano** brother, 6.1

hermoso(a) beautiful, pretty, 1.1

el/la **héroe** hero

higiénico(a): el papel higiénico toilet paper, 12.2

la **hija** daughter, 6.1

el **hijo** son, 6.1

los **hijos** children, 6.1

hispano(a) Hispanic

hispanoamericano(a) Spanish-American

hispanohablante Spanish-speaking

el/la **hispanohablante** Spanish speaker

la **historia** history, 2.2; story

el/la **historiador(a)** historian

histórico(a) historical

la **historieta** little story

la **hoja: la hoja de papel** sheet of paper, 3.1

¡Hola! Hello!, BV

el **hombre** man

¡hombre! good heavens!, you bet!

honesto(a) honest, 1.2

el **honor** honor

la **hora** hour; time

la hora de salida departure hour

¿A qué hora? At what time?, 2.2

¿Qué hora es? What time is it?, 2.2

el **horario** schedule, 13.1

el horario escolar school schedule

horrible horrible

el **hospital** hospital

el **hostal** inexpensive hotel, 12.2

la **Hostia** Host (religious)

el **hotel** hotel

hoy today, BV

hoy (en) día nowadays, these days

el **huarache** sandal

el **huevo** egg, 5.2

humano(a): el ser humano human being

humilde humble

el **humor** mood, 8.1

estar de buen humor to be in a good mood, 8.1

estar de mal humor to be in a bad mood, 8.1

el **huso horario** time zone

I

ida: de ida y vuelta round-trip (ticket), 13.1

la **idea** idea

ideal ideal, 1.2

el/la **idealista** idealist

la **iglesia** church

igual equal

la **ilusión** illusion

imaginado(a) imagined, dreamed of

imaginar to imagine

importante important

imposible impossible

la **impresora** printer

el/la **inca** Inca

incluido(a): ¿Está incluido el servicio? Is the tip included?, 5.1

incluir to include, 5.1

increíble incredible

la **independencia** independence

el **indicador: el tablero indicador** scoreboard, 7.1

indicar to indicate, 11.1

indígena native, indigenous

el/la **indígena** native person

indio(a) Indian

indispensable indispensable

individual individual

el deporte individual individual sport

el **individuo** individual

industrial industrial

la **influencia** influence

la **información** information

informar to inform, 13.2

la **informática** computer science, 2.2

el **inglés** English, 2.2

inmediatamente immediately

inmediato(a) immediate

inmenso(a) immense

inspeccionar to inspect, 11.1

el **instante** instant

la **instrucción** instruction

el **instrumento** instrument

el instrumento musical musical instrument

íntegro(a) integral

inteligente intelligent, 2.1

el **interés** interest

interesante interesting, 2.1

interesar to interest

intermedio(a): la escuela intermedia middle school

internacional international

la **interpretación** interpretation

íntimo(a) intimate

inverso(a) reverse

la **investigación** investigation

el/la **investigador(a)** researcher

el **invierno** winter, BV

la **invitación** invitation

invitar to invite, 6.1

la **inyección** injection, 8.2

ir to go, 4.1

ir a + infinitive to be going to (do something)

ir a pie to go on foot, to walk 4.1

ir de compras to go shopping, 5.2

ir en bicicleta to go by bicycle, 12.2

ir en carro (coche) to go by car, 4.1

ir en tren to go by train

la **isla** island
italiano(a) Italian
izquierdo(a) left, 7.1

J

el **jabón** soap, 12.2
**la barra (pastilla) de
jabón** bar of soap, 12.2
jamás never
el **jamón** ham, 5.1
el **jardín** garden, 6.2
el/la **jardinero(a)** outfielder, 7.2
el **jet** jet
el **jonrón** home run, 7.2
joven young, 6.1
de joven as a young
person
el/la **joven** youth, young
person, 10.1
la **judía: la judía verde**
green bean, 5.2
el **juego** game
el juego de béisbol
baseball game, 7.2
el juego de tenis tennis
game, 9.1
los Juegos Olímpicos
Olympic Games
el **jueves** Thursday, BV
el/la **jugador(a)** player, 7.1
**el/la jugador(a) de
béisbol** baseball
player, 7.2
jugar (ue) to play, 7.1
**jugar (al) béisbol
(fútbol, baloncesto,
etc.)** to play baseball
(soccer, basketball, etc.),
7.1
el **jugo** juice
el jugo de naranja
orange juice, 12.1
el **juguete** toy
julio July, BV
la **jungla** jungle
junio June, BV
junto(a) together
**juvenil: el albergue
juvenil** youth hostel, 12.2

K

el **kilo** kilogram, 5.2
el **kilómetro** kilometer

L

la the (*f. sing.*), 1.1; it, her
(*pron.*)
el **laboratorio** laboratory
el **lado** side
el **lago** lake
el **lamento** lament
la **lana** wool
la **langosta** lobster, 14.2
la **lanza** lance
el/la **lanzador(a)** pitcher, 7.2
lanzar to throw, 7.1
el **lápiz** pencil, 3.1
largo(a) long, 3.2
las them (*f. pl.*) (*pron.*)
la **lata** can, 5.2
lateral side (*adj.*), 13.2
el **latín** Latin, 2.2
latino(a) Latin (*adj.*)
Latinoamérica Latin
America, 1.1
latinoamericano(a) Latin
American
lavarse to wash oneself, 12.1
lavarse los dientes to
brush one's teeth, 12.1
le to him, to her; to you
(*formal*) (*pron.*)
la **lección** lesson, 4.2
la **leche** milk
el café con leche coffee
with milk, 5.1
el **lechón** suckling pig
la **lechuga** lettuce, 5.2
la **lectura** reading
leer to read, 5.1
la **legumbre** vegetable, 14
la **lengua** language, 2.2
el **lenguaje** language
les to them; to you
(*formal pl.*) (*pron.*)

la **letra** letter (of alphabet)
levantar to lift
levantarse to get up, 12.1
el/la **libertador(a)** liberator
la **libra** pound
libre free, 5.1
al aire libre outdoor (*adj.*)
el **libro** book, 3.1
el **liceo** high school
el **lienzo** canvas (painting)
la **liga** league
las Grandes Ligas
Major Leagues
ligero(a) light (cheerful)
limeño(a) from Lima
(Peru)
la **limonada** lemonade, BV
lindo(a) pretty, 1.1
la **línea** line
la línea aérea airline
la línea ecuatorial
equator
la línea paralela
parallel line
la línea telefónica
telephone line
el **lípido** lipid, fat
líquido(a) liquid
listo(a) ready
la **litera** berth, 13.2
literal literal
literario(a) literary
la **literatura** literature, 2.1
el **litro** liter
llamado(a) called
llamar to call
llamarse to be named,
to call oneself, 12.1
la **llegada** arrival, 11.1
llegar to arrive, 4.1
lleno(a) full
llevar to carry, 3.1; to
wear, 3.2; to bring, 6.1; to
bear; to have (subtitles,
ingredients, etc.)
llover (ue) to rain
Llueve. It's raining., 9.1
la **lluvia** rain
lo it; him (*m. sing.*) (*pron.*)
lo que what, that which

local local, 13.2

la **loción**: **la loción bronceadora** suntan lotion, 9.1

loco(a) insane

los them *(m. pl.) (pron.)*

el **loto** lotto

luchar to fight

luego later; then, BV

¡Hasta luego! See you later!, BV

el **lugar** place

lujo: de lujo deluxe

lujoso(a) luxurious

la **luna** moon

el **lunes** Monday, BV

la **luz** light

M

la **madre** mother, 6.1

madrileño(a) native of Madrid

la **madrina** godmother

el/la **maestro(a)** teacher; master

magnífico(a) magnificent

el **maíz** corn, 14.2

mal bad, 14.2

estar de mal humor to be in a bad mood, 8.1

Hace mal tiempo. The weather's bad., 9.1

la **maleta** suitcase, 11.1

la **maletera** trunk (of a car), 13.1

el/la **maletero(a)** porter, 11.1

malhumorado(a) bad-tempered

malo(a) bad, 2.1

sacar una nota mala to get a bad grade, 4.2

la **mamá** mom

la **manera** way, manner, 1.1

de ninguna manera by no means, 1.1

el **maní** peanut

la **mano** hand, 7.1

dar la mano to shake hands

el **mantel** tablecloth, 14.1

mantener to maintain

la **manzana** apple, 5.2

mañana tomorrow, BV

¡Hasta mañana! See you tomorrow!, BV

la **mañana** morning

de la mañana A.M. (time), 2.2

por la mañana in the morning

el **mapa** map

el **maquillaje** makeup, 12.1

poner el maquillaje to put one's makeup on, 12.1

maquillarse to put one's makeup on, 12.1

el **mar** sea, 9.1

el mar Caribe Caribbean Sea

maravilloso(a) marvelous

el **marcador** marker, 3.1

marcar: marcar un tanto to score a point, 7.1

el **marido** husband, 6.1

los **mariscos** shellfish, 5.2

marrón: de color marrón brown, 3.2

el **martes** Tuesday, BV

marzo March, BV

más more, 2.2

más o menos more or less

más tarde later

la **masa** mass

las **matemáticas** mathematics, 2.1

la **materia** matter, subject

el **material: los materiales escolares** school supplies, 3.1

el **matrimonio** marriage

el/la **maya** Maya

mayo May, BV

mayor greater

la mayor parte the greater part, the most

la **mayoría** majority

me me *(pron.)*

la **medalla** medal

media: y media half-past (time), 2.2

la **medianoche** midnight, 2.2

el **medicamento** medicine (drugs), 8.2

la **medicina** medicine (discipline), 8.2

el/la **médico(a)** doctor, 8.2

la **medida** measurement

el **medio** medium, means

el medio de transporte means of transportation

medio(a) half, 5.2

media hora half an hour

el **mediodía** noon

medir (i, i) to measure

melancólico(a) melancholic

menos less, fewer

menos cuarto a quarter to (the hour)

la **mensualidad** monthly installment

el **menú** menu, 5.1

el **mercado** market, 5.2

el **merengue** merengue

la **merienda** snack, 4.2

tomar una merienda to have a snack, 4.2

la **mermelada** marmalade

el **mes** month, BV

la **mesa** table, 5.1; plateau

la **mesera** waitress, 5.1

el **mesero** waiter, 5.1

el/la **mestizo(a)** mestizo

el **metabolismo** metabolism

el **metal: instrumentos de metal** brass (instruments in orchestra)

meter to put, place, 7.1

meter un gol to score a goal, 7.1

el **método** method

el **metro** subway, 10.1; meter

mexicano(a) Mexican, 1.1

mexicanoamericano(a) Mexican-American

la **mezcla** mixture

mi my

mí (to) me *(pron.)*

el **microbio** microbe

microscópico(a) microscopic

el **microscopio** microscope

el **miedo** fear

    tener miedo to be afraid

el **miembro** member, 4.2

mientras while

el **miércoles** Wednesday, BV

mil (one) thousand, 3.2

la **milla** mile

el **millón** million

el **minuto** minute

mirar to look at, watch, 3.1

    ¡Mira! Look!

mirarse to look at oneself, 12.1

mismo(a) same, 2.1; itself

el **misterio** mystery

misterioso(a) mysterious

mixto(a) co-ed (school)

la **mochila** backpack, 3.1; knapsack, 12.2

la **modalidad** mode, type

el/la **modelo** model

el **módem** modem

moderno(a) modern

el **modo** manner, way

    el modo de expresión means of expression

el **molino de viento** windmill

el **momento** moment

la **moneda** coin, currency

el **monitor** monitor

monocelular single-celled

el **monstruo** monster

la **montaña** mountain, 9.2

montañoso(a) mountainous

montar (caballo) to mount, get on (horse)

el **monumento** monument

moreno(a) dark, brunette, 1.1

morir (ue, u) to die

el **mostrador** counter, 11.1

el **motivo** reason, motive; theme

el **motor** motor

mover (ue) to move

el **movimiento** movement

el **mozo** porter, 13.1

la **muchacha** girl, 1.1

el **muchacho** boy, 1.1

mucho(a) a lot; many, 2.1

    Mucho gusto. Nice to meet you.

los **muebles** furniture

la **muerte** death

la **mujer** wife, 6.1

la **multiplicación** multiplication

multiplicar to multiply

mundial worldwide, (related to the) world

    la Copa mundial World Cup

    la Serie mundial World Series

el **mundo** world

    todo el mundo everyone

el **mural** mural, 10.2

el/la **muralista** muralist, 10

el **museo** museum, 10.2

la **música** music, 2.2

el/la **músico(a)** musician

muy very, BV

    muy bien very well, BV

N

nacer to be born

nacido(a) born

nacional national

la **nacionalidad** nationality, 1.2

    ¿de qué nacionalidad? what nationality?

nada nothing, 5.2

    De nada. You're welcome., BV

    Nada más. Nothing else., 5.2

    Por nada. You're welcome., BV

nadar to swim, 9.1

nadie no one

la **naranja** orange, 5.2

el **narcótico** narcotic

la **natación** swimming, 9.1

natural: los recursos naturales natural resources, 2.1

    las ciencias naturales natural sciences

la **navaja** razor, 12.1

navegar to navigate

    navegar por la red to surf the Net

la **Navidad** Christmas

necesario(a) necessary

necesitar to need, 3.1

negro(a) black, 3.2

nervioso(a) nervous, 8.1

nevar (ie) to snow, 9.2

la **nieta** granddaughter, 6.1

el **nieto** grandson, 6.1

la **nieve** snow, 9.2

ninguno(a) not any, none

    de ninguna manera by no means, 1.1

el/la **niño(a)** child

    los niños desamparados homeless children

el **nivel** level

no no, BV

    No hay de qué. You're welcome., BV

    no hay más remedio there's no other alternative

noble noble

la **noche** night, evening

    Buenas noches. Good night., BV

    de la noche P.M. (time), 2.2

    esta noche tonight, 9.2

    por la noche in the evening, at night

la **Nochebuena** Christmas Eve

el **nombre** name

    ¿a nombre de quién? in whose name?, 14.2

el **noroeste** northwest

el **norte** north

norteamericano(a) North American

nos (to) us *(pl. pron.)*

nosotros(as) we, 2.2

la **nota** grade, 4.2

    la nota buena (alta) good (high) grade, 4.2

    la nota mala (baja) bad (low) grade, 4.2

    sacar una nota buena (mala) to get a good (bad) grade, 4.2

notable notable

notar to note

las **noticias** news, 6.2

novecientos(as) nine hundred, 3.2

la **novela** novel

el/la **novelista** novelist

noveno(a) ninth, 6.2

noventa ninety, 2.2

noviembre November, BV

el/la **novio(a)** boyfriend / girlfriend; fiancé(e)

la **nube** cloud, 9.1

Hay nubes. It's cloudy., 9.1

nublado(a) cloudy, 9.1

nuestro(a) our

nueve nine, BV

nuevo(a) new

de nuevo again

el **número** number, 1.2; size (shoes), 3.2

el número del asiento seat number, 11.1

el número del vuelo flight number, 11.1

nupcial nuptial, wedding

la **nutrición** nutrition

O

el **objeto** object

obligatorio(a): el curso obligatorio required course

la **obra** work

la obra de arte work of art

la obra dramática play

la obra teatral play, 10.2

la **observación** observation

el/la **observador(a)** observer

observar to observe

el **obstáculo** obstacle

obtener to obtain

el **océano** ocean

ochenta eighty, 2.2

ocho eight, BV

ochocientos(as) eight hundred, 3.2

octavo(a) eighth, 6.2

octubre October, BV

ocupado(a) occupied, taken, 5.1

el **oeste** west

oficial official

ofrecer to offer

la **oftalmología** ophthalmology

oír to hear

el **ojo** eye, 8.2

la **ola** wave, 9.1

el **óleo** oil

la **oliva: el aceite de oliva** olive oil

once eleven, BV

la **onza** ounce

opcional: el curso opcional elective course

la **ópera** opera

el/la **operador(a)** operator

la **opereta** operetta

opinar to think

oralmente orally

la **orden** order (restaurant), 5.1

el **ordenador** computer

el **orfanato** orphanage

el **organismo** organism

el **órgano** organ

el **origen** origin

original: en versión original in its original (language) version, 10.1

el **oro** gold

la **orquesta** orchestra

la orquesta sinfónica symphonic orchestra

la **ortiga** nettle

oscuro(a) dark

otavaleño(a) of or from Otavalo, Ecuador

el **otoño** autumn, BV

otro(a) other, another

¡oye! listen!

P

la **paciencia** patience

el/la **paciente** patient

el **padre** father, 6.1

el padre (religioso) father (religious)

los **padres** parents, 6.1

el **padrino** godfather

los **padrinos** godparents

pagar to pay, 3.1

la **página** page

la página Web Web page

el **pago** payment

el pago mensual monthly payment

el **país** country, 11.2

el país extranjero foreign country

el **paisaje** landscape

el **pájaro** bird

la **palabra** word

el **pan: el pan dulce** sweet roll, 5.1

el pan tostado toast, 5.2

panameño(a) Panamanian, 2.1

el **panqueque** pancake

la **pantalla** screen, 10.1

la pantalla de salidas y llegadas arrival and departure screen, 11.1

el **pantalón** pants, trousers, 3.2

el pantalón corto shorts, 3.2

la **papa** potato, 5.1

las papas fritas French fries, 5.1

el **papá** dad

el **papel** paper, 3.1

la hoja de papel sheet of paper, 3.1

el papel higiénico toilet paper, 12.2

la **papelería** stationery store, 3.1

el **paquete** package, 5.2

el **par: el par de tenis** pair of tennis shoes, 3.2

para for

¿para cuándo? for when?, 14.2

la **parada** stop, 13.2

el **paraíso** paradise

parar to stop, to block, 7.1

parecerse to look like

parecido(a) similar

la **pared** wall

la **pareja** couple

el/la **pariente** relative, 6.1

el **parque** park

el **párrafo** paragraph

la **parte** part

  la mayor parte the greatest part, the most

  por todas partes everywhere

particular private, 6.2

  la casa particular private house, 6.2

particularmente especially

el **partido** game, 7.1

pasado(a) past; last

  el (año) pasado last (year)

el/la **pasajero(a)** passenger, 11.1

el **pasaporte** passport, 11.1

pasar to pass, 7.2; to spend; to happen

  Lo están pasando muy bien. They're having a good time., 12.2

  pasar por to go through, 11.1

  ¿Qué te pasa? What's the matter (with you)?, 8.1

el **pase** pass (permission)

el **pasillo** aisle, 13.2

la **pasta (crema) dentífrica** toothpaste, 12.2

la **pastilla** pill, 8.2

  la pastilla de jabón bar of soap, 12.2

la **patata** potato

pedir (i, i) to ask for, 14.1

peinarse to comb one's hair, 12.1

el **peine** comb, 12.1

la **película** film, movie, 6.2

  ver una película to see a film, 10.1

pelirrojo(a) redheaded, 1.1

el **pelo** hair, 12.1

la **pelota** ball, 7.2

  la pelota vasca jai alai

el/la **pelotari** jai alai player

la **península** peninsula

el **pensamiento** thought

pensar (ie) to think

la **pensión** boarding house, 12.2

pequeño(a) small, 2.1

la **percusión** percussion

perder (ie) to lose, 7.1; to miss, 10.2

  perder el autobús (la guagua, el camión) to miss the bus, 10.2

Perdón. Excuse me.

el/la **peregrino(a)** pilgrim

perezoso(a) lazy, 1.1

el **periódico** newspaper, 6.2

el **período** period

permitir to permit, 11.1

pero but

el **perrito** puppy

el **perro** dog, 6.1

la **persona** person, 1.2

el **personaje** character

peruano(a) Peruvian

pesar to weigh

el **pescado** fish, 5.2

la **peseta** former monetary unit of Spain

el **peso** peso (monetary unit of several Latin American countries), BV; weight

la **petición** petition

el **petróleo** petroleum, oil

petrolero(a) oil

el **piano** piano

el/la **pícher** pitcher, 7.2

el **pico** peak, mountain

  y pico just after (time)

el **pie** foot, 7.1; down payment

  a pie on foot, 4.1

  de pie standing

la **pierna** leg, 7.1

la **pieza** room

la **píldora** pill, 8.2

el/la **piloto** pilot, 11.2

la **pimienta** pepper, 14.1

el **pincel** brush, paintbrush

la **pinta** pint

pintar to paint

el/la **pintor(a)** painter

pintoresco(a) picturesque

la **pintura** painting

la **pirueta** pirouette, maneuver

la **piscina** swimming pool, 9.1

el **piso** floor, 6.2; apartment

la **pista** (ski) slope, 9.2

la **pizarra** chalkboard, 4.2

el **pizarrón** chalkboard, 4.2

la **pizza** pizza, BV

la **plaga** plague, menace

la **plancha de vela** sailboard, 9.1

  practicar la plancha de vela to go windsurfing, 9.1

planear to plan

la **planta** floor, 6.2; plant

  la planta baja ground floor, 6.2

la **plata** money (income)

el **plátano** banana, plantain, 5.2

el **platillo** base, 7.2; saucer, 14.1

el **plato** plate, dish, 14.1

la **playa** beach, 9.1

  playera: la toalla playera beach towel, 9.1

la **plaza** plaza, square; seat, 13.2

la **pluma** pen, 3.1

la **población** population, people

pobre poor

el/la **pobre** the poor boy (girl)

el **pobretón** poor man

poco(a) little, few, 2.1

  un poco (de) a little

poder (ue) to be able, 7.1

el **poema** poem

la **poesía** poetry

el **poeta** poet

político(a) political

el **pollo** chicken, 5.2

el **poncho** poncho, shawl, wrap

poner to put, 11.1

  poner la mesa to set the table, 14.1

ponerse to put on, 12.1

  ponerse el maquillaje to put on makeup, 12.1

  ponerse la ropa to dress oneself, to put on clothes, 12.1

popular popular, 2.1

la **popularidad** popularity

por for

por aquí over here

por ciento percent

por ejemplo for example

por eso therefore, for this reason, that's why

por favor please, BV

por fin finally

por hora per hour

por la noche in the evening

por lo general in general

Por nada. You're welcome., BV

¿por qué? why?

por tierra overland

el **poroto** string bean

porque because

la **portería** goal line, 7.1

el/la **portero(a)** goalkeeper, goalie, 7.1

la **posibilidad** possibility

posible possible

el **postre** dessert, 5.1

practicar to practice

practicar el surfing (la plancha de vela, etc.) to go surfing (windsurfing, etc.), 9.1

el **precio** price

precolombino(a) pre-Columbian

preferir (ie, i) to prefer

la **pregunta** question

preguntar to ask (a question)

el **premio: el Premio Nóbel** Nobel Prize

preparar to prepare

la **presentación** presentation

presentar to present; to show (movie)

prestar: prestar atención to pay attention, 4.2

prevalecer to prevail

primario(a): la escuela primaria elementary school

la **primavera** spring, BV

primero(a) first, BV

en primera (clase) first-class, 13.1

el/la **primo(a)** cousin, 6.1

la **princesa** princess

principalmente mainly

el/la **principiante** beginner, 9.2

prisa: a toda prisa as fast as possible

privado(a) private

la casa privada private house, 6.2

el **problema** problem

procesar to process

la **procesión** procession

proclamar to proclaim

producido(a) produced

el **producto** product, 5.2

los productos congelados frozen food, 5.2

el/la **profesor(a)** teacher, professor, 2.1

profundo(a) deep

el **programa** program

la **promesa** promise

pronto: ¡Hasta pronto! See you soon!, BV

la **propina** tip, 14.1

la **protección** protection

protector(a): la crema protectora sunblock, 9.1

la **proteína** protein

el **protoplasma** protoplasm

el/la **proveedor(a)** provider

proveer to provide

la **provisión** provision

próximo(a) next, 13.2

en la próxima parada at the next stop, 13.2

proyectar to project, 10.1

publicar to publish

público(a) public

el **público** audience, 10.2

el **pueblo** town

el **puerco** pork

la **puerta** door; gate, 11.1

la puerta de salida departure gate, 11.1

puertorriqueño(a) Puerto Rican

pues well

la **pulgada** inch

el **punto: en punto** on the dot, sharp, 4.1

los puntos cardinales cardinal points

el **puré de papas** mashed potatoes

puro(a) pure

Q

qué what; how, BV

¡Qué absurdo! How absurd!

¡Qué enfermo(a) estoy! I'm so sick!

¿Qué tal? How are you?, BV

¿Qué te pasa? What's the matter (with you)?, 8.2

quechua Quechuan

quedar to remain, 7.1

querer (ie) to want, wish

el **queso** cheese, 5.1

el **quetzal** quetzal (currency of Guatemala)

¿quién? who?, 1.1

¿quiénes? who? (pl.), 2.1

la **química** chemistry, 2.2

químico(a) chemical

quince fifteen, BV

la **quinceañera** fifteen-year old (girl)

quinientos(as) five hundred, 3.2

quinto(a) fifth, 6.2

el **quiosco** newsstand, 13.1

Quisiera... I would like . . . , 14.2

quitarse to take off

R

rápido quickly

la **raqueta** racket (sports), 9.1

el **rato** while

el **ratón** mouse

la **razón** reason

razonable reasonable

real royal

realista realistic

el/la **realista** realist

realmente really

rebotar to rebound

la **recámara** bedroom, 6.2

el/la **receptor(a)** catcher, 7.2

la **receta** prescription, 8.2

recetar to prescribe, 8.2

recibir to receive, 5.1

el **reciclaje** recycling

recién recently

recientemente recently

reclamar to claim (luggage), 11.2

el **reclamo de equipaje** baggage claim, 11.2

recoger to pick up

recoger el equipaje to claim one's luggage, 11.2

el **rectángulo** rectangle

el **recurso: los recursos naturales** natural resources

la **red** net, 9.1

navegar por la red to surf the Net

reducido(a) reduced (price)

reemplazar to replace

reflejar to reflect

el **reflejo** reflection

reflexionar to reflect

el **refresco** drink, beverage, 5.1

el **refugio** refuge

regalar to give

el **regalo** gift, 6.1

la **región** region

regional regional

el **regionalismo** regionalism

regresar to return

regreso: el viaje de regreso return trip, trip back

regular regular, average, 2.2

la **reina** queen

la **relación** relation

relacionado(a) related

relativamente relatively

religioso(a) religious

rellenar to fill

el **remedio** solution

renombrado(a) well-known

rentar to rent

renunciar to renounce, give up

repetir (i, i) to repeat; to take seconds (meal)

el **reportaje** report

la **representación** performance (theater), 10.2

dar una representación to put on a performance, 10.2

representar to represent

la **República Dominicana** Dominican Republic

requerir (ie, i) to require

la **reservación** reservation

reservado(a) reserved, 13.2

reservar to reserve, 14.2

resfriado(a): estar resfriado(a) to have a cold, 8.1

el/la **residente** resident

resolver (ue) to solve

la **respuesta** answer

restar to subtract

el **restaurante** restaurant, 14.1

el **resto** rest, remainder

la **retina** retina

el **retintín** jingle

el **retraso: con retraso** with a delay, late, 13.2

el **retrato** portrait

revisar to inspect, 11.1

revisar el boleto to check the ticket, 11.1

el/la **revisor(a)** (train) conductor, 13.2

la **revista** magazine, 6.2

revolver (ue) to turn around

el **rey** king

rico(a) rich; delicious, 14.2

el/la **rico(a)** rich person

el **río** river

rodar (ue) to roll

la **rodilla** knee, 7.1

rojo(a) red, 3.2

el **rollo de papel higiénico** roll of toilet paper, 12.2

romántico(a) romantic

la **ropa** clothing, 3.2

la **tienda de ropa** clothing store, 3.2

la **rosa** rose

rosado(a) pink, 3.2

rubio(a) blond, 1.1

la **ruina** ruin

el **rumor** rumor

rural rural

la **ruta** route

la **rutina** routine, 12.1

S

el **sábado** Saturday, BV

saber to know (how), 11.2

sabio(a) wise

sabroso(a) delicious

sacar to get, 4.2

sacar un billete to buy a ticket

sacar una nota buena (mala) to get a good (bad) grade, 4.2

el **sacerdote** priest

el **saco** jacket

el saco de dormir sleeping bag, 12.2

sacrificar to sacrifice

la **sal** salt, 14.1

la **sala** room; living room, 6.2

la sala de clase classroom, 4.1

la sala de espera waiting room, 13.1

la sala de salida departure area, 11.1

la **salida** departure, 11.1

la hora de salida departure hour, 13.1

la pantalla de llegadas y salidas arrival and departure screen, 11.1

la sala de salida departure area, 11.1

salir to leave, 10.1; to go out; to turn out

salir a tiempo to leave on time, 11.1

salir bien (en un examen) to do well (on an exam)

salir tarde to leave late, 11.1

el **salón: el salón de clase**
 classroom, 4.1

saltar to jump

la **salud** health

el **saludo** greeting, BV

salvar to save

el **sándwich** sandwich, BV

la **sangre** blood

el **santo** saint

el **saxofono** saxophone

la **sección de (no) fumar**
 (no) smoking section, 11.1

**secundario(a): la escuela
 secundaria** high school, 1.1

sed: tener sed to be
 thirsty, 14.1

seguir (i, i) to follow, 14

según according to

segundo(a) second, 6.2

 el segundo tiempo
 second half (soccer), 7.1

 en segunda (clase)
 second-class, 13.1

la **seguridad: el control de
 seguridad** security
 (airport), 11.1

seis six, BV

seiscientos(as) six
 hundred, 3.2

la **selección** selection

seleccionar to select

la **selva** jungle

la **semana** week, BV

 el fin de semana
 weekend, BV

 el fin de semana pasado
 last weekend

 la semana pasada last
 week, 9.2

el/la **senador(a)** senator

**sencillo(a): el billete
 sencillo** one-way ticket,
 13.1

sentarse (ie) to sit down,
 12.1

el **sentido** meaning,
 significance

el **señor** sir, Mr., gentleman,
 BV

la **señora** Ms., Mrs., madam,
 BV

la **señorita** Miss, Ms., BV

septiembre September, BV

séptimo(a) seventh, 6.2

ser to be

el **ser: el ser humano** human
 being

 el ser viviente living
 creature, being

la **serie: la Serie mundial**
 World Series

serio(a) serious, 1.1

el **servicio** service, tip, 5.1

 **¿Está incluido el
 servicio?** Is the tip
 included?, 5.1

la **servilleta** napkin, 14.1

servir (i, i) to serve, 14.1

sesenta sixty, 2.2

la **sesión** show (movies), 10.1

setecientos(as) seven
 hundred, 3.2

setenta seventy, 2.2

sexto(a) sixth, 6.2

el **show** show

si if

sí yes

siempre always, 7.1

 de siempre y para siempre
 eternally, forever

la **sierra** sierra, mountain
 range

siete seven, BV

el **siglo** century

el **significado** meaning

significar to mean

siguiente following

la **silla** chair

similar similar

simpático(a) nice, 1.2

simple simple

sin without

 sin escala nonstop

sincero(a) sincere, 1.2

singles singles, 9.1

el **síntoma** symptom, 8.2

el **sistema métrico** metric
 system

el **sitio** place

sobre on top of; over; on,
 about

 sobre todo especially

sobresaltar to jump up

la **sobrina** niece, 6.1

el **sobrino** nephew, 6.1

**social: las ciencias
 sociales** social sciences

la **sociedad** society

la **sociología** sociology

socorrer to help

el **sol** Peruvian coin; sun, 9.1

 Hace (Hay) sol. It's
 sunny., 9.1

 tomar el sol to
 sunbathe, 9.1

solamente only

soler (ue) to be
 accustomed to, tend to

solo(a) alone

 a solas alone

 el café solo black coffee,
 5.1

sólo only

soltero(a) single, bachelor

la **solución** solution

el **sombrero** hat

la **sonrisita** little smile

la **sopa** soup, 5.1

el **sorbete** sherbet, sorbet, 14

el/la **sordo(a)** deaf

 su his, her, their, your

 subir to go up, 6.2; to
 board, to get on

 subir al tren to get on,
 to board the train, 13.1

el **subtítulo** subtitle, 10.1

 con subtítulos with
 subtitles, 10.1

el **suburbio** suburb

 suceso: el buen suceso
 great event

 sudamericano(a) South
 American

el **sudoeste** southwest

el **suegro** father-in-law

el **suelo** ground

el **sueño** dream

 sufrir to suffer

 sumar to add

 **superior: la escuela
 superior** high school

el **supermercado**
 supermarket, 5.2

el **sur** south

el **surf de nieve** snowboarding

el **surfing** surfing, 9.1

   practicar el surfing to surf, 9.1

el **suroeste** southwest

el **surtido** assortment

   sus their, your (pl.), 6.1

   suspirar to sigh

la **sustancia: la sustancia controlada** controlled substance

T

el **T-shirt** T-shirt, 3.2

la **tabla: la tabla hawaiana** surfboard, 9.1

el **tablero** board, 7.1

   el tablero de llegadas arrival board, 13.1

   el tablero de salidas departure board, 13.1

   el tablero indicador scoreboard, 7.1

la **tableta** pill, 8.2

   taíno(a) Taino

   tal: ¿Qué tal? How are you?, BV

la **talla** size, 3.2

el **talón** luggage claim ticket, 11.1

el **tamal** tamale, BV

el **tamaño** size, 3.2

   también also

   tan so

el **tango** tango

el **tanto** point, 7.1

   marcar un tanto to score a point

   tanto(a) so much

la **taquilla** box office, 10.1

   tardar to take time

   tarda el viaje the trip takes (+ time)

   tarde late

la **tarde** afternoon

   Buenas tardes. Good afternoon., BV

   esta tarde this afternoon, 9.2

   por la tarde in the afternoon

la **tarifa** fare, rate

la **tarjeta** card, 11.1

   la tarjeta de crédito credit card, 14.1

   la tarjeta de embarque boarding pass, 11.1

   la tarjeta de identidad estudiantil student I.D. card

el **taxi** taxi, 11.1

la **taza** cup, 14.1

   te you (fam. pron.)

el **té** tea, 5.1

   el té helado iced tea, 5.1

   teatral theatrical, 10.2

el **teatro** theater, 10.2

   salir del teatro to leave the theater, 10.2

el **teclado** keyboard

el/la **técnico(a)** technician

la **tecnología** technology

   telefonear to telephone

   telefónico(a) (related to the) telephone

   la línea telefónica telephone line

el **teléfono** telephone

   hablar por teléfono to talk on the phone

el **telesilla** chairlift, 9.2

el **telesquí** ski lift, 9.2

la **televisión** television, 6.2

el **telón** curtain (stage), 10.2

el **tema** theme, subject

la **temperatura** temperature, 9.2

   templado(a) temperate

   temprano early, 12.1

el **tenedor** fork, 14.1

   tener (ie) to have, 6.1

   tener... años to be . . . years old, 6.1

   tener hambre to be hungry, 14.1

   tener miedo to be afraid

   tener que to have to

   tener sed to be thirsty, 14.1

el **tenis** tennis, 9.1

los **tenis** tennis shoes, 3.2

   el par de tenis pair of tennis shoes, 3.2

el/la **tenista** tennis player

   tercer(o)(a) third, 6.2

la **terminal** terminal

   terminar to end

el **término** term

la **ternera** veal, 14.2

la **terraza** terrace (sidewalk café)

   terrible terrible

el **terror** terror, fear

la **tía** aunt, 6.1

el **ticket** ticket, 9.2

el **tiempo** time; weather, 9.1; half (game)

   a tiempo on time, 11.1

   el segundo tiempo second half (game), 7.1

la **tienda** store, 3.2

   la tienda de departamentos department store

   la tienda de ropa clothing store, 3.2

   la tienda de videos video store

   tierno(a) tender

la **tierra: por tierra** by land, overland

el **tilde** accent

   tímido(a) timid, shy, 1.2

el **tío** uncle, 6.1

   los tíos aunt(s) and uncle(s), 6.1

   típicamente typically

   típico(a) typical

el **tipo** type

   tirar to kick, 7.1

   tirar el balón to kick (throw) the ball, 7.2

la **toalla playera** beach towel, 9.1

   tocar to touch; to play (music)

   todavía yet, still

   todo: todo el mundo everyone

   todos(as) everybody, 2.2; everything, all

   por todas partes everywhere

tomar to take, 4.1
  tomar agua (leche, café) to drink water (milk, coffee)
  tomar apuntes to take notes, 4.2
  tomar el bus (escolar) to take the (school) bus, 4.1
  tomar el desayuno to eat breakfast, 12.1
  tomar el sol to sunbathe, 9.1
  tomar fotos to take photos
  tomar un jugo to drink some juice
  tomar un refresco to have (drink) a beverage
  tomar un vuelo to take a flight, 11.1
  tomar una ducha to take a shower, 12.1
  tomar una merienda to have a snack, 4.2
el **tomate** tomato
el **tomo** volume
la **tonelada** ton
  tonto(a) foolish
la **tortilla** tortilla, 5.1
la **tos** cough, 8.1
  tener tos to have a cough, 8.1
  toser to cough, 8.1
la **tostada** toast
  tostadito(a) sunburned, tanned
  tostado(a): el pan tostado toast, 5.2
el **tostón** fried plantain slice
  totalmente totally, completely
  tóxico(a) toxic
  trabajar to work, 3.2
el **trabajo** work
la **tradición** tradition
  tradicional traditionally
  traer to bring, 14.1
el **tráfico** traffic
el **traje** suit, 3.2
  el traje de baño bathing suit, 9.1
  el traje de gala evening gown, dress

el **tramo** stretch
  tranquilo(a) peaceful; calm; quiet
  transbordar to transfer, 13.2
  transformar to transform
  transmitir to send, to transmit
el **transporte** transportation
el **tratamiento** treatment
  tratar to treat; to try
  trece thirteen, BV
  treinta thirty, BV
  treinta y uno thirty-one, 2.2
el **tren** train, 13.2
  el tren directo nonstop train, 13.2
  el tren local local train, 13.2
  tres three, BV
  trescientos(as) three hundred, 3.2
el **triángulo** triangle
la **tripulación** crew, 11.2
  triste sad, 8.1
  triunfante triumphant
el **trombón** trombone
la **trompeta** trumpet
  tropical tropical
  tu your *(sing. fam.)*
  tú you *(sing. fam.)*
el **tubo: el tubo de pasta (crema) dentífrica** tube of toothpaste, 12.2
el/la **turista** tourist, 10.2

U

Ud., usted you *(sing. form.)*, 3.2
Uds., ustedes you *(pl.)*, 2.2
último(a) last
un a, 1.1
la **una** one o'clock, 2.2
único(a) only
la **unidad** unit
el **uniforme** uniform
la **universidad** university
universitario(a) (related to) university

uno(a) one, a, BV
unos(as) some
urbano(a) urban
usar to wear (size), 3.2; to use
utilizar to use

V

la **vacación** vacation
el **vagón** train car, 13.1
  vainilla: de vainilla vanilla *(adj.)*, 5.1
la **vainita** string bean
  ¡vale! OK!
  valer to be worth
  valeroso(a) brave
el **valor real** true value
  vamos a let's go
la **variación** variation
  variado(a) varied
  variar to vary, change
la **variedad** variety
  varios(as) various
el **varón** male
  vasco(a) Basque
  la pelota vasca jai alai
el **vaso** (drinking) glass, 12.1
el/la **vecino(a)** neighbor
el **vegetal** vegetable, 5.2
el/la **vegetariano(a)** vegetarian
  veinte twenty, BV
  veinticinco twenty-five, BV
  veinticuatro twenty-four, BV
  veintidós twenty-two, BV
  veintinueve twenty-nine, BV
  veintiocho twenty-eight, BV
  veintiséis twenty-six, BV
  veintisiete twenty-seven, BV
  veintitrés twenty-three, BV
  veintiuno twenty-one, BV
la **velocidad** speed
  vender to sell, 5.2
  venezolano(a) Venezuelan

venir to come, 11.1
  el viernes (sábado, etc.) que viene next Friday (Saturday, etc.)
la **ventanilla** ticket window, 9.2
ver to see; to watch, 5.1
el **verano** summer, BV
¡verdad! that's right (true)!
verdadero(a) true
verde green, 3.2
  la judía verde green bean, 5.2
verificar to verify, 13.1
la **versión: en versión original** in (its) original version, 10.1
el **vestido** dress
vestirse (i, i) to get dressed
la **vez** time
  a veces at times, sometimes, 7.1
  de vez en cuando now and then
  una vez más one more time, again
la **vía** track, 13.1
viajar to travel
  viajar en avión to travel by air, 11.1
el **viaje** trip

el viaje de regreso return trip
hacer un viaje to take a trip, 11.1
victorioso(a) victorious
la **vida** life
  la vida escolar school life
el **video** video
viejo(a) old, 6.1
el/la **viejo(a)** old person
el **viento** wind
el **viernes** Friday, BV
el **vinagre** vinegar
la **viola** viola
el **violín** violin, 2.1
visible visible
visitar to visit
vital vital
la **vitamina** vitamin
viviente: el ser viviente living creature, being
vivir to live, 5.2
vivo(a) living, alive
la **vocal** vowel
volar (ue) to fly
el **voleibol** volleyball
volver (ue) to return, 7.1
  volver a casa to return home, 10.2
la **voz** voice
  en voz alta aloud

el **vuelo** flight, 11.1
  el número del vuelo flight number, 11.1
  tomar un vuelo to take a flight, 11.1
  el vuelo nacional domestic flight

y and, BV
  y cuarto a quarter past (the hour)
  y media half past (the hour)
  y pico just after (the hour)
ya already; now
la **yarda** yard
yo I, 1.1
el **yogur** yogurt

la **zanahoria** carrot, 5.2
la **zapatería** shoe store
el **zapato** shoe, 3.2
la **zona** zone, area, neighborhood
el **zumo de naranja** orange juice

English-Spanish Dictionary

The English-Spanish Dictionary contains all productive and receptive vocabulary from the text. The numbers following each productive entry indicate the chapter and vocabulary section in which the word is introduced. For example, **3.2** means that the word was taught in **Capítulo 3, Palabras 2**. *BV refers to the preliminary **Bienvenidos** lessons. If there is no number following an entry, this means that the word or expression is there for receptive purposes only.*

A

a un(a)
able: to be able poder (ue), 7.1
aboard a bordo de, 11.2
about (time) a eso de, 4.1
above por encima de
abstract abstracto(a)
academy la academia
to **accept** aceptar
access el acceso
to **accompany** acompañar
according to según
ache doler
  My . . . aches Me duele… , 8.2
acrylic el acrílico
activity la actividad
actor el actor, 10.2
actress la actriz, 10.2
to **adapt** adaptar
to **add** sumar
to **adjust** ajustar
to **admire** admirar
  admission ticket la entrada, 10.1
to **admit** admitir
adorable adorable
to **adore** adorar
to **adorn** adornar
adventure la aventura
African africano(a)
after después de, 5.1;
  (time) y
  It's ten after one. Es la una y diez.
afternoon la tarde
  Good afternoon. Buenas tardes., BV
  in the afternoon por la tarde

  this afternoon esta tarde, 9.2
against contra, 7.1
agent el/la agente, 11.1
  customs agent el/la agente de aduana, 11.1
agreed conforme, 14.2
air el aire
  open-air (outdoor) café (market) el café (mercado) al aire libre
airline la línea aérea
airplane el avión, 11.1
  by plane en avión, 11.1
airport el aeropuerto, 11.1
aisle el pasillo, 13.2
a lot muchos(as), 2.1; mucho, 3.2
alarmed: to be alarmed alarmarse
album el álbum
algebra el álgebra, 2.2
alive vivo(a)
all todos(as)
  All right. De acuerdo.
allergy la alergia, 8.2
to **allow** dejar; consentir (ie, i)
almost casi
alone solo(a)
aloud en voz alta
also también, 1.2
always siempre, 7.1
A.M. de la mañana
American americano(a)
amusement la diversión
analysis el análisis
analytical analítico(a)
to **analyze** analizar
ancient antiguo(a)
and y, BV
Andean andino(a)
anecdote la anécdota

animal el animal
another otro(a)
answer la respuesta
to **answer** contestar
Antarctic la Antártida
antibiotic el antibiótico, 8.2
antiquity la antigüedad
Anything else? ¿Algo más?, 5.2
apartment el apartamento, el piso, el departamento, 6.2
  apartment house la casa de apartamentos (apartamentos), 6.2
to **applaud** aplaudir, 10.2
applause el aplauso, 10.2
apple la manzana, 5.2
to **apply** aplicar
April abril, BV
Aragon: from Aragon (Spain) aragonés(a)
arc el arco
archeological arqueológico(a)
archeologist el/la arqueólogo(a)
archeology la arqueología
area el área (f.), la zona
Argentinian argentino(a), 2.1
argument la disputa
arithmetic la aritmética, 2.2
arm el brazo, 7.1
around alrededor de, 6.2; **(time)** a eso de, 4.1
arrival la llegada, 11.1
  arrival and departure screen la pantalla de salidas y llegadas, 11.1
  arrival board el tablero de llegadas, 13.1
to **arrive** llegar, 4.1

arrogant altivo, arrogante

arsenal el arsenal

art el arte, *(f.)* 2.2

artichoke la alcachofa, 14.2

artifact el artefacto

artist el/la artista, 10.2

artistic artístico(a)

as como

to **ask (a question)** preguntar

to **ask for** pedir (i, i), 14.1

asleep dormido(a)

aspirin la aspirina, 8.2

assortment el surtido

astute astuto(a)

at a, en

  at about (time) a eso de, 4.1

  at home en casa, 6.2

  at night por la noche

  at that time en aquel entonces

  at the end of a fines de

  at what time? ¿a qué hora?, 10.1

athletic atlético

attack el ataque

to **attack** atacar

to **attend** asistir

attention: to pay attention prestar atención, 4.2

audience el público, 10.2

August agosto, BV

aunt la tía, 6.1

  aunt(s) and uncle(s) los tíos, 6.1

Australia la Australia

author el/la autor(a), 10.2

autumn el otoño, BV

average regular, 2.2

B

baby el/la bebé

back to school la apertura de clases

background la ascendencia

backpack la mochila, 3.1

bacteria la bacteria

bad malo(a), 2.1

  to be in a bad (good) mood estar de mal (buen) humor, 8.1

bag la bolsa, 5.2

baggage el equipaje, 11.1

  baggage claim el reclamo de equipaje, 11.2

  carry-on baggage el equipaje de mano, 11.1

ball (basketball, soccer) el balón, 7.1; **(tennis, baseball)** la pelota , 7.2

  to throw (kick) the ball tirar el balón, 7.2

ballpoint pen el bolígrafo, 3.1

banana el plátano, 5.2

baptism el bautizo

bar: bar of soap la barra de jabón, la pastilla de jabón, 12.2

bargain la ganga

base (baseball) la base, 7.2

baseball el béisbol, 7.2

  baseball field el campo de béisbol, 7.2

  baseball game el juego de béisbol, 7.2

  baseball player el/la jugador(a) de béisbol, 7.2; el/la beisbolista

basic básico(a)

basket (basketball) el cesto, la canasta, 7.2

  to make a basket encestar, meter el balón en el cesto, 7.2

basketball el básquetbol, el baloncesto, 7.2

  basketball court la cancha de básquetbol, 7.2

Basque vasco(a)

bat el bate, 7.2

bathing suit el traje de baño, el bañador, 9.1

bathroom el baño, el cuarto de baño, 6.2

batter el/la bateador(a), 7.2

battle la batalla

bay la bahía

to **be** ser, 1.1; estar, 4.1

  to be able poder (ue), 7.1

  to be accustomed to soler (ue)

  to be afraid tener miedo

  to be born nacer

  to be going to ir a

  to be hungry tener hambre, 14.1

  to be included estar incluido, 14.1

  to be named (called) llamarse, 12.1

  to be pleasing gustar

  to be thirsty tener sed, 14.1

  to be tied (score) quedar empatado, 7.1

  to be worth valer, 7.2

  to be . . . years old tener… años, 6.2; cumplir… años

beach la playa, 9.1

  beach resort el balneario, 9.1

  beach towel la toalla playera, 9.1

bean el frijol, la habichuela, 5.2

  green bean la judía verde, 5.2

to **bear (name)** llevar (el nombre)

beau el galán

beautiful hermoso(a), bello(a), 1.1

because porque

bed la cama, 8.1

  to make the bed hacer la cama

  to stay in bed guardar cama, 8.1

bedroom la recámara, el dormitorio, el cuarto (de dormir), 6.2

beef la carne de res, 14.2

before antes de, 5.1

to **begin** comenzar (ie); empezar (ie), 7.1

  beginner el/la principiante, 9.2

  beginning: beginning of school la apertura de clases

behind atrás

being: human being el ser humano

living being el ser viviente

to **believe** creer, 8.2

below debajo (de); bajo

below zero bajo cero, 9.2

berth la litera, 13.2

between entre, 7.1

beverage el refresco, 5.1

bicycle la bicicleta

to go by bicycle ir en bicicleta, 13.2

big grande, 2.1

bilingual bilingüe

bill la cuenta, 5.1

biography la biografía

biological biológico(a)

biologist el/la biólogo(a)

biology la biología, 2.1

birthday el cumpleaños, 6.1

black negro(a), 3.2

black coffee el café solo, 5.1

to **block** bloquear, parar, 7.1

blond rubio(a), 1.1

blood la sangre

blouse la blusa, 3.2

blue azul, 3.2

blue jeans el blue jean, 3.2

board: arrival board el tablero de llegadas, 13.1;

departure board el tablero de salidas, 13.1

to **board** embarcar, 11.2; abordar; **(the train)** subir al tren, 13.1

boarding el embarque

boarding house la pensión, 12.2

boarding pass la tarjeta de embarque, 11.1

book el libro, 3.1

boot la bota, 9.2

to **bore** aburrir

boring aburrido(a), 2.1

born nacido(a)

bottle la botella, 12.2

boy el muchacho, 1.1

boyfriend/girlfriend el/la novio(a)

brave valeroso(a)

bread el pan, 5.1

breakfast el desayuno, 5.2

to eat breakfast desayunarse, tomar el desayuno, 12.1

bright brillante

to **bring** llevar, 6.1; traer, 14.1

broadcast la emisión, 6.2

sports broadcast la emisión deportiva, 6.2

bronze el bronce, 10.2

brook el arroyo

brother el hermano, 6.1

brown de color marrón, 3.2

brunette moreno(a), 1.1

brush el cepillo, 12.2

to **brush one's hair** cepillarse, 12.1

to **brush one's teeth** cepillarse (lavarse) los dientes, 12.1

building el edificio

bus el bus, 4.1; el autobús (la guagua [P.R., Cuba], el camión [Mex.]), 10.1

school bus el bus escolar, 4.1

to miss the bus perder el autobús (la guagua, el camión), 10.1

but pero

to **buy** comprar, 3.1

by (plane, car, bus, etc.) en (avión, carro, autobús, etc.)

C

cafe el café, BV

cafeteria la cafetería

to **calculate** calcular

calculator la calculadora, 3.1

calculus el cálculo, 2.2

called llamado(a)

can el bote, la lata, 5.2

candid franco(a)

canned enlatado(a)

cap la gorra, 3.2

capital la capital

captain el/la capitán; el/la comandante, 11.2

car el carro, el coche, 4.1

by car en carro, en coche, 4.1

cafeteria car el coche-cafetería, 13.2

dining car el coche-comedor, 13.2

sleeping car el coche-cama, 13.2

train car el coche, el vagón, 13.2

card la tarjeta, 11.1

credit card la tarjeta de crédito, 14.1

cardinal: cardinal points los puntos cardinales

careful! ¡cuidado!

carefully: very carefully con mucho cuidado

to **caress** acariciar

Caribbean el Caribe

carrot la zanahoria, 5.2

to **carry** llevar, 3.1

carry-on luggage el equipaje de mano, 11.1

case el caso

cash register la caja, 3.1

cat el/la gato(a), 6.1

to **catch** atrapar, 7.2

catcher el/la receptor(a), el/la cátcher, 7.2

Catholic católico(a)

to **celebrate** celebrar

celebration la celebración

cell la célula

cellular celular

center el centro

central central, 13.2

Central America la América Central

century el siglo

cereal el cereal, 5.2

certainly! ¡claro!

chain (necklace) la cadena

chair la silla

chairlift el telesilla, 9.2

chalet el chalet

chalkboard la pizarra, el pizarrón, 4.2

champion el/la campeón(a)

championship el campeonato

to **change** cambiar

    to change trains (transfer) cambiar de tren, transbordar, 13.2

chapter el capítulo

character el personaje

charming encantador(a)

cheap barato(a), 3.2

check la cuenta, 5.1

to **check luggage** facturar el equipaje, 11.1

to **check one's ticket** revisar el boleto, 11.1

cheese el queso, 5.1

chemical químico(a)

chemistry la química, 2.2

chicken el pollo, 5.2

child el/la niño(a)

children los niños, 6.1

    homeless children los niños desamparados

Chilean chileno(a)

chills: to have chills tener escalofríos, 8.1

chocolate chocolate, 5.1

    chocolate ice cream el helado de chocolate, 5.1

choir el coro

to **choose** escoger

chorus el coro

Christian cristiano(a)

Christmas la Navidad

Christmas Eve la Nochebuena

church la iglesia

circle el círculo

city la ciudad

to **claim (luggage)** reclamar (el equipaje), 11.2

clam la almeja, 14.2

class la clase, el curso, 2.1

    first class primera clase, en primera, 13.1

    second class segunda clase, en segunda, 13.1

to **classify** clasificar

classroom la sala de clase, el salón de clase, 4.1

clinic la clínica

cloth el lienzo

clothing la ropa, 3.2

clothing store la tienda de ropa, 3.2

cloud la nube, 9.1

cloudy: to be cloudy estar nublado, 9.1

    It's cloudy. Hay nubes., 9.1

club el club, 4.2

    Spanish Club el Club de español, 4.2

coast la costa

co-ed mixto(a)

coffee el café, BV

    black coffee, el café solo, 5.1

    coffee with milk el café con leche, 5.1

cognate la palabra afina

coin la moneda

coincidence la coincidencia

cold (illness) el catarro, 8.1

    to have a cold tener catarro, estar resfriado(a), 8.1

cold: It's cold. Hace frío., 9.2

collection la colección, el conjunto

collector el colector

Colombian colombiano(a), 1.1

colonial colonial

colony la colonia

color el color, 3.2

    What color is . . . ? ¿De qué color es… ?, 3.2

comb el peine, 12.2

to **comb one's hair** peinarse, 12.1

to **come** venir

    to come (go) on stage entrar en escena, 10.2

compact disk el disco compacto, 4.2

to **compare** comparar

to **compete** competir (i, i)

competition la competición

complete completo(a), 13.2

compliment: to pay someone compliments echarle flores

composition la composición

computer el ordenador, la computadora

computer science la informática, 2.2

concert el concierto

condominium el condominio

conductor (train) el/la revisor(a), 13.2

confirmed bachelor el solterón

to **connect** conectar

to **conquer** conquistar

to **conserve** conservar, 11.1

to **consider** considerar

to **consist of** consistir (en)

to **consult** consultar

    consultation la consulta, 8.2

contest la competición

continent el continente

to **continue** continuar, 7.2

to **convert** convertir (ie, i)

    cook el/la cocinero(a), 14.1

    copilot el/la copiloto, 11.2

to **copy** copiar

    corn el maíz, 14.2

to **cost** costar (ue), 3.1

    How much does . . . cost? ¿Cuánto cuesta(n)… ?, 3.1

    Costa Rican costarricense

cough la tos, 8.1

    to have a cough tener tos, 8.1

to **cough** tener tos, 8.1

    counter el mostrador, 11.1

    country el país, 11.2

    foreign country el país extranjero, 11.2

    course el curso, 2.1

    elective course el curso opcional

    required course el curso obligatorio

court la cancha, 2.1
  basketball court la cancha de básquetbol, 7.2
  indoor court la cancha cubierta, 9.1
  outdoor court la cancha al aire libre, 9.1
  tennis court la cancha de tenis, 9.1
courtesy la cortesía, BV
cousin el/la primo(a), 6.1
to **cover** cubrir
to **create** crear
credit card la tarjeta de crédito, 14.1
Creole el/la criollo(a)
crew la tripulación, 11.2
Cuban cubano(a)
Cuban American cubanoamericano(a)
to **cultivate** cultivar
cultural cultural
cup la taza, 14.1
  World Cup la Copa mundial
curtain (stage) el telón, 10.2
custom la costumbre
customer el/la cliente, 5.1
customs la aduana, 11.2
to **cut** cortar, 14.1

D

dad el papá
to **dance** bailar, 4.2
dark (haired) moreno(a), 1.1
data los datos
date la fecha, BV
  What is today's date? ¿Cuál es la fecha de hoy?, BV
to **date** datar
daughter la hija, 6.1
day el día, BV
  day before yesterday anteayer
deaf person el/la sordo(a)
death la muerte
December diciembre, BV

to **decide** decidir
to **declare** declarar
to **defeat** derrotar
degree (temperature) el grado, 9.2
delay: with a delay con una demora, 11.1; con retraso, 13.2
delicious delicioso(a), rico, 14.2; sabroso(a)
to **delight** encantar
to **deliver** entregar
deluxe de lujo
departure la salida, 11.1
  arrival and departure screen la pantalla de llegadas y salidas, 11.1
  departure board el tablero de salidas, 13.1
  departure gate la puerta de salida, la sala de salida, 11.1
  departure hour la hora de salida
descendant el/la descendiente
design el diseño
designer el/la diseñador(a)
dessert el postre, 5.1
destination el destino, 11.1
diagnosis la diagnosis, 8.2
dialogue el diálogo
diamond el diamante
to **die** morir (ue, u)
difference la diferencia
different diferente
difficult duro(a), difícil, 2.1
to **dig** excavar
dining car el coche-comedor, el coche-cafetería, 13.2
dining room el comedor, 6.2
dinner la cena, 5.2
  to have dinner cenar
direct directo(a), 11
director el/la director(a)
discipline la asignatura, la disciplina, 2.1
to **discover** descubrir
to **discuss** discutir

to **disembark** desembarcar, 11.2
dish el plato, 14.1
disk: compact disk el disco compacto, 4.2
diskette el disquete, 3.1
to **dive** bucear, 9.1
to **divide** dividir
diving el buceo, 9.1
divorced: to get divorced divorciarse
doctor el/la médico(a), 8.2
doctor's office la consulta del médico, el consultorio, 8.2
to **do** hacer, 11
  to do well (on an exam) salir bien (en un examen)
dog el perro, 6.1
domestic doméstico(a), 2.1
Dominican dominicano(a), 2.1
Dominican Republic la República Dominicana
donkey el asno
door la puerta
dose la dosis, 8.2
dot: on the dot en punto, 4.1
doubles dobles, 9.1
doubt la duda
doughnut (a type of) el churro
dozen la docena
drawing el dibujo
dream el sueño
dreamed of imaginado(a)
dress el vestido
to **dribble (basketball)** driblar, 7.2
drink (beverage) el refresco, 5.1; la bebida
to **drink** beber, 5.1
  to drink water (milk, coffee) tomar agua (leche, café), 14.1
druggist el/la farmacéutico(a), 8.2
drugstore la farmacia, 8.2
dubbed doblado(a), 10.1
during durante
DVD el DVD, 4.2

E

e-mail el correo electrónico
each cada, 1.2
early temprano, 12.1
to **earn** ganar
easel el caballete
east el este
easy fácil, 2.1
to **eat** comer, 5.1
   to eat breakfast desayunarse, tomar el desayuno, 12.1
economical económico(a), 12.2
economics: home economics la economía doméstica, 2.1
economy la economía
Ecuadorean ecuatoriano(a), 2.1
education: physical education la educación física, 2.2
egg el huevo, 5.2
eggplant la berenjena, 14.2
eight ocho, BV
eight hundred ochocientos(as), 3.2
eighteen dieciocho, BV
eighth octavo(a), 6.2
eighty ochenta, 2.1
electronic mail (e-mail) el correo electrónico
elegant elegante
element el elemento
elevator el ascensor, 6.2
eleven once, BV
else: Anything else? ¿Algo más?, 5.2
   No, nothing else. No, nada más, 5.2
emotion la emoción
emphasis el énfasis
to **emphasize** dar énfasis, enfatizar
employee el/la empleado(a), el/la dependiente(a), 3.1

enamored: to become enamored of (to fall for) flechar
enchilada la enchilada, BV
end el fin, BV
   at the end of a fines de
enemy el/la enemigo(a)
energy la energía, 8
English el inglés, 2.2
to **enjoy** gozar
   to enjoy oneself divertirse (ie, i), 12.2
enough bastante, 1.1
to **enter** entrar, 4.1
entire entero(a)
episode el episodio
epoch la época
equation la ecuación
equipment el equipo, 7.1
to **erase** borrar, 3.1
eraser la goma de borrar, 3.1
errant: knight errant el caballero andante
especially especialmente, particularmente, sobre todo
essentially esencialmente
to **establish** fundar
esteemed estimado(a)
ethnic étnico(a)
Europe Europa
evening la noche
   evening gown el traje de gala
   Good evening. Buenas noches., BV
   in the evening por la noche
everyone todos, 2.2; todo el mundo
everything todos(as)
exactly exactamente, 11
to **exaggerate** exagerar, 11
exam el examen, 4.2
to **examine** examinar, 8.2
   example: for example por ejemplo
to **excavate** excavar
excavation la excavación
excellent excelente

Excuse (me). Perdón.
exhibition (art) la exposición (de arte), 10.1
to **exist** existir
expedition la expedición
expensive caro(a), 3.2
expert el/la experto(a), 9.2
to **explain** explicar, 4.2
explosion la explosión
expression la expresión
   means of expression el modo de expresión
extraordinary extraordinario(a)
extreme extremo(a)
eye el ojo

F

face la cara, 12.1
faithful fiel
to **fall asleep** dormirse (ue, u), 12.1
false falso(a)
fame la fama
family la familia, 6.1
family (related to) familiar
famous famoso(a), 1.2
fan (sports) el/la aficionado(a)
fantastic fantástico(a), 1.2
fare la tarifa
fast rápido(a)
   as fast as possible a toda prisa
fat gordo(a), 1.2
father el padre, 6.1
father-in-law el suegro
favorite favorito(a)
fear el miedo, el terror
February febrero, BV
fever la fiebre, 8.1
   to have a fever tener fiebre, 8.1
few pocos(as), 2.1
   a few unos(as)
fiancé(e) el/la novio(a)

field el campo

  baseball field el campo de béisbol, 7.2

  soccer field el campo de fútbol, 7.1

fifteen quince, BV

fifteen-year-old (girl) la quinceañera

fifth quinto(a), 6.2

fifty cincuenta, 2.1

to **fight** luchar

figurative figurativo(a)

film la película, 6.2; el film, 10.1

finally por fin

to **find** hallar; encontrar (ue)

fine bien, BV; Conforme., 14.2

fine-looking gallardo(a)

finger el dedo

first primero(a), BV

fish el pescado, 5.2

five cinco, BV

five hundred quinientos(as) 3.2

flight el vuelo, 11.1

flight attendant el/la asistente de vuelo, 11.2

flight number el número del vuelo, 11.1

floor la planta, el piso, 6.2

  ground floor la planta baja, 6.2

flower la flor

flu la gripe, 8.1

to **fly** volar (ue)

  folder la carpeta, 3.1

  folk healer el/la curandero(a)

to **follow** seguir (i, i)

following siguiente

fond of aficionado(a)

food la comida, 5.2; el alimento, el comestible, 14.2

foolish tonto(a)

foot el pie, 7.1

  on foot a pie, 4.1

for por, para

  for example por ejemplo

foreign extranjero(a), 11.2

fork el tenedor, 14.1

to **form** formar

forty cuarenta, 2.1

to **found** fundar

four cuatro, BV

four hundred cuatrocientos(as), 3.2

fourteen catorce, BV

fourth cuarto(a), 6.2

frank franco(a)

free libre, 5.1

French el francés, 2.2

French fries las papas fritas, 5.1

fresh fresco(a)

Friday el viernes, BV

fried frito(a), 5.1

friend el/la amigo(a), el/la compañero(a), 1.1

frightful espantoso

from de, BV

front: in front of delante de, 10.1

frozen congelado(a), helado(a), 5.1

  frozen foods los productos congelados, 5.2

fruit la fruta, 5.2

to **fry** freír (i, i), 14.1

full (train, bus, etc.) completo(a)

funny cómico(a); gracioso(a), 1.1

furious furioso(a)

furniture los muebles

fury la furia

future el futuro

G

gallant gallardo(a)

game el partido, 7.1; el juego, 7.2

  baseball game el juego de béisbol, 7.2

garage el garaje, 6.2

garden el jardín, 6.2

garlic el ajo, 14.2

gate: departure gate la puerta de salida, 11.1

generally generalmente

generous generoso(a), 1.2

gentleman el señor, BV

geography la geografía, 2.2

geometry la geometría, 2.2

German el alemán, 2.1

to **get a good (bad) grade** sacar una nota buena (mala), 4.2

to **get dressed** vestirse (i, i); ponerse la ropa, 12.1

to **get off (bus, train, etc.)** bajar(se) (del bus, tren, etc.), 13.2

to **get on** abordar; subir, 13.1

to **get on (horse)** montar (caballo)

to **get on board (bus, train, etc.)** subir (al bus, tren, etc.), 13.1

to **get up** levantarse, 12.1

giant el gigante

gift el regalo, 6.1

girl la muchacha, 1.1

to **give** dar, 4.2; **(gift)** regalar

  to give (throw) a party dar una fiesta, 4.2

to **give up** renunciar

  glass (drinking) el vaso, 12.1

  glove el guante, 7.2

to **go** ir, 4.1

  to go by bicycle ir en bicicleta, 12.2

  to go by car ir en coche

to **go back** volver (ue)

to **go down** bajar

to **go home** volver a casa

to **go shopping** ir de compras, 5.2

to **go through** pasar por, 11.1

to **go to bed** acostarse (ue), 12.1

to **go up** subir, 6.2

to **go (walk) around** andar

  goal el gol, 7.1; la portería, 7.1

  to score a goal meter un gol, 7.1

goalie el/la portero(a), 7.1

goalkeeper el/la portero(a), 7.1

godfather el padrino

godmother la madrina

godparents los padrinos

gold el oro

good bueno(a); buen

  Good afternoon. Buenas tardes., BV

  Good evening. Buenas noches., BV

  Good morning. Buenos días., BV

good-bye! ¡adiós!, ¡chao!, BV

good-looking guapo(a), bonito(a), lindo(a), 1.1

Gosh! ¡Dios mío!, 11

gossip: piece of gossip el chisme

grade la nota, 4.2

grammar la gramática

grandchildren los nietos, 6.1

granddaughter la nieta, 6.1

grandfather el abuelo, 6.1

grandmother la abuela, 6.1

grandparents los abuelos, 6.1

grandson el nieto, 6.1

gray gris, 3.2

great gran(de)

  great event el buen suceso

greater mayor

green verde, 3.2

green bean la judía verde, 5.2

greeting el saludo, BV

ground el suelo

group el grupo

to **guard** guardar, 7.1

Guatemalan guatemalteco(a)

to **guess** adivinar

guitar la guitarra

gulf el golfo

gymnasium el gimnasio

hair el pelo, 12.1

half medio(a), 5.2

  half an hour media hora, 14

  second half el segundo tiempo, 7.1

ham el jamón, 5.1

hamburger la hamburguesa, 5.1

hand la mano, 7.1

  to shake hands dar la mano

handsome guapo(a), 1.1

to **hang** colgar (ue)

to **happen** pasar

  What happened (to you)? ¿Qué te pasó?

happy contento(a), 8.1

hard duro(a), 2.1

hardworking ambicioso(a), 1.1

hat el sombrero, la gorra, 3.2

to **have** tener (ie), 6.1

  to have chills tener escalofríos, 8.1

  to have a cold tener catarro, estar resfriado(a), 8.1

  to have a drink (snack) tomar un refresco (una merienda), 4.2

  to have a fever tener fiebre, 8.1

  to have a headache tener dolor de cabeza, 8.1

  to have a sore throat tener dolor de garganta, 8.1

  to have a stomachache tener dolor de estómago, 8.1

  to have to tener que

  They're having a good time. Lo están pasando muy bien., 12.2

he él, 1.1

head la cabeza, 7.1

headache el dolor de cabeza, 8.1

health la salud, 8.1

to **hear** oír

heart el corazón

heartthrob el galán

Hello! ¡Hola!, BV; **(answering the telephone—Spain)** ¡Diga!, 14.2

to **help** ayudar, 13.1

her su, 6.1; la *(pron.)*

here aquí

  Here is (are)... Aquí tiene…

heritage la ascendencia

hero el héroe

Hi! ¡Hola!, BV

to **hide** esconder

high alto(a), 1.1

high school el colegio, la escuela secundaria, la escuela superior, 1.1

hike: to take a hike dar una caminata, 12.2

him lo

his su, 6.1

historical histórico(a)

history la historia, 2.1

to **hit (tennis)** golpear, 9.1; **(baseball)** batear, 7.2

hole el agujero

home la casa, 6.2

  at home en casa

  country home la casa de campo

home economics la economía doméstica, 2.2

home plate (baseball) el platillo, 7.2

home run el jonrón, 7.2

homeless desamparado(a)

homeless children los niños desamparados

honest honesto(a), 1.2

honor el honor

horrible horrible

hospital el hospital, 8.2

hot: It's hot. Hace calor., 9.1

hotel (inexpensive) el hostal, 12.2

hour la hora

  per hour por hora

house la casa, 6.2

  apartment house la casa de apartamentos (departamentos), 6.2

  private house la casa privada (particular), 6.2

how? ¿cómo?, 1.1

  How absurd! ¡Qué absurdo!

  How are you? ¿Qué tal?, BV; ¿Cómo estás?, 8.1

How many?
¿Cuántos(as)?, 2.1

How much? ¿Cuánto?, 3.1

How much does it cost?
¿Cuánto es?, ¿Cuánto
cuesta?, 3.1

How old is (are) . . . ?
¿Cuántos años
tiene(n)… ?, 6.1

human humano(a)

human being el ser humano

humble humilde

hungry: to be hungry
tener hambre, 14.1

to **hurt** doler (ue), 8.2

My . . . hurt(s) me. Me
duele(n)..., 8.2

husband el marido, el
esposo, 6.1

I yo, 1.2

ice cream el helado, 5.1

**chocolate (vanilla) ice
cream** el helado de
chocolate (de vainilla),
5.1

iced tea el té helado, 5.1

idea la idea

ideal ideal, 1.2

idealist el/la idealista

if si

illusion la ilusión

imagined imaginado(a)

immediately enseguida,
inmediatamente, 5.1

immense inmenso(a)

to **imply that** dar a entender

important importante

impossible imposible

in en

in front of delante de

Inca el/la inca

to **include** incluir, 5.1

included incluido(a), 5.1

Is the tip included?
¿Está incluido el
servicio?, 5.1

incredible increíble

independence la
independencia

Indian indio(a)

to **indicate** indicar, 11.1

indicator el indicador, 7.1

indigenous indígena

individual individual, 7.2

individual sport el
deporte individual, 7.2

inexpensive barato(a), 3.2

influence la influencia

to **inform** informar, 13.2

information la información

inhabitant el/la habitante

inheritance la herencia

injection la inyección, 8.2

inning la entrada, 7.2

insane loco(a)

to **inspect** inspeccionar, 11.2

**to inspect (check) the
ticket** revisar el boleto,
11.1

**inspection: passport
inspection** el control de
pasaportes, 11.2

**inspection: security
inspection** el control de
seguridad, 11.1

instant el instante

instruction la instrucción

instrument el instrumento

integral íntegro(a)

intelligent inteligente, 2.1

interest el interés

to **interest** interesar

interesting interesante, 2.1

intermediate intermedio(a)

international internacional

interpretation la
interpretación

interview la entrevista, 4.1

invitation la invitación

to **invite** invitar (a), 6.1

island la isla

it la (f.); lo (m.)

Italian italiano(a)

jacket la chaqueta, el saco,
3.2

jai alai la pelota vasca

January enero, BV

jingle el retintín

July julio, BV

to **jump** saltar

to jump up sobresaltar

June junio, BV

keyboard el teclado

to **kick** tirar (con el pie), 7.1

to kick the ball tirar el
balón, 7.2

kilogram el kilo, 5.2

king el rey

kitchen la cocina, 6.2

knapsack la mochila, 3.1

knee la rodilla, 7.1

knife el cuchillo, 14.1

knight el caballero

knight errant el
caballero andante

knight's attendant el
escudero

to **know** saber, 11.2; conocer,
11.1

to know how saber, 11.2

L

laboratory el laboratorio, 2.1

lady la dama

lady-in-waiting la dama

lake el lago

lamb el cordero, 14.2

lance la lanza

to **land** aterrizar, 11.2

landscape el paisaje

language la lengua, 2.2

large grande

last último(a)

last night anoche, 9.2

last week la semana
pasada, 9.2

last weekend el fin de
semana pasado

last year el año pasado, 9.2

late tarde; con una demora,
11.1; con retraso, 13.2

later luego, BV

  See you later! ¡Hasta luego!, BV

Latin el latín, 2.2

Latin latino(a)

Latin America Latinoamérica

Latin American latinoamericano(a)

lazy perezoso(a), 1.1

league la liga

  Major Leagues las Grandes Ligas

to **learn** aprender, 5.1

to **leave** salir

  to leave late salir tarde, 11.1

  to leave on time salir a tiempo, 11.1

  to leave something behind dejar, 14.1

lecture la conferencia

left izquierdo(a), 7.1

leg la pierna, 7.1

lemonade la limonada, BV

to **lend** prestar, 4.2

lesson la lección, 4.2

to **let** dejar; permitir, 11.1

  let's see a ver

  Will you please let me see your passport? Me permite ver su pasaporte, por favor?, 11.1

letter la carta, 6.2; **(of the alphabet)** la letra, 11.1

lettuce la lechuga, 5.2

liberator el/la libertador(a)

life la vida

  school life la vida escolar

to **lift** levantar

light la luz

to **light** encender (ie)

like el gusto

to **like** gustar

  Lima: from Lima (Peru) limeño(a)

line (of people) la cola, la fila, 10.1

linen el lienzo

to **listen (to)** escuchar, 4.2

  listen! ¡oye!, 1.1

literal literal

literary literario(a)

literature la literatura, 2.1

little: a little poco(a)

live vivo(a)

to **live** vivir, 5.2

living viviente

living creature el ser viviente

living room la sala, 6.2

lobster la langosta, 14.2

local local, 13.2

long largo(a), 3.2

Look! ¡Mira!

to **look at** mirar, 3.1

to **look at oneself** mirarse, 12.1

to **look for** buscar, 3.1

to **lose** perder (ie), 7.1

lotion: suntan lotion la loción bronceadora, 9.1

lotto el loto

lover el/la enamorado(a)

low bajo(a), 4.2

to **lower** bajar

luggage el equipaje, 11.1

  carry-on luggage el equipaje de mano, 11.1

  luggage claim ticket el talón, 11.1

lunch el almuerzo, 5.2

  to have lunch almorzar (ue)

luxurious lujoso(a)

M

ma'am la señora, BV

made hecho(a)

Madrid (native of) madrileño(a)

magazine la revista, 6.2

magnificent magnífico(a)

mail el correo

  e-mail (electronic mail) el correo electrónico

main principal

mainly principalmente

Major Leagues las Grandes Ligas

majority la mayor parte, la mayoría

to **make** hacer

  to make a basket (basketball) encestar, 7.2

  to make the bed hacer la cama, 13

makeup el maquillaje, 12.1

  to put one's makeup on maquillarse, ponerse el maquillaje, 12.1

male el varón

man el hombre, el señor

manner la manera, el modo

many muchos(as), 2.1

map el mapa

March marzo, BV

marker el marcador, 3.1

market el mercado, 5.2

marmalade la mermelada, 5.2

marriage el matrimonio

married: to be married estar casado(a)

marvelous maravilloso(a)

mass la masa

master el/la maestro(a)

material el material, 3.1

mathematics las matemáticas, 2.2

matter: What's the matter (with you)? ¿Qué te pasa?

May mayo, BV

Maya el/la maya

me mí, 5.1; me, 8

meal la comida, 5.2

meaning el significado, el sentido

means el medio, el modo

  by no means de ninguna manera, 1.1

means of expression el modo de expresión

meat la carne, 5.2

medal la medalla

medical office la consulta del médico, el consultorio, 8.2

medicine (drug) el medicamento, 8.2; **(discipline, field),** la medicina, 8.2

medium el medio

melancholic melancólico(a)

member el miembro, 4.2

menu el menú, 5.1

mestizo el/la mestizo(a)

Mexican mexicano(a), 1.1

Mexican American
mexicanoamericano(a)

microbe el microbio, 2.1

microscope el microscopio,
2.1

microscopic
microscópico(a)

middle: middle school la
escuela intermedia

midnight la medianoche

mile la milla

milk la leche

million el millón

mineral water el agua
mineral, 12.2

minute el minuto

mirror el espejo, 12.1

Miss señorita, BV

to miss the bus perder el
autobús (la guagua, el
camión), 10.1

mixed mixto(a)

mixture la mezcla

model el modelo

modem el módem

modern moderno(a)

mom la mamá

moment el momento

Monday el lunes, BV

money el dinero, 14.1

monitor el monitor

monster el monstruo

month el mes, BV

monument el monumento

mood el humor, 8.1

to be in a bad mood
estar de mal humor, 8.1

to be in a good mood
estar de buen humor, 8.1

moon la luna

more más

moreover además

morning la mañana

Good morning. Buenos
días., BV

in the morning por la
mañana

this morning esta
mañana

mother la madre, 6.1

motive el motivo

to mount (horse) montar
(caballo)

mountain la montaña

mountain range la sierra

mouse el ratón

to move mover (ue)

movie la película, 6.2; el
film, 10.1

movie theater el cine, 10.1

Mr. el señor, BV

Mrs. la señora, BV

Ms. la señorita, la señora, BV

much mucho, 3.2

multiplication la
multiplicación

to multiply multiplicar

mural el mural, 10.2

muralist el/la muralista

museum el museo, 10.1

music la música, 2.2

my mi, 6.1

name el nombre

My name is . . . Me
llamo… , 12.1

napkin la servilleta, 14.1

national nacional

nationality la
nacionalidad, 1.2

what nationality? ¿de
qué nacionalidad?

native indígena

natural: natural resources
los recursos naturales

natural sciences las
ciencias naturales

near cerca de, 6.2

necessary necesario(a)

neck el cuello

necktie la corbata, 3.2

to need necesitar, 3.1

neighbor el/la vecino(a)

nephew el sobrino, 6.1

nervous nervioso(a), 8.1

net la red

to go over the net pasar
por encima de la red, 9.1

to surf the Net navegar
por la red

nettle la ortiga

never jamás, nunca

new nuevo(a)

news las noticias, 6.2

newspaper el periódico, 6.2

newsstand el quiosco, 13.1

next próximo(a), 13.2

nice simpático(a), 1.2

Nice to meet you.
Mucho gusto.

niece la sobrina, 6.1

night la noche

at night por la noche

Good night. Buenas
noches., BV

last night anoche, 9.2

nine nueve, BV

nine hundred
novecientos(as), 3.2

nineteen diecinueve, BV

ninety noventa, 2.1

ninth noveno(a), 6.2

no no, BV

by no means de
ninguna manera, 1.1

no one nadie

noble noble

nobody nadie

none ninguno(a), 1.1

noon el mediodía

north el norte

North America la
América del Norte

North American
norteamericano(a)

northwest noroeste, 8

no-smoking section la
sección de no fumar, 11.1

not at all de ninguna
manera

notable notable

note: to take notes tomar
apuntes, 4.2

to note apuntar

notebook el cuaderno, el
bloc, 3.1

nothing nada, 5.2
Nothing else. Nada más., 5.2
novel la novela
novelist el/la novelista
November noviembre, BV
now ahora, 4.2
  now and then de vez en cuando
nowadays hoy día
number el número, 1.2
  flight number el número del vuelo, 11.1
  seat number el número del asiento, 11.1
nuptial nupcial

object el objeto
obligatory obligatorio(a), 2.1
observation la observación
to **observe** observar
observer el/la bservador(a)
obstacle el obstáculo
occupied (taken) ocupado(a), 5.1
ocean el océano
o'clock: It's (two) o'clock. Son las (dos).
October octubre, BV
of de, BV
  of course! ¡claro!
official oficial
oil el aceite, 14.2
OK! ¡vale!
old anciano(a), antiguo(a), viejo(a), 6.1
olive: olive oil el aceite de oliva
on en
  on board a bordo de, 11.2
  on the contrary al contrario
  on the dot en punto, 4.1
  on time a tiempo, 11.1
  on top of encima de; sobre, 9.1
once and for all definitivamente, 11

one uno, BV
one hundred cien(to), 2.1
one thousand mil, 3.2
one-way: one-way ticket el billete sencillo, 13.1
only sólo, solamente
to **open** abrir, 8.2
  to open one's suitcases abrir las maletas, 11.2
opening: opening of school la apertura de clases
opera la ópera, 2.1
operator el/la operador(a)
opinion: What's your opinion? ¿Qué opinas?
optional opcional
orally oralmente
orange (color) anaranjado(a), 3.2
orange (fruit) la naranja, 5.2
orange juice el jugo de naranja, 12.1
order la orden, 5.1
organism el organismo
origin el origen
original: in its original language version en versión original, 10.1
orphanage el orfanato
Otavalo (of or from) otavaleño(a)
other otro(a), 2.2
our nuestro(a)
outdoor al aire libre
outfielder el/la jardinero(a), 7.2
outskirts los alrededores
over por encima de
to **owe** deber

to **pack one's suitcase** hacer la maleta, 11.2
package el paquete, 5.2
page la página
  Web page la página Web
pain el dolor, 8.1
  I have a pain in . . . Tengo dolor de… , 8.2

to **paint** pintar
  painter el/la pintor(a)
  painting el cuadro, la pintura, 2.1
  pair el par, 3.2
  pair of tennis shoes el par de tenis, 3.2
Panamanian panameño(a), 2.1
pants el pantalón, 3.2
paper el papel, 3.1
  sheet of paper la hoja de papel, 3.1
parents los padres, 6.1
park el parque
parka el anorak, 9.2
part la parte
party la fiesta, 4.2
  to give (throw) a party dar una fiesta, 4.2
pass (permission) el pase
to **pass** pasar, 7.2
  passenger el/la pasajero(a), 11.1
  passport el pasaporte, 11.1
  passport inspection el control de pasaportes, 11.2
past pasado(a)
patient el/la enfermo(a), 8.1
to **pay** pagar, 3.1
  to pay attention prestar atención, 4.2; hacer caso
pea el guisante, 5.2
peaceful tranquilo(a)
pen la pluma; **(ballpoint)** el bolígrafo, 3.1
pencil el lápiz, 3.1
peninsula la península
penny el centavo
people la gente
pepper la pimienta, 14.1
percent por ciento
performance la función, la representación, 10.2
  to put on a performance dar una representación, 10.2
to **permit** permitir, 11.1
  person la persona, 1.2
Peruvian peruano(a)
peso el peso, BV

petition la petición

pharmacist el/la farmacéutico(a), 8.2

pharmacy la farmacia, 8.2

photo la foto

photograph la fotografía

phrase la frase

physical education la educación física, 2.2

physics la física, 2.2

piano el piano

to **pick up** recoger

    to pick up (claim) the luggage recoger el equipaje, 11.2

picture el cuadro, 10.2

pig (pork) el cerdo, 14.2

pill la pastilla, la píldora, la tableta, 8.2

pilot el/la piloto, 11.2

pink rosado(a), 3.2

piping (embroidery) el cordoncillo

pitcher el/la lanzador(a), el/la pícher, 7.2

pizza la pizza, BV

place el lugar, el sitio

to **place** colocar, meter, 7.1

    to place one's suitcase poner la maleta, 11.2

plane el avión, 11.1

plate el plato, 14.1

    home plate el platillo, 7.2

plateau la mesa

platform (railroad) el andén, 13.1

play la obra teatral, 10.2

to **play** jugar (ue), 7.1

    player el/la jugador(a), 7.1

    baseball player el/la jugador(a) de béisbol, 7.2

playwright el/la dramaturgo(a)

plaza la plaza

pleasant agradable

please por favor, BV

P.M. de la tarde, de la noche

pocket el bolsillo

pocketbook la bolsa, 13.1

poem el poema

poet el poeta

poetry la poesía

point (score) el tanto, el punto, 7.1

    cardinal points los puntos cardinales

    to score a point marcar un tanto, 7.1

pole: ski pole el bastón, 9.2

political político(a)

poncho el poncho

pool la alberca, la piscina, 9.1

poor pobre

poor boy (girl) el/la pobre

popular popular, 2.1

popularity la popularidad

pork el cerdo, 14.2

porter el/la maletero(a), el mozo, 13.1

portrait el retrato

possibility la posibilidad

possible posible

potato la papa, 5.1

    mashed potatoes el puré de papas

to **practice** practicar

pre-Columbian precolombino(a)

to **prefer** preferir (ie, i)

to **prepare** preparar, 4.2

to **prescribe** recetar, 8.2

prescription la receta, 8.2

to **present** presentar

pretty hermoso(a), lindo(a), bonito(a), bello(a), 1.1

price el precio

priest el sacerdote

primary primario(a)

princess la princesa

principal principal

printer la impresora

private particular, privado(a), 6.2

    private house la casa particular (privada), 6.2

prize el premio

    Nobel Prize el Premio Nóbel

problem el problema

to **process** procesar

procession la procesión

to **proclaim** proclamar

produced producido(a)

product el producto, 2.1

professor el/la profesor(a), 2.1

program (TV) la emisión, 6.2

    sports program la emisión deportiva, 6.2

to **project** proyectar, 10.1

promise la promesa

protoplasm el protoplasma

public público(a)

to **publish** publicar

Puerto Rican puertorriqueño(a)

to **pull out** arrancar

puppy el perrito

purchase la compra, 3.1

pure puro(a)

to **put** poner, 11.1

    to put on a performance dar una representación, 10.2

    to put on clothes ponerse la ropa, 12.1

    to put on makeup ponerse el maquillaje, maquillarse, 12.1

Q

quarrel la disputa

quarter: a quarter to menos cuarto

    a quarter past y cuarto

queen la reina

question la pregunta

    to ask a question preguntar

quetzal el quetzal

quickly rápido

quite bastante, 1.1

R

racquet la raqueta, 9.1

railroad el ferrocarril

    railroad station la estación de ferrocarril, 13.1

English-Spanish Dictionary

railroad track la vía, 13.1

railway platform el andén, 13.1

to **rain: It's raining.** Llueve., 9.1

rate la tarifa

rather bastante, 1.1

razor la navaja, 12.1

to **read** leer, 5.1

reading la lectura

ready listo(a)

realist el/la realista

realistic realista

really realmente

rear (in the) atrás

reasonable razonable

to **rebound** rebotar

to **receive** recibir, 5.1

to receive a good (bad) grade recibir una nota buena (mala), 4.2

recently recientemente

rectangle el rectángulo

red rojo(a), 3.2

redheaded pelirrojo(a), 1.1

reduced reducido(a)

to **reflect** reflexionar, reflejar

reflection el reflejo

refreshment el refresco, 5.1

region la región

regular regular, 2.2

relative el/la pariente, 6.1

religious religioso(a)

to **remain** quedar, 7.1

to **remember** acordarse (ue) de, 3.2

to **renounce** renunciar

to **rent** alquilar, rentar, 10.1

to **repeat** repetir (i, i)

to **replace** reemplazar

report el reportaje

to **represent** representar

republic la república

Dominican Republic la República Dominicana

to **request** pedir (i, i), 14.1

required: required course el curso obligatorio, 2.1

reservation la reservación

to **reserve** reservar, 14.2

reserved reservado(a), 13.2

resident el/la residente

resort: seaside resort el balneario, 9.1

resource el recurso

natural resources los recursos naturales

rest lo demás

restaurant el restaurante, 14.1

to **return** volver (ue), 7.1; **(something)** devolver (ue), 7.2

rice el arroz, 5.2

rich rico(a); con mucha plata

right derecho(a), 7.1

right away enseguida, 5.1

river el río

to **roll** rodar

roll (bread) el pan dulce, 5.1

roll of toilet paper el rollo de papel higiénico, 12.2

romantic romántico(a)

room la sala, el salón, el cuarto, la pieza, 4.1

bathroom el cuarto de baño, 6.2

classroom la sala (el salón) de clase, 4.1

dining room el comedor, 6.2

living room la sala, 6.2

waiting room la sala de espera, 13.1

rose la rosa

round-trip ticket el billete de ida y vuelta, 13.1

routine la rutina, 12.1

row (of seats) la fila, 10.1

royal real

rubber la goma, 3.1

ruin la ruina

rumor el rumor

to **run** correr, 7.2

rural rural

S

to **sacrifice** sacrificar

sad triste

sail (of a mill) el aspa

sailboard la plancha de vela, 9.1

saint el santo

salad la ensalada, 5.1

salesperson el/la dependiente(a), el/la empleado(a), 3.1

salt la sal, 14.1

same mismo(a), 2.1

sand la arena, 9.1

sandal el huarache, la alpargata

sandwich el bocadillo, 5.1, el sándwich, BV

sash la faja

Saturday el sábado, BV

saucer el platillo, 14.1

to **save** salvar

to **say** decir

scale la báscula, 11.1

scene la escena

schedule el horario, 13.1

school schedule el horario escolar

school la escuela, el colegio, 1.1

elementary school la escuela primaria

high school el colegio, la escuela secundaria, la escuela superior

middle school la escuela intermedia

school (pertaining to) escolar

school bus el bus escolar, 4.1

school life la vida escolar, 4.1

school schedule el horario escolar

school supplies los materiales escolares, 3.1

science la ciencia, 2.2

natural sciences las ciencias naturales

social sciences las ciencias sociales

scientific científico(a)

scientist el/la científico(a)

score el tanto, 7.1

to **score: to score a goal** meter un gol, 7.1

to score a point marcar un tanto, 7.1

scoreboard el tablero indicador, 7.1

screen la pantalla, 10.1

sculptor el/la escultor(a), 10.2

sculpture la escultura

sea el mar, 9.1

   Caribbean Sea el mar Caribe

search: in search of en busca de

season la estación, BV

seasoning el condimento, 14.1

seat (theater) la butaca, 10.1; **(airplane, train, etc.)** el asiento, 11.1; la plaza, 13.2

   seat number el número del asiento, 11.1

second segundo(a), 6.2

   second half el segundo tiempo, 7.1

secondary secundario(a), 1.1

secret secreto(a)

security: security control el control de seguridad, 11.1

to **see** ver, 5.1

   See you later! ¡Hasta luego!, BV

   See you soon! ¡Hasta mañana!, BV

   See you tomorrow! ¡Hasta mañana!, BV

   to see a film ver una película, 10.2

to **select** seleccionar

selection la selección

to **sell** vender, 5.2; despachar, 8.2

to **send** transmitir, enviar

sentence la frase

September septiembre, BV

series la serie

   World Series la Serie mundial

serious serio(a), 1.1

to **serve** servir (i, i), 14.1

   service (tip) el servicio, 5.1

   set (theater) el escenario, 10.2

to **set the table** poner la mesa, 14.1

seven siete, BV

seven hundred setecientos(as), 3.2

seventeen diecisiete, BV

seventh séptimo(a), 6.2

seventy setenta, 2.1

several varios(as)

to **sew** coser

sewing la costura

to **shake hands** dar la mano

shampoo el champú, 12.2

sharp en punto, 4.1

to **shave** afeitarse, 12.1

   shaving cream la crema de afeitar, 12.1

shawl el poncho

she ella, 1.1

sheet: sheet of paper la hoja de papel, 3.1

shellfish el marisco, 5.2

sherbet el sorbete

to **shine** brillar, 9.1

shirt la camisa, 3.2

shoe el zapato, 3.2

shoe size el número, 3.2

shoe store la zapatería

to **shop** ir de compras, 5.2

short (person) bajo(a), 1.1; **(length)** corto(a), 3.2

   short story la historieta

shorts el pantalón corto, 3.2

shot (injection) la inyección, 8.2

show la sesión, 10.1; el espectáculo, 10.2

   to see a show ver un espectáculo, 10.2

shower: to take a shower tomar una ducha, 12.1

shrimp el camarón, 14.2

shy tímido(a), 1.2

sick enfermo(a), 8.1

sick person el/la enfermo(a), 8.1

side el lado; *(adj.)* lateral, 13.2

sierra la sierra

to **sigh** suspirar

similar parecido(a), similar

simple sencillo(a); simple

since como; desde, 1.2

sincere sincero(a), 1.2

to **sing** cantar, 4.2

single soltero(a)

single-celled monocelular

singles (tennis) singles, 9.1

sir el señor, BV

sister la hermana, 6.1

to **sit down** sentarse (ie), 12.1

six seis, BV

six hundred seiscientos(as), 3.2

sixteen dieciséis, BV

sixth sexto(a), 6.2

sixty sesenta, 2.1

size (clothes) el tamaño, la talla; **(shoes)** el número, 3.2

   What size do you take? ¿Qué talla (número) usa usted?, ¿Qué número usa (calza) usted?, 3.2

ski el esquí, 9.2

   water-ski el esquí acuático, 9.1

to **ski** esquiar, 9.1

ski lift el telesquí, 9.2

ski pole el bastón, 9.2

ski resort la estación de esquí, 9.2

ski slope la pista, 9.2

skier el/la esquiador(a), 9.2

skiing el esquí, 9.2

skirt la falda, 3.2

sky el cielo, 9.1

to **sleep** dormir (ue, u)

sleeping bag el saco de dormir, 12.2

sleeping car el coche-cama, 13.2

small pequeño(a), 2.1

smile: little smile la sonrisita

smoking (no-smoking) section la sección de (no) fumar, 13.1

snack la merienda, 4.2

   to have (eat) a snack tomar una merienda, 4.2

sneakers los tenis, 3.2

to **sneeze** estornudar, 8.1

snow la nieve, 9.2

to **snow** nevar (ie), 9.2

so tan

so much tanto(a)

soap el jabón, 12.2

bar of soap la barra (la pastilla) de jabón, 12.2

soccer el fútbol, 2.1

soccer field el campo de fútbol, 7.1

social sciences las ciencias sociales

society la sociedad

sociology la sociología

socks los calcetines, 3.2

solution la solución

to **solve** resolver (ue)

some algunos(as), 4.1

something algo, 5.2

sometimes a veces, 7.1

son el hijo, 6.1

soon pronto, BV; dentro de poco

See you soon! ¡Hasta pronto!, BV

sorbet el sorbete

sore throat el dolor de garganta, 8.1

soup la sopa, 5.1

south el sur

South America la América del Sur

South American sudamericano(a)

southwest el sudoeste

Spain España

Spanish español(a)

Spanish American hispanoamericano(a)

Spanish (language) el español, 2.2

Spanish-speaking hispanohablante

Spanish speaker el/la hispanohablante

to **speak** hablar, 3.1

special especial

specialty la especialidad

spectator el/la espectador(a), 7.1

to **spend: to spend the weekend** pasar el fin de semana, 9.1

spoon (tablespoon) la cuchara, 14.1; **(teaspoon)** la cucharita, 14.1

sport el deporte, 7.2

individual sport el deporte individual

team sport el deporte de equipo

sports (related to) deportivo(a), 6.2

sports program (TV) la emisión deportiva, 6.2

spouse el/la esposo(a), 6.1

spring la primavera, BV

square la plaza

squire el escudero

stadium el estadio, 7.1

stage el escenario, la escena, 10.2

to come (go) on stage entrar en escena, 10.2

stairway la escalera, 6.2

standing de pie

star la estrella

state el estado

station la estación, 13.1

subway station la estación de metro, 10.1

train station la estación de ferrocarril, 13.1

stationery: stationery store la papelería, 3.1

statue la estatua, 2.1

to **stay in bed** guardar cama, 8.1

steak el biftec, 5.2

stomach el estómago, 8.1

stomachache el dolor de estómago, 8.1

stop la parada, 13.1

to **stop** parar, bloquear, 7.1

store la tienda, 3.2

clothing store la tienda de ropa, 3.2

department store la tienda de departamentos

stationery store la papelería, 3.1

to **store** almacenar

story: little story la historieta

strategy la estrategia

stream el arroyo

street la calle, 6.2

strong fuerte

structure la estructura

student el/la alumno(a), 1.1; el/la estudiante

student I.D. card la tarjeta de identidad estudiantil

study el estudio

to **study** estudiar, 4.1

stupendous estupendo(a)

style el estilo

subject la asignatura, la disciplina, 2.2

subtitle el subtítulo, 10.1

The movie has subtitles. El film lleva subtítulos., 10.1

to **subtract** restar

suburb el suburbio, la colonia

subway el metro, 10.1

subway station la estación de metro, 10.1

such tal

suckling pig el lechón, 14.2

to **suffer** sufrir

suit el traje, 3.2

bathing suit el traje de baño, el bañador, 9.1

suitcase la maleta, 11.1

to pack one's suitcase hacer la maleta, 11.2

summer el verano, BV

sun el sol, 9.1

to **sunbathe** tomar el sol, 9.1

sunblock la crema protectora, 9.1

Sunday el domingo, BV

sunglasses los anteojos de sol, las gafas de sol, 9.1

sunny: It's sunny. Hace (Hay) sol., 9.1

suntan lotion la crema protectora, la loción bronceadora, 9.1

superior superior

supermarket el supermercado, 5.2

supplies: school supplies los materiales escolares, 3.1

to **surf** practicar la tabla hawaiana, 9.1

to surf the Net navegar por la red

surfboard la tabla
hawaiana, 9.1
surfing el surfing, 9.1
sweet roll el pan dulce, 5.1
sweetheart el/la
enamorado(a)
to **swim** nadar, 9.1
swimming la natación, 9.1
underwater swimming
el buceo, 9.1
swimming pool la
alberca, la piscina, 9.1
swimsuit el bañador, el
traje de baño, 9.1
symptom el síntoma, 8.2

T

T-shirt el T-shirt, la
camiseta, 3.2
table la mesa, 5.1
to set the table poner la
mesa, 14.1
tablecloth el mantel, 14.1
tablespoon la cuchara, 14.1
tablet la tableta, 8.2
taco el taco, BV
Taino taíno(a)
to **take** tomar, 4.1
to take a bath bañarse,
12.1
to take a flight tomar
un vuelo, 11.1
to take a hike dar una
caminata, 12.2
to take a nap echar
(tomar) una siesta
to take a shower tomar
una ducha, 12.1
to take a trip hacer un
viaje, 11.2
to take notes tomar
apuntes, 4.2
to take off (airplane)
despegar, 11.2
to take photos tomar fotos
to take (clothing size)
usar, 3.2
to take (shoe size) calzar,
3.2
to take time tardar
taken ocupado(a), 5.1

to **talk** hablar, conversar, 3.1
tall alto(a), 1.1
tamale el tamal, BV
taxi el taxi, 10.2
tea el té, 5.1
iced tea el té helado, 5.1
to **teach** enseñar, 4.1
teacher el/la maestro(a),
el/la profesor(a), 2.1
team el equipo, 7.1
team sport el deporte de
equipo, 7.2
teaspoon la cucharita, 14.1
technology la tecnología
teeth los dientes, 12.2
telephone el teléfono
to speak on the telephone
hablar por teléfono
telephone (related to)
telefónico(a)
television la televisión, 6.2
to **tell** decir
temperature la
temperatura, 9.2
ten diez, BV
to **tend to** soler (ue)
tender tierno(a)
tennis el tenis, 2.1
tennis court la cancha
de tenis, 9.1
tennis game el juego de
tenis, 9.1
tennis player el/la
tenista, 9.1
tennis shoes los tenis, 3.2
pair of tennis shoes el
par de tenis, 3.2
tenth décimo(a), 6.2
term el término
terminal la terminal
terrace la terraza
terrible terrible
terror el terror
test el examen, 4.2
to give a test dar un
examen, 4.2
thank you gracias, BV
that aquel; eso, 4.1
at that time en aquel
entonces
that's right (true)!
¡verdad!

the el, la, 1.1
theater el teatro, 10.2
theatrical teatral, 10.2
their sus, 6.1
them las (f. pl.); los (m. pl.)
theme el tema
then luego, BV; entonces,
2.1
there allí
there is/are hay, BV
they ellos(as), 2.1
thin flaco(a), 1.2;
delgado(a)
thing la cosa
to **think** pensar (ie), opinar
to think so creer
third tercer(o), 6.2
thirsty: to be thirsty tener
sed, 14.1
thirteen trece, BV
thirty treinta, BV
thirty-one treinta y uno, 2.1
this este (esta)
thistle el cardo
thought el pensamiento
thousand mil, 3.2
three tres, BV
three hundred
trescientos(as), 3.2
throat la garganta, 8.1
to have a sore throat
tener dolor de
garganta, 8.1
to **throw** lanzar, 7.1;
tirar, 7.2
Thursday el jueves, BV
ticket el boleto, la
entrada, 7.2; el ticket, 9.2;
el billete, 11.1
one-way ticket el billete
sencillo, 13.1
round-trip ticket el
billete de ida y vuelta,
13.1
ticket window la
ventanilla, la boletería,
9.2; la taquilla, 10.1
tie la corbata, 3.2
tied (score) empatado(a),
7.1
The score is tied. El
tanto queda empatado.,
7.1

time el tiempo; la vez; la hora
  at times a veces
  at what time? ¿a qué hora?
  on time a tiempo
  one more time une vez más, 12
timid tímido(a), 1.2
tiny diminuto(a)
tip el servicio, 5.1; la propina, 14.1
  Is the tip included? ¿Está incluido el servicio?
  to leave a tip dejar una propina, 14.1
tired cansado(a), 8.1
to **to** a; con destino a, 11.1
toast el pan tostado, 5.2
toasted tostado(a), 5.2
today hoy, BV
together junto(a), 5.1
toilet paper el papel higiénico, 12.2
to **tolerate** consentir (ie, i)
tomato el tomate, 5.2
tomorrow mañana, BV
  See you tomorrow! ¡Hasta mañana!, BV
tonight esta noche, 9.2
too también, 1.2
too much demasiado
tooth el diente, 12.1
toothbrush el cepillo de dientes, 12.2
toothpaste la pasta (crema) dentífrica, 12.2
  tube of toothpaste el tubo de pasta dentífrica, 12.1
tortilla la tortilla, 5.1
to **touch** tocar
touch el contacto
tour la gira, 12.2
tourist el/la turista
toward hacia
towel: beach towel la toalla playera, 9.1
town el pueblo
toy el juguete
track la vía, 13.1
tradition la tradición

traffic el tráfico
trail (ski) la pista, 9.2
train el tren, 13.1
  local train el tren local, 13.2
  nonstop train el tren directo, 13.2
train car el coche, el vagón, 13.1
train station la estación de ferrocarril, 13.1
to **transfer** transbordar, 13.2
to **transmit** transmitir
to **travel** viajar
  to travel by air viajar en avión, 11.1
tree el árbol
triangle el triángulo
trip el viaje, 11.1
  to take a trip hacer un viaje, 11.1
triumphant triunfante
trousers el pantalón, 3.2
trousseau el ajuar de novia
true verdadero(a)
  true value el valor real
trunk (of a car) el/la maletero(a), 11.1
truth la verdad
to **try** tratar
tube el tubo, 12.2
Tuesday el martes, BV
tuna el atún, 5.2
to **turn around** revolver (ue)
twelve doce, BV
twenty veinte, BV
twenty-one veintiuno, BV
two dos, BV
two hundred doscientos(as), 3.2
type el tipo
typical típico(a)

ugly feo(a), 1.1
uncle el tío, 6.1
  aunt(s) and uncle(s) los tíos, 6.1
under bajo, debajo (de)

undershirt la camiseta, 3.2
to **understand** comprender, 5.1
uniform el uniforme
unit la unidad
United States Estados Unidos
university la universidad
university (related to) universitario(a)
until hasta, BV
urban urbano(a)
us nos
to **use** usar, 3.2
usually generalmente

vacation la vacación
vanilla *(adj.)* de vainilla, 5.1
  vanilla ice cream el helado de vainilla, 5.1
various varios(as)
to **vary** variar
veal la ternera, 14.2
vegetable el vegetal, 5.2; la legumbre
vegetarian el/la vegetariano(a)
Venezuelan venezolano(a)
version: in (its) original version en versión original, 10.1
very muy, BV
  very well muy bien, BV
vest el chaleco
victorious victorioso(a)
video el video, 4.2
video store la tienda de videos, 10.1
view la vista, BV
vinegar el vinagre, 14.2
violin el violín, 2.1
visible visible
vital vital
voice la voz
volleyball el voleibol, 2.1
volume (book) el tomo
vowel la vocal

W

to **wait (for)** esperar, 11.1

  waiter el camarero, el mesero, 5.1

  waiting room la sala de espera, 13.1

  waitress la camarera, la mesera, 5.1

to **wake up** despertarse, 12.1

to **walk (around, through)** andar

  wall la pared; **(of a jai alai court)** el frontón

to **want** querer (ie), desear, 3.2

  war la guerra

to **wash oneself** lavarse, 12.1

  to wash one's face (hands, etc.) lavarse la cara (las manos, etc.), 12.1

to **watch** mirar, ver, 3.1

  water el agua (*f.*), 9.1

  watercolor la acuarela

  waterskiing el esquí acuático, 9.1

  to go waterskiing esquiar en el agua, 9.1

  wave la ola, 9.1

  way la manera, el modo, 1.1

  we nosotros(as), 2.1

  weapon el arma (*f.*)

to **wear** llevar, usar; **(shoe size)** calzar, 3.2

  weather el tiempo, 9.1

  The weather is bad. Hace mal tiempo., 9.1

  The weather is nice. Hace buen tiempo., 9.1

Wednesday el miércoles, BV

week la semana, BV

  last week la semana pasada, 9.2

  weekend el fin de semana, BV

  last weekend el fin de semana pasado

to **weigh** pesar

to **welcome** dar la bienvenida, 11.2

well bien; pues, BV

  very well muy bien, BV

west el oeste

what? ¿qué?, ¿cuál?, ¿cuáles?, ¿cómo?, 1.1

  What is he (she, it) like? ¿Cómo es?, 1.1

  What is it? ¿Qué es?, 1.1

  What is today's date? ¿Cuál es la fecha de hoy?, BV

  What time is it? ¿Qué hora es?

when cuando

  for when ¿para cuándo?, 14.2

  when? ¿cuándo?

where donde, adonde, 1.2

  where? ¿dónde?, ¿adónde?

  Where is he (she, it) from? ¿De dónde es?, 1.1

which? ¿cuál?, ¿cuáles?, BV

while el rato

while mientras

white blanco(a), 3.2

who? ¿quién?, 1.1; quiénes, 2.1

  Who is it (he, she)? ¿Quién es?, 1.1

whole entero(a)

why? ¿por qué?

wife la esposa, la mujer, 6.1

to **win** ganar, 7.1

  windmill el molino de viento

to **windsurf** practicar la plancha de vela, 9.1

  winter el invierno, BV

  wise sabio(a)

to **wish** querer (ie), desear, 3.2

with con

within dentro de

woman la dama

wool la lana

word la palabra

work el trabajo; la obra

  work of art la obra de arte

to **work** trabajar, 3.2

world el mundo

world (related to) mundial

  World Cup la Copa mundial

  World Series la Serie mundial

  worldwide mundial

wrap el poncho

to **wrap** envolver (ue)

to **write** escribir, 5.1

  writing pad el bloc, 3.1

Y

year el año, BV

  last year el año pasado, 9.2

  this year este año, 9.2

  to be . . . years old tener… años, cumplir… años, 6.1

yellow amarillo(a), 3.2

yesterday ayer, 9.2

  the day before yesterday anteayer

  yesterday afternoon ayer por la tarde, 9.2

  yesterday morning ayer por la mañana, 9.2

yogurt el yogur, 5.2

you tú (*sing. fam.*), Ud. (*sing. form.*); Uds. (*pl.*); te (*fam. pron.*), le (*pron.*)

  You're welcome. De nada., No hay de qué., BV

young joven, 6.1

  as a young person de joven

young person el/la joven, 8.1

your tu(s), su(s)

youth hostel el albergue para jóvenes (juvenil), 12.2

Z

zero cero, BV

zone la zona

Index

Glencoe would like to acknowledge the artists and agencies who participated in illustrating this program: Matthew Pippin represented by Beranbaum Artist's Representative; Meg Aubrey represented by Cornell & McCarthy; Eureka Cartography; Glencoe; Higgins Bond represented by Anita Grien Representing Artists; Viviana Diaz represented by Irmeli Holmberg; Carlos Lacamara; Beverly Lazor-Behr; Joe LeMonnier; Karen Maizel; Betty Maxey; Rebecca Merrilees; Lyle Miller; Stephen Moore; Ortelius Design, Inc.; David Broad, Susan Jaekel, Jane McCreary and DJ Simison represented by Remen-Willis Design Group; Ed Sauk; Don Stewart; Carol Strebel; Studio InkLink; Diana Thewlis; Ann Barrow and Kathleen O'Malley represented by Christina A. Tugeau; Joe Veno represented by Gwen Walters; Qin-Zhong Yu.

Photo Credits

Cover (t to b)Jeremy Horner/CORBIS, John Hicks/CORBIS, Bo Zaunders/CORBIS, Dallas and John Heaton/CORBIS, (students)Ed McDonald; **iv** (t)Ken Karp, (bl)Suzanne Murphy-Larronde/DDB Stock Photo, (bc)Robert Ginn/PhotoEdit, (br)Antonio Azcona West; **v–vi** Curt Fischer; **vii** (l)Michelle Chaplow, (r)Timothy Fuller, (others)Curt Fischer; **ix** (tl bl)Michelle Chaplow, (tr)Luis Delgado, (br)Morgan Cain & Associates; **x** (t)Andrew Payti, (bl)Larry Hamill, (br)Luis Delgado; **xi** Curt Fischer; **xii** (tl tr)Timothy Fuller, (b)Michelle Chaplow, (l)Suzanne Murphy-Larronde/DDB Stock Photo; **viii** Curt Fischer; **xiv** (l)Suzanne Murphy-Larronde/DDB Stock Photo, (r)Robert Fried/Robert Fried Photography; **xv** (l)Michelle Chaplow, (r)Andrew Payti; **xvi** (l)Michelle Chaplow, (tr)Luis Delgado, (b)Luis Delgado; **xvii** (l)Luis Delgado, (r)Robert Fried/Stock Boston; **xviii** (l)Timothy Fuller, (r)Curt Fischer; **xxi** (l)Andrew Payti, (cr)Randy Faris/CORBIS, (br)Andrew Payti; **xxxiv** (t)Timothy Fuller, (c)Mark Smestad, (b)Curt Fischer; **xxxv** (t)Timothy Fuller, (b)Ed McDonald; **xxxviii** Newberry Library/SuperStock; **1** Timothy Fuller; **2** (t)Ken Karp, (b)Luis Delgado; **3** (tl tc)Michelle Chaplow, (tr)Ken Karp, (bl)Luis Delgado, (br)Timothy Fuller; **4** Luis Delgado; **5** (tl tr)Michelle Chaplow, (b)Robert Frerck/Odyssey/Chicago; **6** Ann Summa; **7** CORBIS; **9** (t)Ken Karp, (c)Chad Ehlers/Stone, (b)David Young-Wolfe/PhotoEdit; **10** CORBIS; **11** Luis Delgado; **12** Boys Climbing a Tree, 1792. Francisco de Goya y Lucientes. Oil on canvas, 141 X 111cm. Museo del Prado, Madrid.; **12–13** Luis Delgado; **14** (l)Curt Fischer, (r)Timothy Fuller; **16** (tr)Timothy Fuller, (bl)Michelle Chaplow, (br)Tom & Therisa Stack/Tom Stack & Associates; **17** (tl)Ken Karp, (tr)Mark Smestad, (others)Aaron Haupt; **18 19 20** Curt Fischer; **21** (t)Ed McDonald, (b)Randy Faris/CORBIS; **22** Curt Fischer; **23** (t)Richard Glover/CORBIS, (b)Macduff Everton/Stone; **24** (tl)Aaron Haupt, (tr)Luis Delgado, (b)Timothy Fuller; **25** (t)Laura Sifferlin, (b)Eye Ubiquitous/CORBIS; **26** (t)Ken Karp, (b)Robert Frerck/DDB Stock Photo; **27** (l)Timothy Fuller, (r)Robert Fried/Tom Stack & Associates, (b)Curt Fischer; **28** (inset)Ed McDonald, (bkgd)Bob Krist/eStock; **29** Tim Fuller; **30** Robert Frerck/Woodfin Camp & Associates; **31** (t)CORBIS, (b)Musee, St. Denis-Seine/1999 Estate of Pablo Picasso/Artists Rights Society (ARS), New York; **32** (t)Luis Delgado, (bl)Norman Tomalin/Bruce Coleman, Inc.; **33** (t)Norman Tomalin/Bruce Coleman, Inc., (b)Organization of American States; **34** (l)Ludovic Maisant/CORBIS, (r)CORBIS, (tr)Andrew Payti, (br)CORBIS; **35** (tl)Curt Fischer, (tr)Andrew Payti, (br)CORBIS; **36** (t)Luis Delgado, (b)Mark Smestad; **39** Robert Frerck/Woodfin Camp & Associates; **41** (t)Timothy Fuller, (b)Curt Fischer; **42** Zurbaran Galeria, Buenos Aires, Argentina/SuperStock; **42–43** Michelle Chaplow; **44** Luis Delgado; **45** (tl tr)Aaron Haupt, (bl)Curt Fischer, (br)Michelle Chaplow; **46** (t)Luis Delgado, (b)Curt Fischer; **47** (t)Ken Karp, **47** (b)Larry Hamill; **48–50** Curt Fischer; **51** Robert Frerck/Odyssey/Chicago; **53** (t)Luis Rosendo/Getty Images, (others)Laura Sifferlin; **55** (l)Doug Martin, (r)John Evans; **56** (t)Larry Hamill, (b)Ken Karp; **57** Ken Karp; **60** (t)Robert Fried, (b)Laura Sifferlin; **61** Sven Martson/The Image Works; **62** Curt Fischer; **63** (l)Luis Delgado, (r)CORBIS; **64** (t)CORBIS, (b)James Ranklev/Stone; **65** (t)Robert Frerck/Odyssey/Chicago, (c)Nicolas Sapieha/Art Resource; **66** (tl)David Young-Wolfe/PhotoEdit, (tc)Chuck Savage/The Stock Market, (tr)Robert Fried/Tom Stack & Associates, (cl)Suzanne Murphy-Larronde/DDB Stock Photo, (c)H. Huntly Hersch/DDB Stock Photo, (cr)Antonio Azcona West, (b)Robert Ginn/PhotoEdit; **67** The Museum of Modern Art, New York. Photograph ©1996 the Museum of Modern Art, New York. National Palace, Patio Corido, Mexico; **68** Timothy Fuller; **69** Andrew Payti; **71** Lindsay Hebberd/CORBIS; **73** Ken Karp; **74** Albright-Knox Art Gallery/CORBIS; **74–75** Robert Frerck/Odyssey/Chicago; **76** Curt Fischer; **77** Timothy Fuller; **78** Luis Delgado; **79** Michelle Chaplow; **80** (c)Luis Delgado, (clockwise from top) (1)file photo, (2–3)John Evans, (4)Esbin-Anderson/The Image Works, (5)Anthony Azcona, (6)Timothy Fuller, (7)Anthony Azcona, (8–10)file photo, (11)Barb Stimpert; **81** (tl)Ken Karp, (tr)Luis Delgado, (cl)Esbin-Anderson/The Image Works, (cr)Curt Fischer, (b)Esbin-Anderson/The Image Works; **82** (c)Antonio Azcona, (b)Luis Delgado, (others)Luis Delgado; **83** (5)Siede Preis/Photodisc, (bl)Ken Karp, (br)Michelle Chaplow, (others)Luis Delgado; **84** file photo; **85** Ken Karp; **85** Luis Delgado; **86** Andrew Payti; **87** (5)Luis Delgado, (others) Andrew Payti; **88** Timothy Fuller; **89** Ken Karp; **90** (l)PhotoDisc, (r)Michelle Chaplow, (b)CORBIS; **92** (tl)Oliver Benn/Stone, (tc)Robert Fried/Robert Fried Photography, (tr)Stephanie Maze/Woodfin Camp & Associates, (cl cr)Loren McIntyre/Woodfin Camp & Associates, (b)Curt Fischer; **93** Courtesy Oscar de la Renta; **95** Esbin-Anderson/The Image Works; **95** Jeff Greenberg/eStock Photo; **96** (t)Matt Meadows, (b)Michelle Chaplow; **98** Curt Fischer; **99** Joe Viesti/The Viesti Collection; **101** Curt Fischer; **102** Schalkwijk/Art Resource, NY; **102–103** Pablo Corral Vega/CORBIS; **104** (t)Photodisc, (tr)Michelle Chaplow, (c)Michelle Chaplow, (b)Michelle Chaplow, (bkgd)Lori Shetler; **105** (t)Ann Summa, (b)Timothy Fuller; **106** Michelle Chaplow; **107** (t)Andrew Payti, (b)Doug Bryant/DDB Stock Photo; **108** Michelle Chaplow; **109** (t)Tom & Teresa Stack/Tom Stack & Associates, (b)Anthony Azcona; **110** (t)Michelle Chaplow, (b)Ann Summa; **111** (t)Aaron Haupt, (b)Philadelphia Museum of Art, A.E. Gallatin Collection; **112** Aaron Haupt; **113** (t)Michelle Chaplow, (b)Antonio Azcona; **114** (t)Ken Karp, (b)Andrew Payti; **116** Mark Smestad; **117** (t)Michelle Chaplow, (b)Dallas & John Heaton/Westlight; **118** Robin Sachs/PhotoEdit; **119** Curt Fischer; **120** Ken Karp; **122** (t)Luis Delgado, (b)Luis Rosendo/FPG; **123** Luis Rosendo/FPG; **124** (t)Mark C. Burnett/Stock Boston, (b)Joe Viesti/Viesti Associates; **125** (t)UPI/Corbis-Bettmann, (b c)Andrew Payti; **126** (l)Luis Delgado, (r)Andrew Payti; **127** Luis Delgado; **128** (t)Michelle Chaplow, (b)Doug Bryant/DDB Stock Photography; **129** Michelle Chaplow; **131** Mark Smestad; **133** (t)Mark Smestad, (b)Luis Delgado; **134** Morgan Cain & Associates; **135** Michelle Chaplow; **136** (tl)Randy Faris/CORBIS, (tc)CORBIS, (tr)CORBIS, (cl)Newscom136, (cr)Bettmann/CORBIS, (b)Reuters; **137** (tl)Newscom, (tc)Richard Cummins/CORBIS, (tr)Anita Calero, (c)AP Photo/Jose Luis Magana, (bl)Sunset Boulevard/CORBIS, (bc)Newscom; **138** (l)STX/The Grosby Group, (tr)Robert Mora/Newscom, (cr br)Newscom; **139** (tl)Getty Images/Newscom, (tr)Time Life Pictures/Getty Images, (cl)Eniac Martinez, (bl)Newscom, (bc)Kevin Winter/Getty Images, (br)Camilo Salas/Reforma-Edred via Newscom; **140** (c)Kactus Foto, Santiago, Chile/SuperStock; **140–141** Telegraph Color Library/FPG; **142** (t)Doug Bryant/DDB Stock Photo, (l r)Ken Karp; **144** Morgan Cain & Associates; **145** Michelle Chaplow; **146** (t)Robert Frerck/Odyssey, (l)Michelle Chaplow, (r)Curt Fischer; **147** (t)Timothy Fuller, (c)Andrew Payti, (bl)Aaron Haupt, (br)Doug Bryant/DDB Stock Photo; **148–149** Andrew Payti; **151** Luis Delgado; **152** Morgan Cain & Associates; **154 156–157** Michelle Chaplow; **158** (t)Curt Fischer, (b)Peter Menzel; **159** Andrew Payti; **160** Michelle Chaplow; **161** Curt Fischer; **162** Andrew Payti; **163** (l b)Andrew Payti, (r)Michelle Chaplow; **164** (9)David Buffington/Photodisc, (10)Andrew Payti, (11)C. Squared Studios/Photodisc, (12)Marshall Gordon/Cole Group/Photodisc; **165** Antonio Azcona West; **168** Schalkwijk/Art Resource, NY; **169** Robert Frerck/Woodfin Camp & Associates; **171** Ann Summa/Getty Images; **172** (t)Ken Karp, (b)Luis Delgado; **173** (t)Larry Hamill, (b)Ken Karp; **175** (inset t tr)Anthony Azcona, (tl)John Evans, (br)Mark Smestad; **176** Michelle Chaplow; **177** (t)Robert Fried/Robert Fried Photography, (c)Andrew Payti, (b)Robert Fried/Robert Fried Photography; **178** Tony Freeman/PhotoEdit; **179** (tl tc tr)Ed McDonald, (b)Luis Delgado; **180** (t)Antonio Azcona, (b)Curt Fischer; **181** Curt Fischer; **182** Michelle Chaplow; **183** Andrew Payti; **184** (t 2 3)Curt Fischer, (1 4)Anthony Azcona; **185** Andrew Payti; **186** Timothy Fuller; **188** Michelle Chaplow; **189** Antonio Gaudi y Cornet; **190** Ann Summa; **191** Prado Museum/Art Resource, NY;

Credits

192 (t)Jacques & Natasha Gilman Collection/Museo Diego Rivera, Mexico City, 192 (b)Pablo Corral V/CORBIS; 193 (t)Anthony Azcona, (c)The Museum of Modern Art, NY, (b)House of El Grecco, Toledo, Spain; 195 (t)Matt Meadows; 198 Ken Karp; 200 Christie's Images/SuperStock; 200–201 Luis Delgado; 202 (l)David Cannon/Allsport, (r)Curt Fischer; 204 David Leah/Allsport; 205 (t)Clive Brunskill/International Stock, (b)Doug Bryant/DDB Stock Photography; 206 (t)Macduff Everton/CORBIS, (l)Curt Fischer; 207 (tl)Curt Fischer, (tr)Image Club Graphics, (cl bl)Aaron Haupt, (cr)Getty Images, (br)Curt Fischer; 208 (t)David Leah/Allsport Mexico, (b)Luis Delgado; 209 Getty Images; 210–211 Luis Delgado; 213 Martin Venegas/Allsport Mexico; 214 (t)Ken Karp, (b)David R. Frazier/Photo Researchers; 215 Michelle Chaplow; 216 Andrew Payti; 217 Curt Fischer; 218 Michelle Chaplow; 220 (t)Paul Marriott/Empics Ltd., (b)CORBIS; 221 Allsport/Getty Images; 222 (t)Doug Persinger/Allsport, (b)David Leah/Allsport Mexico; 223 (l)Tom & Therisa Stack/Tom Stack & Associates, (r)Antonio Azcona; 224 (t)Andrew Payti, (b)Rich Brommer; 225 (t)Rich Brommer, (b)Robert Fried/Robert Fried Photography; 228 Luis Delgado; 229 Simon Bruty/Allsport; 231 Curt Fischer; 232 Luis Delgado; 234 Andrew Payti; 236 (tl)Sergio Pitamitz/CORBIS, (tr)diego Lezama Orezzoli/CORBIS, (b)Art Wolfe/Getty Images; 237 (tl)Galen Rowell/CORBIS, (tr)Erik Rank/FoodPix, (cl)Galen Rowell/CORBIS, (c)Jose Manuel Calvete/CORBIS, (cr)Zuma Press/Newscom, (b)Reuters/Newscom; 238 (t)Ed Kashi/CORBIS, (b)Manuel Zambrara/CORBIS; 239 (t)Courtesy Justo Lamas, (cl)Juan Carlos Algarin, (cr)Newscom , (bl)Telemundo, (br)Dennis Degnan/CORBIS,; 240 Digital Image, the Museum of Modern Art/Licensed by SCALA/Art Resource, NY; 240–241 Timothy Fuller; 242 Curt Fischer; 243 (cr)Ann Summa, (others)Curt Fischer; 244 (t)Michelle Chaplow, (b)Timothy Fuller; 246 (t)Ken Karp, (bl)Aaron Haupt, (br)Curt Fischer, (others)Curt Fischer; 247 Michelle Chaplow; 248 Timothy Fuller; 250 (t)Timothy Fuller, (b)Ken Karp; 251 Aaron Haupt; 253 (t)Andrew Payti, (b)Ken Karp; 254 Robert Fried/Robert Fried Photography; 255 Ken Karp; 257–258 Michelle Chaplow; 260 Andrew Payti, (b)Antonio Azcona; 262 Luis Delgado; 263 (t)Siegfried Tauqueuer/Estock, (b)Courtesy Dr. Antonio Gassett; 264 Curt Fischer; 265 (c)Andrew Payti, (b)Curt Fischer; 267 (t)Timothy Fuller, (b)Andrew Payti; 268 Timothy Fuller; 269 Luis Delgado; 271 Curt Fischer; 272 Whitford & Hughes, London, UK/Bridgeman Art Library, UK; 272–273 Superstock; 274 (tl c)Andrew Payti, (tr)Reuters NewMedia Inc./CORBIS, (bl)CORBIS, (br)Getty Images, (bkgd)Luis Delgado; 275 Timothy Fuller; 276 (t)Luis Delgado, (c)CORBIS, (1 2 3)C. Squared Studios/Photodisc, (4)Doug Bryant/DDB Stock Photo; 277 (t)Digital Vision, (b)Michelle Chaplow; 278 (tr l)Curt Fischer, (br)Buddy Mays/CORBIS; 280 John Curtis/DDB Stock Photo; 283 Luis Delgado; 284 (t)Michelle Chaplow, (b)J.L.G. Grande/Tourist Office of Spain; 286 Ken Karp; 287 (t1 5)Aaron Haupt, (2)Timothy Fuller, (3)Ryan McVay/Photodisc, (4)Curt Fischer, (6)Alaska Stock Images, (7)Thomas Veneklasen, (8)C. Squared Studios/Photodisc, (b)Luis Delgado; 290 (bkgd)Zbigniew Bzdak/The Image Works, (inset) Laura Sifferlin; 292 (l)PhotoDisc, (r)Andrew Payti; 293 (tl)Donald Nausbaum/Getty Images, (tr)Andrew Payti, (b)Andrew Payti; 294 (t)Andrew Payti, (b)Buddy Mays/ImageState; 295 Jeff Curtes/CORBIS; 296 (l)Derke/O'Hara/Stone, (r)Andrew Payti; 297 (t)Harold Castro/FPG, (bl)Andrew Payti, (br)Mireille Vautier/Woodfin Camp & Associates; 298 Marco Corsetti/FPG; 300 (1)Doug Bryant/DDB Stock Photo, (2)C. Squared Studios/Photodisc, (4)Jeff Curtes/CORBIS, (5)Jack Hollingsworth/Stock Photo; 301 Andrew Payti; 303 Superstock; 304 (c)Christie's Images/CORBIS; 304–305 Dave G. Houser/CORBIS; 306 Markow Tatiana/CORBIS SYGMA; 308 (t)Michelle Chaplow, (b)Antonio Azcona; 309 Dallas & John Heaton/Westlight; 310 Culver Pictures; 311 Owen Franken/CORBIS; 313 (t)Andrew Payti, (b)Robert Frerck/Odyssey/Chicago; 315 (t)Michelle Chaplow, (b)Robert Fried/Robert Fried Photography; 316 file photo; 317 Andrew Payti; 318 (t)Aaron Haupt, (b)Juan de Villanueva; 319 Prado Museum, Madrid; 320 Luis Delgado; 322 (l)Luis Delgado, (r)Andrew Payti; 323 Michelle Chaplow; 324 Luis Delgado; 325 (t)Gene Dekovic, (bl)Jorge Contreras Chacel/International Stock, (br)Robert Frerck/Odyssey/Chicago; 327 (l)Suzanne Murphy-Larronde/DDB Stock Photo, (tr)Ulrike Welsch, (c)Doug Bryant/DDB Stock Photo, (br)Robert Frerck/Odyssey/Chicago; 328 Matt

Meadows; 331 Bob Daemmrich/The Image Works; 333 Andrew Payti; 334 Smithsonian American Art Museum, Washington, DC/ArtResource, NY; 335 Thomas D. Mayes, Jr.; 336 337 338 Michelle Chaplow; 339 Andrew Payti; 340 Michelle Chaplow; 341 (t)Andrew Payti, (c)Ismael Jordá/Airliners.net, (b)Michelle Chaplow; 342 Michelle Chaplow; 343 Andrew Payti; 345 Michelle Chaplow; 346 Andrew Payti; 348 (t)Curt Fischer, (b)Thomas Veneklasen; 349 Andrew Payti; 350 (l)Robert Fried, (r)Aaron Haupt; 352 (l)D. Rivademar/Odyssey/Chicago, (r)Jacques Jangouz/Stone; 353 (l)Jay Dickman/CORBIS, (r)Boyd Norton/The Image Works; 354 (t)Reuters NewMedia Inc./CORBIS, (c)Luis Delgado, (b)Andrew Payti; 355 Andrew Payti; 356 (l)Larry Hamill, (r)Curt Fischer; 357 Doug Bryant/DDB Stock Photo; 360 Michelle Chaplow; 361 Andrew Payti; 363–364 Michelle Chaplow; 365 Ken Karp; 366 Photoworks/P. Lang/DDB Stock Photo; 368 (t)CORBIS, (b)Tiziana and Gianni Baldizzone/CORBIS; 369 (tl)Hubert Stadler/CORBIS, (tr)AFP/CORBIS, (bl)Reuters/Newscom, (br)Craig Lovell/CORBIS; 370 (t)AP Photo/Martin Mejia, (bl)Philip Salaverry/FoodPix, (br)Wolfgang Kaehler/CORBIS; 371 (tl tr)AP Photo/Peter McFarren, (cl)Galen Rowell/CORBIS, (cr)Owen Franken/CORBIS, (bl)Tui De Roy/Minden Pictures, (br)Steve Labadessa; 372 Kactus Foto/SuperStock; 372–373 Adam Woolfitt/CORBIS; 374 375 Curt Fischer; 376 Michelle Chaplow; 377 (l)Morgan Cain & Associates, (r)Andrew Payti; 378 (t)Guido Cozzi/Atlantide/Bruce Coleman, Inc., (b)Curt Fischer; 379 (l to r, t to b)Antonio Azcona, (tl)Curt Fischer, (bl)Luis Delgado, (br)Michelle Chaplow, (2 6 7)Andrew Payti, (3–5)Curt Fischer; 381 Curt Fischer; 383 Michelle Chaplow; 384 (t)Timothy Fuller, (b)Ken Karp, (1 4–6)Timothy Fuller, (2 3) Aaron Haupt; 385 Michelle Chaplow; 386 388 Luis Delgado; 390 (l)Robert Frerck/Odyssey/Chicago, (r)Luis Delgado; 391 Robert Fried/Robert Fried Photography; 392 (bl)Robert Frerck/Woodfin Camp and Associates, (br)Massimo Borchi/Atlantide/Bruce Coleman, Inc.; 392 K. Gillham/Photo 20-20; 393 Robert Frerck/Odyssey/Chicago; 394 (l)Luis Delgado, (r)Reuters NewMedia Inc./CORBIS; 395 (t)Bernard P. Wolfe/Photo Researchers, (b)Andrew Payti; 397 Ken Karp; 398 (t)Curt Fischer, (bl)Curt Fischer, (bc)Andrew Payti, (br)Andrew Payti; 399 CORBIS; 401 Curt Fischer; 402 The Stapleton Collection/The Bridgeman Art Library; 402–403 Luis Delgado; 404 (t b)Michelle Chaplow, (inset)Luis Delgado; 405 Andrew Payti; 406 Luis Delgado; 408 (t)Michelle Chaplow, (b)Doug Bryant/DDB Stock Photo; 409 (tr)Andrew Payti, (cr)Photodisc, (bl)Doug Bryant/DDB Stock Photo; 410 (t)Luis Delgado, (b)Michelle Chaplow; 411 (l)CORBIS, (tr)Ken Karp, (br)Robert Fried/Robert Fried Photography; 412 Andrew Payti; 413 Ken Karp; 414 House of El Greco, Toledo Spain; 415 Yoichiro Miyazaki/FPG; 416 Robert Fried/Robert Fried Photography; 417 Ken Karp; 418 420 Luis Delgado; 421 (t b)Robert Fried/Robert Fried Photography, (c)Telegraph Color Library/FPG; 422 (t br)Robert Fried/Robert Fried Photography, (c)Robert Fried/Stock Boston, (bl)Robert Frerck/Odyssey/Chicago; 423 Andrew Payti; 425 (t)Curt Fischer, (b)Michelle Chaplow, (others)Luis Delgado; 426 Morgan Cain & Associates; 427 file photo; 428 Andrew Payti; 429 Robert Fried/Robert Fried Photography; 431 Luis Delgado; 432 Kactus Foto/SuperStock; 432–433 Luis Delgado; 434 Curt Fischer; 435 (t)Andrew Payti, (cl c cr)Doug Bryant/DDB Stock Photo, (bl)Doug Bryant/DDB Stock Photo, (br)Aaron Haupt; 436 (t)Ed McDonald, (b)Luis Delgado; 438 Curt Fischer; 439 (t bl)Timothy Fuller, (br)Curt Fischer; 440 Michelle Chaplow; 443 (t)Ken Karp, (b)Morgan Cain & Associates; 445–446 Ken Karp; 448 (l)Curt Fischer, (r)Timothy Fuller; 449 National Palace, Mexico City; 450 (t)Curt Fischer, (tr)Michelle Chaplow, (br)Andrew Payti; 451 (t)Robert Fried/Robert Fried Photography, (b)Laura Sifferlin; 452 (bl)Andrew Payti, (others)Curt Fischer; 453 Michelle Chaplow; 454 Timothy Fuller; 456 Curt Fischer; 459 (t)Timothy Fuller, (b)Curt Fischer; 460 Luis Delgado; 462 Timothy Fuller; 463 Michelle Chaplow/Andalucia Slide Library; 464 (t)Sandy Perez, (c)Bettmann/CORBIS, (l to r)Franz-Marc Frei/CORBIS, (1)Jon Bradley/Getty Images, (2)Jon Bradley/Getty Images, (3)Eric & David Hosking/CORBIS, (4)Sheldan Collins/CORBIS; 465 (t)Frank Veronsky, (bl)AP Photo/Cristina Quicler, (br)Royalty Free/CORBIS; 466 (tl)Pablo Sanchez/Newscom, (tcl)Rufus F. Folkks/CORBIS, (cl)Fred Prouser/Newscom, (bl)David Cruz/Newscom, (bc)Sergio Perez/Newscom, (1)Visual Arts Library/Art Resource, (2 3)Archivo Icongrafico/CORBIS,